COLONIALISM AS
CIVILIZING MISSION

COLONIALISM AS CIVILIZING MISSION

Cultural Ideology in British India

Edited by
HARALD FISCHER-TINÉ
AND
MICHAEL MANN

Anthem Press is an imprint of
Wimbledon Publishing Company
75–76 Blackfriars Road
London SE1 8HA

First published by Wimbledon Publishing Company 2004

British Library Cataloguing in Publication Data
Data available

Library of Congress Cataloging in Publication Data
A catalog record has been applied for

ISBN 1 84331 091 0 (hbk)
ISBN 1 84331 092 9 (pbk)

1 3 5 7 9 10 8 6 4 2

Typeset by Regent Typesetting, London

CONTENTS

'Torchbearers Upon the Path of Progress': Britain's Ideology of a 'Moral and Material Progress' in India.

An Introductory Essay[1]

MICHAEL MANN
FernUniversitaet in Hagen

> We cannot presume from the past state of any people, with respect to improvement in arts, that they would, under different circumstances, for ever continue the same. The history of many nations who have advanced from rudeness to refinement, contradicts such hypothesis; according to which, the Britons ought still to be going naked, to be feeding on acorns, and sacrificing human victims in the Druidical groves. In fact, what is now offered, is no more than the proposal for the further civilization of a people, who had very early made a considerable progress in improvement; but who, by deliberate and successful plans of fraud and imposition, were rendered first stationary, then retrograde.
>
> Charles Grant, *Observations on the State of Society among the Asiatic Subjects of Great Britain* (1792)[2]

1. An Ideology Turned Upside-down

To explain the impact of the British 'civilizing mission' upon India it seems sensible to have a brief look at the results and effects of the colonizer's perpetual efforts to ensure the 'material and moral progress' of the country and its people. Therefore, let us skip to the British Empire's final days in the Indian subcontinent. Clearly, the zenith of British Indian colonial enthusiasm had been passed in the aftermath of the First World War[3] when the East was no longer regarded as a career, as Benjamin Disraeli had proudly put it in his 1847 *Tancred*. At the end of the 1930s, only half of the Indian Civil Service's covenant officers were Britons indicating that the once famous 'steel frame' of British India was considered as a burdensome, and hence, fairly unattractive institution, which outweighed all positive notions of the 'white man's burden' ideology. The image of the exhausted yet well-intended and deeply committed British officer, as partly depicted on the cover of this volume, had disappeared.[4] One of the many frustrated British officials in the late colonial service was Eric Blair, better known under his *nom de plume* as George Orwell. Born in India in 1903, he spent his youth in Burma as a member of the Indian Imperial Police from 1922 to 1928. He started his literary career in the early 1930s when he wrote down his colonial experiences in *Burmese Days*, published in 1934. Set in a small district headquarters in the middle of nowhere in Upper Burma, Orwell's own, basically pessimistic, view of Albion's imperial enterprise is mirrored in his depiction of the few members of the British colonial society who are bored, frustrated, sarcastic and aggressive. Ironically, while on the verge of quitting the country, they reminisce about the good old days of the 'imperial heyday'. Thus the novel reflects perfectly, and probably authentically, the situation of the interwar period.

In the initial chapters of *Burmese Days*, the protagonist Mr Flory, a British merchant who came to Burma to exploit her timber resources, is irritated by the imperial racism of his countrymen who rudely discuss the admittance of the only Indian doctor in town, Dr Veraswami, to the sacrosanct 'club'. Turning away in disgust, Flory visits his friend Veraswami who invites him to have a seat on the veranda and offers him drinks ranging from beer to whisky, which reflect what the Indian considers as the taste of all Britons. In the ensuing conversation it turns out that Veraswami is not only familiar with British drinking habits but that he is also impressed by the sort of 'progress' and 'modernization' the British have brought to the Orient. Flory, however, who is a member of the 'imperial race', appears critical of the British presence in India and Burma. He points to the exploitative character of the colonial economy and the appropriation of wealth by a foreign people to the detriment of the said countries. Although he opposes this sort of colonial relationship, Flory admits frankly that he is in Burma precisely for the purpose of making money, but that he hates the hypocritical talk of the 'white man's burden'. Moreover, Flory criticizes the moral pretensions of the British in the colonies: they seem to be solely interested in boozing and womanizing, in stark contrast to their claims to be a highly civilized people setting an example to backward nations.

Veraswami, who has apparently internalized the attitudes and aims of the British civilizing mission, is appalled by Flory's defeatist utterances.

But truly, truly, Mr Flory, you must not speak so! Why iss it that always you are abusing the pukka sahibs, as you call them? They are the salt of the earth. Consider the great things they have done – consider the great administrators who have made British India what it iss. Consider Clive, Warren Hastings, Dalhousie, Curzon. [. . .] And consider how noble a type iss the English gentleman! Their glorious loyalty to one another! The public school spirit. Even those of them, whose manner iss unfortunate – some Englishmen are arrogant, I concede – have the great, sterling qualities that we Orientals lack.[5]

Yet Flory insists upon the exploitative role of the British, calling the empire a device for giving trade monopolies to themselves. Veraswami replies that the Burmese would not themselves be able to trade because the British had brought all the machinery, the ships, railways and roads. In fact, the Burmese would be helpless without the colonizers and he is glad that the British have come to civilize them. Subsequently, Veraswami points towards the latent eastern agony and superstition that could only have been overcome by British standards of law and order, prisons and schools. British civilization at its worst would be an advance for the East. 'I see the British, even the least inspired of them, ass – ass – [. . .] torchbearers upon the path of progress.'[6]

Prison is the most controversial subject that the two friends debate; Veraswami regards prisons as necessary because they symbolize the rule of law and the overall *Pax Britannica*. Flory, on the other hand, is disgusted by the kind of progress manifested in bricks and bars. In his defence of colonial policy the Indian doctor cites the usual list of British achievements:

> Consider that there are also other achievements of your countrymen. They construct roads, they irrigate deserts, they conquer famines, they build schools, they set up hospitals, they combat plague, cholera, leprosy, smallpox, venereal disease – ?[7]

The two points of view seem hardly compatible and the discussion could have continued. But soon Veraswami turns the internalized version of the British 'civilizing mission' against its initiator. Turning the representative character of colonial rule in the Orient – in the sense of Edward Said – upside down, he tells Flory that if he disapproved of the British Empire as strongly as he pretends he would not confine himself to talking about it privately but would speak out in public. 'I know your character, Mr Flory, better than you know it yourself.'[8] In this moment western civilization is represented by a self-confident, positive-thinking, 'manly' Oriental, who has successfully adapted the moral and material values of the civilizing mission. Although, of course, the doctor represents Europe's 'effeminate other', he depicts a paradoxical situation. Defending the values and morals of Europe, which Flory belittles, the sensible, reasonable grown-up Oriental 'child' Veraswami is now willing to follow and, in a distant future, to catch up with the paternalistic 'torch-bearers of progress'. At the point where the colonizers are about to give up their role as civilizers, the colonized ask to continue as objects of a civilizing mission – truly 'twisted worlds' in those days. As well as being a masterly literary criticism of imperialism, Orwell's story at the same time suggests that Britain's civilizing mission in South Asia is a success story, because parts of the colonized population accept their oppressor's hegemonic claims. Leaving aside for a while the solution to this tricky matter, the following sections of this introductory essay attempt to trace the development of the idea that the British were not only entitled to educate and 'improve' their Indian subjects but had a duty to do so.

2. The Initial Phase of the Civilizing Mission

All European powers claimed to pursue a civilizing project in their colonies from the late eighteenth century onwards. What the English initially called 'improvement' or 'betterment' and, later on, 'moral and material progress' will be, therefore, subsumed under the term 'civilizing mission'. This notion and the term is borrowed from the French *mission civilisatrice*, which became the latter's imperial ideology and official doctrine in the heyday of imperialism, especially after 1895. The idea of a civilizing mission rested upon the twin fundamental assumptions of the superiority of French culture and the perfectibility of humankind. Also, it implied that colonial subjects were too backward to govern themselves and that they had to be 'uplifted'. Since the middle of the eighteenth century, the French had aimed at institutionalizing universal principles, thus exporting the ideas and concepts of the Enlightenment and the French Revolution. By the end of the nineteenth century, they were convinced of their material and moral superiority. This was particularly true for western sciences and technology.[9] Basically the *mission civilisatrice* rested upon the idea of mastery – or, in other words, 'to be civilized was to be free from specific forms of tyranny: the tyranny of the elements over man, of disease over health, of instinct over reason, of ignorance over knowledge and of despotism over liberty'.[10] However, in spite of this 'enlightening agenda', the concept of the *mission civilisatrice* was used above all for the self-legitimation of colonial rule.

The same was true, of course, for British attitudes towards their Indian empire and the non-white colonies. Indeed, colonialism – as with any -ism – can hardly be understood without the element of self-legitimation inherent in it. The legitimacy of British colonial rule was constructed on two fundamental principles. First, the British tried to articulate their sovereignty in an Indian idiom. They felt a lack of legitimacy within India after the successive acquisition of territorial rights in the second half of the eighteenth century. Nominally, the Mughal was still sovereign in (not 'of') India, sharing his sovereignty with the major princes of the subcontinent. Yet the further the British expanded in India, the more the legitimacy of their rule was questioned. It was not until the 'Great Rebellion' of 1857–9, when the British deposed the defeated Mughal, that they declared their monarch the sovereign of India, claiming the right of a victorious conqueror. It is important to note that within the Indian context of legitimacy and legitimate rule, the succession to the Mughals was the sole justification for the Indian princes, nobles, elites and the bulk of the population to accept the British as the sovereign power.[11]

Second, the British felt obliged to justify their rule in a European idiom. The most powerful tool of self-legitimation was the colonizer's claim to improve the country and to bring the fruits of progress and modernity to the subject peoples. As will be argued in subsequent chapters, it is inherent in the logic of colonialism that people who were different because they were regarded as inferior had to be made similar and, hence, equal by being civilized. This was the self-inflicted 'duty' of the 'white man' whose 'burden' derived from the permanent atonement for original sin as well as from the sympathetic attitude of the philanthropic Enlightenment. However, once the colonized peoples were equal and in consequence could justly demand emancipation (to continue with the vocabulary of Enlightenment), the basis of colonial rule would vanish, likewise destroying the foundation of self-legitimation. This ultimately explains why the colonizers could never admit similarity, let alone equality, between themselves and the subject peoples in the colonies.[12] Interestingly, legitimate colonial rule was always more closely connected with the notion of self-legitimation than with Indian concepts of legitimate rule, which may point to a core problem of European self-perception.

From the beginning of their colonial rule in India, the British regarded the country and its people as subjugated by political regimes that they characterized as 'Oriental despotism'. Early British historiography, chiefly written by officials of the East India Company, stigmatized India in that manner. Robert Orme, for instance, contrasting the 'unhappy system of oppression' [13] prevailing in Mughal India with the enlightened government of England, ended his comparison with the following words:

> The sons of Liberty may here behold the mighty ills to which the slaves of a despotic power must be subject: the spirit darkened and depressed by

ignorance and fear; the body tortured and tormented by punishments inflicted without justice and without measure: such a contrast to the blessings of liberty, heightens at once the sense of our happiness, and our zeal for the preservation of it.[14]

In the course of the later eighteenth and nineteenth centuries, the liberation from such 'Oriental oppression' became the justification for British expansion on the subcontinent. At the same time, this historiography established the 'Oriental' picture of a weak and primitive people, unfit for self-government due to the crippling influence of long-lasting subjugation that, again, argued for a strong paternalistic government as the most appropriate form for an uncivilized people. Accordingly, the Indian population was placed in a master and servant, teacher and pupil, parent and child or – as Ashis Nandy has demonstrated[15] – husband and wife relationship that justified the imposition of discipline, education and upbringing. In short, the 'civilizing mission'.

However, the transformation of such early British civilizing attitudes into a more coherent form began with the growth of England's awakening Christian movement in the second half of the eighteenth century. Initiated by John and Charles Wesley and John Whitfield, the 'Methodists' attracted England's lower classes because, in contrast to the established Anglican Church with its purely rational understanding and interpretation of the Gospel, the early evangelical revival favoured an emotional Christianity. Moreover, the Methodists developed new forms of discipline and social behaviour – hence their name. The new religious movement assumed wider importance when it began to find adherents and supporters in the English upper-middle classes in the last decades of the eighteenth century, it made a significant impact on the British society and, as a moral agency, paved the way for Victorian 'respectability'. Since it would be beyond the scope of the present essay to investigate the specifics of the evangelical movement, it may suffice to characterize briefly the movement of the so called 'Evangelicals': they promoted discipline as a means for the world to win salvation and pursued a 'vital religion' founded on a practical and personally-experienced Christianity. In essence, Evangelicals believed in a morally pure way of life and represented a revival of seventeenth-century Puritanism.[16]

Simultaneously, Evangelicals opposed French enlightened atheism and deism, so their moral attitudes had strong political implications. Evangelicalism drew many of its motifs from the antagonism to 'Jacobinism' and the French Revolution and sought to prevent similar widespread unrest in England through a religious campaign to keep the lower classes in obedience and subordination. Also, an educational programme would support the social fabric of the state: it was thought that the state is as secure in proportion as the people are attached to its institutions. Naturally, this 'social programme' attracted the English upper classes and some backed the Evangelicals. However, the latter led a vicious assault on the moral imperfection of the ruling elites, merchants as well as gentry and aristocracy. At best, a moral reform of the elite would disseminate through the population, thereby reforming society at large. It is supposed that in the middle of the nineteenth century about 20 per cent of the English population could be described as Evangelicals, which gives some idea of the extent of their possible influence.[17]

Evangelicals also pursued political aims, as became obvious with the 'Clapham Sect' whose members were of intellectual, mercantile and political backgrounds. William Wilberforce, MP for Yorkshire, and Thomas Babington, a Lancashire landowner and Cambridge graduate, were its most prominent early members.[18] It became well known first for its successful campaign for the abolition of slavery, then for its fight in support of the admission of the Christian mission to the territories of the East India Company.

Charles Grant was not only a highly esteemed Company official with solid experience of India but also an Evangelical hard-liner who, soon after his return from India in 1790, insisted on an overt civilizing programme for the religious and moral improvement of the country. This was duly backed in Parliament by Wilberforce. Yet the initiative failed at the time of the Company's charter renewal in 1793 and the admission of Christian missionaries to India had to wait until the next charter renewal in 1813. It is interesting in this context to note that even before official missionary activities began after 1813, Christian literature on the civilization of India's peoples was published in Scotland and England demanding the diffusion of the Christian religion throughout India. This was regarded as the best means to civilize her people, and the proponents of missionary activity argued in favour of a general 'civilizing mission' as a project for the enhancement of India's moral standards.[19]

> Civilization is a comparative term, and admits of several significations. In its common and popular acceptation, it denotes that state in which man finds himself placed in the more advanced stages of society, and by which he is distinguished from the rude and uncultivated savage, whose knowledge extends not further than to supply the common and returning wants of his nature. In this sense of the term, the natives of India rank high amongst the civilized nations of the world. [. . .]
>
> Civilization [. . .] supposes man to enjoy the benefit of those institutions, which it is the province of political science to devise, for the regulation of his conduct, in a social state, in as great perfection as the circumstances of this state will admit; and to be put in that state of

happiness and freedom, which, consistent with the objects society has in view, is the possible he can attain. [. . .]

To promote the progress of civilization among a people, whom the fortune of war has brought under our subjugation, will be allowed to be an undertaking, worthy of a humane and liberal nation to encourage.[20]

The notion of 'improvement of humankind' was prevalent among the political and economic elite of Great Britain during the last decades of the eighteenth century, and extended to the moral and material improvement of British India; in both societies, the British elite regarded betterment as a mandate to civilize the 'masses'. Hence, the British civilizing mission was not restricted to the colonies but included society at home. However, the colonies in general, and India in particular, became a kind of vast laboratory where the ideology of a civilizing mission towards an uncivilized people was worked out by various groups and individuals who dominated the public and political spheres of both the metropolis and the colonial periphery. It is against this background that the civilizing mission was used to justify British rule in India.

In addition to the Evangelicals, there existed a secular group of civilizing missionaries. Scottish Enlightenment, and later on Utilitarianism, supplied the reformers with the instruments necessary to develop their ideology. Civilization could be characterized and measured according to principles like the rule of law and good government. Of course, Britain embodied the said two principles and was therefore at the top of such a ladder of civilization, along with or above other European countries, while countries of the East or the Americas were placed at its lower end. The tools of Enlightenment worked well, since the construction of difference took shape with regard to civilizations. In India, early Orientalists like William Jones and Nathaniel Halhed, encouraged by Governor General Warren Hastings (1772–1785), constructed the approach of the difference of civilizations. India, they maintained, had possessed a grand ancient civilization, which had degenerated over the course of history. The first generation of British administrators, therefore, felt obliged to uplift contemporary India and reform the country according to its old traditions. Therefore Hastings and his Orientalist contemporaries were in search of old texts representing true Indian values. Reforms would take place partly in accordance with western ideas of reform yet with an Indian content in order that they were acceptable to the Indian people. This was deemed an appropriate means of liberating India from 'Oriental despotism'. Nevertheless, most of the Britons involved agreed on the necessity to rule the Indians firmly, and took it for granted that they were *a priori* good rulers and the Indians good subjects.[21] The corresponding concept of 'benevolent despotism' remained popular until well into the twentieth century.

The 'good government' that the British wanted to establish had to be based on sound principles, like the 'rule of law'. Consequently, the introduction of western ideas and institutions of governance into India was considered the appropriate instrument for the general improvement of the country and its people. This view was not always shared by the subject population. As Margret Frenz's article argues, the British were confronted with a mighty local kingdom in Malabar whose *raja* was highly respected by the population, which made it difficult to establish colonial rule after the conquest of the Malabar Coast between 1792 and 1799. Questions of legitimate rule based on the right of conquest and the concept of good government dominated the discussion between the British and the Malabarians for decades and provoked fierce resistance by the Malabarian *raja*s and the local population. Despite negotiations, British power was only established by bayonet. Pacification was never completed satisfactorily and Malabar Province remained an 'unruly' territory prone to rebellions and disturbances until the end of colonial rule in India.[22]

The crucial question about the civilizing mission was the extent to which a country like India could be transformed by its 'benevolent' rulers – what sort of institutions could be introduced or even transferred from Britain, and which Indian institutions and traditions should be preserved. Early Orientalist attempts to reform India in accordance with what was perceived as her 'traditional' knowledge and institutions resulted in a reinvention of Indian legal traditions according to the British–European notion of an ancient civilization's cultural merits. Nathaniel Halhed's *Hindu Code*, published in 1776, is the most striking example of such a reinvention, and is a random collection of the Hindu laws needed by the British administration. Apart from this, the British interfered with the jurisdiction of Bengal. In their early effort to claim the prerogatives of sovereignty, the British stipulated that the 'feudal' powers of the intermediary local rulers involved in revenue collection and jurisdiction, as well as the personal jurisdiction of a creditor over his debtor, were to be transferred to the supreme authority. The Company state thus began to extend its own punitive jurisdiction in place of the punitive and restitutive claims of its subjects against each other. The result was extended 'public justice' in contradistinction to 'personal injury'.[23]

It is in this context that the early colonial state's effort to wrest the right to confirm death sentences and usurp capital punishment from the *nawab* of Bengal sheds light on the true purposes and mechanisms of colonial rule. On a superficial level it aimed at the preservation of 'ancient institutions', yet these, disguised as modern reforms, were designed to benefit the colonial regime. The unequal application of laws, such as those against the highway robbers (*dacoits*) and 'criminals by birth' – the most notorious being the famous Thugs[24] – later regarded as 'criminal tribes', and thus not chargeable with individual crimes or subject to individual guilt – soon turned the colonial state's jurisdiction into a fairly despotic regime.[25] The case study of capital punishment as the supreme prerogative of the sovereign refers to this concept. Governor General Warren Hastings failed, but his successor Lord Cornwallis successfully usurped control of capital punishment on grounds of the sovereign's 'privilege of taking life'.[26] Nevertheless, this core of judicial reform could only be accomplished because Cornwallis changed the law, deceiving the people of Bengal, as will be demonstrated in the first chapter of this book.[27]

Cornwallis did not want to rely on British institutions to assist in his improvement policies: he viewed the Indian people as unready to participate in such unfamiliar bodies, which would be, in his estimation, barely intelligible to them. Instead, he promoted the introduction of the abstract 'rule of law' into India because he regarded it as the appropriate instrument to implant a 'spirit' of rationality that, he hoped, would be ultimately disseminated among the peoples of the subcontinent. Of course, Cornwallis was aware of the limited effect and success of his reforms, but he was convinced that the improvement's 'spirit' would influence large parts of society and enable the colonial state to introduce further reforms at a later stage. The enactment of the Civil and Criminal Procedure Codes in India in the 1860s bears testimony to this design, which guided the British policy of improving and modernizing India until 1947.[28]

3. The Progress of History: The Political Utility of Historiography

A swing towards a more straightforward policy of reform in India took place during the course of the Napoleonic Wars in Europe and the victories of the British-Indian forces in India in the second decade of the nineteenth century: the awkward question of legitimate rule had provoked a vivid debate on the legitimacy of colonial rule. Within a short time, the subject had become a prime topic on Britain's political agenda. What was the standing of British rule in India, and how was continued military expansion to be justified?

In 1792, Charles Grant took a strong stance against British reformist attitudes in India. In his *Observations on the State of Society among the Asiatic Subjects of Great Britain*, addressed to the directors of the East India Company and written against the background of the Company's charter renewal, due in the following year, Grant opposed the 'Orientalist' attitudes of Warren Hastings and William Jones, and opted for radical reforms because of the 'vile and exceedingly depraved' state of Indian society, which could only be uplifted by a thorough transformation.[29]

According to Grant, light had to be brought into darkness. Consequently, religious reforms should be put in train, emphasizing the universal truth of Christianity, which would improve Hindu society. Selfishness, he declared, was the main mark of 'Hindu character', which could be seen from the absence of parental affection and conjugal love in most Hindus. Women were doomed to a life of near slavery, often suffering premature violent death. He considered Hinduism despotic, and therefore responsible for the corrupted state of Indian society. Reforms were to include an education programme to be run by Christian missionaries, initially for the Indian elites but in the long run for the majority of the population. Grant strongly recommended English as the sole administrative language in which knowledge, which comprised natural philosophy, useful literature and the principles of mechanisms, would be disseminated. The most important innovation, though, would be the introduction of Christianity.[30]

Even though Charles Grant believed in the universal validity of Christian values, he doubted that they could be wholly applied to India because it seemed unlikely to him that the reforms would produce the same results as they would within a European society: 'effeminate' Indians lacked the 'manly character' of Europeans.[31] For that reason, it also seemed unlikely that Indians would demand independence, as the American colonists had. Grant argued that England's retention of India was more of an atonement for original sin than an indication of her persistence. He envisaged a permanent connection between India and Britain, which would be secured with the reforms, which would 'have established, in their minds such an affectionate participation in our lot, such an union with our interests [. . . that the people would] identify their cause with ours'. Grant thus suggested for the first time the 'principle of assimilation', against that of equality, as the basis of legitimacy for a colonial state and future guidance for an imperial power.[32] Indians were no longer considered potential equals in the Christian sense but as inherently inferior, which justified 'keeping the subjects in obedience and subordination'.[33]

The idea of reform gained new momentum in Britain with the emergence of the 'Utilitarians', who promoted radical reforms of society at large; Jeremy Bentham was the protagonist of this movement. He suggested administrative and legislative reforms based on simple principles to facilitate the greatest happiness for the greatest number. His ideas were spread among the young Britons at the East India Company's Haileybury college. As future members of the Indian Civil Service they went out to India with the notion that free trade and a cheap, efficient government were the best means by which to set in motion the modernization of India. Evangelicalism and Utilitarianism were movements of individualism, both seeking to liberate the individual from slavery and custom, and from the tyranny of nobles and priests. To achieve this, men had to be educated until they could discipline themselves. A severe schoolmaster or father was necessary in the form of harsh laws. In contrast to the Evangelicals, the Utilitarians substituted human for divine justice: good government and law became the keystone of modern society. James Mill applied this philosophy to India, simplifying the problem of promoting her civilization to three core issues: the reform of government, the nature of laws and the mode of taxation.[34]

It seems as if Grant's *Observations* served as a blueprint for James Mill's *The History of British India*, published in five volumes in 1817, the most influential piece of historiography published during British colonial rule in India, although the influence of Grant's *Observations* has been underestimated until now.[35] Referring to the established enlightened notion of a cultural difference between Europe and India, Mill starts his *History*: 'Rude nations seem to derive a peculiar gratification from pretensions to a remote antiquity'[36] and goes on to launch a vicious attack on India's civilization. In his eyes, India was a 'lost country' that had never acquired a high degree of civilization, and had degenerated under the influence of continued 'despotic Oriental regimes' as well as an arbitrary and corrupt priesthood, built on a most superstitious form of religion. Hence Indian society remained backward, its people the most enslaved in the world. To free the country from oppression and stagnation, Mill proposed the introduction of the Utilitarian panacea: light taxes, and rational, codified, accessible laws – which would induce social revolution. Otherwise his proposals were not new: Cornwallis had been pursuing a similar policy. The important point is that Mill, like Grant before him, con-demned all Indian institutions as being unfit for reform.[37]

According to Mill, every society possessed superior spirits capable of generating the best ideas of their times and accelerating the progress of society. These specialists had to be selected for governance to improve the country. In India, the ruling elite, of course, was not composed of Indians but of British administrators employed in the East India Company. For India, because of its 'rude and ignorant' state of civilization, Mill suggested a simple form of arbitrary government tempered by European moral, political and intellectual standards, as the only form of government appropriate to rule the country. However, he regarded the contemporary British government in India as incapable of sufficient improvement to transform India and lobbied for a fundamental change in politics, strongly recommending the introduction of western institutions.[38] In a way, Charles Grant and James Mill forced the gates of the so-called 'Age of Reform' in India, which lasted from the late

1820s to the late 1850s. During this period, Evangelicals and Utilitarians had a decisive influence on Indian society in the introduction of radical reforms.[39]

British administrators, like Governor General William C Bentinck (1828–35), Charles Metcalfe, secretary, and Thomas B Macaulay, member of the British-Indian law commission in the 1830s, were outstanding representatives of the new British policy in India determining Utilitarian-cum-imperial attitudes. The new generation of administrators was guided by British upper middle class ideas of reform, in respect of the moral and material betterment of society, and favoured immediate reforms from a western perspective as well as their rapid enactment. The days of trial and error seemed to have gone. Instead, as John William Kaye's *The Administration of the East India Company* – written at the beginning of the 1850s – demonstrates, historiography again pioneered the civilizing mission and offered prospects for the future development of India. A masterpiece of Orientalist literature and an immediate outcome of utilitarian *Weltanschauung*, British historiography described colonialism as a 'history of progress', as the subtitle of Kaye's work suggests.[40]

What was hitherto considered as the more or less unsystematic 'improvement' of the Cornwallis era was reshaped and newly moulded in a form of systematic and stringent advancement. British rule in India became synonymous with the country's progress. The new contemporary European leitmotif was duly applied to British politics in India. However, the title of Kaye's book is somewhat misleading because he refers not only to the administrative history of India but also to her technological, educational and economic development. Indicating the continuity of British attitudes towards India, even in the aftermath of the 'Great Rebellion', the first volume of the newly published periodical *Moral and Material Progress and Condition of India*, dating from 1859–60, reported on the proceedings of the civilizing mission. Subjects like 'Geological Survey of India', 'Suppression of Human Sacrifice and Female Infanticide in the Hill Tracts of Orissa', 'Vital Statistics, Sanitation &c.', and 'Forests', next to more general subjects like 'Finances', dominated the tables of contents and bore testimony to the civilizing mission's all-embracing progressive programme.[41] Reflecting the Victorian rhetoric of progress, the following two sections of this introduction will explore in more detail the changes introduced between 1830 and 1940 to further the country's 'material and moral progress'.

4. Issues of 'Material Progress': Technology, Public Health and Economic Development

In light of nineteenth-century technological innovations and Britain's industrial revolution, reformers in the British-Indian administration connected the progress of society with the equipment technology provided.[42] Steamboats on India's rivers and, later, railways linking her major cities, as well as the telegraph, became highly promoted icons of improvement.[43] Ravi Ahuja demonstrates in his article that the British regarded the building of railways in India as a major contribution to the improvement of the country and to the civilization of its people. His analysis of Rudyard Kipling's 'The Bridge-builders' shows that such technical 'improvement' can be seen as the replacing of Indian gods with the fetishes of modernity. The subsequent case studies of the railways of Orissa and the pilgrim trains to Puri show that, within a short time, a self-confident Indian 'agency' emerged, demanding better trains, better connections and better service. However, British administrators did not feel obliged to comply with the requests of the Indian pilgrim-customers. On the contrary, denying any kind of 'agency' to the petitioners, British commentaries stated that Indians were unable to understand or deal with modern machines and their 'conundrums'. The colonial subjects were again reduced to a childlike status, to second class citizens in need of guidance by benevolent paternalists. As a result, improvement remained largely the preserve of the British.[44]

Besides the transfer of western technology to India, the spread of western medicine was also increasingly seen as a landmark contribution to the material betterment of the country. At the outset, it was a highly contested field between Indian knowledge and European 'science'. From the late eighteenth century to the second half of the nineteenth, the colonial medical service was one of the principal scientific agencies in India: surgeons provided a large number of the botanists, geologists, foresters and other specialists who became deeply engaged in the investigation of the environment. Additionally, medicine represented the direct intervention in, and interaction with, physical, social and cultural aspects of the lives of the population. Until the 1830s, parts of the Indian medical system were regarded as worthy of adoption into the scientific canon of western medicine. It was only gradually that British administrators came to treat it as irrational, superstitious and unscientific. After 1835, Indian medical institutes were increasingly replaced by colonial medical colleges, which produced hundreds of Indian doctors serving in the major cities of British India and in the princely states. Nevertheless, western medicine remained an imperfect, purely empirical science, which could not provide cures for epidemics of, for instance, cholera and smallpox.[45]

Colonial medicine was also considered a useful tool for ruling the country[46] in its potential for colonizing and civilizing the bodies of the people.[47] This was especially apparent when the British tried to introduce western modes of prophylactic vaccination to prevent smallpox. The question of whether to adopt vaccination or to continue with the traditional Indian variolation was hotly debated among British medics; any preference, of course, could not be founded on empirical data generating scientific knowledge. As Nils Brimnes elaborates in his article, it was not the European doctor who argued against his Indian 'colleague' but the British administrator of the East India Company, pursuing the interests of his government, who was compelled to give preference to European 'science' in order to demonstrate British superiority and justify legitimate British rule.[48]

Vaccination was debated between British and Indian physicians, trained according to western methods, and Indian ayurvedic practitioners in the aftermath of the plague epidemic of 1896–7. Questions of urban hygiene and sanitation were on the municipal and medical agendas in Britain, and had been in India since the middle of the nineteenth century, but the discussion on public health became prominent in the subcontinent only at the turn of the nineteenth century.[49] Then, the emphasis gradually shifted from an entirely curative to a more preventive medical policy, as Mridula Ramanna's case study on Bombay city illustrates.[50] It was generally agreed that only an education scheme would improve the deplorable situation: wider knowledge of sanitation would lead to improved awareness of hygiene among the Indian urban population. Indian doctors were considered as the most important intermediate agency in this – the success of public-health policy rested on their cooperation. Interestingly, Indian doctors not only supported the British public-health policy but also criticized British institutions, like the railway authorities, for lack of cooperation. Unlike the Indian railway pilgrims to Puri, they were listened to. But again, as in the case of the early vaccination programme in south India, Indian medical knowledge was soon regarded as inferior and duly ruled out by legislative measures.[51]

The British treatment regime in lunatic asylums appears to have been another instrument of the overall civilizing mission. As James Mills argues in his article,[52] psychiatry did not aim primarily at the medical cure of the patients but pursued a policy of rehabilitating inmates as useful members of the colonial society. This implied a self-regulating, obedient and, above all, economically productive colonial subject. A lunatic was regarded as 'corrected' when he or she could work again. Moreover, asylums reflected (or became laboratories of) the paternalistic British view of an ideal colonial society separated according to castes, religions and gender. These communal identities and distinctions drove a wedge between the colonized groups and prevented them identifying the British as their common enemy.

The emphasis placed on the formation of orderly, useful and productive subjects in the native lunatic asylums points to another aspect of the civilizing mission: the trope of economic development. Yet material improvement for

India, as envisaged by the British colonizers, primarily comprised an economic development for Britain, who wanted to enrich herself from the output
of India's economy, in cash and in kind. The politics of material progress
started with the well-known Bengal Permanent Settlement of 1793. It fixed,
once and for all, the revenues from the land, and created a class of revenue
contractors with vaguely defined rights in the soil, crudely mirroring the
British notion of 'private property'. For quite some time, economic improvement was viewed mainly as an extension of the cultivated area and an
intensification of agriculture to increase crop output. As with the colonies in
the Americas, India was treated as a supplier of agricultural products.
Industrial development was never considered, at least as far as competing
industries were concerned. India became only partly industrialized in the
second half of the nineteenth century, when the jute industry of Calcutta, the
cotton industry of Bombay and Ahmedabad, and the Tata Iron and Steel
Company in Jamshedpur were established. As with railway construction, this
development did not include a transfer of knowledge and technology
but merely exploited the cheap labour and lax legal provision for industrial
workers in India.[53]

It was only between 1918 and 1939, and especially during the Great
Depression from 1929 to 1939, that it became clear that British India needed
to enhance her economic potential to cope with a rising population and an
accelerating world economy based on a speedy exchange of industrial
goods.[54] It also became clear that Britain had failed to modernize India,
despite her official ideology – the civilizing mission.[55] The notion of a colonial
development 'programme' as part of an economic framework to justify colonial rule was born in the 1930s, when it was argued that a benevolent colonial
regime was still preferable to concepts of home rule or self-government.
Even the British Labour Party conceptualized 'development' as an evolutionary process, recommending 'socialism' in certain colonies rather than self-
government or independence.[56] 'Development' became the modern term for
'civilizing', since it still operated on the principle of imagined differences and
hierarchies. Consequently, the antonym 'underdevelopment' was introduced
into the political-cum-economic discourse after 1945, with the colonies being
on the threshold of independence.[57]

At a quite early stage, Indians themselves acknowledged the 'backwardness' of their country's economy and deemed 'economic development' a
central issue in the debates on modernization and nation building. Soon these
discussions also comprised the means of development. While some political
leaders surrendered to western models of modernity, others tried to reconcile
them with eastern values and Indian culture – the debate is reminiscent of the
Orientalist–Anglicist controversy on the improvement of India a hundred

years earlier. Generally Gandhi rejected the western notion and definition of backwardness, because of its cultural implications. Instead, he argued in favour of economic concepts set within an Indian context. Although his ideas in this area seemed nebulous and far from practicable as the basis for a future national economic policy, Indian modernizers conceded that his proposal for village industries might be included in an overall scheme of economic development, which, nevertheless, should be founded on science, technology and industrialization for India's national, not Britain's imperial, benefit.[58]

Some of Gandhi's disciples, such as J C Kumarappa, who had been awarded his academic degrees in the USA, were authorized to interpret his sometimes inconsistent writings on economics and disseminate them to a wider public. As Benjamin Zachariah shows, Kumarappa's major book *Why the Village Movement?*, published in 1936, was an annotated commentary, from a Gandhian perspective, on contemporary discussions about India's development. However, Kumarappa is not able to free himself from the colonial discourse: he sticks to the binary Orientalist framework of differences between East and West. He turns arguments upside-down: the West becomes morally deficient and the East claims superiority. He separates modernity from the West and claims it for the East – surely a twisted form of an internalized civilizing mission, which meant giving the foreign linguistic phrasing a 'new' meaning.[59]

5. Issues of 'Moral Progress': Education, Character Building, and the Fight Against 'Social Evils'

Railways, hospitals, clean cities and a modern economic programme were visible signs of the material improvement and progress of India. The moral improvement turned out to be a more difficult task, because the envisaged principle of dissemination or permeation was idealistic and hardly controllable. Legal reforms were supposed to have a positive impact on the 'superstitious beliefs', 'irrational thinking' and 'partially barbaric behaviour' of the Indian people. Starting with the eighteenth-century legal reforms of Warren Hastings and Lord Cornwallis, the aim for moral improvement through legal measures was reintroduced in a much more straightforward manner in the 1830s.

What, in the first place, appeared as reform of the 'superstitious' Hindu religion, in the abolition of *sati*, discussed by Jana Tschurenev, was another attempt by the colonial regime to enforce its right to reform India's society. Neither general human rights nor the position of women in contemporary Indian society were on the agenda of the British-Indian government. *Sati* was simply the most spectacular issue of reform: all Europeans knew about the practice of a widow's self-immolation on her husband's funeral pyre, though it did not often occur. However, Britons regarded *sati* as the most outrageous and horrifying religious ritual. Sensationalism, combined with sexuality, violence and the desire to abolish the atavistic practices of a rude society, guided reform politics. Among contemporaries the abolition of *sati* was controversial: Indian reformers, like Ram Mohan Roy, a *brahmin*, supported the British position while others opposed any interference with Hindu religious customs. Even present-day debates on singular cases of *sati* that took place in the 1980s and 1990s demonstrate the emotion that the issue still provokes. Advocates of *sati* insist on cultural and religious freedom, but critics opine that participants have not liberated themselves from the colonial notions of modernity on the one hand and superstitious beliefs on the other.[60]

Taming the savages of India became the special task and greatest challenge for the 'men on the spot' of the civilizing mission. Although the peoples of India were generally believed not only to be inferior in mind and character but also effeminate, the manly colonial officer's duty consisted chiefly of administering their lot. The civilizing mission had degenerated into forms of supervision and control while a truly 'manly' mission seemed impossible. This proved to be different with the robust hillsmen of the north-west frontier, as well as with the 'savages' – the wild tribes in Chota Nagpur, south Bihar, western Bengal and the Western Ghats, where the British civilizing missionary had to deal with a fierce, hence manly, opponent.[61] This double-tiered Indian society and, accordingly, mission project characterized colonial rule. To identify the object of the civilizing mission, the British separated their colonial antagonists into classes, clans, castes and various communities.[62] It was not only the wild tribes of India that were considered savages and, therefore, 'manly' objects of their civilizing attitudes: 'warrior' tribes or clans, like the Nepalese Gurkhas, and strong, 'proud' ethnic groups like the north Indian Rajputs, were all considered worthy of being fought, subdued, pacified and civilized.[63]

Malavika Kasturi has worked out the changing role of the Rajputs in the second half of the nineteenth and the beginning of the twentieth centuries. Her article takes a different angle on the ritually and socially founded killing of girl children. While *sati* was in the public arena, female infanticide took place in the domestic sphere. She argues persuasively that, in that period, the importance of marriage as a means of power was reinforced when the political and social system, based on honour, exchange and military service, collapsed in the aftermath of the 'Great Rebellion' of 1857–9. The formerly esteemed Rajput soldiers were dismissed from the British-Indian army on suspicion of having taken part in the revolt. It was only at this point that the British colonial state started to investigate their social circumstances and customs. The cruel and abhorrent custom of female infanticide, which was not practised to control birth rates but to check marriage costs and to secure the social status of the family and the clan of Rajput society, was regarded as sound reason to interfere. Families suspected of practising female infanticide were put under special surveillance so that the law of 1870, which prohibited the custom, could be enforced. However, the colonial state could never effectively control female infanticide and consequently, the Female Infanticide Act of 1870 was abolished in 1912. Again, as with *sati*, the status of women was not paramount in the debates on female infanticide.[64]

In both cases, of *sati* and female infanticide, the British pretended to reform India in accordance with the old Hindu scriptures and, therefore, referred to the opinions and findings of the *brahmins*. From the late eighteenth century, Britons and *brahmins* launched a hitherto unknown, modern 'brahminical renaissance', starting with the reconstruction of the ancient Hindu law as well as the Muslim law of India. The way that the British urged *brahmins* to elaborate the non-Hinduistic practice of *sati*, based on old Sanskrit texts – as in the case of the 'Hindu Code' in 1776 – indicates the attempt to (re)construct Indian religion according to their own understanding of how Hinduism ought to be – less superstitious and more rational. Also, *brahmins* and *maulavis* were compelled to produce *vyavasthas* and *fatwas* (written legal opinions) according to British stipulations. The same pattern was used in the case of *sati* and female infanticide when *brahmins* had to produce legal opinions and principles consistent with British reform purposes. This not only reflected a purely brahmanic view of the law but also a narrow aspect of the multifarious interpretations inherent in it. Codification through legislation systematically reduced Indian laws to British needs of governance.

Next in the abolition of 'cruel practices', the British administrators of the Age of Reform made the education of India's population a cornerstone of their reform scheme. After 1813, the officials of the East India Company observed with suspicion the ensuing 'classless' educational activities of the Evangelical mission in India: they considered books with egalitarian Christian ideas dangerous because they might cause discontent and even upheaval. Instead, they favoured books that advocated punctuality, honesty, diligence, loyalty and sexual restraint. In a break from all of the previously debated ideas of education, Thomas B Macaulay took up Charles Grant's earlier suggestion to establish English as the sole administrative language in British India. As is well known, the education debate of the 1830s was highly controversial and its results, despite the 'compromise settlement' of 1839 and the educational review of 1854, extinguished all benevolent Orientalist reform ideas that took into account Indian cultural heritage, traditions and values.[65]

Contrary to the early Orientalist reformers, Macaulay did not aim at an overall education of the Indian population but restricted his programme to create a class of Indians educated in the English language to assist the British in the administration of India, a class '[. . .] English in taste, in opinion, in morals and in intellect'.[66] It seems that he did not intend to transform India's society *in toto*, and even the aspect of dissemination was not clearly elaborated, although he envisaged a politically independent India, one that would have embodied an '[. . .] imperishable empire of our arts and our morals, our literature and our laws', to quote once again his infamous 'Minute of Education' of 1835.[67] The educational improvement of India was visualized chiefly for the intellectual élite of the country as she surfaced in the second half of the nineteenth century. Parts of this élite founded the Indian National Congress in 1885 to participate in the politics of colonial India, which ultimately turned against her educators in demanding independence, as Macaulay had rightly predicted.

Indian reform movements were initially dominated by British ideas yet, in the nationalistic climate of the late nineteenth and early twentieth centuries, Indians also searched for independent and indigenous sources for their modernizing initiatives. Vacillating between religious and social reconstruction and overt political agitation, Hindu reform organizations, like the Arya Samaj, developed their own programmes, which included the quest for a national education. For the emerging Indian middle classes, traditional religious education was not an alternative to British-run high schools and colleges. From the 1870s on, a multitude of educational institutions was founded, which endeavoured to combine the best of East and West. Students were to be provided with the necessary qualifications to start a career in the colonial administration as well as being endowed with an independent mind and a feeling of 'national pride'.[68]

As Harald Fischer-Tiné shows in his contribution to this book, the Gurukul Kangri, founded in 1902, is the most striking example of such an educational experiment, reflecting the social and political visions of the Arya Samaj. The educational reformers had internalized the early British historiography of India's high state of ancient civilization and its degeneration theory after the Muslim conquest and therefore demanded that India should reform herself on the basis of her old values contained in the Vedic scriptures. These values and virtues had to be rediscovered (some were reinvented) to provide India with a class of national leaders fit to govern the country. Repeatedly internalizing the concept of the British civilizing mission, the promoters of the Gurukul Kangri envisaged India's independence within an indefinite time-span. Interestingly, educational notions like character building and manliness reflected contemporary British public-school values. Yet the Gurukul Kangri did not simply copy British elite education schemes but also provided a critique of colonial rule. They were suspicious of the British, although they were partly willing to promote the institution as a positive example of the civilizing mission aims. The article exemplifies some of the inconsistencies in Indian educational reform attitudes as well as the British colonial regime's contradictions in respect of legitimizing their rule at the beginning of the twentieth century.[69]

As is already evident in the educational agenda of the Gurukul Kangri, moral improvement extended to physical development. Sport was seen as an ideal means to combat idleness and unruliness, and develop physical prowess and a sense of discipline. In a wider sense, sport provided dutiful, hard-working and useful members of the colonial society. In British eyes, sport embodied the Victorian concept of manliness as it was taught in Britain's public schools and, of course, the military. Above that, the qualities developed and trained through sport were regarded as the reason for Britain's superiority over Orientals *and* over westerners like the Germans and the French.[70] Although the British recognized the benefits of physical exercise they also saw the danger inherent in it: Indians could not be allowed to become as physically powerful as themselves. Physical tests for Indians before gaining admission to colonial public institutions became a hurdle many an Indian candidate failed to leap, thus confirming British racial stereotypes and cultural prejudices.

Paul Dimeo argues in his article that, ultimately, the British civilizing mission in the field of sport failed because British officials assumed that Indians preferred inertia over activity.[71] Soon, football became the game Indians did not play for the British Empire but for themselves. Understandably, this caused anxiety among British imperialists, and made them question their assumptions. Between 1918 and 1939, Indians had gained equal representation on the sport's governing bodies without showing the weaknesses accepted as normal in colonialism. At the same time, they did not change the colonial parameters: they stuck to the rules of the game set up by the British; they still wanted to gain British respect and they also respected football's (sport's) inherent manly virtues. The legacy of this aspect of the civilizing mission is complex but, as Dimeo shows, the internalization has led to feelings of physical inferiority that can still be observed today.[72]

Another example of the civilizing mission's internalized results is presented by Markus Daechsel.[73] Ghulam Jilani Barq (1901–84) was an educationalist and publicist who traversed the Punjab tirelessly to persuade his Muslim countrymen to embrace an Islam that incorporated all positive aspects of western civilization. He was especially referring to hygiene, education and science. Barq viewed himself as a preacher and prophet, and as an Indian who continued the work of renowned European enlightened philosophers. He challenged traditional Islam and voiced opinions that most of his Muslim contemporaries would not have dared utter for fear of causing insecurity and desperation. Barq represents the collision between the ideas of Islam and western science, inferiority and superiority, and the relationship between the individual and the universe. Having internalized the aims of the civilizing mission, Barq also adapted the simplistic civilizational ideas of fascism – in short, might is right – which left him in the uncomfortable position of deciding whether he should opt for the overall superiority of the west and accept the historic failure of Islam, or whether Islam could be retained and, therefore, hailed as a universally true belief. In this ambiguity he is typical of modern Muslims in India and Pakistan.

A discussion of the ideology of the British civilizing mission cannot be concluded without reference to race and caste. Cultural differences, which had predominated British perceptions of India in the eighteenth and the first half of the nineteenth centuries were gradually replaced by a racial concept to explain the superiority of European over Asian people. Racial theories, as they were developed in Europe in the wake of the newly-established natural sciences, provided colonialists with additional ammunition in the fight for their civilizing mission. Similar to the ordering of civilizations on a hierarchical scale, Europeans ordered 'invented' races according to the principles of superiority and inferiority. India's races were viewed as 'primitive' for biological reasons, thus reflecting the cultural category of 'uncivilized'. However, the concept of races was seemingly inconsistent since the Aryan race comprised Indians as well as Europeans. Consequently, the British constructed (or invented) an immigration-cum-mixing of races on the subcontinent that caused the racial degeneration of the Indian Aryans and an overall decline of the Indian races.[74] Referring to established Indian concepts of certain essential differences between humans, the British treated some Indian races as martial, such as the Sikhs or the Afghans who had a fair complexion, and regarded them as an even more formidable enemy.[75] This, again, represents the double-edged 'manly' concept of colonial rule in contrast to the general perception of a weak and lazy Oriental embodied in the 'effeminate' Bengali.[76] What was at issue, then, was not race itself but processes of history and culture in which race became an additional argument and convenient marker of differences, indicating one of the many inconsistencies of colonial concepts and constructions.[77]

Race and caste became closely intertwined in the western discourse on India in the late nineteenth and twentieth centuries. Although caste is an Indian historical as well as a sociological reality, an all-India caste system derived from the British imagination of India's population as a strictly divided society. Relying on Indian informants, mostly *brahmins* but also village headmen, the colonial administrators identified hundreds of castes and depressed groups (for example, the 'pariahs' or 'untouchables') to protect the latter from the evils of the system. Hence, the hierarchical caste system is the outcome of cooperation between colonial officials and representatives of certain Indian social groups. India's social fragmentation reflected the British concept of divide and rule, which was used to explain her disunity in respect to the idea of a nation. For this reason, India was to be governed by the British because Indians were regarded as unfit to govern themselves. Once again, colonial rule was legitimized by the lack of civilization.[78]

Melitta Waligora uses new findings on social structure in India to give a more precise picture of how the idea of a so-called all-Indian caste system developed during the nineteenth century. The main idea is that the British did not invent caste but changed the 'spirit' according to their self-imposed civilizing mission. With reference to the empirical data collections and interpretations of Francis Buchanan, writing at the beginning of the nineteenth century, and H H Risley, writing at the end, she points out some remarkable shifts in the approaches of these colonial ethnographers. Whereas for Buchanan the principles of power and wealth were important for the hierarchical structure of Bengali society, Risley tried to insert the theory of race to explain social hierarchy and to combine this principle with the brahminical idea of sacred hierarchy and purity. In the end he failed because his own empirical material, which tells us much about the social realities of Bengal, does not fit his theoretical approach. But colonial administrators were not interested in this material and, once the theory of race proved to be wrong and the principles of power, wealth and importance dropped out, the remaining concept was caste as the religious basis of Indian society. This coincided with the fact that caste increasingly became the point of reference for the judicial and fiscal administration of the country. Risley's writings accelerated this process because they became the blueprint for the ensuing generation of colonial administrators to deem India 'caste ridden'. Instrumentalized by the judges, caste penetrated deep into India's society. Again, as in the case of the vaccination–variolation debate, it was the colonial administrator, rather than the specialist working on a specific region or subject, who took decisions on political grounds supportive of British needs to maintain colonial rule.[79]

6. The British 'Civilizing Mission' in India: A Success Story?

It was through dichotomies that Europeans perceived the non-European world. Since the appearance of Edward Said's *Orientalism*, scholarly attention has also been focused on the dichotomies that reduced highly complex interactions and interrelationships to the simple binary system of the 'self' and the 'other'. Extending the argument, Gyan Prakash has recently reminded us that

[t]he writ of rationality and order was always overwritten by its denial
in the colonies, the pieties of progress always violated irreverently in
practice, the assertion of the universality of Western ideals always
qualified drastically. Paradoxes and ironies abounded, as did the
jurisdiction of the gap between rhetoric and practice on the grounds
of expediency and the exceptional circumstances of the colonies.[80]

These paradoxes and contradictions comprised anomalies, such as spreading
civic values and virtues by military power or propagating the text of *The Rights
of Man* while simultaneously prolonging slavery in India and setting up the
system of indentured labour. As has been pointed out, the basic contradiction
of the civilizing project was, however, the fear of the colonizers that the
colonized might become civilized and, hence, equal. In many of the essays and
articles included in this book, such paradoxes and inconsistencies are dealt
with in detail. What has to be stressed is that they were not simply irregularities but an integral part of the civilizing mission ideology, which enabled the
British to react flexibly to changing colonial parameters and to 'improve' the
means and mechanisms of self-legitimation. An analogy may illustrate this
statement: it has not been the case that the internal contradiction of capitalism
has caused its collapse, as Karl Marx predicted. Instead it has secured its
survival, as both economic and political leaders were forced to respond openly
to societal contradictions. If we bear this in mind, it seems justified to characterize the civilizing mission as the sole ideology of British colonialism in India
and elsewhere in the world, except in the white-settler colonies.

What the French overtly described as the *mission civilisatrice*, which, as has
been convincingly argued, also included paradoxes, contradictions and inconsistencies,[81] was called by the British 'material and moral improvement' and,
later on, in modern (positivistic) terms, 'moral and material progress'. Both
concepts had, again like their French counterpart, the same implications. To
pave the way for the civilizing mission, protagonists basically concurred on
the subject, differing only on its means. As we have seen, there was little
difference between the Orientalists William Jones and Warren Hastings and
early Anglicists, like Charles Grant and Lord Cornwallis, concerning the
extension of the state's legal and punitive claims. The main topic for discussion was the strategy to be used to secure the sovereign rights of the state.[82]
The same was true for the British administrators in India who followed, such
as the Governor Generals William Bentinck and James Marquess Dalhousie,
who strongly emphasized the right to rule and regulate the colonial state in
trying to push reforms to the utmost. This policy included technological
innovation and science, which the Utilitarians considered necessary to rule
the country efficiently and firmly.

In Great Britain, the emerging Conservative Party reflected by and large the positions of the Anglicist, while the Liberal Party harboured the former Orientalist attitude towards India. For both imperialists and liberals, the timetable of colonial rule – that is, the duration of the civilizing mission in India – seems to have been unclear and lacked perspective. Imperialists never took the end of empire into close consideration and created an illusion of permanent colonial rule – Winston Churchill frankly admitted that he had not become prime minister to preside over the dissolution of the British Empire. Liberals more or less envisaged a future independent India but continuously postponed it on the political agenda, which points towards a latent imperialist attitude. As mentioned above, even the Labour Party favoured a 'socialist regime' in India over her independence. Until the end of the Second World War, almost no British politician could imagine an independent India during his lifetime.[83]

Hence, the majority of British politicians probably agreed with the words uttered in the heyday of imperialism by the most outstanding imperialist ever, the Governor General and Viceroy of India, Lord Curzon, who gave the following simple definition of the civilizing mission's aim. The purpose that sustained the empire was

> [t]o fight for the right, to abhor the imperfect, the unjust or the mean, to swerve neither to the right hand nor to the left, to care nothing for flattery or applause or odium or abuse [. . .] but to remember that the Almighty has placed your hand on the greatest of his ploughs [. . .] to drive the blade a little forward in your time, and to feel that somewhere among these millions you have left a little justice or happiness or prosperity, a sense of manliness or moral dignity, a spring of patriotism, a dawn of intellectual enlightenment, or a stirring of duty, where it did not before exist. That is enough, that is the Englishman's justification in India.[84]

This bold statement also sheds light on the question of whether the civilizing mission was a success story or whether it failed. There is no easy answer. As the case studies have shown, it depends on the subject or the field of the civilizing project as to whether its implementation can be regarded as successful or not. Perhaps, from the colonizer's view, one might conclude that the civilizing mission almost completely failed. But from the point of view of the colonized, the cultural and civilizational changes and deformations are evident. The effects of the civilizing mission will have to be decided on individual cases: a balance sheet would be the most inappropriate conclusion.

With very few exceptions,[85] historians who have written so far on the multifarious colonial attitudes towards British India and the other colonies have never paid close attention to the British civilizing mission in India and elsewhere as programme, concept and ideology. For this reason, this book brings together essays dealing with a broad variety of perspectives of the British civilizing mission in India, including subjects seldom dealt with in this context. As will be seen from the articles, their subject matter and conclusions provide much fresh, innovative and stimulating food for thought for students of British imperialism as well as readers interested more in South Asian history or the post-colonial era. However, the book does not claim comprehensiveness: it is evident that even more aspects of the civilizing mission deserve to have been included. To some degree, the articles have been arranged chronologically, although four main sections mark the stages of progress according to subjects within the history of the colonial civilization programme.

PART I:

TRIAL AND ERROR

1

Dealing with Oriental Despotism: British Jurisdiction in Bengal, 1772–93[1]

MICHAEL MANN

FernUniversitaet, Hagen

> With regard to the rules by which justice was to be administered, the Hindoo and Mohamedan codes were in general to be the standard for the respective subjects of them, but tempered, in some instances where they are barbarous and cruel, by the mildness of British sentiments, and improved in others which have relation to political economy.
>
> Charles Grant, *Observations on the State of Society among the Asiatic Subjects of Great Britain*, 1792[2]

1. The Idea of Reform

During the last decades of the eighteenth century, intellectuals, clergymen and politicians in Britain dominated a general discussion about the moral improvement of human beings and society at large. This debate dealt with the universal betterment of mankind through social reforms. Leading figures were to be found in Robert Young's Philanthropic Society, but individuals, like William Jones, the ardent parliamentary reformer of the 1770s who went to India as puisne judge of Calcutta's Supreme Court in 1783 and Colin Miles of the Royal Humane Society, bear testimony to a general reform approach in terms of an overall societal enhancement.[3] As will be seen, this discussion had an immediate influence on contemporary colonial politics in India where the idea of improvement was introduced into the political discourse by Governor General Charles Cornwallis (1786–93). Its other proponent, as the epigraph indicates, was Charles Grant, the ardent 'Evangelical' administrator and later director of the East India Company in India and first European theoretical reformer of Indian society.[4]

The colonial constellation, however, is characterized by an unbridgeable hiatus between Indian and European civilizations more or less from the beginning. The character of Indians was thought inferior, as was their administration of the country, especially with regard to revenue and justice. In the early days of colonial rule, Alexander Dow, a servant of the East India Company, brought out his translation of Ferishta's *History of Hindostan* (1770–72), commenting on the miserable condition of the Indian polity, manifested in its arbitrary jurisdiction as well as in the inert Indian population, which was in stark contrast to the British sense of good government and civil society:

> The history now given to the public, presents us with a striking picture of the deplorable condition of a people subjected to arbitrary sway; and of the instability on empire itself, when it is founded neither on law, nor upon the opinions and attachments of mankind [. . .]. In a government like that of India, public spirit is never seen, and loyalty a thing unknown. The people permit themselves to be transferred from one tyrant to another, without murmuring [. . .].[5]

Since the 1780–4 war of the East India Company against Tipu Sultan of Mysore (1782–99), whom the British regarded as the prototype of an oriental despot and his state as a Muslim tyranny *par excellence*, the British had promoted the idea of their own beneficial rule in contrast to that of any Indian prince. The more they became involved in Indian warfare and politics the more they constructed the differences between Indian and British civilization to support the legitimacy of their rule. To appear as beneficial rulers, whose moral and civil duty it was to liberate by a just war an oppressed people from an unjust and cruel ruler, and to set up a just government as a means of civil improvement, became the core of British self-justification and helped to shape the future self-image of British rule in India.[6]

It is interesting to note that the discussion on the moral and material improvement in British India was part of a general discourse on overall human betterment and that in both societies the British elite regarded betterment as a mandate to civilize the 'masses'. Therefore, the British civilizing mission was not restricted to the colonies but extended to society at home. But India became a 'laboratory' in which the ideology of a civilizing mission for subordinate and uncivilized people was promulgated, starting with reform in the revenue and judicial departments. In this article we will concentrate on moral improvement with regard to judicial reform because jurisdiction became the most contested field between the British and the Indian governments.

Reorganization and reform of Bengal's judicial system became of critical importance after 1765, when the East India Company had acquired the *diwani* of Bengal. Five different courts already existed in the city of Calcutta, with different areas of responsibility in respect of the resident British and other European traders and, in a much more limited capacity, of the Indian inhabitants.[7] Apart from that, the British were now vested with the civil jurisdiction in the Mughal *suba*s (provinces) of Bengal, Bihar and Orissa. The various courts and laws created a confusing situation. The early British colonial administrators quickly realized that, in the long run, they would not be able to administer Bengal's jurisdiction properly, and that the current way of dealing with the laws of Bengal would neither stabilize the fairly ephemeral British rule nor be advantageous to the indigenous population. After Warren Hastings had become governor of Fort William in 1772, the East India Company's Court of Directors in London informed him that he and his government in Calcutta should 'stand forth as Duan'.[8] Whatever they meant by this, they left it to Hastings and his council to set up a plan for the future management of Bengal's, as well as Bihar's and Orissa's, fiscal administration along with the administration of civil justice as the *diwani* comprised both these rights and obligations.[9]

Hastings took seriously the dual obligations of his new post and began with the reform of revenue administration in Bengal.[10] Simultaneously, he launched a reform programme for the judicial administration with the plan of the Committee of Circuit in Bengal, dated 15 August 1772. It was never implemented but served as a blueprint for the judicial reforms in the 1780s and the reforms of 1789–93. Hastings and his government tried to organize the judicial system of Bengal according to British needs rather than the Bengalis' common good, shown by Elijah Impey's procedural code in 1781. The Supreme Court's judge compiled a set of regulations to establish how everyday business in Bengal's civil courts should be implemented. These regulations were supposed to diffuse into Bengal society and end corruption, while enforcing a reliable jurisdiction. On top of that, the British attempt to take over the right to administer the death penalty sheds light on the rather unsuccessful early colonial rule characterized by many trials, and many errors. Therefore, this article will, in the first place, deal more with the failure of the civilizing mission in the eighteenth century than its success, which only took shape in the nineteenth.

British-Indian history is closely connected with the reforms of Cornwallis, Governor General in India from 1786 to 1793, and the 'Cornwallis Code', beginning with its first regulation, the Permanent Settlement of 1793. Fiscal reform was integrated in a grand scheme for the improvement and betterment of the Indian people. 'Improvement' became Cornwallis's *leitmotif*. The term is usually applied to the Utilitarian attitude towards India, particularly to the ambitious Governor General William Cavendish Bentinck (1828–35). A disciple of Jeremy Bentham (1748–1832), Bentinck wanted to modernize India according to western notions of administration, organization and, most importantly, morals.[11] Among many, the abolition of *sati* was the most infamous attempt to improve the – in British eyes – degenerate morals of the Indian people.[12] It was under the administration of Bentinck that Thomas B Macaulay, chairman of the first Law Commission (1834–7) on the future administration of justice in British India, drafted his equally infamous 'Minute of Education', strongly favouring English against Persian as the future administrative language of British India in the wider context of root-and-branch reforms of the Indian judiciary.[13]

But this 'fundamental improvement' was not on the political agenda of the colonial state in its initial phase. Besides, the British were bound by treaty to administer law according to the valid laws of Bengal.[14] At this early stage of colonial rule, the power and position of the British in Bengal were still too weak for them to break with the treaty stipulations and act politically according to their own legal code. However, when taking a closer look at Cornwallis's correspondence at the end of his Indian career, it becomes clear that the idea of improvement as Cornwallis expressed it resembles Bentham's and Macaulay's assumption of 'reform' as a matter of correcting the individual's relationship to government and society and, therefore, a step towards general improvement that would create a better mankind.[15]

It will be argued that, from the beginning of their rule in Bengal, the British were concerned with the reform of the existing dual fiscal and civil judicial system, as the *diwani* provided for it. The British felt that the *diwani* showed fundamental organizational defects and, therefore, had to be restructured on sound rational principles according to contemporary European understanding. The idea of reform was not only related to the administrative needs of the colonial regime: it was also meant to root out rampant bribery as well as ransom decisions – in short, Oriental despotic rule manifested in an arbitrary jurisdiction. The development of British attempts at administrative judicial reforms towards a judicial code with the aim of overall improvement in 'civilization' was brought to a temporary end with the reforms of Cornwallis, anticipating the Utilitarian concept of improvement as a civilizing mission for the material and moral progress of the people of India.

2. The Taming of the Despot

To start with, we should look at Hastings's reform scheme of August 1772 as it was outlined by the Committee of Circuit, since it delineated the main aspects of the future judicial reforms of Cornwallis in 1790 and 1793.[16] In an

accompanying letter to the plan the Committee of Circuit stressed its familiar-
ity with the existing legal traditions: 'the general Principles of all despotic
Governments, that every degree of Power shall be simple and undivided,
seems necessarily to have introduced itself into the Courts of Justice.'[17] The
Committee's members considered themselves as the executors of a governmental system that was both accommodating and serviceable to the Indian
people because of the undivided and simple form of administration it promoted, which was regarded as 'benevolent despotism' or 'paternalism' – India
needed to be ruled by a strong hand.[18] The British favoured their own ideas of
government by describing the actual conditions euphemistically: the modern
western European state claimed to be 'undivided and simple', which anticipated Utilitarian thought, expressed by British officials in Bengal. The
Commissioners' intention was to free the indigenous administration from
arbitrary Oriental habits and, of course, to establish British control.

According to the plan, two courts – one for criminal and one for civil law –
were to be established in every district: the *mufassil diwani adalat* and the *faujdari
adalat*. Special clauses regulated the details.[19] The two High Courts, the *sadr
diwani adalat* and the *sadr nizamat adalat*, were to have their seat in Calcutta and
serve as courts of appeal for the cases of the *mufassil* courts.[20] Criminal jurisdiction remained in the hands of the *nawab*, whose technical sovereignty consisted of the right to confirm as chairman (*daroga*) of the *sadr nizamat adalat* the
candidate put forward by the British. The final decision on capital punishment also rested with the nawab. The plan tied in perfectly with existing
administrative structures, and modified them only slightly.[21]

At the same time Hastings was eager to reform the application of capital
punishment according to contemporary understanding of it as a deterrent as
well as punitive measure.[22] Article 35 of the reform plan from August 1772
became symptomatic of the approach of the colonial jurisdiction and its
civilizing mission. Since the British were unable to control the activities of the
*dacoit*s (bandits) with the police forces and even the military, Hastings considered draconian punishments:

> [. . .] that it be therefore resolved that every such Criminal on
> Conviction shall be carried to the Village to which he belongs and be
> there executed for a Terror and Example to others, and for the
> further prevention of such abominable Practices, that the Village of
> which he is an Inhabitant shall be fined according to the Enormity of
> the Crime & each Inhabitant according to his Substance, and that
> the Family of the Criminal shall become the Slaves of the State, and
> be disposed of for the General Benefit of the Government.[23]

Dacoits were regarded as professional criminals by birth who could not be compared to British criminals and to whom, therefore, British law could not be applied. Their execution would show the force of the law. Enslaving their families was supposed to serve as a means of a moral improvement for the population.[24] It was assumed that an Indian *dacoit* had a lower cast of mind than a British thief. And as Islamic law was inferior to British law, the latter could not be applied to the *dacoits* in the first place. With Regulation XXXV from 21 August 1772 the order was approved, and thus the inferiority of Indian people and institutions was established. At the same time the idea gained strength of the need to improve the population's moral fibre and was increasingly regarded as a duty.[25]

Now and then, the British colonial administration tried to intervene in criminal jurisdiction, but the imposition of capital punishment remained in the hands of the *nazim*, that is the nawab in his function as supreme criminal judge. Technically, he was supposed to confirm the sentences, while the trial and the execution were conducted by the British. Hastings formulated the principal aims for reforming the criminal law. At the top of the list for the British-Bengal government in Calcutta, the Calcutta Council and the Governor General, was the right to investigate all criminal offences. Here, though, drastic intervention in Bengal criminal law was necessary: first, the abolition of the distinction between weapons used in a crime as proof of intent to kill or murder, as made in the Hanafi school prevalent in Bengal; second, the removal of the right of a victim's family to pardon a murderer – that is, transferring murder from the private sphere of civil law into public law; and third, in cases of murder within a family, prohibiting execution of the murderer by a member of the family.[26]

This all fitted with Hastings's personal perception of legality and punishment.[27] It is important to note here that British jurisdiction at the time was much harsher than the contemporary Bengal or 'Indian' version. The protection of private property was more important in Britain than the protection of human life: capital punishment for theft was the order of the day. Murder and manslaughter were also punishable by death, and the British judiciary was not squeamish about imposing it.[28] This explains the severe punishments for *dacoits* who deserved the death penalty, according to British law; in Bengal law, however, they did not because murder had to be proved in concomitance with robbery.[29] The British had soon established a three-tier law system to distinguish between 'white' and 'black' offenders, and criminal acts of whites against blacks: British delinquents were never sentenced to death for the murder of an Indian.[30]

The discussion on greater severity in criminal law never went any further than that. In 1772, the Calcutta Council decreed that all criminal cases in the province of Bengal were to be submitted to it for confirmation. Although the British professed that they did not want to interfere with the *nizamat*'s responsibilities, they felt that the arbitrary jurisdiction of the Muslim courts demanded that, for the safety and happiness of the Bengal people, they were closely monitored.[31] However, the decree was never put into practice, as neither the Calcutta Council nor the provincial councils were able to enforce it. Various forms of resistance by Bengal court 'subalterns' prevented the successful implementation of the decree.

Therefore, the supervisors tried to intervene in current proceedings and influence sentencing. In many cases, they demanded the death penalty. They were urged to tighten the law in compliance with British ideas, but had little success in doing so. The Bengal judges demonstrated their independence by conspicuously and continuously ignoring the supervisors' petitions. Consequently, Hastings went a step further: he arrogated the right to correct sentences by taking up the Islamic tradition that, although the ruler could not pass judgment, he could examine the sentencing and make alternative suggestions.[32]

Although we profess to leave the Nazim the final Judge in all Criminal cases, and the Officers of his Courts to proceed according to their own Laws, Forms, and opinions, independant of the Controul of this Government, yet many cases may happen, in which an invariable observance of this Rule may prove of dangerous Consequence to the Power by which the Government of this Country is held, and to the Peace and Security of the Inhabitants. Wherever such cases happen the Remedy can only be obtained from those in whom the Sovereign Power exists. It is on these that the Inhabitants depend for Protection, and for the Redress of all their Grievances, and they have a right to the accomplishment of this Expectation, of which no Treaties nor (Casuistical) distinctions can deprive them. If therefore the Powers of the Nizamut cannot answer these salutary Purposes, or by any Abuse of them, which is much to be apprehended from the present reduced state of the nazim, and the little Interest he has in the general Welfare of the Country, shall become hurtful to it, I conceive it to be strictly conformable to Justice and Reason to interpose the Authority or Influence of the Company, who as Dewan have an Interest in the Welfare of the Country, and as the governing Power, have equally a right and obligation to maintain it, I am therefore of opinion that wherever it shall be found necessary to supersede the Authority of the Nizam to supply the deficiencies or to correct the irregularities, of his Courts, it is the duty of this

Government to apply such means as in their Judgement shall best promote the due course of ends of justice.[33]

The Calcutta Council expressed its general agreement with Hastings's view in a special meeting. Its members were also convinced that there had to be an authority to monitor the sentences passed by Muslim judges, as the sovereigns of all Muslim states had the right to intervene to prevent abuse. But the Council also made it clear it knew how delicate the situation was and that, therefore, the *naib diwan* (deputy *diwan*) should keep his post as mediator between Indian law administration and British–Indian jurisdiction.[34] The Governor General was to exercise his 'full power' for two years only, from 1773 to 1775, when he was ordered to restrain himself by the London authorities. The East India Company's Court of Directors was afraid that, by widening their claims to power, the British would stretch their legitimacy too far.[35] Shortly after this, Hastings returned his 'office' to the renowned and reliable *naib diwan* Muhammad Reza Khan, and the *sadr nizamat adalat* was transferred back to Murshidabad.[36]

During the two years that Hastings had usurped supervision of the *nizamat*, he corrected a large number of sentences according to his European ideas of reason and humanity as well as his personal estimation.[37] Far more death sentences were imposed and carried out for manslaughter than would have been possible under Islamic law.[38] After 1775, the British no longer interfered with criminal jurisdiction. The first clumsy attempts had drained too much energy. Principally, the Bengal judges were urged to adhere to the *sharia* more strictly, but it seems they rarely did. It was only in 1788, that Jonathan Duncan, the British Resident in Banaras, dared to defy the local judges by ordering the first public hanging and having it carried out. For the first time, gallows were erected in Banaras, a significant omen for the future jurisdiction of the colonial state.[39] Nevertheless, the first attempt to usurp control of the death penalty had utterly failed.

3. The Usurpation of Control of Capital Punishment

The reform of the Bengal judicial system had come to a halt at the beginning of the 1780s. The colonial administration thought it necessary to continue, but the insecurity caused by Hastings's term in office had prevented all activity. Before the advent of the British, civil jurisdiction had been adapted according to the needs of the day, but the colonial regime was more interested in criminal jurisdiction, especially in the execution of capital punishment, as this was a central-governmental right. Warren Hastings had realized this and had looked for ways to tie legally and legitimately all criminal jurisdiction, and especially the death penalty, to the British courts in Bengal but actually to himself as Governor General.

After Cornwallis took over as Governor General in Calcutta in 1786, the efforts towards reform gathered new drive, and by the end of 1789 he had prepared for extensive judicial reforms. Beforehand, Jonathan Duncan had alerted him to blatant cases of wrong judgments being passed by judges in Banaras in two letters, in which he also expanded on the general shortcomings and absurdities of the prevalent jurisdiction, especially in the case of physical and capital punishment.[40] It had been obvious for about two years that the criminal judiciary in Bengal had fallen into an intolerable state. This had been caused principally by Hastings: in 1772 he had cancelled the annual payments of 16.00.000 rupees to the *nawab*, which he received for his services as *nazim*, so that he was 22.86.666 rupees in debt fifteen years later.[41] This had led to the neglect of judicial duties, and also to an increase in corruption. Cornwallis ended this sad state of affairs by giving the colonial state control over the criminal judiciary.[42] In achieving this, he sent out questionnaires to the 25 collector-magistrates to discover their view of the condition of the criminal judiciary in Bengal; the questions were often phrased in a tendentious way.[43]

The tenor of the replies confirmed Cornwallis's suspicion that the Bengal-Islamic judiciary lacked the criterion of equity and that some judgments were absurd, especially in the sentencing of murderers: the right of a family to pardon a murderer was regarded as perverted. The collectors were in favour of higher sentences, but considered corporal punishment, such as mutilation, as inhumane and suggested imprisonment as an alternative. Generally, the prevalence of corruption was criticized, as well as the arbitrary nature of court proceedings, if they took place at all. Judgments that resulted in prison sentences 'during pleasure' became common.[44]

Like Hastings, Cornwallis did not envisage a fundamental reform of the judicial system but aimed at reforms within the administration of the judiciary. In principle, the Bengal judicial system was to be retained, and only to be modified in those parts where the British idea of justice and the principle of equity were in stark contrast. Cornwallis began by reforming the administration of the criminal judiciary, thereby seeing through what his predecessor had started in 1772. He referred to Warren Hastings's 'plan' of 15 August 1772 for the reform of civil and criminal jurisdiction, although it had never been officially approved – but neither had it been rejected, limited or expanded.[45] One of his first measures was to relieve Muhammad Reza Khan of his duties; he went into retirement after 27 years of commendable cooperation under the *nawab*s and the British.[46] With Cornwallis's suggestions from 3 December 1790, which received legal status on 1 January 1791, the existing hierarchy of the judicial system was emphasized by the establishment of a court of appeal that paralleled the administration of the civil judiciary. Next to *sadr diwani adalat*, there now existed the *sadr nizamat adalat* in Calcutta, which took over the powers that had previously been invested in Muhammad Reza Khan.[47]

Legislation and jurisdiction concerning capital punishment deserve closer scrutiny. With a stroke of the pen, the Calcutta Council tried to eliminate, in cases of murder, presentation of evidence in accordance with the Hanafi school and to replace it with that of the Yusef and Imam Muhammad school. From then on, *fatwa*s had to be drawn up based on the intentionality of the crime.[48] Basically, the reformers stayed within the boundaries of existing law and seemed only to change the presentation of the evidence. This was to avoid giving the impression of arbitrary interference with the jurisdiction.[49] Again, Cornwallis's plans tied in perfectly with Warren Hastings's commentary. After reassuring himself, with the help of his completed questionnaires, that he was supported Cornwallis ordered the application of a legal concept that was not usual in Bengal. In order to fully establish a jurisdiction that was exclusively controlled by the state, it was essential to eliminate private prosecution as practised according to the *sharia*. Therefore, a special clause prohibited the right of victims' relatives to pardon a perpetrator.[50]

Apparently, there were many difficulties in implementing the new regulations, as the *qasi*s and *mufti*s did not go out of their way to establish the modified legal practices in their *fatwa*s. The state could not rely on the cooperation of the legal experts. Therefore, nine months later the Calcutta Council felt it necessary to force the result they wanted by detailed legislation. The recently established Courts of Circuit were given the following order:

> When any private person or persons shall be convicted of murder, the Judge shall cause to the reference prescribed in such cases by the Muhammadan Law to be made to the heir of the slain. If the heir shall require the murderer to be punished with death, Judges shall pass sentences accordingly. But when heirs shall require Daiat (blood money), or pardon the murderer, the Judges shall not pass any sentences, but shall forward the record of the trial, including the Futwa of the Law officers and the requisition of the heir, to the Nizamut Adaulat, and wait the sentence of that court.[51]

On the same day, the Governor General made a decision with the following wording:

> In cases of murder, in which the murderer would be liable to Kissaas or capital punishment should the heir of the slain demand it, if the

heir shall pardon the murderer, or shall require from him Deyut or
fine for the price for blood, the will of the heir shall not be allowed to
operate, but the Court of Nizamut Adaulut [. . .] shall sentence the
murderer to suffer death.[52]

When relatives wanted to exercise their right to pardon, the British judge at
the Court of Circuit gave them the impression that the whole trial would be
referred to the Court of Appeal together with the traditional legal reports,
where the case would then be decided according to the usual legal practices.
The highest criminal court, consisting of the Governor General and the
members of the Council, was now urged to impose the death penalty in all
cases of murder. The colonial government only managed to usurp control
over life and death with this deception.[53] But the *fatwas* of the *qasis* and *muftis*
still seemed to take the wishes of the heirs of a murdered relative into account.
The Calcutta Council made short work of this by decreeing that the Courts of
Circuit were to try these cases as if there were no relatives. The *nizamat adalat*
was ordered to do the same.[54] The *fatwas* had to be submitted after the trial
was closed, under the pretence that an heir of the plaintiff had been present.[55]
   This separation between British ideas of justice, concerning capital punishment and the Bengal-Islamic legal practice in cases of murder, relied on
established fictions according to which the *fatwas* were drawn up. Technically,
no new legal system but rather a frame of theoretical constructs, that transformed real cases into fictional ones, was established. The *fatwa* remained
within the boundaries of the Islamic legal tradition, but was increasingly
modified according to British expectations. As it was impossible to change the
law, the particulars that were the basis for the *fatwa* were changed to achieve
the preferred result.[56] The method described was well known: the eleven *brahmins* compiling the Hindu Law since 1771 had often been incapable of establishing the firm legal principles and laws that the British wanted because of
the greater flexibility of their own legal principles, so Hastings and his
colleagues had already felt it necessary to set fictional cases, in accordance
with which a judgment could be passed and which would serve as a legal basis
for the British. It was not valid law that was the prerequisite for a sentence,
but the other way round: the sentence became the basis for the jurisdiction.[57]
   Detailed regulations in the judiciary were supposed to simplify jurisdiction.
An intervention from the side of the legislation surely lay in the introduction
of testimonies of non-Muslims against Muslims in cases of murder.[58] Again,
capital punishment was the subject of reform. The Calcutta Council reserved
the right to make the final decision in such cases with Regulation IX of 1793;
they probably knew that they had reached the limit of what was possible.[59]
The only direct intervention into the legislation, which at the same time

expressed the European humanitarian ideals of the Enlightenment, was the commutation of mutilation sentences into imprisonment: for each limb that would have been severed, the culprit got seven years imprisonment instead.[60]

The courts of law were often far away so only a few plaintiffs had access to them, and the magistrates were therefore ordered to pay compensation to the persons involved in the court cases. This practice was unusual even in Europe. Moreover, the decision to pay for rehabilitation for all prisoners with sentences lasting longer than six months to prevent them committing new offences sounds downright modern.[61] 'Humanity' is often given as the reason for the introduction of these regulations, but it cannot obscure the fact that reasons of practicability and the acceptance of the colonial judicial system were more important than such concerns. It was cheaper to rehabilitate former inmates rather than to risk a huge backlog of trials that would have rendered the judiciary immobile. Moreover, humanity in the Indian penitential system was limited: culprits were still summarily executed and officially flogged; branding of convicts' foreheads only ceased in 1849, the bodies of the executed were displayed to the public until 1836, and the public gallows stood outside the Madras Penitentiary as late as the 1880s.[62] What the British viewed as 'Oriental barbarity' continued under their rule, camouflaged as the humanity of British benevolent paternalism, which often had to teach Indians a lesson.

Cornwallis was aware that there were limits to his reforms, and concluded his famous 'minute' on the reforms within the judiciary with the words:

> A regard to the religious prejudices of the Muhammadans will probably prove an insurmountable obstacle to our making those alterations in the law which the good of the community requires. But if we cannot introduce a system of jurisprudence as perfect as might be wished, it is the interest as the rulers of the country, and duty we owe to our subjects, to see that the Law, as it exists, is duly administered; that the evils resulting from maladministration of it may not be superadded to those which are consequent of its inherent defects.[63]

Elsewhere he told the Court of Directors in August 1791:

> We are of opinion, that notwithstanding its many defects, no material alterations, except those already adopted, should be attempted, until the minds of the people, by a more intimate acquaintance with the enlightened principles of European policy, are prepared for the reception of other laws more consonant to reason and natural justice.[64]

Cornwallis mainly regarded himself as presiding over a government that had to take into account the commonwealth of its subjects, and to achieve a general improvement in their living conditions through reform. The idea of moral progress becomes clearly discernible and was important to Cornwallis in both the current and future reforms. Apart from that, he seems to have been aware of the judicial reforms' limited effects, especially regarding capital punishment. As long as the law was to be duly administered, the colonial regime's intended 'good government' would, more or less, come true. But it is evident that Hastings, and even more so Cornwallis were eager to improve the moral defects of their Indian subjects: a good judicial system, properly implemented, was one aspect of their ambitious scheme. However, British reforms, with regard to the judicial proceedings as they were set up and implemented, seemed much more effective for British civilizing purposes.

4. The Dissemination of Civilization

Though basic forms of bureaucratic administration seem to have been established according to British ideas, the British thought them insufficient, inefficient and corrupt. The process of judicial administration is amply described by Robert Orme, the official historian of the East India Company, as an ill-working apparatus:

> The wealth, the consequence, the interest, or the address of the party, become now the only consideration [. . .]. The friends who can influence, intercede; and, excepting where the case is so manifestly proved as to brand the failure of redress with glaring infamy (a restraint which human nature is born to reverence) the value of the bribe ascertains the justice of the cause.
>
> Still the forms of justice subsist; witnesses are heard; but browbeaten and removed; proofs of writing produced; but deemed forgeries and rejected, until the way is declared for a decision, which becomes totally or partially favourable, in proportion to the methods which have been used to render it such [. . .].
>
> The quickness of the decision which prevails in Indostan, as well as in all other despotic governments, ought no longer to be admired. As soon as the judge is ready, everything that is necessary is ready: there are no tedious briefs or cases, no various interpretations of an infinity of laws, no methodized forms [. . .].[65]

As mentioned earlier, in 1780 Hastings had submitted another plan for reforming the judiciary.[66] Essentially, it aimed to separate civil jurisdiction from fiscal administration. But perhaps its most outstanding characteristic features are the sections on putting down all proceedings in writing and keeping them in files, which led to a discernible increase in filing.[67] This can be regarded as the beginning of colonial bureaucratization in Bengal. On top of that, the plan established a scale of charges and fees, which had to be paid for copies of legal documents that were to be used at another court as well as for the opening of a trial. In order to recover the costs of the legal proceedings, the courts were given the right to increase the fees accordingly.[68]

Irregularities and scandals within British judicial practice not only annoyed the Bengali population but also gave rise to insecurity among the British, which they could ill-afford at that infant stage of their power. In order to guarantee a proper judiciary, including established methods of proceeding and their control, Sir Elijah Impey, senior judge at the Supreme Court in Calcutta (1775–82), compiled a civil code of procedure.[69] It consisted of different regulations, orders and rules, as they had been decreed during the preceding years, with some new ones. All in all, it contained ninety-five clauses, which replaced all former decrees concerning civil court cases. The collection was linked to practical application with translations into Persian and Bengali.[70]

All courts were to be equipped with a regulated number of court ushers, clerks and employees, who were to be sworn in. The *mufassil diwani adalat*s received the right to establish their own codes of procedure, as long as they were approved by the *sadr diwani adalat* and the Calcutta Council and thus became legally binding for all *mufassil* courts. Accordingly, standardization was supposed to take place step by step 'from below'. A registry had to be established at the courts, which had to be in session three days a week. Certain forms of procedure had to be strictly adhered to, be it the written petitions of the lawyers, the forms of testimony, or establishment of time and place. After this, a trial had to be held.[71] Regulations concerning the keeping of daily registers, in the plans of 1772 and 1778, were abolished so that the courts were not held up with superfluous paperwork.[72] All judges were forbidden to hand over court cases to court employees or take extra money for their services.[73]

When an appeal was lodged, only the public prosecutor and the defending lawyer had the right to speak in front of the court without being expressly asked to do so. If the persons lodging a complaint were unable to testify in court, they could submit their testimony beforehand, in writing; the document had to bear the signature of two witnesses and the lawyer. All legal cases, including the verdicts, had to be filed in a special ledger. The witnesses also had to be listed in the verdict, which the judge had to date and sign before it was sealed. A 'true copy' of this had also to be drawn up, including the court seal and the judge's signature.[74] Under Cornwallis, this procedure was implemented when he put the early suggestions of Hastings's 1772 plan into practice and from then on the British judicial administration gradually permeated Bengal institutions. Case files had to be drawn up at the district courts and summaries of these, including the verdict, had to be transmitted to the two courts of law in Calcutta.[75] The trials themselves were also restructured according to British ideas.[76] Codes of procedures, according to which courts of law in Bengal were in keeping with local traditions, became obsolete.[77]

In spite of all his efforts, Impey did not manage to carry through the principle of 'rule of law' in British Bengal's jurisdiction. But he realized rightly that every centralist administration could only work with the help of decrees fixed in writing. Thus he paved the way for Cornwallis, who later followed up and tried to implement Impey's suggestions with all possible resolution. However, the growing obstacles within day-to-day legal practices prevented successful implementation of the 'Impey Code'. It seems that the British never quite understood the Bengal–Indian judiciary system and left it in the hands of local lawyers. The language barrier also contributed to misunderstandings and defiance. At the same time, the Bengalis were confronted with a judicial system that alienated them, with its lengthy proceedings and the volume of paperwork required. As all petitions in a lawsuit had to be submitted in written form, which is why illiterate farmers could no longer appear in court without a lawyer. The paperwork often took away their own language from them. Finally, British judges in their wigs and robes were disturbing figures to those who had to appear before them. The British judges, clothes symbolizing their authority had a doubly alienating effect, as foreign judges in grotesque disguises applied unknown or unfamiliar laws.

The reforms had an effect, but contrary to what was desired, as the following example illustrates. Within only a few years, the establishment of the professional group of lawyers, for which Cornwallis had worked, had paralysed all court proceedings. The code of procedure prescribed the submission of testimonies and written statements from both parties, which were then translated into Persian and then into English. This practice turned out to be a rich source of mistakes. The British judge had increasingly to reach a verdict on the basis of procedural errors.[78] The 'rule of law' collapsed into absurdity when the code of procedure strangled both civil and criminal law.

The Bengal *wakil*s (lawyers) were soon exploiting the situation for the benefit of both plaintiffs and defendants. This becomes apparent when we look at the reasons for summonses at court. Corruption, attempted bribery of court personnel or government officials, and incitement to bribe public servants were among the most popular offences, next to arrangements with the lawyer representing the opposing party and illiteracy of the plaintiff or defendant.[79] The backlog in the court cases filed and the slim chance of getting justice within a reasonable time frame led inevitably to the re-emergence of the old corruption and the people of Bengal soon found themselves confronted with the same obstacles they had encountered when trying to get justice under the previous regime. Cornwallis's reforms never took effect and 'rule of law' remained nothing but a *desideratum* in British India.[80] But what becomes clear are the energetic efforts of both the Hastings and the Cornwallis administration to gain acceptance for the jurisdiction by implementing a unified system of legal administration on the one hand and, on the other, to achieve an effect of diffusion for the code of procedure and the administration of justice into the population through the sheer amount of legal proceedings in progress.

The most prestigious instrument of British colonial rule, and doubtless the most influential in terms of lasting effects, was the 'Cornwallis Code'. The Court of Directors had pointed out repeatedly to the Calcutta Council that they should introduce 'simplicity, energy, justice and economy' into the judicial administration.[81] By compiling his regulations in 1793, starting with the decree of the Permanent Settlement, Cornwallis complied with the demand. All in all, the 'Cornwallis Code' consists of 48 regulations and represents the 'constitution' of the British colonial state in Bengal. Each regulation was preceded by a preamble explaining its background and the reason for its existence. This helped the judges to discern the unambiguous scope of the law, and placed the legal regulations into a general context. An inner structure divided each regulation into sections that, again, could be divided into different clauses. From then on, it was possible to amend or repeal individual clauses, sections or whole regulations through other new regulations.[82] For both the judicial and the civil administration, there now existed a clear codex of rights, decrees, restrictions and regulations, which were binding for both British and Bengali citizens and which had to be expressly referred to when applying them.[83]

All regulations issued during one year were entered, listed, numbered, printed and published in the Judicial Department. At the end of each year, they were bound into a book and handed out to the courts and officials of the colonial administration. Ten copies had to be sent to the Court of Directors.[84] The index was constantly updated, which made the codex simple to use.[85] Moreover, in order to achieve a high level of distribution for the codex and easy access to the law, the British government in Bengal was instructed to translate the regulations into Persian and Bengali.[86] Regulation XLI of 1793 stressed the general accessibility of the Code and emphasized the claim for legal.[87] With this, the civilizing character of the legal collections as a direct product of a superior political regime was underlined. Simple formalization of procedures and regulations was regarded as the proper instrument to start the diffusion of civilization into the Indian society.

Cornwallis systematically completed the regulations that had been in effect since Warren Hastings's term of office, according to the right of the Council in Calcutta – valid since 21 Geo. III, c. 65, s. 23 (1781) – to pass legal decrees for the provincial courts and provincial councils. The system of the 'Bengal Regulations' is vaguely reminiscent of the 'British Statutory Acts': in the famous *Fifth Report from the Select Committee* of 1812, the importance of the 'Cornwallis Code' is alluded to, both the compilation itself and its transference to the presidencies of Madras and Bombay: '[. . .] and the code of regulations thus framed, may be considered as the statute book of the British government'.[88]

Institutionalization and the separation of the individual administrative areas surely were necessary prerequisites for a more efficient administration, but this alone was not binding to the people working in it. In that respect the 'Cornwallis Code' did pioneering work. Several regulations contained specific formulas for official oaths binding British as well as Indian government employees.[89] While the India Act of 1784 already prescribed that collectors had to be sworn in, and the judicial regulation of 1781 contained a special clause on the oath for judges,[90] several regulations now contained formulas for oaths for British and Indian governmental employees. The oath concerned the rendering of public duties in a conscientious and correct way and the fulfilment of the individual's responsibilities according to the best of their ability. There was also a special oath in which the officials had to swear that they would neither accept presents nor other donations, especially money. This applied to both 'covenanted servants' and Bengal employees. The oath became the guarantee for an administration that functioned smoothly as it superseded personal involvement and the interests of the individual in material security, channelling them collectively into the interests of the state.

The British got into unexpected difficulties when they tried to implement their 'rational' conception of official oaths. As soon as they attempted to expand the religious oaths of Muslims and Hindus to the benefit of the colonial state, its institutions and representatives, they were met with resistance. Members of both religious communities feared that the oath, which now had to be taken by plaintiffs, defendants and all witnesses, would lead to social pollution and/or degradation. Also, many Indians did not see the point of swearing a religious oath to uphold an institution.[91] Not without reason, they feared the abuse of a holy ritual for something devoid of spiritual meaning. William Jones, Impey's successor to the office of senior judge at the Supreme Court in Calcutta, was driven to despair in his search for an official oath that would be binding to both Hindus and Muslims.[92] At least during the eighteenth century, the British had been forced to allow affidavits in front of the court next to the oaths taken by plaintiffs.[93] Instead of levelling social favouritism by way of egalitarian access to the law, this concession led to the paradox that the British courts contributed to the traditional privileges of individual social strata and classes.

But in the long run, the swearing-in process generated a relationship that reminded British employees and all subordinate Indian servants of their loyalty to the state. The cadre of European employees in the administration was formed by the Covenanted Civil Service of India from the renewal of the East India Company's charter in 1793. Future personnel were educated by the East India Company at Haileybury College from 1805 onwards. It was a 'corps of civil servants', which was strictly organized and well trained, and existed in India long before anything similar developed in Britain and large parts of Europe. The Indian Civil Service became well known as the frame-work of the British Indian Empire.

5. The Idea of Improvement

From the beginning of their colonial rule in Bengal the British regarded Indian society as inferior to western concepts and ideas of civilization. This became more obvious the further British administrators got involved in the governmental business of Bengal and other parts of India. Her political regimes and her administrative systems were thought unjust, corrupt and arbitrary – in short, despotic. When the British were vested with the *diwani* in 1765, they were deeply concerned about the necessity of reforming the existing administrative system. From the outset of their semi-professional academic research 'Orientalists', as the learned people around Warren Hastings were later called, began to establish the supposed inferiority of the Indian civilization that rendered improvement necessary. They only differed from the more Utilitarian-minded 'Anglicists' of the first half of the nineteenth century in respect of the ways and means by which the British should reform Indian society and improve her people's mind, consciousness and character.

The civilizing mission's attitude and stern intention of improvement becomes clear in the context of the Orientalist perception (in the sense of Edward Said) of Bengal society and its dire need for reform. We can certainly observe some kind of early antecedent civilizing mission with the foundation of the exclusively white Royal Asiatic Society of Bengal in 1784 and its successful attempt to establish a cultural gap between the British and the Indians. Sciences, such as linguistics, history, archaeology and botany, were used in the service of the colonial state: it was important to get to know the country by gathering all available information about the land and its inhabitants.[94] The 'Orientalists' wanted to reform India's degenerate civilization along the lines of the highly esteemed ancient Indian culture and tradition.[95] Simultaneously, the same colonial regime turned the scientific findings and results against its subdued people in order to justify some sort of educational mandate.

In the field of administration, the implementation of a hierarchical and centralized judiciary became one of the main tools with which the colonial regime could discipline the putative despotic system. The usurpation and reform of capital punishment, however, was primarily supposed to serve the British and, subsequently, to make the Bengal population '[. . .] conform to the dictates of the law', as Cornwallis bluntly put it.[96] He clearly aimed at the people of India's submission under the law and its administrative personnel, in order to establish a political regime based on sound principles that ultimately should serve the progress of India. In reaching this target of betterment in terms of civilization, Cornwallis pursued a policy of material and moral improvement. He elaborated on the idea of a moral improvement, next to material improvement, in the course of his correspondence with the home authorities concerning judicial and fiscal measures between 1789 and 1793. For this reason the Governor General is the core figure, or perhaps a 'missing link', between the early phase and the climax of reform – that is, the period of the initial six decades of 'direct' British colonial rule in India (1772–1835).

In his famous minutes on the introduction of the Permanent Settlement in Bengal, dated 18 September 1789 and 3 February 1790, Cornwallis mentions the term 'improvement' eighteen times.[97] Mostly he speaks of a general material improvement of the country, the peasants and the *zamindars* (landlords and revenue collectors) or of the economic situation, hinting at the 'future prosperity of the country'. In his terms the British administration's duty of 'improvement' became the decisive means of promoting '[. . .] the prosperity, happiness and wealth of their [Indian] subjects' since the state would protect the individual to his own benefit with '[. . .] the enaction of good laws, [which are c]onsistent with justice, policy, or humanity'.[98] With regard to India, Cornwallis enlarged the civilizing mandate with this notion and the contemporary idea of improvement as it emerged in Europe and as it became regarded as one of the principal duties of a modern government and state.

In contrast to the 'Orientalists' of the early years, the Cornwallis administration increasingly aimed at the moral correction of the individual's character by '[. . .] a spirit of improvement [which] is diffused through the country [. . .]'.[99] Certainly, the Governor General was aware of the limited effects of purely judicial reforms as a route to moral improvement. Therefore, laws and the judiciary were only intended as means to rule the country and help its administration run smoothly. Methods of civilizing attitudes could only be provided by the gradual diffusion and dissemination of a superior judiciary's procedures accompanied by an efficient administration's proceedings. A more advanced polity, based on the principles of equality and humanity, was thought to influence and change the Indians' evil habits and bad character in the long run and to enhance their culture in terms of a 'modern' civilization. The above-mentioned 'spirit' was viewed as the vehicle of the civilizing mission to further the country's moral and material progress. Besides, this spirit was of recent western origin and therefore guaranteed 'modernity'.

In the course of the emerging concept of 'improvement', the construction of differences between the Orient and the Occident took a new shape and paved the way for the Anglicists' impact on Indian politics. Cornwallis introduced the *leitmotif* of the later utilitarians into Indian politics in its 'straightforward' sense and thus caused a linguistic-cum-conceptual shift from reforms hitherto guided by 'internal' principles to those based on 'external' concepts, which became more aggressive in terms of civilizing and modernizing India. The reforms of Bengal's judiciary and court proceedings were regarded as prime tools to facilitate this transformation, as can be seen during the course of the nineteenth century and, ultimately, the introduction of the Civil Procedure Code, the Evidence Act and the Transfer of Property Act in the 1860s.

2

'A Race of Monsters': South India and the British 'Civilizing Mission' in the Later Eighteenth Century

MARGRET FRENZ

Centre for Modern Oriental Studies, Berlin

> It has been much the custom of late to represent the Malabar Rajahs as a race of Monsters: But they appear to me only like other men in a rude state of society who can be supported in this situation to possess an imperfect code of morality and must be guilty at times of acts of power, that could not be tolerated in more civilized communities. We behold then the body of people in Malabar in their society less cultivated than the other Inhabitants of India and not yet advanced to that state to admit of the introduction of the best laws.[1]

This Minute, most probably written by an administrative officer of the East India Company (EIC) in April 1798, comprises the main characteristics of British policy towards India, and particularly Malabar, having been driven by a spirit or sense of mission to bring 'civilization' to the natives. As complex as the individual motives of the persons who came to India were, the 'civilizing mission' reveals many aspects of the British quest to build an empire. If we take a closer look at the above statement it appears that the British viewed themselves to be in possession of a superior state of body, mind and soul. For those taking this attitude seriously it involved improving others who did not have the privilege to live in a 'civilized community'.

Malabar seemed an especially dreadful place: the local population and its rulers, according to the above quotation, did not even match up to the standard found elsewhere in India. The manifold appearances of the civilizing mission were manifest in all sections of society. To govern the newly-conquered country, with its vast geographical dimensions, numerous peoples and myriad customs, India had to be sorted out in a way familiar to the British sense of order and hierarchy. For this purpose many surveys on different subjects were carried out and written down, forming essential tools for the British to set up an administration according to the new categorizations in India. Only by categorizing the complex Indian reality were the British able to make themselves familiar with the local way of life and govern the country. For the British, values like the rule of law and the right to property were of primary importance. As values defining a 'civilized people', they represented a 'demarcation of an essential quality of difference' that characterized the British in their own eyes as 'modern' and 'civilized' people. Only after complete implementation of British standards did Malabar seem secure in British hands.[2]

Economic ambitions led the British to Malabar and were a major reason behind their efforts to gain political control over the country. Pepper played a key role during the British appropriation of rule, the 'black gold' being the main attraction of the Malabar coast. The British strove to take control of the spice and especially the pepper trade,[3] yet not even direct political control of Malabar could guarantee their monopolization of pepper. The newly-created province was intended to be self-sufficient: the cost of any government measures should be paid by the province itself.

This article seeks to investigate the concept of rule, as well as the methods of achieving it applied by the British in India and particularly in Malabar. The focus is given to the concepts of sovereignty the British had in mind when coming to India and involving themselves in administrative matters. With what expectations had they arrived? What conditions did they find there? How did they legitimize their demand for sovereignty in India, a country that was foreign to them? Which motives were behind their 'civilizing mission'? Is it possible to regard the establishment of British power in Malabar as a success story?

While analysing the period of transformation from indigenous to colonial rule in India in the late eighteenth century one should bear in mind that at this time the ambition to administer the country had just taken root in British ideas and imaginations. A decisive step towards establishing the desired authority and sovereignty of the British in India was the granting of the East India Company charter of 1813. It declared the EIC to be the administrative body of India rather than just a trading company representing a far-away ruling elite. From this time on the sense of mission within EIC officials could be openly disseminated, and was emphasized by permitting missionary societies to come to India, which also had an impact on the political situation.

After the mutiny of 1857 and the proclamation of Queen Victoria as Empress in 1858 the manifold measures taken to impose British rule – that is, the 'right civilization' – in India bore fruit. A parallel process to the elaboration of the imperial protocol can be noticed in the development of an Indian elite striving for responsible government.

1. British Ideas of Sovereignty

Looking at the European, and more specifically the British, concept of sovereignty,[4] we must be aware that at the time Britain assumed power in India the British system as we know it today was still in a process of formation. The theoretical foundations of the concept had been laid by philosophers like Jean Bodin (1529/30–96). Bodin applied the undivided authority of a state to the bearer of sovereignty, who should use it with regard to justice and general welfare; Thomas Hobbes (1588–1679) had traced back sovereignty to a 'contract of society', while Jean-Jacques Rousseau (1712–78) also referred to a *contrait social*. In his *Two Treatises on Government* (1690) John Locke (1632–1704) declared equality, liberty and the right of invulnerability of the person as the highest legally protected rights. Locke spoke up for the principle of dividing the executive from the legislative power in a state, the same vehemently demanded later by Charles Montesquieu (1689–1755), preparing the way for the separation of powers in today's democratic states. According to Montesquieu, the people should decide on the type of government; his thoughts influenced the Declaration of Independence of the United States of America in 1776 as well as the French constitution of 1791.

The aforementioned aspects constitute the basis of the concept. To put it into practice in India, the British had to introduce corresponding institutions. As the concept of sovereignty is closely interwoven with legitimation, the British had to find ways to legitimize their establishment in India. The systematic organization of state affairs enables the administrative body to act with a kind of self-legitimizing power, and an essential aspect of the European conception of the state was its legitimation through technical, administrative and legal proceedings. In this context 'legal proceedings' should be understood 'as the logical cohesion of real actions [. . .], legitimation as a transfer of binding decisions into a separate decision-making structure'.[5] Niklas Luhmann assumes that the proceedings are not a criterion of 'truth' itself, but that they promote decision-making and its correctness, that they enable and channel communication, and that they also help to avoid foreseeable disruptions to the ascertainment of the truth. The aim of proceedings is to find the 'true justice'. However, 'truth' in such a narrowly defined sense does not always guarantee the resolution of problems, since legal proceedings do not call in all the elements of a case when seeking to ascertain the 'truth'. In the final analysis 'truth' is not the decisive factor, but rather power and its legitimation through administrative proceedings.[6]

In late-eighteenth-century Britain, the concept of sovereignty thus went hand in hand with a codified constitution, the state unit being held together by bureaucratic administrative actions and legislation within a clearly defined territory. The concept that was taken to India in the minds and thoughts of Company officials, later comprising the administrative staff of the 'new' territories within the empire, took root in institutions like courts, police and military stations. An important aspect regarding the conduct of British officials in India was that they were conscious of acting as deputies of the Crown, which thereby legitimized everything they undertook in India, including armed combat. The feeling of having power also determined their dialogue with the 'Other', the Indian population or local elites.

To ensure a continuous British administration, Haileybury College was founded in 1806. Its curriculum not only comprised practical and administrative training, but also moral conduct, creating a new sense of imperial spirit or consciousness. The most important things to be transferred to India were British liberty, the British character and the British constitution.[7] The EIC, being systematically organized to a certain extent, therefore had, besides the legitimation of administrative bodies as described above, the necessary manpower to establish its administration in India. The more institutions it created there, the more power it usually had to command. The EIC helped in continuing the process of colonizing new 'shores', as well as the local population.[8]

Getting back to the concept of sovereignty, the British seemingly had a fairly clear idea of what it should look like. As they wanted to implement their concept in India thoroughly, bearing in mind that the British colonies in North America had already taken the liberty of freeing themselves from British rule, the necessity to take this concept as the 'only true and right' one was obvious. Though the general attitudes of EIC officials were the same, by and large, their policy on the spot might take different shapes. For example, Lord Charles Cornwallis (1738–1805, Governor General 1786–1793) pursued a slow Anglicization of the Indian people by reforming property rights hoping for the establishment of a new landholding class, while Richard Wellesley (1760–1842, Governor General 1798–1804) continued to conquer new territories, personifying an imperial attitude towards the country. This example illustrates the scope for action of the men on the spot, which included furthering their own business ends, one major reason why they had been attracted to go to India.[9]

The conviction of the British that they belonged to a superior civilization was further developed and supported by most of the missionary societies, which were legally allowed to work in India from 1813 onwards. Although the government followed a policy of strict separation between political and Church matters, the two spheres were interconnected, through individuals or political-administrative fields like education (here the missionary schools played a major role well into the twentieth century). The rather frequently quoted and famous *Minute on Education* of 1835 by Thomas B Macaulay (1800–59) reflects the wish to form a westernized stratum within the Indian population for the good of the 'civilized community': 'We must at present do our best to form a class who may be interpreters between us and the millions whom we govern – a class of persons, Indians in colour and blood, but English in tastes, in opinions, in morals, and in intellect.'[10] One should keep in mind these nineteenth-century developments while investigating the early phase of transformation from local to colonial rule in India.

The term 'civilizing mission' proves descriptive of several processes that took place during the formation of the British Raj, or, looking at it from another point of view, during the transformation of traditional Indian rule to colonial rule. The fundamental characteristic of the 'civilizing mission' was based on judging the world as a dual system, neatly dividing it into oppositions like black-white, traditional-modern, despotic-democratic. This was combined with the will of many Britons to proselytize the Indians according to their vision of world, state and society – in short, to influence them in every area of life. In the beginning the Indians were thought able to catch up with the ideas of a 'modern' state, European concepts of administration and science. They just had to learn and imitate, the small Indian elite serving as an example for the population. Later on, however, this image of a child or 'effeminate' man who would catch up with the European 'adult' became subject to a more racist view: the Indian civilization was inferior to the European one.[11] The men on the spot of the 'pioneering' years of empire laid the foundation for the later sense of mission to India.

2. Transforming a South Indian 'Way of Life'

Having taken control of Malabar in 1792 in the peace settlement of Srirangapattanam, the British had to provide the recently-won province with institutions capable of government according to the British definition. In this they partially fell back on the structures created in Malabar by Haidar Ali and Tipu Sultan. However, the primary aim in taking control in Malabar was to turn the province into a prosperous source of income.[12] To reach this goal, the British used economic as well as administrative means. Here I restrict myself to exemplify the measures taken with regard to administration, land law, tax policy and, since this is of unique significance to Malabar, the policy regarding the pepper trade.

British Administrative Intervention in Malabar

After annexing Malabar the government in Bombay decided to form a commission in order to assess conditions; they started work in 1792,[13] charged with recording the political situation of the day and its historical background.[14] It is evident from the instructions drawn up by General Robert Abercromby[15] that the aim of the commission was to establish a fully functioning administrative system in Malabar, which was to be in a position to collect the taxes levied by the British on a regular basis.[16] One of its most important aspects concerned the British government's intention to direct affairs within the province, which they thought anarchic, along well-ordered paths. Abercromby's strategy was to implement the British administrative system step by step.

In order not to offend the Malabar *raja*s outright Abercromby instructed the commissioners to adopt a cautious approach. This happened after he had ascertained that the treaties signed with the *raja*s of northern Malabar in 1790 had not been formulated as comprehensively as the British would have liked them to be. The treaties promised the *raja*s independence from Tipu, but did not spell out explicitly the dependence of the Malabar princes on the British.[17] The commissioners had a weighty argument in their favour that could make the *raja*s compliant when it came to their demands for independence: the princes had not complied with the most important article of the previous treaties, namely the exclusive supply of pepper to the EIC. Consequently, in future treaties with the *raja*s the commissioners were to stipulate that they should pay tributes in natural produce for their protection by the British.

Only a few months later a policy of intervention was favoured instead of the policy of 'mild language',[18] aiming for economic profits by assuring the EIC of a monopoly on pepper. A chief characteristic of this policy was to strip the Malabar princes of their sovereignty and to seal with them appropriate treaties on tax. The aim of the treaties was, first, to refuse all claims to sovereignty made by the Malabar princes and to ensure their long-term dependence on the EIC; second, to have the tax collections guaranteed for the British by restoring the strength of Malabar's economic production through its primary crop of pepper; and third, to create an administrative and legal structure. Thus the 'civilizing mission' took off right at the beginning of British control in Malabar, thereby combining the political ambition to rule it with the economic ambition to make a profit from its products.

The *raja*s, however, were not willing to give up their sovereignty so easily. In their first set of negotiations, with W G Farmer and A Dow, they assumed they would be regarded as allies of the British, and therefore insisted upon their principalities being returned. In the end, they were forced to give in to British demands: they were allowed internal sovereignty over their lands on condition that they permit the British to collect taxes, and that they themselves regulate internal affairs.[19] Furthermore, the British endeavoured to countermand a large part of the Malabar *rajas*' basis of legitimation by depriving them of their rights to sovereignty. For example, they forbade them to accept gifts from the people at the festivals of Onam and Visu[20] and, in doing so, struck at one of the fundamental pillars for the basis of legitimation within the redistributive system. Indeed, while the commissioners called themselves sovereign in Malabar on behalf of the EIC,[21] the *rajas* considered the EIC usurpers: '[. . .] considering the state of this country [Malabar], and more particularly the peculiar situation of the British Government in respect to the exercise of their sovereignty in it (which, to hide nothing, the rajas look upon rather as a [*sic*] usurpation on our part than a legal rule), [. . .].'[22] But in the end the *rajas* had to accept the conditions of the British, and signed treaties with them.[23]

Regarding the civil administration of Malabar, the first significant act to be passed by the commissioners was the guidelines for the new government of what was known as 'Malabar Province' on 11 March 1793.[24] The head of the government was the 'supravisor' (or general magistrate) to whom two superintendents were assigned. The superintendents exercised both fiscal and administrative powers, but military decisions could be made only by the supravisor. All of them were obliged to make trips around the country aimed at making it easier to exercise administrative control, to maintain peace and justice, collect taxes and keep an eye on the mint.[25] As a support to the superintendents and the supravisor the British took on a certain number of assistants, who were employed in public accountancy, as court administrators and in any miscellaneous tasks that arose.[26] The new style of government was announced officially to the Malabar *rajas* and the population on 18 March 1793.

Analysing the level of administration introduced by the British, we can conclude that they did not take into account the structures that had previously developed in Malabar, apart from the retention of their name: The old *desams* were brought together into a larger administrative unit, the *amsams*.[27] *Adhikaris*,[28] administrative officials, as the head of the *amsams*, were appointed by the British government. The primary function of the *adhikaris* was to collect taxes for the British. They were thus the most important people in British eyes for passing on information to the population and carrying out orders. In return the *amsadhikaris* were afforded the status of powerful men. The British usually attempted to satisfy the *adhikaris* to ensure their loyalty as subordinates and also benefited from using them as middle men in communicating with the local population. The British frequently recruited these employees from the numbers of *desavazhi*s and *natuvazhi*s, formerly the administrative officials of the Malabar *raja*s who had lost their privileged position due to the new British administration.[29] Therefore the *adhikari*s were well acquainted with the land and its people, which meant that administrative costs could be kept low as they received lower wages than British EIC officials; pressure on already limited British finances was therefore avoided. Additionally, the *adhikari*s might present the British administration in a more favourable light to the population, diffusing the blessings of a 'modern civilization'.

There were still further changes in the administrative structure of British Malabar: in 1800 the British government divided the province into ten districts, each run by a revenue collector who also had limited legal authority. In the same year the British government took away the civil and military administration of Malabar from the Bombay Presidency and handed it to the Madras Presidency, although the department of trade still remained with the Bombay Presidency.[30] The British hoped that this measure would quell the rebellions still latent in Malabar and thus leave them in a position to build up an effective administration in this province. It was placed under the responsibility of a principal collector to whom three subordinate collectors were assigned.[31] The reorganization was based on the Cornwallis system for administration introduced to the Madras presidency in 1802, but applied in Malabar only from 1806.[32] Closely connected with the administrative takeover of the province was the disarmament of the population, one of the British government's principal tasks in Malabar. A ban was enacted against the production and carrying of weapons.[33] Ultimately, the British demanded that all weapons in use be handed over for a small fee; from this time on only authorized government employees were allowed to own one. However, the *raja*s did not submit to this demand: they considered disarmament an attack on their sovereignty.[34]

With an administrative structure characterized by British concepts introduced in Malabar, changes and breaks had occurred in the traditional structure of society. One of the most striking examples of these changes is the restructuring of the Nayar *taravatu*s (family house-and-land unit). The women within the *taravatu*s were hit especially hard: the legislation introduced by the British was favourable to patrilinear structures and women were only allowed to hold the post of *karanavarti* (eldest member of the family with decision-making power) if a British court acknowledged their right to have it. Furthermore, the authorization to hold this post could be taken away from them at any time.[35] Already by the end of the nineteenth century the implementation of British law had gone so far that the traditional, matrilinear right of women to occupy the position of *karanavarti* was unheard-of by some British judges.[36] After the introduction of British law the *taravatu*s were not destroyed in physical terms, but they were broken as a political, social and ritual unit through the fundamental redefinition of their appearance and functions.[37] Besides, the British did not recognize their major function and importance within society; they stripped the Nayars of their political freedom, their right to share in decision-making and also their economic independence. As a result they were denied their traditional responsibilities, i.e. the management of the land and its people, and the leadership and implementation of the local administration. Matriliny had to give way to patriliny.

The British policy, marked on the one hand by persistent ignorance of existing social structures in Malabar, and on the other by visions of a state modelled on European bureaucracy, increasingly countermanded the traditional state system in Malabar, which had already been weakened by the Maisurian occupation in the mid-eighteenth century. This ultimately resulted in the widespread elimination of traditional structures within society and state, and their replacement by British forms of state control. It was not only the changes forced by British policy but also the methods employed to achieve this that found little favour with the local population. This is exemplified in the dissatisfaction caused by the British restructure of administration. The aim of British policy was to achieve greater control over the land and its people while attaining the most effective economic exploitation possible in the form of trade monopolies and tax collections, and all this at the lowest possible cost.[38] Therefore, in the course of negotiations with the British, the Malabar princes must have detected that the concessions wrested from them were intended to weaken their position and to strengthen that of the British. Some *raja*s, who did not consider it acceptable for the British to take away their rights of sovereignty made a stand against them. The result was a period of rebellions lasting almost ten years.

Legal Interventions

The British system was introduced not only in administrative lines but also in the field of law and order. *Iustitia*, in the form of a British court, settled in Kozhikodu over which the members of the commission presided. One of the purposes of this institution was to impress the locals with the establishment of a judicial system guaranteeing them rights and property.[39] In case of dispute the population could choose whether to turn to this court or to the *raja*s for traditional judgment. The British, however, reserved the right to amend judgments made by any *raja* in those cases where the parties concerned were not satisfied with the result.[40] The jurisdiction in the courts followed the Bengal Code. Within the seven local judicial administrations the British also employed local people as policemen and court administrators.[41] To guarantee their good conduct and integrity the British withheld an annual salary for local employees (*adhikari*s) as a kind of deposit-cum-personal-commitment. In addition, employees had to swear an oath that they would meet their obligations and not abuse their position to make financial gain.[42] Thus, imposing the 'right' conduct could be achieved by manipulating wages as pedagogical measures. A modification was made to the Bengal Code in October 1797: this was partially designed to keep in check the growing influence of the *raja*s, while at the same time establishing British supremacy and enabling a reduction in the expenditure of the EIC.[43] At the end of 1797 civil servants and tax assistants, who had been sworn in, were employed across the entire district.[44] Despite all these measures, confidence in British institutions, for example the courts, could not be fully established: people still turned to traditional courts. Here, the limits of the 'civilizing mission' were reached.

With the establishment of British courts and the orientation of jurisdiction towards Anglo-Saxon conventions, Indian common and traditional law were almost entirely remodelled according to British standards. Traditional institutions were consequently ignored and substituted by the western, in particular the British, system without any thought as to whether this was suited to the customs of the country. Yet the British government found it impossible to bring about 'law and order' to its satisfaction, since the new system did not operate with sufficient efficiency: the population trusted neither the courts nor their staff, and the operation of the system entailed high costs for the EIC. Nevertheless, the British regulations laid the foundations for a modern jurisdiction as well as legislature based on the western model, although the colonizers did not enjoy any real success in the initial years following the takeover of administration.[45]

British Taxation Policy

Before the British introduced their own taxation scheme, they first tried to ascertain what sums Haidar Ali and Tipu Sultan had raised in their annual tax collections. When determining British tax policy the commissioners rejected both Tipu's over-taxation of Malabar and his monopolization of internal trade.[46] After negotiations in the spring of 1792, the British sealed treaties with the Malabar princes, limited to a certain length of time, in which the *raja*s were given a relatively free hand on internal matters in their regions, yet accorded the EIC the highest level of authority. Two British officials per principality were to be responsible for tax assessment.[47] In spite of these agreements the issue of tax assessment was to prove problematic.

For example, in one of his letters about the Nambyars of Iruvazhinatu,[48] the supravisor in Malabar, W G Farmer, describes and complains about the

freedom-loving Malabarians: the *raja*s insisted that they collect taxes themselves and without supervision by employees of the EIC, which Farmer
regarded as impudent. Ultimately Farmer withdrew to the position where the
Nambyars were allowed to nominate one of their own as a contact person for
the EIC, via whom Farmer would be able to agree on tax collection in
Iruvazhinatu.[49] The self-governance that had been practised until then, which
was now defended and demanded by the Nambyars of Iruvazhinatu and also
by the *raja*s and other local elite groups in Malabar, caused the British to comment that the Malayalees were a people with a particularly pronounced sense
of freedom.

In October 1792 one-year treaties were signed with the princes of
Malabar.[50] Nevertheless, negotiations had not been easy for the British and
they had required prolonged discussions with Pazhassi *Raja* of Kottayam
especially, since he refused to pay what was demanded of him. They
described him as the 'most untractable and unreasonable'[51] of the *raja*s. In the
end, however, Pazhassi *Raja* had to agree, first, to hand over the entire pepper
production (at least five hundred *kanti*s[52]) to the British, and second, to pay a
sum of 20,000 rupees, either in cash or natural produce, in two instalments
one year in arrears.[53] This minimum payment did not seem to be enough for
the British treasury, since in the spring of 1793 the commissioners made
amendments to the treaty of October 1792: in Kottayam there was to be a
tax collection of 55,000 rupees and at least 700–800 *kanti*s of pepper.[54]
Pouring oil on troubled waters, the British confirmed Vira Varmma, *Raja* of
Kurumpranatu as the appointed tax collector of Kottayam in May 1793.
Additionally the EIC upheld Vira Varmma's subsequent request for an assistant to facilitate tax collection.[55] Thus at that time two treaties existed with
two different princes over tax collection in Kottayam; the execution of either
was therefore bound to lead to confrontation. Pazhassi *Raja*'s opposition to
British policy deepened considerably, because he seemingly felt that his previous loyalty to the British was not being recognized.[56]

An example of Pazhassi *Raja*'s opposition to British tax policy was his
refusal to collect taxes in Kottayam until November 1793. Where this practice
could not be put into operation Pazhassi *Raja* saw to it that all pepper plants
were destroyed to prevent them being used to calculate taxes.[57] The systematic attempts of the British to secure tax collection by contract enjoyed such a
low level of success that the supravisor of Malabar was forced to give concessions to the *raja*s. Finally, an agreement was made between Pazhassi *Raja* and
the supravisor in December 1793, which concerned the taxation of some districts of Kottayam. Other points in question were agreed upon as well: estates
that belonged to temples were to be exempt from tax for a year, a fifth of taxes
were to go towards Pazhassi *Raja*'s upkeep because he had remained loyal to

the EIC during the battles against Tipu Sultan, and another fifth of taxes were to support the temples.[58] These more or less liberal conditions brought some stability to the strained situation.

However, the peace did not last because Vira Varmma, *Raja* of Kurumpranatu, had started collecting taxes in Kottayam on the basis of agreements with the British. The population of Kottayam did not care to accept the appointment of a British puppet as ruler instead of their own *raja*, i.e. Pazhassi *Raja*; they demanded to be led by the ruler who had stood by them in wartime. Furthermore, Vira Varmma turned the operation of tax collection to his favour in those regions under his control: as intended by the British the population of Kottayam had to pay him four times the amount expected; this is evident from the complaints issued by Kottayam's nobility.[59] Many poor farmers left the country for this very reason, which in turn had a negative effect on pepper production. Thus the high taxation destroyed the inhabitants' fundamental way of life. The local people of Kottayam demanded the reinstatement of their king, Pazhassi *Raja*, as the responsible tax collector: 'So we made a representation about all these affairs to Pazhassi *Raja* and await his decision. [. . .] Now we request you, Sahib [Christopher Pili], to be kind enough to entrust Pazhassi *Raja* to collect the taxes due to the Company from 72 [972 M.E./1796–97 A.D.] onwards and to remit the same to the Company. This would solve our problem and save us.'[60] Nevertheless in April 1797, when the British were busy issuing new treaties, tax collection in Kottayam was once again entrusted to the Kurumpranatu *Raja*. This happened despite clear knowledge of the resulting and ongoing conflicts, documented in the aforementioned petition by the nobility of Kottayam.

As the treaties of 1797 maintained the status quo regarding tax collection in Kottayam, with Vira Varmma the responsible collector, Pazhassi *Raja* continued his policy of opposition: by August 1798 the British had still not received any payment from him. Furthermore, he was reported to have prevented attempts by British officials in Kottayam to collect taxes there. He opposed the taxation of houses in particular.[61] In the spring of 1799, he was largely able to prevent payment of the pepper tax.[62] The government in Bombay expressed its dissatisfaction over the level of taxes being brought in from Malabar, and the government there was ordered to take appropriate measures and increase levels of tax:[63] the superintendents told local officials from Malabar to submit reports on tax collection, and to face questions on the state of affairs within the country.[64] On the basis of the current tax situation, which was no longer viable for the British, the inhabitants of Kottayam were instructed to hand over their taxes to none other than the EIC collectors.[65]

Still, the story went on: in 1802 a new tax assessment, including a redefinition of the exchange rate in Malabar, was carried out.[66] This meant an increase in taxation for each individual by 20 per cent in gold *fanams* and by 10 per cent in silver *fanams*, while the government's share of rice production was increased from 35 to 40 percent, based on a dubiously accurate assessment of farming production. The yield for one coconut palm, for example, was put at 48 nuts instead of a realistic estimate of 24 nuts.[67] As a result the financial situation of the Malabar population became even more precarious: many had to sell all of their movable property just to cover tax payments.[68] This did not go unnoticed by the British: one EIC official stated that in the previous year the province had reached a slump in economic and demographic terms; he even admitted that the British government might have made some errors in this regard. He did not refer to that statement, however, when he implemented the tax increases in Malabar in 1802. Instead he cited the subjection of the population to their *raja*s as one of the causes of the precarious situation.[69] Again we come across an argument quite common to British documents regarding India: as soon as problems arose with the local elite they were attributed to the subjection of the people by the 'despotic' power of the *raja*s. The British sought to portray themselves as helping the population to throw off this yoke – thereby establishing their version of 'just and fair' rule.

3. Roots of Conflict

For a better understanding of why conflicts arose between the British and the local inhabitants, we have to look at the Indian concept of sovereignty, which differed fundamentally from the European notion. When examining Indian states and their structures, it is essential not to take as a starting point any preconceptions of a western-style state. Only by distancing oneself from the Eurocentric concept of state, which is understood as a firmly-defined entity with political, economic and administrative structures, is it possible to grasp the structures of traditional Indian society. It follows from this that the western concept of state cannot do justice to the Indian concept in all its complexity. This primarily concerns having a share in power, 'i.e. in the legitimate participation in the honour of social standing befitting the elite, and in the distribution of produced goods amongst those who were not producers themselves'.[70] To a large extent, the Indian concept of state, and of state rule, came from proportional exercise of power and not from any attempt to secure a monopoly on power. The aim of every ruler was to occupy the highest position in the state structure, thereby being the head of a hierarchy of kings, and to hold the title of *maharajadhiraja*, the king of kings. This title was reserved for the 'great king', who was able to amass for himself the most titles. Even though he occupied the highest position in the hierarchy of the kings the great king was not omnipotent: the rulers stationed beneath him commanded a share of his power. A further indispensable element of the Indian concept of state was that of political and religious acts, which served to determine and illustrate the rulers' relations with one another.

According to traditional state doctrine, especially strongly embodied in southern India, the nature of state was characterized by seven elements: the king (*svami*), the minister (*amatya*), the land (*janapada*), the fort (*durga*), state reserves (*kosa*), the army (*danda*) and the allies (*mitra*).[71] Although the king held the most important position, he was a part of – neither outside nor above – the state structure: the king was always linked with the other elements that constituted this model and, more especially, by a structure of relationships defined by political and ritual acts. Since the king's power sprang from the *dharma* (code of conduct), which he, as the head of the administration, had to support and implement, he was not able to act alone at his own discretion.[72] Moreover, there were advisers and institutionalized committees to which the king was accountable; thus he did not enjoy absolute status.[73] The *dharma* can also be regarded as the rule of interdependency, which can be attributed to natural conditions, and which is necessary for the maintenance of social order.[74] In addition to his political and administrative functions the *raja*, according to the *rajadharma*, was charged with looking after the welfare of the people in his kingdom.

The concept behind the *rajadharma* was multi-faceted and involved the consequential activities of the *raja*.[75] Prosperity and harmony required not only the settlement of conflicts, but also the pleasing of the gods with gifts and rituals.[76] Thus, on the one hand, the gods were involved in government while on the other, the king took on a partially divine quality.[77] A king legitimized his power within the redistributive system: that is, he validated and manifested his rule through political and ritual actions, for example through the patronage of temples and the upkeep of religious ceremonies. The main concern was that he exercised his power for the welfare of the people – a goal firmly in accordance with the traditional canon of duty for a king. In Malabar, as in other regions in India like parts of Orissa and Tamil Nadu, the state was run as a 'little kingdom'. The 'little king' shared his status with other little kings and legitimized his rule by taking a share in the power of the great king. His status was determined by his ever-shifting relationship with administrative officers, his fellow little kings, and to the great king.[78]

Disputed Sovereignty

The administrative actions taken by the British, as described in the previous section, triggered varying reactions from the Malabar princes. One option was to refuse to adopt – and fight against – British claims to power, while another was to cooperate, thereby supporting the establishment of British rule. These two divergent reactions are exemplified in the respective behavioural patterns of Kerala Varmma Pazhassi *Raja* and Vira Varmma of Kurumpranatu. After several attempts by diplomatic means, Pazhassi *Raja* decided to mount resistance against the British. Vira Varmma, however, opted to cooperate with them.

Vira Varmma of Kurumpranatu was usually one of the first to sign treaties proposed by the British, which he believed would increase his power. It is no longer possible today to reconstruct with any great certainty whether Vira Varmma's gain in material goods led him to overlook the fact that the price to be paid was loss of sovereignty, or whether he knowingly accepted it. The assessment of him in contemporary British texts is as a *raja* concerned only with material gain, who forgot his traditional commitments. At the least he seems to have spotted the chance to make personal gains, whether financial or political, from the conflict with the British. To this end he also schemed against Pazhassi *Raja*. It seems likely that he attempted to turn Pazhassi *Raja*, who had been on good terms with the British until 1792, against them.[79] One might suspect that Vira Varmma's enigmatic behaviour was often the cause of misunderstandings between Pazhassi *Raja* and the British.[80] When Pazhassi *Raja* turned to resistance, Vira Varmma was able to portray himself to the British as the comparatively 'good' *raja*, always at their service. Another tactic he used was to comply speedily with British orders: he sent daily reports on events in Kottayam and recommended the British to crush the rebels.[81] Such a policy made it easier for the British to take control of Malabar.

How did negotiations run between Vira Varmma of Kurumpranatu and the British? Vira Varmma appeared open-minded about the proposed British treaties: as mentioned above he was one of the first *rajas* to sign them. The considerable advantage he had enjoyed since the first treaties with the British was that he was not only appointed as tax collector for Kurumpranatu but also for Kottayam. In this way he was indirectly given the opportunity to take sovereignty of another Malabar principality, albeit restricted by the British.[82] The advantage in this for the British was that Vira Varmma played the part of a cooperative middle man for them, and furnished them with insider information and recommendations. Thereby they gained access to details of internal affairs in Malabar that would otherwise have remained hidden, which helped them to move closer towards achieving their goal: control over Malabar. A casual assessment of the situation may indicate that Vira Varmma and the employees of the EIC were pulling in the same direction, particularly over tax collection in Kurumpranatu and Kottayam. Nevertheless, one can safely assume that they were motivated by differing goals. As a little king, Vira Varmma used his alliance with the British to extend the area over which he exerted power; it is still unclear as to whether he wished to advance to the status of great king. For their part, however, the British strove for absolute sovereignty in Malabar, which fitted the European-British model, and they used the treaties to attain this objective. The manipulation of local elites helped them achieve their goal.

Pazhassi *Raja*'s relationship with the British was formed in a different way: he called upon them to acknowledge his sovereignty in Kottayam, to take into account the needs of the local people and to grant him rule over the part of Vayanatu to which he had been entitled since time immemorial. Yet his insistence on his rights of sovereignty inevitably led to conflict with the British, because they were intent on stabilizing economic dominance in Malabar; their chief concern lay in the creation of a monopoly on the pepper trade through territorial supremacy and improvements to administration – 'their euphemism for raising the level of taxation'.[83] The British demand for sovereignty in Malabar and Pazhassi *Raja*'s defence of his sovereignty in Kottayam and Vayanatu, for the British on account of important pepper cultivation areas, collided with one another at this point. This clash of sovereignty[84] only was resolved in 1805 when the British used military force to eliminate Pazhassi *Raja*.

Pazhassi *Raja* was firmly convinced that the sovereign rights over Kottayam and Vayanatu were his, and he held the same conviction over his duty to looke after his people's needs. For him any renunciation of his sovereign rights, and thus his responsibility for governmental affairs in Kottayam, would signify a neglect of his duty as ruler. He was not prepared to give up these rights voluntarily. Over several years he tried to use diplomatic means when negotiating with the British over areas of responsibility and power in Kottayam and Vayanatu. When the attempts had finally failed, however, he was forced to acknowledge that it would be impossible to make any alliances with the British as their equal partner. His attitude towards the British, which had initially been loyal, became hostile when they failed to hold to a number of different agreements, and he mounted resistance, in the form of guerrilla warfare, from 1796 to 1805. The British had to take seriously the rebellions he led, and they were not free of them for many years. Had Pazhassi *Raja* not agreed to the British desire for peace in 1797 it would have been almost impossible for them to consolidate their power in Malabar at the beginning of the nineteenth century. The rebellions of Pazhassi *Raja* and his supporters cast serious doubt over the British position in Malabar.[85] Only after a colossal military armament in Malabar and the stubbornness of Subcollector Thomas H Baber, who pursued the rebels into the farthest corners of Vayanatu was it possible for the British to gain control of the politically unstable situation. Ultimately it took Pazhassi *Raja*'s death to break the spirit of resistance among the local population and finally seal British dominance.

On 8 December 1805 the principal collector of Malabar issued an official proclamation by which the death of Pazhassi *Raja* was made known to the population. He emphasized that any rebellion against the British would be useless, and pointed to Pazhassi *Raja* as an example. The proclamation stated that it was therefore in the local population's own best interests to place itself under the authority and protection of the British.[86] To keep up appearances the British granted Pazhassi *Raja* a funeral with full honours, and he was laid to rest in Manantavati.[87] Finally the British had paved their way to 'liberate' the population from its 'despot' and to shower 'civilization' on their subjects.

The examples given here of the *raja*s' reactions to British claims over rulership and land in Malabar show that patterns of conduct towards the British were varied, and even conflicting. As far as the British were concerned, Pazhassi *Raja*'s conduct hindered their aspirations to power, while Vira Varmma's policy of cooperation smoothed their way into the circle of Malabar princes.

4. Conclusion

A few years later the *raja*s of Malabar still did not fit in with the British idea of authority of the state and its subjects' duty, that is, to carry out government orders. The British considered the conduct of the Malabar princes rebellious and ungrateful; this might have been why they described them as 'a race of monsters'. A characteristic of the Malabar *raja*s, as well as of the local magnates, mentioned repeatedly in British documents is their desire for freedom. Two more quotations, the first one by an employee of the EIC, illustrate the British judgement of local rulers and people:

> I have only to observe, that the peculiar habits and prejudices of the People, and a spirit of independence, which, the difficult nature of the country, and their mode of Life, has enabled them in a greater comparative degree, to preserve, renders them less subservient to authority, and always prone to avail of the advantages they possess, to relieve themselves from the operation of such measures, as materially affect their Interests, and which they conceive to be burthensome, or have been unaccustomed to sustain.[88]

William Bentinck, the president and governor of Fort St George, commented in a similar vein:

Independence of Mind, seems to be the Characteristic which distin-
guishes them from our other Subjects. [. . .] But the independence in
Malabar is said to be generally diffused, through the Minds of the
people. They are described of being extremely sensible of good treatment and impatient of oppression. To entertain a high respect for
Courts of Judicature and to be extremely attracted to their Old
Customs.[89]

Written in 1803–4 these citations reveal that after more than a decade
British efforts to convert Malabar into a smoothly working province with
'proper' administration, tax and land policy, as well as to provide financially
profitable undertakings, still did not show the desired results. Moreover, the
*raja*s and the population seemed as convinced of their right to independence
as ever, in opposition to the British view that they should submit to the new
government. As a result, the 'civilizing mission' proved difficult to implement
in Malabar; the processes of negotiation between the local people and the rising colonial power continued to be fractious. The local elite and the *raja*s used
different ways to counter the challenge imposed by the British.[90] However,
with regard to the economic efforts of the British limits existed to their policy:
the failure of the British policy on pepper can be attributed to various factors,
inter alia the strong influence of the *raja*s on the pepper producers and their
opposition to the British monopolization of pepper, and also the private trading affairs of EIC officials. As a result, the EIC did not achieve the economic
advantages they had hoped would come from the annexation of Malabar.[91]
The *raja*s and the local population, by and large, thwarted the British attempt
to monopolize pepper.

Besides their claim to sole sovereignty, the economic squeeze imposed by
the British may explain the rebellions of Kerala Varmma Pazhassi *Raja* and
his followers, in particular the heavy taxation of the entire population,
whether in trade or farming. Rebellions, social unrest and suchlike had been
relatively absent from Malabar until the eighteenth century. The first rebellions in the region took place during the Maisurian rule, but it was only under
British colonial rule that Malabar became an enduring trouble-spot; this can
be traced back to the British intention completely to restructure its society.[92]
The implementation of colonial legislature and jurisdiction[93] forced a clear
separation of the traditionally interwoven spheres of politics, the economy,
society and religion. Indeed, this was clearly evident in Malabar itself: with
the aid of legal proceedings as a basis of legitimation, the British worked on an
administrative and tax structure that corresponded to their conceptions, but
ultimately they were able to implement it only by force and against the wishes
of a large section of the local population. The pre-colonial state system in

Malabar was brought to collapse by British unwillingness to use and add to the existing system. Their intention to adopt their own model of state and its implementation in Malabar (and India) as far as possible without prior modification denoted the end of the pre-colonial system. Although some elements of the traditional structures of society remained in place, such as the *taravatu*s, they were given new functions that had scarcely anything to do with their original purpose.[94] In place of the indigenous structure, the British aimed to create an entirely new order for Malabar based on the western model, and consequently fostered tension.

The question arises as to how the British came by the notion that they could claim sovereignty in a country foreign to them. Different motives for the 'civilizing mission' are to be found in the abovementioned instances: though the main objective of the East India Company was economic profit, this was not the only motive for the 'civilizing mission'. Another was the missionary spirit of Christianity. The British claim to sovereignty in Malabar can be attributed partly to their view that they were the 'better', superior civilization.[95] At the same time they also claimed a moral obligation, on account of their superiority, to liberate the Indian people from the rule of 'despots'. This self-image inclined the British to the idea that their law was superior to that of other systems, and that it was therefore unnecessary to take any notice of the existing law of a conquered country. The British were able to justify their claim to rule, and its associated sovereignty, only by preserving the difference between colonizers and colonized, which implied the 'savageness' of the latter. There is also the fact that no codified, written system of law existed in Malabar, which relegated Malabar society to one of the lower levels within the 'ranking' of societies. Moreover, it was, paradoxically, their own 'gentlemanliness' that gave the British ample self-justification for their imperialistic behaviour.

3

Between Non-interference in Matters of Religion and the Civilizing Mission: The Prohibition of *Suttee* in 1829

JANA TSCHURENEV

Humboldt-University, Berlin

Of the rite itself, of its horror and abomination not a word need be said. Every rational and civilized being must feel anxious for the termination of a practice so abhorrent from humanity, and so much at variance even with the otherwise mild principles of the Hindu religion itself. But to the Christian and to the Englishman, who by tolerating sanctions, and by sanctioning incurs before God the responsibility of this inhuman and impious sacrifice not of one, but of thousands of victims, these feelings of anxiety must be and ought be extreme. The whole and sole justification is state necessity – that is, the security of the British empire, and even that justification, would be, if at all, still very incomplete, if upon the continuance of the British rule did not entirely depend the future happiness and improvement of the numerous population of this eastern world.'

Government Circular on *suttee* addressed to military officers, 10 November 10, 1828[1]

In early nineteenth century Bengal the newly established British administration faced a fundamental dilemma: it was torn between the declared principle of non-interference in local matters of culture and religion and the idea of having a moral responsibility to save the lives of innocent victims.[2] The dilemma could be boiled down to the question of which was the lesser evil:

either to accept thousands of widows being killed in the name of religion, or to jeopardize the stability of British rule in India. The decision became even more difficult for two reasons: first, it was not only considered a moral duty to save the lives of the widows: the creation of stable British rule in India was held necessary for the sake of the colonized people, and to civilize and educate the Indians was considered the best and safest solution for problems such as *suttee*.[3] Second, it was not possible to define clearly what *suttee* specifically denoted and where it could be placed within the broader context of the Hindu religion.

In the circular to military officers quoted above, Governor General William Bentinck (1828–35) mentions two concurring principles that British rule in India was supposed to follow. The first addresses in practical terms the need to focus on political and military stability to ensure the economic success of the East India Company (EIC). From this point of view there was no need for interference in the religious and cultural practices of the local population since an intervention of this kind might cause trouble and instability. The theoretical concepts underlying this strategy can be found in the early 'Orientalist'[4] approach to India. The first phase of British rule in India was accompanied by the process of western 'discovery' of the Indian society and past. The collection of information and the building of knowledge was not only precipitated by the practical need to understand the colonized people, it was also driven by an interest in understanding the functioning and structure of Indian society – an interest that, initially, was not governed by the wish to enforce social change. English political theorists justified this first approach to British rule in India. Edmund Burke, for instance, considered interference in matters of the local population to be an act of tyranny.[5]

It is well known that the establishment of British rule caused considerable change in Bengal society, even if at first this was not deliberate. The *diwani* taken over by the Company in 1765 consisted not only of the right to collect revenues in the territory under British control: according to common practice it was also connected with tasks in the civil judiciary. Thus, the need arose to establish legal institutions and to clarify legal norms.[6] It was in keeping with the British non-interference policy to follow the legal tradition of each religious community in matters of civil law. In case of the Hindus, *jatis* (endogamous caste groups) determined legal questions of marriage, divorce and inheritance within different institutions such as caste cutcherries or councils.[7] Thus, local legal institutions existed, but no uniform legal code. Instead, a variety of (Brahmin) religious law texts, *dharmaśāstras*, *dharmasūtras* and commentaries, subsumed under the term *shastras* or *shasters* by the British Orientalists, served as the scriptural basis of legal activity. Initially, the British judges had to ask Brahmin pundits to compose *vyavasthās* – that is, legal

opinions varying from case to case. But then the texts were translated –
mainly as an initiative by William Jones – and categorized. This process of
collecting Hindu law and of its codification in English, according to European
ideas of legal standards is particularly well reflected in the British regulation of
Bengali social practices such as *suttee*. Thus, even if the British tried to treat
customs of the Bengal population according to Muslim and Hindu legal
standards, they caused fundamental changes by their practical policy.[8]

The creation of a modern bureaucratic administration also caused major
social transformation. A new sector of employment developed in which
Indians had to adapt to European professional codes of behaviour. Agricultural production was restructured through the Permanent Settlement in
1793. Land became an economic commodity, which could be sold and
bought freely. Furthermore, it could be used for speculation and profit-
making. These changes had negative implications for the peasants, but other
classes took advantage of the new profit-making opportunities.[9] New urban
Calcutta-based elites formed a middle class between the British rulers and the
Bengali population. They called themselves *bhadralok*, honourable folk, to
differentiate themselves from the *chotolok*, the common people.[10] This group
was characterized by high social mobility and the traditional position of the
jatis was questioned and changed. Several scholars writing about *suttee* in the
colonial context hold that the practice was concentrated on the *bhadralok* at
the beginning of the nineteenth century.[11]

The *bhadralok* formed a modern public sphere with its own media, educational institutions and associations. In 1828 the main organization of the
social reformers, the Brahmo Samaj, was founded, followed in 1830 by
the Dharma Sabha.[12] The *bhadralok* engaged in social reform fell into two
factions: the 'conservatives', who belonged to the Dharma Sabha, and the
'modernists', those of the Brahmo Samaj. The main difference between the
two was their respective view on the relation between society and religion.
The modernists, such as Rammohan Roy and Dwarkanath Tagore, regarded
social organization as dependent on religion. In this context, religion had to
be reformed before social change could be achieved. The conservatives,
around Gopimohun Deb and his son Radhakanta Deb, did not consider this
connection: from their more secularist point of view, religion and society
should be independent of each other. Modernizing society was seen as
desirable, but interference with religion could not be justified. These two
parties also formed the pro- and contra-*suttee* lobbies in the debates over legal
prohibition of the practice.

Scholars following the 'subaltern studies' approach pointed at another area
of fundamental change within Bengal society due to the establishment of
colonial rule: the organization of gender relations. The restructuring of land

ownership and the spreading of *brahmin* legal norms especially deprived lower-caste women of their freedom of action. In the developing labour market, which offered jobs in administration, education or production, women rarely had equal chances of employment. Therefore, several writers share the opinion that, with the creation of colonial rule, existing inequalities between women and men were enhanced and irrevocably institutionalized.[13] These large-scale changes form the background for the British policy on *suttee*.

In the 1820s there was a shift in the theoretical understanding of India. James Mill and Jeremy Bentham paved the way for Utilitarianism, the ideology that expressed the desirability of reforming and restructuring Indian society according to the European model, which had implications in terms of potential interference in certain religious customs: if these customs were considered intolerable it was the moral duty of Christians and civilized humans to abolish them. At this point, the idea of Britain's civilizing mission in India comes into play. For a long time *suttee* was used as one of the main examples to prove the necessity to civilize Indian society – to save women from the barbarity exerted on them by their male relatives and the priests.

It is not surprising that a dilemma arose for the British administration on *suttee*. The practice of burning widows alive had fascinated European witnesses and missionaries for at least two centuries. It prompted a variety of reactions, ranging from abhorrence to admiration. The meaning of the practice was never clear so it was considered either as a ritual of Hinduism (which was, anyway, barely comprehensible to western visitors) or as an ancient practice to defend a man's honour. However, European travellers, merchants and missionaries were only detached observers, in a different situation from that in which servants of the East India Company, who had taken over governmental duties since 1765, found themselves. As rulers, the British magistrates and judges had to deal with the social phenomena they observed.

From the 1770s on – and especially between 1805 and 1832 – a debate took place about how to handle *suttee*, its legal status within Hindu law, its religious basis, and the possibility of forbidding it. From 1815 on, the new urban middle class in Calcutta increasingly took part in this debate, which Lata Mani analysed and characterized as a colonial discourse.[14] In short, two parties developed: first, those who advocated or defended *suttee* as an essential part of the Hindu religion; and second, those who supported abolition. It was the subject of the first modern public controversy in Bengal. Within the debate the modern image of *suttee* was shaped and the dilemma of how to deal with it came to the fore.

In this article, I want to focus on the development of British policy towards *suttee*.[15] This, however, is inseparable from the process of defining what *suttee* denotes. At the beginning, I will show briefly which European images of *suttee* already existed before the British administration had to develop a policy towards the practice. Therefore, the main questions will be: which image of *suttee* developed in the discourse of the colonial administration? How did this happen? How did this shape British regulation policy? And, finally, how had the dilemma with which Governor General Bentinck was faced in 1829 been constructed? I will also focus on the active role the Bengal *bhadralok* played in this defining process.

The process of defining, constructing and (re)inventing *suttee* has not been concluded until now, as the final section of this paper will demonstrate.[16] At the beginning of the twentieth century, two more or less academic approaches to it existed, and both used it to defend their views on the colonial rule.[17] Then, *suttee* was still used as justification for continuing colonial rule and for the necessity of civilizing Indian society. Even nowadays there are discussions about it in the Indian media. A passionate intellectual debate emerged at the end of the 1980s after the young widow Roop Kanwar burned herself in Deorala, Rajasthan. It seems that the discussions have not been completely freed of ideology until today. Furthermore, academic discussions on *suttee* after 1987 point out the implicit civilizing mission of modernity as well as questions about respecting or inventing one's own traditions. Hence, it is not possible to write about *suttee* and the civilizing mission without focusing on the controversial discussions that have surrounded it.

1. **Admiration, Pity and Abhorrence:** *Suttee* **in European Travellers' and Missionaries' Accounts**

In the eyewitness accounts written by European travellers and missionaries in the seventeenth and eighteenth centuries, two different positions developed on the practice of burning living wives with their deceased husbands. On the one hand, the accounts revealed admiration for the courage of the woman and her willingness to sacrifice herself for the sake of love and fidelity; on the other, they expressed abhorrence at the cruelty of the practice and the superstition behind it. Between these two extremes we find a kind of astonishment mixed with pity, especially if the woman was young and beautiful.

The American merchant Benjamin Crowninshield wrote in 1789 when visiting Calcutta: 'Whether it is right or wrong, I leave it for other people to determine [. . .]. It appeared very solemn to me. I did not think it was in the power of a human person to meet death in such manner.'[18] The admiration expressed here is often mixed with a certain ambivalence and a moral distance. The Flemish artist Balthazard Solvyns exemplifies this point of view: in 1799, he published four etchings representing different forms of *suttee* in

Bengal with explanations and commentaries. He concludes: 'We cannot refuse our pity to the poor Hindoo women who are sacrificed to this ancient and barbarous custom; but their courage, firmness, and resignation, entitles them to some share of admiration.'[19]

However, clear disapproval and rejection of the practice is more wide-spread. Missionary statements in particular fall into this category. The widow is seen as the victim of cruel priests, greedy relatives, or her own superstition and religious delusion. The French traveller Tavernier wrote sarcastically: '[. . .] the idolators do not only burn the bodies of their dead, but the bodies of the living. They scruple to kill a serpent, or a louse, but account it a meritorious thing to burn a living wife with the body of the deceased husband'.[20]

The seventeenth century French traveller François Bernier described a *suttee* 'struggling to leave the funeral pyre when the fire increased around her, but was prevented from escaping by long poles of the diabolical execution-ers'.[21] Some reports tell us about efforts by European travellers to rescue the *suttee* – especially when she was young.[22] Sometimes they were successful and led to marriage.[23]

William Ward, a Baptist missionary from the Serampur mission,[24] de-scribed *suttee* as 'a singularly shocking practice' and 'another proof of the amazing power which this superstition has over the minds of its votaries'. His observations 'fill the mind of the benevolent with the deepest compassion for the miserable victims of this shocking superstition'.[25] He sees *suttee* as an example of the 'abhorrence of idolatry', and condemns it along with other ascetic suicidal practices such as throwing oneself before the Jaganath cart. These phenomena are reason enough for the necessity of British rule in India: 'Since the commencement of the brahmanical system millions of victims must have been immolated on the altars of its gods; and, notwithstanding the influence of Europeans, the whole of Hindoost'han may be termed 'a field of blood unto this day.'[26]

Generally speaking, the *suttee* can only be a victim in Ward's eyes: she never acts voluntarily or consciously. In most cases the 'poor wretch' or 'slaughtered victim' is murdered by her greedy relatives, by an excited crowd or unscrupu-lous *brahmins*. However, there have been cases in which no physical or psycho-logical violence was used. He quotes a woman who had explained her intention to him: 'It is right that a wife leave the world with her husband; a son can never be for his mother what a husband is to a wife; the extinction of life is the work of a minute; by strangling, by drowning, how soon does the soul leave the body: there are no terrors then in the funeral pile, and I shall at once enter on happiness! What multitudes have died in this manner before me; and if I live, I have nothing but sorrow to expect.'[27]

It is not possible to assess the authenticity of this statement. At any rate, Ward shows *suttee* as a means to acquire religious merit, and happiness in life after death as well as an expression of faithfulness in marriage beyond the grave. He also mentioned a worldly motive: to avoid the 'disgrace of widow-hood'.[28] Moreover, *suttee* brings honour to the family. The main reason for *suttee*, however, lies in the Hindu view of life and death. Death is understood as a transformation, and not as the end of a biological cycle. Thus, a woman can decide to become a *suttee* without being forced into it. However, even in this case she is – from the missionary point of view – led by false religious beliefs, and her decision cannot be called voluntary. This point was also emphasized by Mani in her analysis of the colonial discourse on *suttee*. Hindus, women as well as men, are presented as people incapable of acting rationally, but led by the teaching of their priests. In this interpretation, the possibility of conscious decision making on the part of the *suttee*s is denied.[29]

The missionaries did not only observe incidents of *suttee*. From the begin-ning of the nineteenth century, three Baptist missionaries from Serampur, William Ward, William Carey and Joshua Marshman, attempted to influence the administration into prohibiting *suttee*. In 1803, 1804 and 1812 they collect-ed data on which to base their arguments.[30]

Thus, when the British East India Company started to debate how to handle it, certain images and stereotypes of the practice already existed.

2. The Suttee Practice: a Religious Custom, Enforced by Hindu Law

It is not possible to identify a clear starting point for the discussion on *suttee* between British administrative officials and judges including Orientalists such as W W Wilson. On several occasions a district magistrate was confronted with a case of *suttee*. He was shocked and decided to consult his superior how to react and whether he could forbid the practice. The cases were brought to the *nizamat adalat*, the court presided over by two British judges in Calcutta. The main question was: is the practice legal according to Hindu law? This approach was in line with general practice of law, which stated that civil or private matters had to be judged according to the law of the religious community concerned. Thus, the *nizamat adalat* asked *pandit*s and Hindu law scholars to compose *vyavasthā*s, (legal opinions) according to their interpreta-tion of the *shastra*s. Using these, the *nizamat adalat* formulated guidelines for intervention and supervision in cases of *suttee*, which were distributed among the district magistrates.[31]

The first official statement in February 1779 was provoked by the un-authorized prohibition of a *suttee* by M H Brooke, a revenue collector in the

Shahabad district. His intervention was appreciated, but he was recommended to use unofficial influence in further prevention of *suttee* because '[t]he public prohibition of a ceremony authorized by tenets of the religion of the Hindus, and from the observance of which they have never been yet restricted by the ruling power would in all probability tend to increase rather than diminish their veneration for it'.[32]

This advice expresses several basic assumptions about *suttee*, which are repeated in later documents. First, *suttee* is seen as a religious ceremony. Second, the prohibition by law would most likely lead to results other than those intended: there was a real danger that the number of *suttee* cases would increase rather than diminish. It also becomes clear that the first officials confronted with cases reacted with revulsion, not admiration. And this view was shared by the higher administrative levels.

In 1805, J R Elphinestone, who was district magistrate in Bihar, prevented a twelve-year-old intoxicated girl being burned with the body of her husband. The question of whether or not he was authorized to do so was brought to the *nizamat adalat*. To decide on the case, the court tried to explore 'how far the practice (of widows burning with the bodies of their husbands) is founded on the religious opinions of the Hindoos'.[33] If the practice was not sanctioned by the Hindu religion, a general prohibition would be possible. The question was forwarded to the *pandit* Ghanshyam Sharma 'whether a woman is enjoined by the Shaster voluntarily to burn herself with the body of her husband, or is prohibited; and what are the conditions prescribed by the Shaster in such occasions?'.[34] Ghanshyam Sharma gave the answer in March 1805:

> Having duly considered the question proposed by the court, I now answer it to the best of my knowledge: – every women of the four castes (Brahmin, khetry, bues, and soodur) is permitted to burn herself with the body of her husband [. . .] This rests upon the authority of Anjira, Vjasa and Vrihaspati Mooni. There are three millions and a half of hairs upon the human body, and every woman who burns herself with the body of her husband, will reside with him in heaven during a like number of years.[35]

In general, according to some scriptural authorities, any woman is permitted to become a *suttee*. The *pandit* also mentions the exceptions, cases in which *suttee* is forbidden by the *smrtis* or is contrary to usage. The widow must not be 'under the age of puberty', pregnant, or 'in the state of uncleanness'. Also, care for her infants must be secured by her family.[36]

In June, the *nizamat adalat* forwarded its own interpretation of the *pandit's vyavasthā* to the Governor General.[37] In this letter, *suttee* is defined as a 'practice of widows burning themselves with the bodies of their deceased husbands'. It is also called a 'custom', based on the religious beliefs of the Hindus and prescribed by the Hindu legal texts: '[*Suttee*] is founded on the religious notions of the Hindus, and is expressly stated, with approbation, in their law.' In this interpretation, a uniform Hindu law is assumed. The differentiated statement of the *pandit*, his explicit mention of some texts (but not all) is simplified in order to find a clear position. Thus, knowledge of Indian reality was constructed from political needs, based on the prejudice of the colonial officials.[38]

Starting with the interpretations of the *pandit*, legal and illegal forms of *suttee* are distinguished. Apart from the cases he described as forbidden, intoxication was also declared illegal. 'Ideally [t]he practice [. . .] is voluntary on the part of the widow, and grounded on the prejudice respecting the consequent benefit to herself and her husband in another world.'[39] Therefore, a certain religious motive was assumed to underlie the practice, not social reasons. It is also remarkable that its purpose seemed to be happiness in life after death and not, as one might be induced to assume, salvation from the circle of rebirth.

However, it becomes clear that in spite of the assumption that *suttee* was voluntary on the part of the widow the court was reluctant to accept the practice for moral reasons and, thus, considered prohibition desirable: 'This court is fully sensible how much it is to be wished that this practice, horrid and revolting even as a voluntary one, should be prohibited and entirely abolished.'[40] There was also much scepticism about how voluntary it actually was. The widow had to decide under circumstances that proved psychologically demanding. She could not avoid persuasion by priests and relatives and was afraid of becoming a social outcast if she refused.

Much doubt was expressed about the feasibility of prohibition. *Suttee* was considered deeply rooted in the consciousness and imagination of all castes. Hence, the court was afraid to cause resistance, protest or social disorder with interference of this kind.[41] Therefore, prohibition was considered desirable but 'impracticable at present time'.[42] It is remarkable that the court came to this conclusion, although it was widely known and written in the same document that certain Hindu princes had regulated the practice already. In order to contain *suttee* it was recommended that illegal or criminal practices should be prevented: the widow's age should be checked, and it should be confirmed that her decision had been made voluntarily. A policeman should observe the practice, help the widow if she wanted to leave the pyre, compile monthly reports about the cases and bring illegal practice to court.

Until 1812 there were no further discussions or regulations. After this date, however, the government took up the recommendations of the *nizamat adalat*, maybe because Indian affairs and the reconfirmation of the EIC's charter were debated again in Parliament. In a letter from the secretariat of the Bengal government[43] it was stated that the burning of widows was a practice 'recognized and encouraged' by Hindu law and therefore could not be prohibited. This interpretation still rested on the legal opinion of Ghanshyam Sharma. It was a basic principle of British politics in India 'to allow the most complete toleration in matters of religion, to all classes of native subjects',[44] an overt expression of the principle of non-interference.

In 1813, the regulations regarding 'the ceremony denominated 'Suttee'' were forwarded as guidelines to the district magistrates.[45] The term was applied to describe the practice of burning wives. In the same year, Claudius Buchanan[46] published a list of *suttees*, including names, age, number of children and the husband's caste. The data had been collected in May and June 1812 in an area between Kasimbazar and the mouth of the Hughly. Of the sixty-six *suttees*, twenty-three were of *brahmin* families, four *kayastha* and four *kaibarrtha*. A concentration within the higher castes is visible in these figures.[47] In 1815 some further regulations were added. Brahmin women were then only allowed to perform the 'Hindoo rite of suttee' as *sahamarana*: they could burn themselves with the body of their husband immediately after his death, not years later with an object of his personal property.[48] At the same time, the *nizamat adalat* ordered the district officials to report all *suttee* incidents including name, age and caste of the widow and the same data for her husband. From 1822, the profession and living circumstances of the husband had to be mentioned as well.

Thus, the administration tried to understand the phenomenon with the help of numbers. In 1820, the Governor General reported the following numbers of cases in the Fort William presidency to the Court of Directors in London: 378 incidents in 1815, 442 in 1816, 707 in 1817, and 839 in 1818.[49] Between 1818 and 1829, the annual number of cases in the Bengal Presidency, counted by EIC officials, vacillated between five hundred and six hundred.[50] Thus, from 1815 to 1818 the number of counted *suttee* incidents had increased considerably. This gave rise to speculation and controversial discussion, not only among the British administration, judges and Orientalists but also in academic explanations of *suttee* in nineteenth-century Bengal. Anand Yang and V N Datta explain this increase as resulting from better methods of collecting statistical data or coincidence.[51] However, Ashis Nandy, Lata Mani and Romila Thapar interpret it as a genuine increase in cases caused mainly by the transformation of society induced by the beginning of colonial rule.[52]

The politics of sanctioning *suttee* were never supported by all British officials. Walter Ewer, superintendent of the police in the Upper Provinces, wrote a letter to the legal department secretary W B Bayly in November 1818 wherein he sharply criticized the assumption that the widows acted voluntarily. He assumed that *suttee* sprang from the law of inheritance practised in Bengal, the *dayabhaga*, which made the widow the heir of her husband if no son had been born to the marriage. This fact, he supposed, would induce greedy relatives to persuade her into burning herself. Also, the widow could not revise her decision to climb on to the pyre because it was a spectacle for the whole village. So she was 'scarcely ever a free agent at the performance of the *suttee*'.[53] He also questioned the religious sanction: this could be only an error or misinterpretation of the scriptures. As a result, he did not accept any justification for not prohibiting *suttee*.

Doubts about the results of the legalizing strategy are also expressed in the above mentioned letter from the Governor General to the Court of Directors. The increasing tendency to perform *suttee* was explained by two facts: the more intensive efforts of the local police officers in reporting the incidents, and a cholera epidemic that led to a higher death rate. But the government also feared that the politics of legalizing and therefore sanctioning *suttee* might have caused the increase. People felt safer after knowing for sure which cases were allowed and which were not. Also, the continuing debate made sure that *suttee* remained on the agenda and thus led to an 'excitement of religious bigotry by the continual agitation'.[54]

The Court of Directors responded in 1823. They asked for cautious policies to be followed regarding matters of religion. British courts were not considered the right place to discuss what was allowed in Hindu law and what was not. It was doubted furthermore whether *suttee* was really prescribed by the Hindu religion: 'But connected with the opinions expressed by many intelligent men, [. . .] the practice of Suttee is not a tenet of Religion, to which the people are enthusiastically attached; but rather an abuse fostered by interested Priests or Relations.'[55] After this, a modernization argument becomes important for the first time: education would lead the Hindus to understand how absurd and 'corrupted' a practice like *suttee* was. Five years later, H H Wilson also pinned his hopes on the spread of a common morality in India through the establishment of European education, as the only way to abolish such practices.[56]

During the following years the statistical results were observed attentively and speculation continued about the reasons for increasing and decreasing figures. The issue was also discussed by the public in Britain, which could not be ignored in Bengal. Between 1813 and 1830, British women's associations engaged in the campaign for the prohibition of *suttee* through petitions to Parliament and support of the missionary activities in Bengal.[57] The Serampur trio tried to influence governmental policy with their published writings, personal contacts and petitions.[58] The main argument for abolition was that homicide and suicide were forbidden not only by Christianity but also by presumed universal moral norms and humanity. Thus the government could not tolerate them. Between 1818 and 1826 the *Friend of India*, the main journal of the missionaries, regularly published articles arguing in a similar way.[59]

Public opinion in Britain was largely shaped by the presentation of *suttee* in the newspapers. In the 1820s the *suttee* was usually portrayed as victim – in accordance with the missionary view. The description of central features included the use of physical violence and drugs as well as emphasizing the barbarity of a religion which supported the murder or the suicide of innocent women.[60] In 1827 *London Magazine* represented the *suttee* as the victim of cruel relatives:

> She soon leaped from the flame, and was seized, taken up by the hands and feet, and again thrown upon it, much burnt; she again sprung from the pile and running to a well hard by laid herself down in the water course, weeping bitterly . . . an uncle swearing by the Ganges, that if she would seat herself on the cloth (which he proceed) he would carry her home; she did so, was bound up in it, carried to the pile now fiercingly burning, and again thrown into the flames.[61]

Until the end of the 1820s the opinion spread in Bengal too that humanity and Christianity would not allow any further toleration of this practice. But the success of prohibition was questioned more than ever. In his letter to the military secretary of the government H H Wilson reached the conclusion that *suttee* was recommended by the holiest texts of the Hindus, whose statements were regarded as obligatory by pious Hindus:

> These promises [of paradise to the widow and her husband] and injunctions are set forth not by writers of recent date or disputable authority, but by those whom the Hindus universally class amongst the divine and inspired founders of their system. They have therefore the weight of commands, as far as opposed without violence to the conscientious belief of every order of Hindus.[62]

Therefore 'the *suttee* cannot be put down without interference with the Hindu religion'.[63] This estimation of the situation was shared by a large number of government officials. The main question in 1828 was whether and how the abolition of *suttee* – as interference with the Hindu religion – would endanger the stability of British rule in India. Hence, Governor General Bentinck summarized the dilemma developed during the last decades in his Minute on Suttee: there could be no justification for tolerating this 'first and most criminal of their customs', this 'inhuman and impious rite', which 'costs the lives of hundreds of innocent victims' every year – if the British government had the power to stop it. But disturbing the Hindus in their religious rites – and *suttee* was certainly understood as such now – would be a risk for the security of the 'British Empire' in India.[64]

To assess the probability of riots or rebellion following a prohibition, Bentinck asked forty-nine experienced British military officers how their Indian troops would react, if they regarded prohibition as interference with their religious freedom or even as a general attempt to promote Christianity in India and, most importantly, if they were prepared to mutiny.[65]

In the administrative correspondence the opinion is expressed that religion played a central role in the life of the Hindus and that they would be sensitive to interference. Interestingly, most of the military officers asked did not share this impression. Only five feared their troops would be ready to rebel; some recommended caution since twenty-four officers supported immediate general prohibition. 'I believe our sepoys, Hindu and Brahmin, care less for their religion than they do for the Company's service,' Lieutenant Colonel Porderi said.[66] Lieutenant Colonel Tapp prophesied that Hindus would be 'perfectly indifferent' to prohibition by law.[67] Robert Hamilton's remarks show the same tendency:

> Apathy is the strongest feeling if I may use the expression, that pervades the Hindus, coupled with an inordinate desire to scrape together money, and I feel persuaded that the observance of the most strictly enjoined ceremony would be quitted were it likely to entail any possible contingent loss or hindrance in any of the affairs of life.[68]

On 12 December 1829 *suttee* was prohibited by law and declared a crime. The practice 'hurt the feelings of humanity' and it was 'nowhere enjoined by the religion of the Hindus as an imperative duty'.[69] The second legitimizing argument was to deny the free will of the women concerned – they could only be victims and thus had to be rescued from a forced act of burning. After building up the – never disputed – image of *suttee* as a religious custom, it was now prohibited with the claim that it was not a religious duty. This can only be understood by focusing on the voices of the Bengali in this debate. At this point Bentinck took up the main argument of the well-known Bengali opponent of *suttee*, Rammohan Roy, with whom he was in personal contact.

3. Defending and Opposing Concremation[70]

Prohibition of *suttee* caused neither riots nor rebellion among the population or the Indian troops, but an ambivalent reaction among the Bengali public. In January 1830, the inhabitants of Baksar wrote to Bentinck expressing their gratitude because they had been able to prevent a *brahmin* widow burning herself.[71]

At the same time, however, the Dharma Sabha was founded as a direct reaction to the abolition of *suttee*. The association stated: 'Through the absence of all religious authority in this country, religion suffers great detriment. It has therefore become necessary that the excellent and the noble should unite and continually devise means for protecting our religion and our excellent customs and usages.'[72]

One of its initial activities was to raise funds to send a petition to the British Parliament asking for revision of the Act. An anonymous letter to the editor of the *India Gazette* criticized its efforts sarcastically, stating in the name of the prisoners of Allypore jail: 'The Government should recognize that murder, robbery and theft are ancient customs amongst the prisoners and therefore should not be punishable.'[73]

The petition of the Dharma Sabha was sent to Parliament by Dr Lushington in 1831. There, '[h]e proceeded in the first place to show that the religious rite and custom of *suttee* was an integral and essential doctrine of the Hindoo religion, as appeared from the concurring opinions which had been obtained from some of the most celebrated pundits [. . .]'.[74] A counter-petition 'in defence of the regulation prohibiting the practice of *suttee*' praising abolition and asking for maintenance of the law was brought to London by Rammohan Roy. This document calls *suttee* a 'barbarous and inhuman practice [. . .] abhorrent to all the feelings of nature'.[75] *Suttee* is denied for moral reasons and abolition is seen as an invaluable gain for the Indian population.

Rammohan Roy's mission was successful: Parliament reconfirmed prohibition and the Brahmo Samaj sent a letter of thanks to the King, expressing their gratitude 'for this beneficial measure'[76]. However, the *Samachar Chandrika*, the journal associated with Dharma Sabha, lamented: 'In anguish and distress, with great grief and affliction, overwhelmed in a sea of sorrow, swimming in a river of tears, we now publish the sad intelligence respecting Suttees. [. . .] When such an injury against religion as this is committed, we must conclude, that justice has departed from earth.'[77]

When Bengali voices joined the British debate on *suttee* in 1815, the main question was already established. Is *suttee* a religious duty sanctioned by Hindu law? The *bhadralok* took up this issue, and used some British statements as reference for their own position and for revising it. The focus of this section will therefore be the Bengali arguments for and against the abolition of *suttee* and how the Bengali population reacted to the set of assumptions established in the British debate.

The most active, or at least best-known, opponent of the practice, Rammohan Roy, published two pamphlets in 1818 and 1820 and many articles in which he developed three main arguments against *suttee*.[78] First, he argued that the practice lacked sanction by the *shastras*. Some texts left two options to the woman after the death of her husband: ascetic widowhood or concremation. The *Mānavadharmaśastra* or *Manusmṛti* prescribed that the widow should live an ascetic life and practise austerity.[79] Roy considered Manu the highest authority on this question: 'Therefore, the laws given by Ungira and the others who you have quoted, being contrary to the law of Munoo, cannot be accepted; because the Ved declares, "whatever Munoo said is wholesome" and Vrihusputi, "whatever law is contrary to the law of Munoo is not commendable".'[80]

This statement, which he repeated in 1831, clearly contradicts Wilson's conclusion drawn in 1828 that the practice is recommended 'not by writers of recent date or disputable authority, but by those whom the Hindus universally class amongst the divine and inspired founders of their system'. This claim had been made by *suttee* defenders several times. Rammohan Roy stressed that Aṅgira and the other legislators who recommend *suttee* have no authority equal to Manu, 'the most ancient, and highest legislative authority of the Hindoos'.[81]

Moreover, according to Manu, 'self-destruction with the view of reward is expressly prohibited'.[82] Thus, Roy's second argument referred to the religious meaning of the practice. The question was whether *suttee* made sense as a religious rite. According to the *Bhagavadgītā*, the 'essence of all the Smritis, Poorans, and Itihasas'[83], in Roy's interpretation, seeking reward through the practice of certain rites was not only wrong but useless, because such actions sprang from human desires. Following the *Bhagavadgītā*, one should overcome one's desires to gain knowledge and salvation.

Two religious notions concur here. Roy did not see a long stay in heaven promised to the *suttee* and her husband as her goal, but salvation. Moreover, *suttee*, he thought, was in contradiction to the neo- or reform-Hindu break with the ritual in general. Finally, Roy argued passionately against *suttee*, stressing moral ideas. It contradicted his concept of justice. Hence, '[s]uch an argument [the scriptural sanction] is highly inconsistent with justice. It is in every way improper to persuade to self-destruction by citing passages of inadmissible authority.'[84]

In this view, concremation was not sanctioned by law since Manu did not mention it. It is, rather, a useless ritual according to Rammohan Roy's new concept of Hinduism with its strong reference to the *Bhagavadgītā*. But by far the strongest argument defined *suttee* just as murder – owing to the common practise of binding the widow or holding her down with sticks.[85]

Rammohan Roy's pamphlets are structured as a debate between an opponent and an advocate of *suttee*. He presented each side as agreeing on the assumption that women should never live independently or unsupervised. Since this, in the defender's view, was one reason to burn a widow the opponent stressed that supervision could be provided by the family. Finally the misogynist concepts underlying *suttee* were criticized. The widow was sentenced to death out of caution: to prevent her bringing shame to the family.[86]

The petition against the prohibition did indeed argue in this way. The concremation required only one moment of bravery and causes only brief pain, while ascetic widowhood called for discipline and strength over many years, difficult for a weak woman: she would endanger her own salvation as well as the family's honour if she departed from decent behaviour. She could avoid these considerable risks by becoming a *suttee*.[87]

Rammohan Roy considered women inferior to men in physical strength and energy. But as long as they did not have the same opportunities in education, nothing could be said about their mental inferiority. On the contrary, *suttee* showed the high degree of psychological strength and bravery of which women were capable.[88] In the end, he accused the defenders of *suttee* of lack of compassion for the pain women suffered on the pyre. He compared them to those who worshipped Kali with cruel sacrifices and advised them to learn from the compassion and pity of the Vaishnavas.[89]

Even though he opposed concremation so explicitly, Rammohan Roy did not support prohibition by law. When Bentinck asked him for his opinion in 1829, to include it in his Minute on Suttee, he recommended a discreet strategy for abolition because he feared it might be interpreted as interference with freedom of religion and as a measure to promote Christianity in India. Bentinck quotes: 'While the English were contending for power they deemed it politic to allow universal toleration and to respect our religion, but having obtained the supremacy their first act is a violation of their profession, and the next will probably be, like the Muhammadan conquerors, to force upon us their own religion.'[90]

This position towards legal regulation was not the consensus view among opponents of *suttee*. In 1819 when the defenders engaged in lobbying for a revision of the regulations passed in 1815 and 1818, the opponents counterpetitioned: they denied to Governor General Hastings the scriptural sanction – as Roy did several times – and reported on cruel practices such as the binding of the women on the pyre, which contradicted 'common feelings of humanity'. They accused the other party of not knowing their own religion and of declaring themselves representatives of the opinion of the majority of educated Hindus in Calcutta. They appealed to the 'known humanity of the British nation' to abolish *suttee*, just as it had prohibited female infanticide.[91]

The main arguments of the defenders of *suttee* can be found in the petition against prohibition in 1830.[92] It was signed by the founders of the Dharma Sabha, among them Radhakanta and Gopimohan Deb. They demanded a withdrawal of prohibition because it marked an interference with the religion and customs of the Hindus – even though the Governor General and even parliament had ensured that the customs, rites, religion and law of the religious communities of India were respected. The Hindu religion was based on 'usage' as well as 'precept'. *Suttee*, 'the sacrifice of self-immolation', was sanctioned by both principles. The petitioners relied on several statements and measures taken by the government authorities, which showed that the British considered *suttee* an element of the Hindu religion. However, this was a question only to be answered by learned *brahmins*. And they had come to the conclusion that *suttee* was permitted by the *shastras*:[93] according to Aṅgira the only duty left for a woman after her husband had died was to burn herself with his body because her life and duties were inextricably bound with his.

The *Vishnusmirti* and other *shastras* mention concremation before the alternative of ascetic widowhood, and from this the conclusion was drawn that it was the preferred solution. Moreover, Manu permitted *suttee*; the version referred to by its opponents was forged. Finally, *suttee* was legitimized by the Veda, the highest authority.[94]

The spiritual merits of the *suttee* were described: she would extinguish the sins of three families: her father's, her mother's and her husband's. Personally she 'partakes of bliss with her husband as long as fourteen Indrus reign'.[95] Moreover, she was presented as acting voluntarily for her own happiness in life after death, as well as for her husband's and their families' sake. It would be unjust and intolerant to forbid her to follow her religious beliefs. As an illustration, they mention the case of a woman who starved herself to death after she was prevented from burning herself.

Thus, it was argued that the British government had no right to interfere: first, because it was neither competent nor authorized to judge about the religion of the Hindus; second, because a policy of non-interference had been ensured. Finally, the Bengali *suttee* opponents had misunderstood the *shastras* and were not authorized to interpret them.

In the debate between British government officials, judges and academics a certain image of *suttee* was constructed, one could even say invented. Based on the interpretation of a *vyavastha* demanded by the *nizamat adalat*, *suttee* was understood as a matter of religion, sanctioned by the Hindu law. This opinion spread and was taken up by Bengalis regardless of whether they were against or in favour of *suttee*. Since Rammohan Roy tried to convince his readers that *suttee* was not legal because Manu did not mention it and that it was useless according to his understanding of religion he still held that it was founded in religious beliefs – even if these beliefs were false. Thus, he shared to some extent the opinion that prohibition was interference with the religion. The defenders of *suttee* referred to British official statements that the practice was based on the religion of the Hindus. By combining this picture with the assumption that religion played a central role in the life of a Hindu – a notion widespread among officials and orientalists, but not shared by military officers who had a closer contact with the people – abolition of *suttee* seemed a dangerous venture. To legitimize prohibition the developed picture of *suttee* had to be partly deconstructed again – and to this end the opinions of Bengali *suttee* opponents were used, as can be seen in the prohibition Act.

It is interesting to note that the image of *suttee* constructed in the debates between Rajput princes and their British 'advisers' differed from the one prevalent in Bengal. In this context it was not religion that formed the central point but honour, social prestige and family tradition.[96] Therefore, a historian may conclude that British officials brought themselves into this difficult situation – without knowing it – and that it was hard for them to find a way out of their dilemma.

In the debate a shift in the approach to *suttee* can be observed, although certain basic assumptions did not change. Initially, the focus was indeed to clarify whether *suttee* was legal according to Hindu law. Later, however, the moral responsibility for saving the lives of innocent victims was emphasized. The fact that these victims were women plays an important role. The British gentlemen had to rescue the Hindu women from the cruelty of their own male relatives or, at least, from self-destruction relating to superstition. As Spivak puts it: 'White men saving brown women from brown men.'[97]

However, one may question whether the efforts to regulate *suttee* and the debates were really concerned with the women's fate. According to Mani, the subject of the colonial discourse was never the woman. It was rather about inventing and defining Hindu tradition, about the authority of certain *shastras*. The *suttee*s with their pain on the pyre were just the battleground for 'a complex and competing set of struggles over Indian society and definitions of Hindu tradition'.[98] Thus, *suttee* was an 'alibi for the colonial civilizing mission on the one hand, and on the other hand, a significant occasion for indigenous autocritique'.[99]

Sumit Sarkar disagrees on this point:

> It soon becomes clear that the real purpose of establishing such a
> unifying structure is to imply that the reformist advocates for the

discouragement or banning of suttee were not in any meaningful
sense more progressive or humanistically inclined than their opponents. Improvement of the lot of women was no more than the
means to the end of establishing the priority of classical texts.[100]

Indeed, in the statements of *suttee* defenders one misses any concern for the
suffering of the *suttee*s – in a rather cynical way it was described as the less
painful alternative to ascetic widowhood. But at least some local British
government officials and, more importantly, Rammohan Roy mentioned
moral reasons for the abolition of *suttee*. And Roy seemed emotionally affected
by it. However, his main interest was the promotion of a new form of
Hunduism.

In my opinion, the debate on *suttee* arose from several political needs. When
the EIC took over governmental responsibilities – initially from profit-making
interests – the officials had to cope with the social practices of the population
they ruled. Political measures are led by practical needs, but also by theoretical concepts on how to govern a society. And here we find both the early
Orientalist model, which stated that the British should interfere as little as
possible with the religion and culture of the colonized people, and the shift to
Utilitarian politics of social reform. The prohibition of *suttee* can be seen as
justified by the civilizing ideology.

4. Lack of Social Morality vs. Superiority of Hinduism

This is not the end of the history of *suttee* and the civilizing ideology. After the
Indian mutiny the prohibition of *suttee* and the politics of social reform in
general were questioned again. There was much doubt as to whether this
approach had been responsible, to some extent, for the discontent of the
Indians and had contributed to their rebellion. This view can still be interpreted in terms of looking for the best policy towards 'Indian traditions'. In
the late nineteenth century a romantic idealization of *suttee* in literature and
art became fashionable in Britain. *Suttee* was seen as an expression of deep love
of a wife for her husband.[101] But in the 'heyday of imperialism' it became
obvious that *suttee* was an ideal example of the need to civilize the Indians.
This view was expressed by Edward Thompson in plain terms in the first
historical analysis of *suttee*. He appreciated the prohibition of *suttee* as necessary
and criticized the hesitation of the British administration in the 1820s and,
thus, the delay of the final prohibition Act: 'The abolition of *suttee*, so far from
being, like the abolition of slavery, an example of our greatness as a nation
and an empire, is an example of our timidity.'[102]

According to Thompson the abolition of *suttee* was an important step in

civilizing Indian society. The existence of such customs justified the continuation of British rule in India:

> Infanticide had an economic cause. But *suttee* cut to the very roots of
> social morality, and the society which practised it and gloried in
> made itself an outcast from the civilized comity of nations. It is often
> made a reproach against the British that, after a century and a half of
> predominance in India, they have not advanced the people any
> further along the road of fitness for self-government. [. . .] I have no
> doubt whatsoever that such things like *suttee* kept back Indian political
> progress by many years; until the rite was abolished, even a begin-
> ning in self-government was impossible.[103]

The social morality was inextricably bound to the notion of Hinduism.
Thompson found *suttee* rooted in Hinduism, in the belief that the widow was
spiritually responsible for the husband's death. Thus, she had to atone for her
sin by *suttee*.[104] But without paying much respect to religious beliefs he
described the degradation of the wife to the level of her husband's property as
the main cause of the practice: 'Hinduism from the first was consistent, and
increasingly and inexorably diligent, in one aim – that of surrounding the
male creature with every comfort and dignity. [. . .] *Suttee* was for the aggrandizement of the husband, who took with him when he died the most valuable
and personal of his possessions.'[105]

Thompson was astonished that even educated Hindus defended *suttee* and
respected it as an expression of an idealized connection of husband and wife:
'The nonsense about the wonderful purity and spirituality of the Hindu
marriage ideal cannot survive examination.'[106] This statement can be interpreted as a swipe at Ananda Coomaraswamy, half Indian, living in America,
who played an important role in Hindu-traditionalist thinking of his time. His
defence of *suttee*, written in 1924, has been discussed in India until recently.
He is still used as a reference,[107] as well as strongly criticized and refuted.[108]
Writing about the *suttee*, he stated:

> The root meaning of the word is essential being, and we have so far
> taken it only in a wide sense. But she who refuses to live when her
> husband is dead is called *Suttee* in a more special sense [. . .] This last
> proof of the perfect unity of body and soul, this devotion beyond
> grave, has been chosen by many Western critics as our reproach; we
> differ from them in thinking of our 'suttees' not with pity, but with
> understanding, respect and love. So far from being ashamed of our
> 'suttees' we take pride in them; that is true even among the most pro-
> gressive among us.[109]

In this view *suttee* was proof of the superiority of Hinduism over the western 'industrial' society because it was an expression of the feeling of one's duty (*dharma*) and the fulfilling of one's social role. These roles were unequal and clearly defined: 'When man of necessity spent his life in war or in hunting, when woman needed personal physical as well as spiritual protection, then she could not do enough for him in personal service; we have seen in the record of folk-song and epic how it is part of women's innermost nature to worship man.'[110]

This differentiation of roles had nothing to do with oppression or slavery. On the contrary, it offered Oriental women the opportunity to be 'a woman': 'The Eastern woman is not, at least we do not claim that she is, superior to other women in her innermost nature; she is perhaps an older, purer and more specialized type, and it is precisely here that the industrial woman departs from type.'[111] Thus, the superiority of the Hindu-society became visible in the superiority of Indian women.

Therefore Indian society must not seek orientation in the European mode of life, but find its own way. Coomaraswamy sharply criticized colonial rule:

> Aside from all questions of mere lust for power [. . .] untold evils have resulted from the conviction that it is our God-given duty to regulate other people's lives – the effects of the current theories of 'uplift' and of the 'white man's burden' are only single examples for this; and even when the intentions are good, we need not overlook the fact that the way to hell is often paved with examples of this.[112]

The ideas of both authors, Thompson and Coomaraswamy, can only be understood in their colonial context. Both focus on the role of colonial rule. Both compare the western European with the Hindu culture. Both use *suttee* to demonstrate certain characteristics of the Hindu culture or religion that seem to be inseparable. For the British historian Thompson, *suttee* was a unique example of the lack of social morality in India and the necessity of the British civilizing mission. Coomaraswamy saw the *suttee* as a symbol of the superiority of the Hindu culture with its faithful marriages, spirituality, sense for duty and sacrifice.

Again we find the gender issue as a means to defend or fight the idea of the civilizing mission. On the one hand the woman was seen as enslaved, degraded to mere property of her husband; therefore white men had to rescue her from practices such as *suttee* as well as from social oppression. On the other, the Oriental woman was claimed to be superior to the industrial western woman, which meant that the Hindu society to which she belonged could not be inferior – so there was no justification for the civilizing mission.

Thompson's position, which might be characterized as western modernist, was for several decades the dominant approach in academic literature. Also, Indian authors followed this view in a less radical way. But it was common to interpret the abolition of *suttee* as a step towards modernizing Indian society even if the authors had, in general, a critical view of colonialism (see, for instance, Majumdar). Coomaraswamy's standpoint of Hindu traditionalism did not prevail in academic discourse, but rather in some press reviews of the late 1980s and early 1990s.

5. A Post-colonial Modernizing Project Following the Colonial Civilizing Mission?

Since the 1970s the British role in the process of abolishing *suttee* has been judged critically by historians deconstructing the modernizing images of colonial history. This did not happen because prohibition was seen as interference with an ancient, deep rooted tradition of the population but, on the contrary, because it was regarded as the construction of a tradition:[113] a high caste phenomenon, used primarily as a status symbol, had been declared a common tradition among Hindus. But the British did not only get themselves into trouble by constructing an image of *suttee* as a religious ritual enforced by Hindu law, but contributed to a visible increase in *suttee* incidents. Ashis Nandy[114] speaks about an 'epidemic' of *suttee* in nineteenth century Bengal, an outcome of the 'pathology of colonialism' and the 'anomic' situation.

After the historical discourse about *suttee* in the colonial context a passionate debate about *suttee* in post-colonial India arose in the late 1980s and 1990s following the case of the young widow Roop Kanwar, who burned herself in Deorala, Rajasthan.[115] Again, there was discussion on the feasibility and legitimacy of the prohibition of *satīpūja* (*suttee* worship).[116] The issue of the civilizing mission is still on the agenda: first, in efforts to modernize Indian society and, second, as a reproach against those in favour of prohibition of *satīpūja*. Even though Madhu Kishwar, editor of the feminist journal *Manushi*, does not support *suttee* she accused the western-influenced social reformers of having interfered as arrogantly as British colonial officials in the life of India's rural population to enforce their own norms:

> It is understandable that the British should resort to such distortion and defamation as part of the imperial game of convincing Indians that they were 'uncivilized' and hence unfit for self-governance. But if reformers in post-Independence India operate with the same colonial categories when dealing with the traditions of their own people, it only goes to prove that the brown sahibs of India have

learnt to treat the people of this country with the same contempt as
did our colonial masters.[117]

Her standpoint is that social reform is too complex to be influenced by law:
it is a long process. The customs of the rural population must be tolerated,
even though the urban elites do not like them. More radically, Ashis Nandy
criticized the 'modernist' *suttee* critics. He claimed that they condemn *suttee*
naïvely without understanding the underlying spiritual notions, that they were
alienated from their own tradition while taking over the colonial perspective
on Indian society: 'It is remarkable how, since the Deorala event, there has
been a revival of efforts by anglophone, psychologically uprooted Indians –
exactly the sector that produced the last epidemic of *suttee* in eastern India – to
vend *suttee* as primarily a stigma of Hinduism, not as one of the by-products of
the entry of modern values into India.'[118]

C K Vishwanath argued against this position stating that it idealized the
Indian past and the village traditions:

> The intellectual position of Ashish Nandy and Madhu Kishwar is
> afraid of challenging the *suttee* and the romanticizing the tradition of
> Indian society. Urban intelligentsia, the most important opinion-
> makers of Indian society, have been living with the Sangh *parivar*
> myth of a golden past of India and have failed to see the harsh
> realities of Indian society, ignoring oppressive social practices.[119]

Narasimhan found the *suttee* debate in post-colonial India embedded in the
context of the numerous conflicts in the society.[120] Controversial notions of
Indian society, of decolonization, tradition and identity come into play.

The ideas of spirituality, altruistic sacrifice, faithfulness of the wife underlying *suttee* according to Coomaraswamy and Nandy are defended as a certain
emancipation from the (former) colonial rule. The rediscovery of one's 'own'
tradition – in this case *suttee* – is part of ideological decolonization. But *suttee*
critics ask: '[W]hy should we accept this kind of anti-colonialism which care-
lessly legitimizes the worst of indigenous practices?'[121] They emphasize that
suttee is unjustly defended as a common Hindu tradition or even as symbol for
the Hindu tradition as a whole. People opposing the prohibition of *satīpūja*
accuse the *suttee* critics of being intoxicated by western ideas to the extent that
they were no longer able to understand their own culture. On the other hand,
the defenders of *satīpūja* are criticized for declaring a phenomenon to be a tradition without reflecting upon it. They, it is said, only try to promote a
traditional role model for women according to the Hindu nationalist world-
view. Thus,

an attempt is being made [by the current defenders of *suttee*] to transfer a ritual associated with a small segment of upper caste society to
entire society with the claim that it is the rite/right of the Hindu community. [. . .] The justification incorrectly sought from Hindu *dharma*
is an attempt to legitimize it so that it can be treated as universally
applicable.[122]

The question of interference or non-interference is no longer important.
The questions discussed rather address the problem of how to design Indian
society from within: How can we deal with colonial history? How can we promote women's rights and 'modernize' Indian society without falling into a
colonial or western perspective?

PART II:

ORDERING AND MODERNIZING

4

'The Bridge-Builders': Some Notes on Railways, Pilgrimage and the British 'Civilizing Mission' in Colonial India*

RAVI AHUJA
South Asia Institute, Heidelberg

1. Introduction

Railway construction in colonial India proceeded with particular dynamism in the two concluding decades of the nineteenth century when the existing network of 8,995 miles of railway line was expanded to 23,627 miles, or almost trebled.[1] The construction of railway lines (as well as of other so-called 'public works') was by then not merely a keystone of political and economic imperialism but also one of the most effective practices in generating 'basic legitimacy' for colonial rule – a legitimacy derived from the display of the regime's awe-inspiring 'organizational efficiency'.[2] Consider, for instance, the construction of iron-girder bridges for railways – bridges that were pre-produced in British factories to the last rivet, transported via the recently opened Suez Canal to modernized colonial ports by steamships and from there onwards to the interior of India by rail, where they were assembled to span her mighty and previously uncontrollable rivers.[3] If 'engineering [. . .] became an integral part of late-nineteenth-century British imperialism'[4] one implication of this 'engineering imperialism' was that its monuments were powerful and highly

* Research for this article was conducted as a contribution to the Orissa Research Programme of the German Research Council (DFG). An earlier version was presented to a panel of the International Convention of Asia Scholars, 9–12 August 2001, Freie Universität Berlin. I owe thanks for their critical comments to the participants of this panel, especially to Dr Michael Mann and Prof. Dietmar Rothermund and, as always, to Nicole Mayer-Ahuja. Archival locations are indicated by the following abbreviations: NAI: National Archives of India, New Delhi; NMM&L: Nehru Memorial Museum and Library, New Delhi; OIOC: Oriental and India Office Collections of the British Library, London; OSA: Orissa State Archives, Bhubaneswar.

visible symbols of the 'superiority' of 'European civilization'[5] and created an air of finality: the British raj, they were to tell the passing 'native', had come to stay.

Railways derived their symbolic power not solely from their massive materiality and technological novelty but, even more importantly, from their ability to transform the everyday experiences of millions: communications development remoulded the geographical as well as social topography of the colony according to the extractive interests of the colonizers, brought about higher levels of socio-economic, political and cultural integration and signified, therefore, as British 'civilians' loved to put it, that India was 'opened up' towards 'civilization'. Hence, 'railways' were, to all intents and purposes, used as a synonym for 'civilization' in the late nineteenth-century political discourse of colonial legitimacy.

2. Engineer as Civilizer: Rudyard Kipling's Short Story 'The Bridge-Builders'

It was in this atmosphere of 'engineering imperialism', 'railway frenzy' and colonial self-legitimation through 'public works' that Rudyard Kipling wrote his short story 'The Bridge-Builders'. It was first published in the Christmas issue of the *Illustrated London News* in 1893, at a time when writings on engineering in India apparently could hope to find a large audience in Britain.[6] As a journalist, Kipling had already written two articles on such bridge works for the *Civil and Military Gazette*, both of which were published in 1887.[7] Kipling's acquaintance with and keen interest in minuscule organizational and technical details of bridge construction in colonial India, as well as his ideological commitments, render this short story an interesting source for historians of South Asian society. Moreover, it can be read as a literary rendering of a late nineteenth-century ideological construct that celebrated the colonial engineer (whose presence was increasingly felt in colonial India from the 1850s)[8] as the incarnation of Britain's 'civilizing mission'. In fact, Kipling has been considered one of the most eminent propagators of this ideology.[9] It is for this reason that this short story has been chosen as a starting point for our discussion.[10]

'The Bridge-Builders' is carefully constructed as regards both setting and plot. The clash of 'European modernity' and 'timeless Hindu tradition', which is at the core of the story, is indicated by the choice of location: Kipling relates an imaginary incident during the construction of 'Kashi bridge', a fictitious bridge across the holy river Ganga near Varanasi, the ancient centre of 'Hindu' culture, learning and pilgrimage.[11] The protagonists of the story are, first, the experienced civil engineer Findlayson who is in charge of the works, second, his British assistant Hitchcock who is on his first assignment in India after graduating from the Royal Indian Engineering College at Cooper's Hill in Surrey and, third, an Indian subcontractor named 'Peroo' from the region of Kacch in Gujarat. Peroo used to be a *serang* (a recruiter and foreman of sailors) on British steamships, possesses, therefore, extraordinary skills for difficult hauling operations and now commands a gang of *lascars* (sailors) all of whom he has enlisted in his home village. The rest of the five thousand people working on the construction site do not possess recognizable faces, not even the five hundred European 'fitters and riveters'. The story commences at a point when only a few substantial tasks remain to be done before the completion of the bridge. Findlayson and his assistant permit themselves to take a retrospective view of the work of three years, recount natural, social and political obstacles that had to be overcome, reassess the technical and organizational arrangements they have made. Their self-satisfied reflections are cut short by a telegram informing them that heavy rains have set in prematurely at the upper course of the Ganga and a massive flood is impending. Few hours remain to secure the incomplete bridge and to remove machinery and materials from the riverbed. The large labour force is promptly set to work and executes its tasks as smoothly as a machine until the river starts to rise and nothing but waiting remains to be done. Findlayson, aware that his reputation depends on whether the bridge withstands the flood or not, is in a state of extreme anxiety, keeps rechecking his static calculations and is able neither to rest nor eat. To calm himself, he accepts opium pills from his foreman Peroo. Unaccustomed to the drug, he gets heavily intoxicated and throws himself into the river to save the bridge with his bare hands. He is saved, in turn, by Peroo who drags him into a little boat, which is driven off by the river to a mound that has become an island in a vast expanse of flooded land. Here Findlayson and Peroo rest and both of them slide into an (opium) dream in which they overhear an assembly of Hindu gods.

Mother Ganga, the river goddess, has called on her fellow deities to assist her in destroying the chains the 'bridge-builders' have imposed on her. In the ensuing debate, some gods lend her support, others take a more benign stance towards the insignificant efforts of humans, while yet others claim that railways and bridges have brought them new worshippers and will, on the whole, enhance the power of India's Hindu pantheon. Shiva even argues that

[. . .] Kali knows that she has held her chiefest festivals among the pilgrimages that are fed by the fire-carriage. Who smote at Pooree, under the Image there, her thousands in a day and a night, and bound the sickness to the wheels of the fire-carriages, so that it ran from one end of the land to the other? Who but Kali? Before the fire-carriage came it was a heavy toil. The fire-carriages have served thee well, Mother of Death.[12]

At this point Krishna enters the stage, depicted as the god of the people, ridiculing his fellow deities' deliberations and telling them that the destruction of the bridge was futile since they, the ancient Hindu gods, were doomed already:

> It is too late now. Ye should have slain at the beginning when the men from across the water had taught our folk nothing. Now my people see their work, and go away thinking. They do not think of the Heavenly Ones altogether. They think of the fire-carriage and the other things that the bridge-builders have done, and when your priests thrust forward hands asking alms, they give a little unwillingly. That is the beginning [. . .].[13]

When Krishna leaves, the opium loses its power over the two men's minds and a new day dawns. The British engineer and his faithful Indian foreman are saved from their island by a steam launch and learn, as we might have guessed, that the bridge has withstood the flood.

3. 'The Bridge-Builders' and the Limits of the Colonial 'Civilizing Mission'

Gyan Prakash has recently argued that '[p]ortraying a railway bridge over the Ganges River as a symbol of imperial rationality, Kipling's short story depicts the triumph of reason over India's unruly nature and mythic culture'.[14] And so it does: the 'day's work', the sunlit manifestation of European science and industry, prevails over the nocturnal horrors of a raging tropical nature and of Oriental opium dreams. Yet there is more to this text, and the picture that emerges from a close reading of 'The Bridge-Builders' is far less unequivocal than Prakash's comment suggests. For the short story is not *solely* focused on the 'advancement of reason': another central theme is 'hierarchy'. The two themes blend into each other but are not fully reconcilable thus creating a tension within the text.

Kipling is mainly concerned with the propagation of *technological* and not of *social* 'reason' and 'progress'. Consider, for instance, the social values propagated in Kipling's short story, which are certainly *not* those of a liberal bourgeois society of 'free' individuals who seek their advantage on the basis of property and legal equality.[15] This is clearly borne out by the narrative of the bridge's erection, which makes up the first half of the short story and introduces the reader to the workings of a construction camp. Here it is obvious that the creation of (formally) 'free' labour, the commodification of labour power, is not considered by Kipling as being of any importance for a 'triumph of reason' and civilization of his liking. On the contrary, his prose not merely vindicates but virtually *celebrates* elements of forced labour: the appointment of the assistant engineer as 'a magistrate of the third class with whipping powers, for the better government of the community' (that is, the construction camp) is specially mentioned; even the technicalities of corporal punishment inflicted on labourers are spelled out as Kipling insists that the 'two feet of wire rope frayed at the ends', which Peroo used to discipline his gang, 'did wonders'.

Moreover, what keeps the 'bridge-builders' going in Kipling's story is not economic reason but a rather aristocratic sentiment: 'honour and credit which are better than life'. Work is conceived not as social activity for individual profit but as a kind of secular worship: the phrase 'the day's work', which is casually inserted in the story and gave the title to the collection in which it was published, seems to refer to a Bible word carved into the mantel-piece of Kipling's study by his father.[16] Findlayson's ambition, we are informed in the first lines of the story, is not material gain but to be raised to a CSI, a Companion of the Order of the Star of India. Since only the engineer and his assistant are remorselessly sacrificing their lives to that aristocratic quest for honour, it is only these two who count in the end: 'the bridge,' insists Kipling, 'was two men's work'. The only other person to whom the author concedes a minor share in this achievement is Peroo, the *lascar*, who is, how-ever, ridiculed for his boastfulness. If Peroo has any claim at all to be reckoned among the 'bridge-builders' it is precisely because he is 'not within many silver pieces of his proper value' – he is paid badly according to custom but works well for his honour. As for the rest of the labour force, to whom this ethical urge means less or nothing, another kind of non-economic compulsion needs to be employed: 'two feet of wire rope frayed at the ends' – well-measured doses of violence.

In the meantime, Peroo is represented as an Indian avatar of the mythical, undemanding and fearless, childlike and fully committed white workman of good old times whose demise was often lamented in contemporary gentle-manly discourse. He reminds us of the ancient British sailor Singleton in Conrad's novel *The Nigger of the Narcissus* (first published in 1897, about the same time as 'The Bridge-Builders') who stands for the assumedly ordered maritime world of labour of the past as opposed to the unruly one of the present: Singleton is a *child* 'of the mysterious sea' while his successors 'are the grown-up children of a discontented earth. They are less naughty, but less innocent; less profane, but perhaps also less believing; and if they have learned how to speak they have also learned how to whine.'[17]

This nostalgia for childlike subalterns indicates a growing gentlemanly fear of what was understood to be dangerous side-effects of 'civilization' and industrialization: the dissolution of supposedly 'organic', paternalistic and hierarchical social relations which entailed a growing assertiveness of the 'masses' in general and of the 'dangerous' and working classes in particular. David Cannadine has reminded us recently of the obsession of British imperialism with the preservation and celebration of social hierarchy – an obsession that grew in the late nineteenth century in proportion to the increasing unease of the British upper classes about processes of 'moderniza-tion' in the metropolitan country. The anxieties of these classes (from which the colonial administrative elite was recruited) were at the heart, in Cannadine's view, of their anti-modernist attempts to stifle such develop-ments in the 'Indian Empire' and other colonies.[18] Rudyard Kipling, it has been noted by Edward Said and others, shared this taste for hierarchy in an age when the (European) world was turned upside-down and gave it a literary expression in 'The Bridge-Builders' as well as in other writings.[19] In 'The Bold 'Prentice', another, less-known railway story, he even praised the 'beauty of caste', the reinvention of a caste hierarchy in India's railway service as an admirable arrangement preventing industrial disputes and strikes that were troubling the upper and middle classes in contemporary Europe.[20]

The growing pessimism about social and political results of the process of 'civilization' in the European metropolises entailed a partial reformulation of the idea of the British 'civilizing mission' in India from about the 1850s onwards. Earlier in the century, this idea had been more holistic in the sense that it referred to the spread of 'improvement' and 'reform' to all spheres of human existence, though many colonial officials had recommended even then a low pace in the transformation of Indian society as non-interference with 'native customs' was deemed necessary for securing their subjects' com-pliance.[21] Now, an optimistic progressivism was still at large, as far as the sciences, technology and economy were concerned, while pessimistic or 'anti-modernist' voices grew more insistent and influential in respect of transforma-tions of culture and society not merely in the Indian Empire but also on the British Isles themselves. In other words, scientific discoveries and transforma-tions in industry were, on the whole, still appreciated and celebrated by a large majority of contemporary ideologues and writers while political and social changes were noticed with an increasing sense of apprehension if not with outright hostility.[22] For in many European societies a growing pressure was felt to concede rights of political participation to a larger part of the population – a tendency that was opposed not only by conservatives but also by many liberals who concurred in the opinion that the so-called 'masses' were unable to make 'reasonable' use of such rights. Such reservations were, of necessity, even more determined in respect of colonies where European dominance had drawn much of its legitimacy even earlier from the assertion that the 'natives' could not rule themselves because of a deficiency of 'reason', which more and more ideologues considered racially determined and thus not subject to 'progress'.

The effects of these developments on the idea of the 'civilizing mission' can be summed up as follows: *functionally* it continued to be the collective illusion of a dominant social force that its particular interests were identical with those of humanity at large (in the metropolis as well as in the colonies) – 'functionally' because this illusion had practical implications for the prevailing mode of dominance: it motivated the agents of colonialism and legitimized their rule.[23] Regarding its *content*, however, the concept was cut down to size: the civilizing mission was reduced to an enterprise with more limited liability and goals – it was *predominantly* in the sphere of technology, science and economy that it continued to provide an optimistic progressivist outlook.

G W MacGeorge, a senior bureaucrat of the colonial Public Works Department, would, for instance, claim in 1894 that the 'most potent factor in this truly wonderful resurrection of a whole people', which would inevitably raise India 'to a high level of power and civilization', 'is unquestionably the railway system'.[24] Yet while MacGeorge was still as enthusiastic about the imminent social and cultural implications of railway construction (namely the breakdown of 'caste prejudice' and of 'religious superstition')[25] as Governor General Lord Bentinck had been a half-century earlier,[26] the tone in Kipling's 'The Bridge-Builders' (as well as in other writings) is rather more muted and cautious. Yes, Peroo, the *lascar*, is shown to be increasingly doubt-ful of whether ancient gods like 'Mother Ganga' possess more power than modern technology, and at the end of the story he is set upon giving the 'use-less' *guru* of his work gang a severe lashing. And yes, in the passage quoted above, Kipling has Krishna argue that Indians have started to realize that modern technology is more effectual than their old gods, which is why they will also pay less respect to *brahmins*. Hence Kipling predicts, much like earlier writers had done, the faltering of 'traditional' systems of hierarchy. However, he qualifies this point in two important ways: first, he allows for a temporary *boost* of religiosity (and, by implication, of 'indigenous' hierarchy) in the wake of technological modernization, taking account of the enormous increase of pilgrim traffic which actually occurred after the opening of the railways.[27] Second, he is rather careful in his prediction as to the time span in which the demise of the ancient gods and of brahmanical power is to be expected: his Krishna contends that it may take long if measured in human time, but not according to the chronometer of the gods.[28] 'Prejudice' and 'Hindu' deities would, no doubt, have to retreat to the jungles, but later rather than sooner.

While the old systems of belief and hierarchy were thus found to be more persistent than had been expected, the establishment of new, colonial varieties of rationality and hierarchy met with unforeseen difficulties. For a long historical period the white man would have to shoulder his burden without expecting any thanks from the 'new-caught, sullen peoples' who were, after all, as Kipling wrote in his most infamous poem, not only 'half child' (that is, minors requiring paternal direction) but also 'half devil' that is, in need of exorcism).[29] It was this latter, innately uncivilized and unreasonable half of the 'native' population who induced them to appropriate technological innovations to purposes that were quite at variance with the intentions of the missionaries of civilization: railways had, as Kipling had Shiva point out, the immediate effect of *increasing* the number of pilgrims (see above). This development entailed, in the view of many contemporary colonial commentators, not merely a continuation of 'superstitious' practices but also a loss of lives and revenue. For mass pilgrimage (rather than the combined effects of structural poverty and modern transport infrastructure) was asserted to be the *main* cause of cholera epidemics,[30] the utilization of railways for this 'unreasonable' objective was made responsible for the rapid spread of the disease across the subcontinent.[31]

On a more general level, Kipling's emphasis on 'unreasonable' appropriations of modern technology points at another limitation of that ideological construct 'civilizing mission'. So far we have argued that the growing pessimism of the British upper classes concerning the social and political implications of modern 'civilization' *in their home country* set certain limits to the concept of 'civilizing mission' in the colony. Now we are confronted with corresponding limitations that arose in South Asia itself: from the last decades of the nineteenth century, sharp observers like Kipling did not fail to realize that 'civilizing' interventions into South Asian society never quite produced the results intended by colonial administrators since these innovations were immediately *appropriated* by the Indian 'masses': various social interests sought to obstruct, deflect, remould or utilize these interventions according to their own needs and perceptions. These practices of appropriation constituted a challenge to the aspirations of the colonial elite to erect the 'organic', paternalistic and hierarchical system of governance in India, which they felt was being destroyed by the processes of 'modernization' in Britain.

The prompt appropriation of new transport technologies, of steamships and railways, by hundreds of thousands of Indian pilgrims for practices that seemed to the colonial official's mind blatantly 'unreasonable', 'uncivilized', 'morally degrading' and even dangerous is only one case in point. Yet it is an interesting one since numerous conflicting interests focused on the issue of 'railway pilgrimage' that implied direct dealings between the representatives of the colonial state and the Indian 'masses' on many counts. 'Railway pilgrimage' consequently became a matter of intense debate in the newly emerging Indian public sphere and an issue that gave rise to demands on the part of Indian social groups for participatory rights. Though these demands were brought forward in the beginning by a rather small group of Indian notables, these tendencies conflicted with the pseudo-manorial paternalism of upper-class colonial officials in general and with the 'technocratic paternalism'[32] of colonial engineers in particular. Moreover, they seemed to foreshadow the emergence of 'mass politics' – the very phenomenon that many British 'civilians' despised most in their home country.

The analysis of the conflicts about 'railway pilgrimage' permits us, therefore, to mark out contradictions and limitations of the ideological construct 'civilizing mission'. Such an analysis requires, however, changing our perspective and, accordingly, the corpus of sources we refer to. We now have to put aside the literary sources and turn to rather less engaging material from the colonial archives. This material was produced, too, within the ideological framework of British imperialism but it permits further insights into concrete constellations of interest and conflict. In the following section we will mainly confine ourselves to discussing material concerning steam technologies of transport in respect of one of the main centres of pilgrimage in South Asia: the town of Puri, located on the shores of the Bay of Bengal in the eastern region of Orissa.

4. Colonial Images of the Pilgrimage to Jagannath

While the temple of Jagannath (literally 'the Lord of the World') had attracted high caste pilgrims from beyond Orissa (especially from north India) from the thirteenth century, it was only in the sixteenth century that the stream of pilgrims widened as came to include affluent peasants, many of them from the adjacent region of Bengal. By 1803, when the British annexed coastal Orissa, organizational patterns of mass pilgrimage were firmly established, Jagannath temple had become more accessible to lower castes and in June/July the annual *rath jatra* (chariot festival) regularly attracted a crowd of pilgrims several times larger than the usual population of the town of Puri.[33] In the early nineteenth century, British Christian missionaries spread the (misleading) rumour of the annual self-immolation of numerous pilgrims in Puri. They were allegedly instigated by cruel *brahmins* to throw themselves under the massive wheels of the chariot on which the idols of Jagannath and his siblings were drawn through town.[34] 'Juggernaut', as the British called the deity and sometimes the town, thus became another name for the barbarity of Hindu religious practices. In the English language, the word soon acquired a more general meaning and came to designate an unrelenting force of destruction, a *moloch*. It is in allusion to this well-established cliché that Kipling let Shiva, in a passage of 'The Bridge-Builders', which I have already quoted (see page 000), not refer to the pilgrimage to nearby Varanasi but to faraway Puri when conjuring up images of the superstitious irrationality of pilgrims: 'Who smote at Pooree, under the Image there, her thousands in a day and a night, and bound the sickness to the wheels of the fire-carriages, so that it ran from one end of the land to the other?'

Though rumours about human sacrifices during the *rath jatra* lost their plausibility in the course of the nineteenth century, the Jagannath cult continued to be painted in dark colours in colonial writings. Biswamoy Pati has recently pointed out that '[p]ilgrimage centres like Puri haunted the colonial imagination and emerged as a metaphor for disease and death'.[35] British medical officers considered Jagannath, in fact, to be among the most dangerous destinations of pilgrimage in South Asia: the main festival coincided with the beginning of the monsoon rains when the risk of epidemics was highest.[36] Orissa, therefore, acquired the reputation of being the 'home of cholera',[37] while Puri was regarded a 'cholera centre'[38] or even a 'valley of death'.[39] This image was no doubt grounded in genuine experience – there are numerous reports on epidemics during large *melas* (festivals) in the town of the 'Lord of the World' and even more on large numbers of people dying from cholera, dysentery and general exhaustion on the 'Orissa Trunk Road', the main pilgrim route from Bengal. Though his figures are of a rather speculative kind, W W Hunter's 1872 estimate that the annual death toll of the Jagannath pilgrimage amounted to ten thousand lives gives an impression of the scale of misery connected to this cultural practice.[40] In the ideologically framed perception of the British colonial oligarchy, such experiences provided proof of the ignorance and stubborn irrationality, the mental minority of the 'Hindus' and, consequently, of their continuing need for paternalistic regulation.[41]

The exceptional ill repute of the Jagannath cult among colonial officials was further grounded on what they considered to be immoral practices connected to the Puri pilgrimage. David Smith, sanitary commissioner for Bengal, took on the prevailing atmosphere in colonial circles when he remarked that the pilgrims' 'moral blindness, their wickedness, their very degradation have but too frequently been made the subject of uncharitable declamation'.[42] The *pandas*, temple priests who were called 'pilgrim-hunters' in colonial documents, were deemed to be the embodiment of immorality, fraud and abuse. *Pandas* went to the same far-away villages every year in order to recruit pilgrims whom they guided to Puri in exchange for various payments and donations. Many accusations were related to the fact that generally a very large proportion of the *jatri*s were women, while the pilgrims attending the *rath jatra* were even said to consist overwhelmingly of widows and other females from Bengal. British gentlemen and apparently also a few Bengali *bhadralok* were deeply worried about the indecency of women travelling without husbands or fathers: they suspected that women went for the thrill of independence or, if they were young widows, even to 'satisfy their carnal desires'. These commentators inferred a high level of promiscuity from the fact that these women walked with men to whom they were not related, washed themselves in the same *ghat*s and slept in the same pilgrim hostels as their *panda*s and male fellow-travellers. There was also the suggestion that some female pilgrims were forced into illicit relationships, found themselves in Muslim *zenana*s after having been enslaved and sold by their *panda*s or ended up in Calcutta brothels because they could not return to their families.[43] Once again it is highly probable that these perceptions were in some way founded on genuine experience – there is no point in denying practices of gender discrimination and violence associated with Hindu pilgrimage.[44] Yet it is also necessary to acknowledge that these phenomena were perceived by British (and Indian) gentlemen within the conceptual framework of a patriarchal ideology from which they arrived at conclusions that were, once again, paternalistic: in order to fight back immorality and indecency, existing gender hierarchies (that is, the permanent minority of females) had to be reinforced. To put it in contemporary words, women had to be prevented from 'cast[ing] away infant children from their own breasts' only to meet on their pilgrimage with 'an untimely death and thereby leave their husbands and children in wretchedness'![45]

To sum up the foregoing paragraphs: pilgrimage to Jagannath epitomized India's lack of civilization in the eyes of her British rulers on various counts. In the case of Orissa, a contradiction of British traffic policy became, therefore, more visible than elsewhere: the creation of modern means of transport, usually deemed, as we have seen, to be a crucial element of Britain's civilizing mission, was likely to result in an increase of 'uncivilized' practices and the reinforcement of brahmanical hierarchy. Hence when the colonial government was under missionary pressure to disassociate itself from the Jagannath cult in the 1830s by abolishing the pilgrim tax, it was admitted by British officials that the 'natural effect' of 'improved facilities for internal communication which have taken place within the last few years' [*sic!*] had been 'to augment the resort of pilgrims'. Yet it was 'incumbent upon a humane Government' to provide improved means of communications to save the lives of pilgrims who were 'blinded by superstition'.[46]

5. 'Public Works' Beyond Public Control: Pilgrims and Colonial Traffic Policy in Orissa

In fact, the British colonial oligarchy was not only realistic enough to accept that the practice of pilgrimage could not be stopped by government intervention without putting their power at risk. Moreover, they realised the provision of improved transport facilities for the pilgrim traffic could also be a profitable undertaking. The colonial administration consequently pursued a traffic policy in Orissa that primarily served imperial interests but could also be appropriated by various segments of Indian society, including the pilgrims. Hence the construction of the 'New Jagannath road' was commenced in 1809 only after a pious and rich Bengali *zamindar* had made a very substantial donation to the Bengal government for this purpose, which provided the British not merely with a comparatively cheap line of communication between Calcutta and their administrative headquarters in Orissa but also with increased returns from the taxation of pilgrims.[47] By the same token, two early British promoters of railway construction in India, Marshman and Stephenson, took the trouble to get 'the assurance of the *Dharma Sabha* of Calcutta that a pilgrim might ride in a train without losing his caste and the merit of his pilgrimage'.[48] Similarly, when colonial bureaucrats started discussing the introduction into Orissa of modern means of communications in the 1850s and 1860s, pilgrim traffic was always a factor in their calculations of the profitability of their schemes.[49]

If Orissa was connected to the Indian railway system only by the late 1890s, the reason was clearly *not* that the British government wished to restrict pilgrim traffic to Puri, but that the expectation of large numbers of passengers was not sufficient by itself to render this project a priority item on their 'public works' agenda. The main concerns of colonial railway policy in India, as Lord Dalhousie had already clarified in his famous Minute of 1853, were to provide greater military efficiency, to create markets for British industrial products and channels for the extraction of natural resources and tropical products. Yet Orissa was, then and in the subsequent decades, of minor importance both from the point of view of imperial strategy and in terms of colonial economics.[50]

However, the region was not totally excluded from the spread of steam technologies of transport prior to the turn of the century: what was constructed instead from the 1870s was a system of canals in the Orissa coastal plains, some of which were navigable. Steamboats plied these canals and could, for a while, attract tens of thousands of pilgrims from Bengal who preferred this mode of travelling to the more cumbersome road transport of the time.[51] Yet this combined system of irrigation and inland navigation ran far from smoothly, never paid back the large investments and was altogether abandoned less than half a century after its inauguration.

Before turning to the issue of railway construction and policy it is worth taking a brief look at this 'Orissa Canal Scheme' since it appears to be a perfect example for the operation of 'Civilizing Mission Ltd'. I have already argued above that the civilizing mission, in the context of late-nineteenth-century colonial India, was increasingly reduced to the spheres of science, technology and economics, while the political implications of 'modernization' (or, more precisely, of higher levels of social integration), such as the tendency towards increasingly participatory politics were resisted as far as possible by the colonial oligarchy. This proved to be disastrous in the case of the Orissa Canal Scheme in more than one way. For one, the scheme seems to have been opposed by large parts of the population of Orissa's coastal plains right from the start. The main reasons for this unpopularity were (a) that the canal embankments impeded the drainage of the land from the water of regularly occurring floods; (b) that parts of the country were thereby cut off from regular fertilization by the silt that was carried along with the floods; (c) that embankments cut across fields and created barriers for local communications; (d) that the rates demanded by the administration for irrigation water were too high.[52] Therefore, the canal scheme became a target for peasant resistance, while even the largely loyalist Indian notables of the region had regularly voiced their disapproval of canals and their preference for railways in the emergent Oriya press since the mid-1870s.[53] This simmering conflict between the colonial regime and Orissa's population was mainly due, as Rohan D'Souza has argued, to the antagonism between the inflexible imperatives of colonial revenue policy and the flexible requirements of agriculture in a specific ecological environment.[54] Yet it was also the result of a policy that persistently disconnected technological innovation from the creation of such mechanisms of political participation that were becoming more indispensable as levels of social and economic integration rose and infrastructural measures were realized on a larger scale.

The same holds true for the second drawback of the canal scheme: the attractions of inland steamers stayed limited as an uninterrupted voyage was never made possible, and the journey from Cuttack to Calcutta still took from five to eight days. Moreover, serious complaints abounded about overcrowding and ill-treatment of passengers on sea-going as well as inland steam vessels, which went largely unnoticed, probably because the managing agencies who operated these lines (for example, Hoare, Miller and Co.) were closely connected to the upper echelons of the colonial administration in Calcutta.[55] Hence the Orissa Canal Scheme was never tuned to the requirements of pilgrims and the population in general and, therefore, resulted in a major débâcle. Inland steam navigation virtually ceased in the 1920s. As for the Orissa Coast Canal, which had solely been built for shipping purposes, a government commission stated in 1928 that 'no one would to-day propose a navigation canal between Orissa and Bengal, still less a canal on this alignment'.[56]

Railway construction in Orissa commenced, as has been mentioned before, only in the 1890s when most other Indian regions were already linked to the railway system. Yet there had been some talk about the construction of an Orissa railway as early as the 1850s and 1860s.[57] In 1866, the colonial administration had also received and disregarded a 'Petition of the Inhabitants of Cuttack' (that is, of a number of Indian notables) for the construction of a light railway line between Howrah (Calcutta) and Puri for the benefit of Jagannath pilgrims.[58] Further appeals for an Orissa railway were apparently written and turned down in 1874 and 1878.[59] However, it was only in the 1880s that the debate intensified: a 'Balasore Railway Committee', consisting of notables of northern Orissa and headed by a local *zamindar*, Baikuntha Nath De, was founded in 1881 and sent a carefully prepared memorial to the government of Bengal. They propagated the construction of a direct rail link between Calcutta and Madras through the Orissa coastal plains and of a branch line to Puri. This railway, they argued, would not only provide a faster and safer means of transport to Jagannath pilgrims, but would also reduce the incidence of cholera epidemics by improving the pilgrims' lot and could, furthermore, serve as a famine protection line. The large number of pilgrims travelling to Puri, which they estimated to be between five and six hundred thousand annually, would guarantee handsome profits to investors.[60]

From the early 1880s these arguments were repeated time and again in Oriya (and sometimes also in Bengali) newspapers who urged the colonial government to construct a railway to Cuttack and Puri either from Varanasi via Chota Nagpur and the mountainous 'Garjat' hinterland of Orissa or from Calcutta across the coastal plains. An analysis of official summaries of relevant articles reveals a growing sense of exasperation among the largely loyalist correspondents: interventions from a newly emerging Indian public sphere were clearly not appreciated and usually ignored by the British administration.[61] The point was not that Orissa's colonial administrators were averse to the construction of a railway line. In fact, they argued on similar lines as the Indian notables. Yet the commissioner of Cuttack plainly refused to cooperate with the 'Balasore Railway Committee'.[62] When the construction of the Bengal–Nagpur Railway (BNR) was taken in hand in the early 1880s, the colonial government of India seriously considered a 'Benares–Cuttack–Pooree pilgrim line' and had two alternative routes surveyed and estimated.[63] Again, there were high expectations of attractive dividends for the railway shareholders from an increasing pilgrim traffic as well as the prediction that a railway line would dispel Orissa's bad reputation as the 'home of Cholera' and could serve as a 'famine protection line'.[64] However, this interesting project, which would have entailed a path of regional integration very different from that actually experienced in Orissa, was repeatedly postponed and finally shelved – the traffic policy of the colonial government always seemed to have other priorities and so had the Bengal–Nagpur Railway Company, which was chiefly interested in getting direct access to Calcutta.[65]

In 1887, the campaign for an Orissa railway reached a new pitch when the *Sir John Lawrence*, a seagoing steamer that had left Calcutta for Puri with over eight hundred passengers, sank on 25 May due to the shipmaster's irresponsible navigation. Hundreds of mainly female pilgrims were drowned, many of whom were from well-to-do Calcutta *bhadralok* families.[66] It was now that more widely distributed Bengali newspapers took the lead in the campaign and that the tone became more insistent: 'Railway lines have been constructed in all directions for the benefit of Europeans and of their trade. The interests of natives of India have been sacrificed to the interests of Europeans,' wrote the *Bangabasi*. And it went on to present the Orissa railway as an issue for the whole 'Hindu community': 'A railway line to Puri will be hailed with delight by 16 crores of Hindus, for it will lessen the dangers and difficulties, and put an end to their sorrows and fears.'[67] The *Dainik* argued on similar lines:

> It is the fault of Government that a railway to Puri has not yet been opened. The Darjeeling Railway has been constructed for the convenience of hill-going Europeans; railways have been constructed in Assam for the benefit of tea-planters; and arrangements are in progress for constructing railways to the different sanatoriums of the different Governments. But no railway has yet been constructed for the safety of the hundreds of thousands of Hindu pilgrims to Puri. In vain have the people of Orissa and the whole Hindu Community of 16 crores of people repeatedly prayed for a railway to Puri.[68]

In other words, the British railway policy was identified as the pursuit of a particular interest and not, as the colonial oligarchy claimed, as an activity for the benefit of their subjects. The self-representation of the colonial government as the corporate patriarch and missionary of 'civilization' was, thereby, put into question. Large-scale infrastructure projects on the part of the colonial state with deep implications for larger segments of the population gave rise to demands for political participation – demands that the British

administrators sought to put off as long as possible. Until independence they
pursued a policy, as will be shown in the remainder of this paper, of keeping
the so-called 'public works' beyond public control.

In the case of the Orissa railway, public pressure had little effect. The
project was again repeatedly postponed and it was only in 1895 that the construction of the 'East Coast Railway' from Calcutta to Cuttack, with a branch
line to Puri, was finally sanctioned by the government of India.[69] When
the line was opened in 1899, the *Indian & Eastern Engineer*, a mouthpiece of
imperial engineering, sneered at the 'apathetic East' for not being sufficiently
jubilant about this new achievement of imperial 'Railway Power'.[70]
Uninterrupted railway journeys from Calcutta to Madras became finally
possible in 1900 when the bridges over the major rivers of Orissa had been
completed.[71]

6. Appropriating the Railways: Pilgrimage and
Steam Technologies of Transport

By this time, the Indian railway system had long been appropriated by
pilgrims to Hindu shrines and even by those who ventured to Puri. In the
early 1880s it was believed that pilgrimage to Gaya had more than doubled
after the construction of the railway.[72] From the same decade onwards, there
was also a marked increase of pilgrimage to Jagannath which was at least
partly due to improved railway communications: pilgrims from north or
central India could travel by rail to locations in Bengal or (after the opening of
the BNR in 1891) Chhattisgarh from where they continued their journey by
road or waterway.[73] It was obvious, by then, that an Orissa railway would
readily be embraced by large numbers of pilgrims. And so it was. Yet this
appropriation not only entailed a considerable increase but also qualitative
changes in the rhythm and organizational patterns of Puri pilgrimage.[74] For
one, the time when pilgrims wandered for several months along an extensive
chain of numerous local pilgrimage sites came to an end. As late as in 1881
the road journey from the railhead of Raniganj in western Bengal to Puri had
taken twenty-six days;[75] from the turn of the century the journey from
Calcutta to Puri could be done in twelve hours.[76] A 'Pilgrim Committee',
which was installed by the colonial government of Bihar and Orissa in 1913,
thus noted that temporal patterns of pilgrimage had changed: participation in
great festivals like the *rath jatra* increased markedly, but not as steeply as the
annual figures. Pilgrim traffic thus came to be distributed more evenly
over the year though at certain seasons, when work was less in agriculture,
unexpected rushes occurred as villagers used the opportunity for a short
pilgrimage to Puri.[77] The social base of pilgrimage thus seems to have

widened further. Moreover, as the Calcutta middle classes acquired a taste for trips to Puri that combined traditional pilgrimage with modern tourism, clever entrepreneurs began to develop the facilities of a holiday resort.[78]

Not all Hindu notables appreciated the changes accompanying 'railway pilgrimage'. Insisting in 1909 that '[g]ood travels at a snail's pace' and charging the railways with having rendered the 'holy places of India [. . .] unholy',[79] Gandhi echoed ideas that had been aired for years. One Bengali newspaper correspondent had warned, for instance, in 1895 that 'all means of rapid locomotion are [. . .] impediments in the way of acquiring religious merit'.[80] Romesh Chandra Dutt (who had earlier been a collector in Orissa) also underscored the superior value of traditional forms of pilgrimage to Jagannath by having the protagonists of his novel *The Lake of Palms* (1902) prefer the slow pilgrimage by palanquin to the railway journey.[81]

Yet, for all objections that were uttered, the 'modernization' of pilgrimage seems to have been pervasive. One aspect of this modernization consisted in a transformation of the economy of pilgrimage – pilgrimage was now combined with commercial activities in other ways than before the coming of the railway. The *panda*s who were, as we have seen, perceived by the British as 'pilgrim-hunters' and major adversaries of their civilizing efforts in Puri, were far from rendered obsolete by the construction of the Orissa railway. Previously, a *panda* had annually visited a few villages where his family had usually recruited pilgrims for generations, had been donated land and had, thereby, knitted close networks with local society. Now, the railways were permitted to operate on a larger scale: powerful pilgrimage entrepreneurs emerged who bought, rented or simply invaded the rights and privileges of other *panda*s. Pilgrim registers, in which such claims were carefully entered, became valuable and transferable assets. More powerful *panda*s ceased to go to the villages themselves and preferred to send out agents while they diversified their economic activities in Puri town. Traditional hierarchy was thus neither conserved nor dissolved by the introduction of the new steam technologies of transport. Instead, since quite a few *panda*s were not slow to grasp the opportunities that emerged from rising levels of geographical and social integration, some were able to transform the organization of pilgrimage into more extensive commercial enterprises.[82] Kipling's expectation that the pilgrims' donations to *brahmin*s would slowly dry up was thus disappointed: the pursuit of the civilizing mission created, once more, results very different from the intentions of the colonial rulers.

7. 'Inundated with Complaints': The Politics of Colonial Railway Administration

Therefore, despite the fact that pilgrim traffic was an immensely profitable business for the colonial state, for British-owned railway companies and other entrepreneurs, British officials were never quite at ease with the prompt appropriation of the railway network by Indian pilgrims. If they had argued, before the construction of the Orissa railway, that steam locomotion would relieve the region from the scourge of cholera as pilgrims would be removed from the unhealthy conditions of Puri much faster,[83] they soon came to perceive the threat that, as Kipling put it, the sickness might be attached 'to the wheels of the fire-carriages', that cholera epidemics might be spread from Puri to distant parts of the subcontinent.[84] These perceptions appear to have been not totally unfounded – in 1912, when the *rath jatra* was attended by almost a quarter of a million of pilgrims, the minimum figure for Puri pilgrims who had died of cholera on the train during their return journey was 251.[85]

Yet British railway and government officials, like those in the Bihar and Orissa 'Pilgrim Committee' of 1913, were never quite prepared to admit fully that appalling sanitary conditions in trains and stations were important contributing factors to such outbreaks. In their view, pilgrimage and epidemics were inevitably connected. Interestingly, this inevitability seems to have been far less plausible to many pilgrims. On their round trip to various pilgrimage sites in Bihar and Orissa, the members of the committee made the bewildering discovery that Indian pilgrims were far from being petrified with awe and gratefulness in the face of the new 'fire-carriages' that had been bestowed on them by their colonial masters. The gentlemen found, instead, that '[w]herever we went we were inundated with complaints regarding the manner in which pilgrims are carried and treated in their journeys by rail'. This kind of appropriation of the railways by Indian society was clearly at odds with the colonial oligarchy's obsession with paternalistic order and the corresponding expectation of undemanding submissiveness from their subjects, which has been discussed above. Therefore, it may be in order to quote the report's relevant passages at some length:

> Quick to appreciate the comforts and advantages of railway travelling in these days, the educated and well-to-do people of this country have interested themselves greatly in all matters of railway administration. This branch of public affairs occupies their attention very largely and they are continually asking for the extension and improvement of the railway system throughout the country. The numerous questions in the Legislative Council show how keenly the

shortcomings of the railway are scrutinized all over India. It is not strange then that the railway arrangements during the festivals at places of pilgrimage should come in for a good deal of adverse comment. The trains are crowded to their utmost; often there is no seat to be found; it is very difficult to get a ticket; trains are frequently delayed; food and water are not readily procurable: the discomforts are too well known to everyone to need detailed enumeration. The educated passenger finds that travelling at the time of a great religious festival is a very different thing from an ordinary railway journey. His acquaintance with the railway, however, is too short for him to understand that much of this discomfort is unavoidable and that, go where you will in the world, wherever there is a rush of travellers there will, and must, be similar discomforts. Railways are new and it is not fully realised in this country as elsewhere that at times the rush and the overcrowding are inevitable. The Indian has a trusting belief that he has but to make a complaint and someone will find the remedy.

What was even worse, however, was that these complaints were not confined to *babu*s or 'educated classes', whose demands were generally considered by the British oligarchy to be unrepresentative of the 'true mind' of the people:

> The patient villager is slow to voice his grievances but will, if questioned, likewise add his protest against the railway arrangements. The same villager who will cheerfully submit to any overcrowding in his panda's house, to any sort of shelter at the fair, to any crushing or weary waiting at the temple door, to any exactions from his priest, reserves his grumble for the railway. This seems strange but is largely due to the newness of the railways: it has always been his experience that fairs are crowded and priests greedy but that railways are generally comfortable; his acquaintance with the latter is too short for him to understand that there are times when lapses from the normal must be expected.[86]

These lines would merit closer examination but we shall confine ourselves here to two brief observations. First, the committee's report betrays the feeling that colonial authorities could not instil the same kind of unquestioning obedience in their subjects' minds as the representatives of 'traditional' hierarchy (the *panda*s and priests) could. In other words, there is a sense of inadequate 'basic legitimacy' and a lack of hegemony. Second, the committee's explanation for the permanent criticism of railway arrangements for pilgrims is of some interest. In their view, the main reason for the numerous complaints was not to be found in the prevailing conditions, though they admitted, for instance, that 'trucks used for carrying cattle are much better provided with ventilation than those generally used in the pilgrim traffic'.[87] The point was rather that the 'acquaintance' of both 'educated passengers' and 'patient villagers' with railways was too brief: Indians were lacking experience – therefore, they just couldn't understand. This argument brings us back to the paternal ideologies of colonial rule we have discussed above: in this case, the very refusal of Indians to accept social minority was used as proof of their continuing incapability of political participation and need of paternal regulation. Hence the committee members felt no need to explain why the railway companies were averse to making use of volunteers in the organization of pilgrim traffic though 'Indian gentlemen' had offered assistance at various places.[88]

This seems to have been typical of the prevailing attitude of railway authorities towards Indian pilgrims – an attitude that relied more heavily than in the metropolitan country on the enforcement of obedience and made considerably less effort to muster cooperation. This attitude expressed itself in numerous quotidian practices of authority, which were experienced by millions of Indians. A study of these experiences may well permit new insights into the everyday structures of colonial power but is beyond the scope of this paper. However, the following quotes from the memoirs of John W Mitchell, a railway official who had once been in charge of the Puri section of the BNR, may permit us to catch a glimpse of such structures. 'The Bengal–Nagpur Railway,' wrote Mitchell proudly, 'has built up a most efficient system of handling the masses of ignorant, illiterate, grown-up children who crowd its trains to Puri bound.'[89] And he also gave an example for the workings of this system at Puri's railway terminal:

> Four huge roofed steel pens, permanent and solid, each capable of accommodating 1,500 pilgrims, have been erected. To prevent over-crowding and possible chaos, never more than approximately 1,000 passengers are allowed to enter at one time. No one is admitted to the platforms without first passing though these pens which segregate the pilgrims according to their ticket colours. One can hardly imagine an English railway administration attempting to pen off its football crowds and shoe traffic passengers this way. Steel bars would never suffice for them. They would have to be reinforced by asbestos to withstand the sulphurous language from the enraged inmates. This is India, however, and other countries, other peoples, other ways.[90]

Once again, the children of the East had to be 'handled' differently from the grown-ups of the West, and never the twain were to meet.

8. Conclusion

We will conclude this paper by returning to our argument that the ideological construct 'civilizing mission' became to a higher degree focused on spheres of science, technology and economy from the mid-nineteenth century onwards. This 'Civilizing Mission Ltd' continued to be a 'practical illusion' of the ruling political force of colonial India, which motivated the regime's officials and legitimized, though with decreasing efficiency, the rule of a thin layer of white colonizers over three hundred million Indians. The content of this illusion was not identical with that of the dominant illusions of the European 'Age of Revolution' before the mid-nineteenth century. Accordingly, the declared objective of colonial social engineering was neither a brisk breakdown nor a gradual dissolution of 'traditional' paternalistic forms of social and political hierarchy but the substitution of one such hierarchy for another. The arche-type of the colonial official was thus not Prometheus, the mythical embodi-ment of enlightenment who emancipated humanity from the gods by teaching them the use of fire. In a way, the objective was rather to substitute new gods for the old. 'Not half a bad thing to pray to, either,' commented Kipling's bridge-builder Findlayson on being told that Peroo had 'prayed to the low-pressure cylinder' when he first saw the engine-room of a steamer.[91] The colonial oligarchy's favourite poet indulged in a day-dream, in a reactionary Utopia, of which he probably knew it was not to materialize. In this dream, the eastern idol of 'Mother Ganga' was supplanted by an idol of empire, 'Kashi bridge'; the 'barbaric' temple chariot that carried the idol of Lord Jagannath was replaced by the 'steam-carriage', the idol of the non-universal, but superior civilization of the West.

Almost five decades after the first publication of Kipling's 'The Bridge-Builders', after nationalist critique and popular movements had severely damaged the colonial regime's legitimacy and the 'practical illusion' of its functionaries, John W Mitchell, the Puri railway official, put the same techno-cratic day-dream in words of negligible literary quality but of admirable clarity. Recounting how crowds of pilgrims greeted the 'Lord of the Earth' on their arrival in Puri by exclaiming, '*Jai*, Jagannath *ki jai*,' he gave his readers the benefit of the following reflections:

> Do the unlearned, unlettered, inarticulate mass appreciate the many wonders of the wheel [the railway, R. A.]? It is to be feared not. Many of those who profess to voice the aspirations of India's peoples

oft-times unreasonably reject or biasedly ignore its manifold bless-ings.

Standing then on the Puri platform almost under the shadow of the ancient symbol, listening still to the age-old challenge, we feel that these thanksgiving children, perhaps with less reverence but with greater truth, could cry, '*Jai Charka ki Jai*,' which, interpreted, might read, 'Hail! Thou Wheel! Lord of the World!'[92]

5

Taming the 'Dangerous' Rajput; Family, Marriage and Female Infanticide in Nineteenth-century Colonial North India

MALAVIKA KASTURI
University of Toronto

1. Introduction

This chapter studies nineteenth-century colonial interventions in the 'domestic space' of Rajput lineages in the north-western Provinces[1] (the term 'domestic space' is used here to refer to the private world of the household and family). More specifically, it seeks to examine the contradictions and pressures influencing colonial efforts to civilize the 'inner world', through a study of Rajput marriage strategies and their concomitant, female infanticide. In this context, it will also attempt to highlight evolving British policies towards status, gender and kinship hierarchies,[2] as officials dealt with Rajput landholding lineages, whose martial identities were seen at different points either as a threat or a stabilizing influence in nineteenth century north India.

When the East India Company wrested control of the Ceded and Conquered Provinces from Nawabi Awadh between the 1780s and 1818, it found that, in agrarian society, Rajput lineages constituted the locally dominant elites, commanding enormous amounts of economic and symbolic capital and controlling the largest proportion of the land. All Rajput lineages, or *biradari*s, were corporate kinship groups of varying genealogical depth with claims to a service tradition and *kshatriya* status. *Biradari*s traced their origins, history and traditions to the supposed progenitors of their respective clans. Members of socially and ritually hierarchical clans were bound together by claims to a shared ritual status and fictive genealogies.[3]

Officials observed that not all Rajput clans were of the same ritual status.

Some clans were perceived as being of purer *kshatriya* origin as compared to others and were accorded a higher position in the cultural and ritual hierarchy of the 'imagined' Rajput community. Having said that, Rajput clans and lineages were open and fluid social categories. Claims to 'Rajput-hood', inextricably linked to the assertion of martial masculinity, were achieved by a variety of social groups through participation in the military labour market, the assertion of rights of kingship, or alternatively through intermarriage with families claiming high Rajput status. However, ritual status alone did not determine Rajput identity. The localized social standing of Rajput *biradaris* also derived in large part from their access to economic and political power and their relationship with state structures. Indeed, land, lineage and honour were closely linked in the world-view and power struc-tures of Rajput lineages, whose sphere of influence in Nawabi Awadh was determined by the extent of their control over resources and manpower. Thus, while Rajput lineages were subject to the revenue, administrative and judicial machinery of the Nawabi, they exercized great influence in local society,[4] struggling over land and position in contests that shaped their marriage practices and the rates of female infanticide

From the beginning of its rule, the East India Company came into conflict with dominant Rajput elites, for it asserted a monopoly over the use of force and claimed absolute sovereignty over the territories under its control. Indeed, from the eighteenth century, the British attempted, through pacifi-cation, demilitarization and disarmament to delimit conflicts between elite lineages over territoriality and authority on the one hand, and tear the link-ages binding land and service to political power on the other. The network of alliances among the *biradaris* under study, based on kinship and marriage, friendship and dependence, were especially perceived as an obstacle in the path of the expansion of the Company's coercive and administrative power. Nonetheless, the evidence indicates a very complex relationship between the Rajputs and the British. From the early nineteenth century, the 'domestica-tion' and 'civilizing' of Rajput 'wild' and 'primitive' traits by British officials accompanied the valorization of the 'masculinity', 'pride' and courage of these lineages. Even after 1857, when the coercive power of the state came down heavily on offending brotherhoods, efforts were made to avoid alienat-ing a dominant landholding group, who crowded the imagination of policy-makers and ethnographers obsessed by caste and race. Official ambivalence towards the Rajputs was never clearer than when legislating on matters relating to the 'domestic' space and more specifically to women, an especially sensitive subject in this period.

The evidence of recent research indicates that colonial subjects saw them-selves as free from interference in the private world of the household.[5] In this arena, among elite Rajput lineages, women represented and perpetuated male claims to honour and status and were viewed more as property and as instruments of exchange. *Biradari*s controlled the sexuality and mobility of their women and primarily utilized them to contract alliances of superior position. The cultural ideology and strategies of high-ranking lineages devalued women, sought to limit their agency in the public space and re-inforced conservative caste and gender hierarchies.[6]

British policymakers, on the other hand, saw the family as the repository of indigenous 'tradition', religious norms and values, a site that was alternately left alone or reformed.[7] While Company officials believed that intrusion into the 'domestic proceedings' of its subjects would lead to resistance, they also gave in to the need to monitor and normalize those subjects' private lives whenever their 'traditions' were deemed 'threatening' to new normative definitions of 'civilization'.[8] In the realm of civil and criminal law, the Company was guided by the Regulating Act of 1781. This declared that the authority of 'fathers' and 'masters' of families in the new colony would be preserved in accordance with the religion and manners of the Company's new subjects, in so far as they did not contravene the 'due execution of the laws and attainment of justice'.[9] What this meant, as Radhika Singha persua-sively argues in the case of criminal law (our main focus of interest), is that 'certain manifestations of the patriarchal prerogative were rejected as 'exces-sive' because they were bound up with an older political order which clashed with the ideological, fiscal and pacificatory imperatives of the colonial state'.[10] In particular, she suggests that Company criminal law interfered in instances such as female infanticide, in which its moral codes and sovereign and legal claims over the life and death of its subjects were challenged.[11] At the same time, norms, values and rights that strengthened paternal and conjugal rights of men over women were sanctioned by law. The intervention of criminal law in the 'domestic space' by the 1840s, therefore, was open to a number of conflicting pressures.

I would like to take off here from this argument to investigate the trajectory of official policy towards female infanticide. This practice went beyond the neglect of female infants and the denial of basic nutrition to them, a state of affairs common to other castes and, unlike *suttee*, occurred in the private space. The inevitability of colonial efforts to eradicate the systematic elimina-tion of girl children cannot be taken for granted. While officials had viewed women as objects of 'brutish', 'uncivilized' and 'unnatural' acts perpetrated by men from the beginning of British conquest, they did not wish to prohibit local cultural practices reinforcing patriarchal control over women unless they were proscribed by religious and customary 'traditions'.[12] This was because the East India Company had made an early equation between law, scripture and social and religious identities. By the 1840s, however, the state seemed confident about 'civilizing' Rajput masculinities to eradicate female infanticide, especially as the Hindu scriptures proscribed the practice.

This chapter focuses on the period between 1840 through 1912, when official interest in female infanticide peaked. Colonial policies influenced by various ideological, administrative and political considerations played themselves out in two phases. In the first, officials seeking to avoid punitive action attempted to make sense of and reform those aspects of Rajput marriage systems influencing female infanticide. In the second, beginning in the 1870s, criminal law sought concomitantly to punish and 'normalize' Rajput lineages suspected of the practice by putting these *biradaris* under special surveillance and monitoring all domestic events. The following analysis investigates the reasons behind this shift in policy, asking what made the colonial state overcome its earlier inhibitions about policing the Rajput household. Here, it examines to what extent the early ambivalence in criminal legal attitudes towards the 'domestic space' was carried over into the latter half of the nineteenth century. Additionally, the chapter probes the manner in which the relationship between patrilineal honour, marriage and status shaped choices exercised in relation to girl children. This analysis will provide a background against which to study the private world in which the punitive rules hoped to make a dent and examine how status and gender hierarchies defined and limited British efforts to eliminate female infanticide.

The issues raised above are investigated in four parts. First, the chapter locates the 'civilizing mission' of the colonial state towards female infanticide against the broader backdrop of British strategies to domesticate Rajput masculinities in the public space. It suggests that an examination of this theme is crucial in understanding the direction taken both by Rajput matrimonial strategies and colonial policies towards female infanticide. The second section gives a quick overview of the evidence relating to female infanticide and its connections with marriage and status hierarchies to place the evolution and limitations of colonial policies in the domestic space in perspective. Third, the chapter examines the official debates revolving around marriage and female infanticide and the nature of early state intervention in the Rajput household to resolve this problem. Fourth, it examines official attempts forcibly to domesticate Rajput masculinities by proscribing female infanticide after the passage of Act VIII of 1870.

2. Domesticating 'Unbridled' Masculinities in the Public Space

The nineteenth century resonated with contradictions in British attitudes towards the Rajputs. On the one hand, if their chivalrous and courageous qualities were lauded, the *biradaris* under study were also feared as pugnacious and violent, with a fierce temperament driven by primitive instincts. The central paradox was that the British simultaneously reified Rajput codes of warriorship and kingship and attempted to domesticate the 'savage' and 'violent' impulses of the lordly Rajput man of prowess.[13] The systemic crisis in the articulation of Rajput martial masculinities gave a special edge to contradictory colonial 'civilizing' policies towards these lineages in the public and private space.

In pre-colonial north India, Rajput identity was a collective one, applied to members of open status groups in search of patronage and *naukari*.[14] Service was part of a wider martial culture of masculinity, feeding into the north Indian political system, establishing hierarchies and affirming common identities in the public space.[15] Through service, Rajput caste identities were in a constant state of fluidity and redefinition, as various socially mobile groups participated in the unending search for status and position.[16] Moreover, upwardly mobile Rajput *biradaris* affirmed their position in the 'imagined' Rajput community, and negotiated their position and power through cultural strategies of collective violence called *bhumeawat*. *Bhumeawat* may be described as the fight for identity, status and territory arising out of a sense of commitment to the homeland, or *bhum*. Through *bhumeawat*, and its constituents, rebellion against the state, feuding and banditry, all of which were inextricably linked, boundaries were constantly redrawn between various Rajput factions, *biradaris*, other social groups and the state.[17] The more the territory and resources owned or coveted by powerful *biradaris*, the more intense the conflict between them. In the colonial period, elite Rajput *bhumeawat* became more defensive than offensive in nature, as lineages struggled to preserve a resource base no longer assured of renewal, and to protect indigenous patterns of kingship, prestige, and martial identities from outsiders, whether other lineages or a new, predatory and threatening state structure. Increasingly, *bhumeawat* became a political and cultural expression of protest against a changing order, based on unfamiliar conceptions of an all-enveloping sovereignty and territoriality, new knowledge systems and ideologies that threatened the assertion of Rajput martial culture and power.[18]

Having said that, British responses to the articulation of Rajput authority and identity were complicated. In the early nineteenth century, as Company officials privileged and reinvented several high-profile codes of indigenous masculinity, they glorified *kshatriya* martial culture, arguing that it exemplified bravery, chivalry and sacrifice and could be harnessed to realize British ambitions on the subcontinent.[19] Despite various ideological and policy shifts, the cornerstone of colonial political and economic policy in India in the nineteenth century remained the 'urge of improvement', industry and order. The effort was to create an environment in which India's commercial connection to Britain could best be exploited, coupled with the desire to appropriate, dominate and control the distribution and allocation of resources and 'civilize' social spaces and peoples. In pursuit of these aims, a new 'rule of property', deeply influenced by Physiocratic doctrines, attempted to convert Rajput lineages into 'economical' and 'prudent' landlords, trustees of the 'public interest', who would help enhance the value of private property, encourage agrarian expansion, the 'rule of law', increase land revenue, and buttress colonial power.[20] Moreover, it was hoped that once the threatening bonds tying lineages together were effectively weakened, and their pristine primitivism suppressed, their good qualities could be harnessed, not merely to colonize the agrarian wastes but also to fight in the Company army.

Thus, while British rule led to the reduction if not the gradual disappearance of the pre-colonial military labour market, with the disbanding of the armies of princely states and magnates of all types, the British Indian army remained one of the few viable arenas of military service, for 'Rajput' martial culture in our period. By 1840, the Rajputs from the north-western provinces and Awadh, increasingly praised as a 'fine race of men both as to bodily symmetry and personal character'[21] were recruited in large numbers into the Company's regiments. Before 1857, every village from the region contributed at least one member to the army.[22] The consistency of pay and employment made the army an attractive proposition, while it was also an important outlet for elite Rajput *biradaris* for the maintenance and improvement of their warrior traditions, high-caste Hindu status and social prestige.[23] Rajput peasants, in particular, used military service to emulate and compete with their richer clansmen.[24] However, after the Great Rebellion, while ethnographers such as Sherring continued to assert that the 'physique of the Rajpoot, in the opinion of military men, peculiarly adapts him for the life of a soldier,'[25] Rajput lineages from north India were no longer recruited into the army by a suspicious colonial state. This shift in British policy affected the prosperity of brotherhoods dependent on military incomes in these areas. More importantly, it led to a crisis in the perceptions of rank, status and position of those asserting a lordly Rajput status.

The Great Rebellion also brought to the fore the concern that the unbridled masculinity of the Rajputs, as expressed through *bhumeawat*, constituted a threat to 'order' and 'civilization'.[26] Indeed, from the 1780s, the

Company had sought, with a limited degree of success, to encroach upon the power of these lineages in the public space by questioning the right of Rajput elites to maintain independent spheres of influence, revolt against state power and conduct *bhumeawat* in efforts to enhance their strength. Initially, this policy was not an unqualified success, and was marked by ambivalence. Indeed, the period between the 1780s and the 1830s was one of caution and limited experimentation by the Company, as the power of the state was more circumscribed than envisaged due to a multiplicity of pressures. By the 1840s, halting steps were taken to bring 'turbulent' Rajput lineages to heel; their armies were disbanded and their *garhi*s or forts demolished if they refused to pay revenue or rebelled against the state. After 1857, the colonial resolve to force powerful *biradaris* to operate within the framework of colonial administrative, legal, cultural and ideological codes and norms intensified. Now, more than ever before, conquering the forces of 'primitivism' with the use of force represented a victory for British political and coercive structures and colonial masculinity. Lineages who had participated in civil rebellion against the colonial state had their land confiscated, were forcibly disarmed and their forts systematically destroyed, while drives were launched against feuding and banditry to eliminate *bhumeawat* once and for all.[27] Having said that, the British could not afford to alienate completely elite Rajput *biradaris*, and, as the evidence on female infanticide indicates, policymakers continued in many ways to placate these dominant and influential elites in the latter half of the nineteenth century.

The British attack upon Rajput martial masculinities and power in the 'outside' world, however conflicted, had profound repercussions on gender hierarchies and cultural practices in the home, such as marriage and female infanticide. It also directed the gaze of colonial criminal law to the family, in an effort forcibly to normalize those among its Rajput male subjects who systematically eliminated their girl children. The British interest in policing the 'inner world' coincided with the transformation of social relationships and cultural strategies within the Rajput family. In the pre-colonial period Rajput martial culture based on aggrandizement, power and rank, had been reflected within the domestic space through the composition of the elite household, its consumption patterns and network of alliances. Now, as colonial political culture, underwritten by a different set of 'civilizational' and normative definitions, slowly took centre-stage, there was a fundamental shift in the arenas in which power was articulated by Rajput elites.[28]Increasingly, as Rosalind O'Hanlon suggests, as a result of 'declining opportunities for the expression of martial masculinity' and the 'contraction of the outdoor world in which these identities were affirmed', their attention was 'focused more closely on the indoor realm of household and family'. [29] Now, the 'crucial asset' helping dominant and upwardly mobile Rajput elites survive these developments was a hitherto undue emphasis on 'pure' bloodlines, 'pristine' genealogies and high ritual status as the only signifier of Rajputhood. In this scenario, cultural practices such as marriage, which had always fixed, symbolized and transmitted relations of power among Rajput elites in pre-colonial kingdoms,[30] came under especial scrutiny. These historical changes, I suggest below, structurally impinged on the status of Rajput women, given the connection between marriage and female infanticide.

3. The Lineage, Marriage, and Female Infanticide

Ester Boserup pointed to the linkages between production, labour and female infanticide. She suggested that the status of women was linked to marriage systems based on dowry or bride-wealth. Matrimonial strategies, in turn, were influenced by female participation in production and the differential position of women in various social strata. In Boserup's reckoning, infanticide exists only in those regions and communities of South Asia (including Rajputs) where the division of labour in 'male' plough-sharing systems is such that the engagement of women in manual labour is considered highly degrading and polluting and they are increasingly removed from the field, relegated to the domestic sphere and pay dowry to the groom. In contrast, in areas of plough cultivation among lower caste/class rural communities, where women are valued as economic assets, bride-wealth is paid to the family of the bride as compensation for the loss of an active working member.[31]

There are, however, important deviations in the female infanticide registers in our region and period, which Boserup's hypothesis cannot fully explain. The 'suspected' groups included not merely high-ranking elite Rajput *zamindars* (or landholders), but upwardly mobile rich Rajputs of low status and Jat and Ahir families, belonging to social groups who, with their women worked in fields and often received bridewealth from the groom at the time of marriage. It appears that the existing relationship between production, labour and the status of women only offers a partial explanation for the incidence of female infanticide.

Officials assumed that female infanticide was the consequence of poverty amongst high status lineages unable to pay large dowries. Evidence indicates, however, that female infanticide was practised by localized lineages *across* the economic spectrum who claimed high ritual status. These included wealthy lineages, who were either already at the pinnacle of the social and political ladder, and upwardly mobile families, whose self-conscious claims to status were bolstered by capital. It also included influential families, whose resource base was fast contracting. Thus, it was noted that among the Pundir brotherhoods in Saharanpur who practised female infanticide, 'the majority of the villages are well to do, a few are rich and several poor . . . villages guilty of infanticide are . . . distinguishable from their neighbours by excessive pride of caste, but not by any other circumstances'.[32] However, this observation, which assumed that the demands of ritual status alone caused disproportionate male:female sex ratios, was only partially correct. As we have noted above, the shifting relationship between Rajput ritual status and economic/ political power played a profound role in shaping marriage strategies and female infanticide.

An examination of the archival evidence from the north-western provinces indicates that the fallout of the nineteenth century shifts in political economy (which I have examined in depth elsewhere)[33] had a differential impact upon Rajput status, power and their grip over land. By the time the *mahalwari* settlement was put in place in north India, the British had also launched an assault on property rights, which resulted in the contraction of the Rajput resource base and the auction, sale and confiscation of land among *biradaris* of high and low ritual status in revenue *mahals*. This situation is relevant, given that after 1857, as the military labour market completely dried up, lineages claiming Rajput status fell back on shares to land, even as their property was confiscated as a punishment for having instigated rebellion against the state. The extent to which brotherhoods retained control over land was largely dependent on local circumstances and how they responded to the vagaries of fate. The Rajput experience in north India was not uniform as lineages were divided along the lines of class and status. Indeed, rank, wealth and power existed in various permutations and combinations among our *biradaris*. Within the same district, brotherhoods belonging to the same clan could be locally dominant and prosperous in one zone, and poor and lacking in power and influence in another. Further, conflict and feuding between the rich and poor within landholding brotherhoods intensified, in response to the structural shifts taking place in agrarian society. Among elite lineages, prosperous co-sharers bought land from their indebted brethren, who slipped to the position of the upper cultivating peasantry and took to the plough, a practice scorned by elite families. Likewise, many Rajput families of lower rank took advantage of the high turnover of land to increase their social standing in agrarian society. Consequently, the relationship between economic, ritual and social ranking grew exceptionally complicated, for many poor Rajput lineages declining in power claimed a high ritual status, while the claims of rich brotherhoods to status and *izzat* (honour) were often not recognized by their compatriots. While these disparities were not new in themselves, I suggest they were bound to have a profound impact on the marriage practices of lineages at both ends of the economic and power ladder in the colonial period, as the Rajput social and political world retreated into the shadows.[34]

Marriage had always impinged directly on the improvement, conservation and dissipation of the economic and 'symbolic' capital of the lineage and was one of the major mechanisms of the 'social reproduction' of the latter in pre-colonial Awadh. Marriage alliances, as political expressions of kinship, played a fundamental role in enlarging the spheres of influence of various lineages. All Rajput lineages claimed to belong to hierarchical exogamous clans, which intermarried with each other.[35] Unlike lineages of lower status, which exchanged their daughters for bride-wealth, elite lineages practised localized hypergamous marriages, whose contours were determined by the relative ritual, social and political status of both families sealing the alliance. Hypergamous alliances between lineages belonging to different clans con-formed to the main principle of *kanyadana* marriages, in which the daughter was given as *dan* or gift to a family of superior ritual status with a dowry to earn spiritual merit and to form an alliance of mutual benefit. Hypergamous Rajput marriage patterns had always encouraged female infanticide among elite families claiming very high ritual status in the pre-colonial period. These groups were usually of exalted social standing or upwardly mobile and in search of expanding influence and power. However, not all families practising such alliances killed girl children. Female infanticide seemed to occur when Rajputs at the top of the marriage ladder took the desire for precedence to unrealistic heights, acknowledging few clans as their equals and limiting the number of families with whom they could intermarry. Consequently, some families, who by definition could not marry their daughters to anybody of equal or higher status, were faced with a possible surplus of unmarried girls.[36] Dowries added to the problems of restrictive alliances for families with several girls, unwilling to shoulder what they perceived as an unnecessary financial burden. In such situations, these *biradari*s often resorted to female infanticide. By limiting the number of their female children, I contend, they attempted to minimize the potential loss to their rank and wealth if not altogether avert it.[37]

It has been argued that that, under colonial rule, networks based on caste and kinship, including marriage alliances, were separated from power when the political and social system based on gifts, honour, exchange, military rights and service broke down.[38] However, I argue in contrast that in this period the importance of marriage as a means to power was reinforced for these very reasons. As noted in the previous section, as efforts by brother-hoods to enlarge their sphere of influence through territorial expansion, feuding and warfare were curbed by the coercive machinery of the colonial state, elite Rajputs turned inwards to the domestic space for the affirmation of identities and martial masculinities. In this environment, marriage alliances, more than ever before, took centre stage as one of the primary sites for the social and political articulation of power and rank by patrilineages seeking to compensate for their gradual displacement in the public arena. Through marriage, lineages claiming high ritual status and power in a fast-changing world sought to indicate to their wider audience the multiplicity of their social and political networks, their potential for alliances, wealth and power through the maintenance of social exclusiveness, caste and ritual purity, and delimitation of social boundaries within the 'imagined' Rajput community. As a result, the role of women as the definers, instruments and carriers of status, both ritual and social, and honour at the time of marriage was reinforced, even as their status declined.

In both the eastern and western districts of the north-western provinces, Rajput clans largely practised female infanticide in regions where they predominated as the main landholding elites and were most conscious of ritual and social rank. There were a larger number of clans suspected of female infanticide towards the western districts partly because they claimed a higher ritual status. Within these areas, investigators found that only specific localized lineages as opposed to a whole clan displayed abnormal sex ratios.[39] The largest number of suspected villages in any district was located where 'scores' of settlements of the same clan were clustered in the same neighbourhood in large estates. In contrast, in areas where they were 'weak' and 'scattered', the same clans, preserved their daughters.[40] In such zones, lineages, although of high ritual status, had few claims to influence, land and power.

By the mid-nineteenth century, brotherhoods in clan settlements, who were susceptible, wealthy and seeking to expand their sphere of influence, were increasingly open to a greater degree of social pressure and rivalry in the relentless hunt for 'suitable' grooms if they consciously limited their marriage circles. Among powerful lineages, fast losing their grip over economic resources and unable to participate in the military labour market, the demands of status and identity revolving around marriage were also mounting.[41] Before 1857, for example, the affluent Surajbansi and Gautam *biradaris* of Amroha, Nagar and Basti had earned a bad name for infanticide because of their marriage practices. After the rebellion, although numerous men belonging to these clans were adjudged rebels and had their lands confiscated, there was little diminution of ambition and social pressure underlying the desire for prestigious alliances. Poverty perhaps reinforced the incentives behind female infanticide among families pursuing authority and position.[42] While it is difficult to indicate precisely whether the rate of female infanticide increased or decreased on the basis of the existing figures, we may speculate that it did not remain stationary or decrease in our period. In fact, the evidence suggests that the material and social conditions created by more than a century of British rule were probably conducive to the intensification of infanticide among rich, poor and upwardly mobile lineages seeking to expand their influence as the gap between the haves and have-nots widened.

Rich and poor Rajputs claiming high status did not practise female infanticide if they adopted pragmatic compromises as restrictive marriages based on *kanyadana* were not compulsory. As their fortunes waxed and waned, many brotherhoods contracted alliances with lineages of similar status, often called *barabari ki shadi* or 'equal marriages'. Girls of families fallen on hard times often underwent a ceremony called *dharam byah*, in which the bridegroom paid for the ceremony and no dowry was given. Some families, especially former co-sharers who were now mere tenants, albeit with special rights, even changed their matrimonial strategies and demanded bride-wealth instead.[43]

Even wealthy lineages preserved their female babies if they could be reconciled to sons-in-law of equal or lower status.[44] There also existed families who preserved as many daughters as they thought they could marry satisfactorily, killing the rest. Sometimes kinship groups practising female infanticide preserved little girls if hopes of a male heir were entirely lost. Girl babies born in their maternal grandparents' house, or who had already been suckled by the mother, had higher chances of survival. The statistics betrayed the tension between the multiple choices exercized by a variety of families. Their struggle to reconcile their urge to keep girl children was at odds with their desire to destroy them in order to forestall a decline in status.[45]

In most cases, it seems that only 'legitimate' offspring were destroyed. Girls considered 'illegitimate' by the British – the children of concubines and slaves – were usually preserved if they were the consequence of a relationship with a social inferior. In such cases, daughters were seen as belonging to the mother and were not under as much threat.[46] If possible, Rajput fathers made arrangements for them to get married. If not, these children either became dancing girls or were sold to other Rajputs as wives.[47]

Female infanticide had unintended consequences. There was a great demand for women among high-ranking Rajputs, as there were many unmarried men in villages in which girl children were destroyed. The scarcity of girls in many clans of higher status led to the kidnapping of women of lower castes, who were sold to high-ranking lineages for matrimonial purposes.[48] These sales were *bona fide* for the purposes of marriage and those guilty often could not be prosecuted under the penal code.[49] More commonly, women of lower ritual and economic position were given in marriage to men in groups higher up in the status and power hierarchy to meet the acute scarcity of marriageable brides. Consequently, large numbers of men among localized clans of lower ritual status were deprived of wider choices as relatively few women were available to them at the bottom of the marriage ladder. Often these men either remained unmarried or, in some communities, resorted to a whole series of palliative measures such as widow-remarriage, levirate marriages and alliances with lower-caste girls from Jat and Gujar communities.[50] In some cases women from semi-nomadic communities were also married to 'Rajput' bridegrooms of this level in exchange for bride-wealth.[51] Thus, female infanticide contributed indirectly to the blurring of identities in the generic category 'Rajput' at the lower end of the scale. It also widened the gap between those of 'high' and 'low' ritual status. These tendencies were probably reinforced in our period.

As noted before, high-ranking Rajput ideals of position, honour and marriage were adopted all the way down the social scale by upwardly mobile Rajputs of low ritual status.[52] The magistrate of Etawa observed that the Gahlots, Bamungors and Bais 'kill their daughters if they are rich, but make a profit from their marriages if they are poor'.[53] It appears that such *biradaris* were more likely to adopt dowry marriages and practise female infanticide if they lived in the vicinity of high-ranking lineages, who tended to ignore their claims to upward social mobility. Officials in the Farrukhabad district suggested that the Gaurs, Chandels, Nihumbhs and the Rathors of low rank had apparently been 'corrupted' by the example of their neighbouring high-ranking Rathors.[54] Similar evidence was available for the peasant castes such as the Chaudhary Jats of Bijnor, the Phatuk Ahirs in Mainpuri and the Gujars in Saharanpur, who had been settled by the British by the 1850s on some of the richest land of the western districts of the north-western provinces. All these groups, who were challenging elite Rajput cultural and economic hegemony by the end of the nineteenth century, were concentrated in areas where they constituted the most powerful sections of the population, such as the prosperous irrigated agricultural zones of the Meerut and Rohilkhand divisions.[55]

The adoption of female infanticide by families of lower rank, I argue, was both a symptom as well as part of a complex response to the conflict over identity, gender, rank, class and power taking place under colonial rule. In challenging the claims to social pre-eminence by elite Rajputs, such families adopted an ideological and behavioural commitment to a specific lifestyle supposedly separating the 'pure' Rajput from all comers, in a period in which claims to *kshatriya* identity were primarily defined through cultural practices such as marriage. These changes were reflected in the relationship between land, labour and production. Women were gradually secluded and removed from the fields in rich and status-conscious households among these castes.[56] The self-inflicted pressures of rank and power associated with marriage strategies perceived as Rajput may have encouraged female infanticide among such families. To achieve a measure of success in its policies to eliminate female infanticide, the colonial state had to work its way round the barriers erected within the household by gender and status hierarchies favouring the low incidence of girl children.

4. From Reform to Repression: Female Infanticide and Early British Objectives

The Company had evinced an interest in Rajput marriages and female infanticide from the 1780s, ever since Jonathan Duncan discovered that the Rajkumar brotherhoods in the Benares division of the north-western provinces selectively killed girl children to avoid having to arrange 'expensive' alliances for their daughters. From the beginning, the status of Rajput women was never paramount in official debates on female infanticide. Girl children were only important in so far as they were viewed as symbols of a society hidebound by 'barbaric' traditions. Horror was heightened after details of the practice became known. The ways devised for disposing of unwanted girl children were manifold and included drowning, strangling, poisoning and asphyxiation by drawing the umbilical cord over a baby's face to prevent respiration. In many families, infants were left to die without nourishment. Often, if they survived the first few hours after their birth, infants were fed poison.[57]

All strains of opinion unreservedly viewed female infanticide as a 'deviant' activity 'subversive of the principles of the natural and revealed Christian religion'.[58] By the 1820s, those advocating intervention to eradicate the practice also used the Hindu scriptures to bolster their arguments, confident that these measures would be in consonance with indigenous religious tenets. Thus that verse of the *shastras* was quoted, which said that 'to kill one woman is equal to one hundred brahmins, to kill one child is equal to one hundred women' while 'to kill one hundred children is an offence too heinous for comparison'.[59]

The official approach towards female infanticide was not ambivalent: the right of Rajput lineages to kill girl children was questioned by colonial law and the moral values it tried to perpetuate from the beginnings of Company rule, once it was clear that female infanticide occurred in an insidious manner within the home and was hard to detect. Consequently, for a long time the Company continued to be perplexed by the nature of intervention required to abolish the practice. While Regulation III of 1804 contained some provisos for the prevention and punishment of female infanticide, these were inadequate for the task at hand and impossible to enforce. Although there is evidence to suggest that persons committing female infanticide were tried by the criminal courts as early as 1806, all of them were let off on grounds of ignorance of the regulations and lack of evidence.[60]

While the possibility of the surveillance of suspected Rajput households was considered extremely early on, it was argued that 'such a measure would lead to much intrusion into the most private and domestic proceedings of the superior castes (among whom alone Infanticide prevails) [. . .]' [61]while the chances of success of this policy would not 'compensate' for the resistance it would create'. Company officials were obviously unwilling unnecessarily to antagonize lineages they were still trying to tame in the public space. They argued instead, in favour of eliminating female infanticide through reason and persuasion, not coercion.

Before the 1840s, pleas for the abolition of the practice on humanitarian grounds by missionaries and others were secondary to the colonial preoccupation with the impact of the demands of status and expensive marriage practices linked to female infanticide on the position of Rajputs. The increasing importance given to Rajput marriages took place against the backdrop of a growing British concern linking the weakening position of the agrarian elite to the loss of land and the feeling that they wasted large amounts of money on festivals, rites and rituals, both secular and religious, especially marriage. Now, conspicuous consumption and the theory of 'improvidence' assumed great significance in official eyes. The anxiety revolving around the impact of Rajput 'family pride' and 'avarice' on the amounts spent on marriages (especially the dowry given to the bridegroom) was reflected in the attempt to induce patrilineages to reduce the amount of money needed to uphold status during marriage ceremonies, in the hope that female infanticide would be eliminated in time.[62]

Agreements were increasingly signed in earnest with various Rajput landholders, seeking to limit the amount given as dowries and that spent on pomp and splendour. These codes tried to fix status hierarchies. For example, in November 1851, Charles Raikes collected the *raja* of Mainpuri with other important Chauhan headmen and chiefs in his camp at Sumaon. The Chauhans decided to regulate expenses according to four grades in descending order of social and economic hierarchy. In the first grade applicable to *raja*s and *taluqdar*s, the most powerful magnates, the dowry to be demanded on behalf of a son from the parents or guardians of a marriageable daughter was not to exceed 500 rupees: one-third to be paid at the period of the *lagan*, or engagement, one-third at the door of the girl's father when the marriage procession arrived, and the remainder in the shape of *kanyadana*. In the second grade, consisting of *zamindar*s, or smaller landholders, a ceiling of 250 rupees was placed on wedding expenditure. Those in the third grade, or families in 'easy circumstances', were not to spend more than 100 rupees in total on marriages. Finally, those in the fourth grade consisting of 'all other decent people' or *bhale manas*, were to expend only *one* rupee on the marriage and gifts to the bridegroom's family. The agreement implicitly recognized the fluidity of the marriage system and the continuous emergence of lineages claiming Rajput status into the social system.[63]

The agreement maintained that if the father of any marriageable girl chose of his own accord to give more dowry to the groom than was specified it was on his own responsibility, but 'if the father of any youth *demands* more than has been specified in the resolution we will remonstrate with him. If he persists we will put him out of the *biradari* or brotherhood, because he has from his own avarice brought dishonour to the father of the damsel'.[64]

To prevent 'needless expenditure' in crowded wedding processions or *barat*s, the Chauhans also undertook to invite a moderate number of persons to weddings depending on the social grade to which they belonged. Such agreements were by no means legally binding on the signees and depended for their success on good faith. Ironically, at Sumaon and elsewhere, lineage heads and others signed the resolutions in order of precedence and position. Far from undermining the role of status, all efforts at reform tended to confirm and reinforce the divisions between the various classes of landholders.

The concern with controlling the economic repercussions of status demands was voiced until 1870 and went hand in hand with appeals to give up female infanticide. In this period, some pamphlets were also written by 'concerned' members of the community, advocating a reduction of 'expensive' marriages by the Rajputs to forestall a decline in their strength and power. While debating the bill on female infanticide, some policy-makers even toyed with the idea of making sumptuary regulations a part of the Female Infanticide Act.[65] Indeed many Rajputs suggested to officials that 'If you will put a visible and active repression on our expenditure, so that it may be universally known among our community that the fear of the law alone prevented our displaying a proper dignity, then perhaps we may keep our good name and our money too.'[66] In the light of these suggestions, a school of opinion proposed that the state appoint marriage commissioners.[67] These men would examine all presents whether livestock, clothes, jewellery or cash, count the number of guests at weddings and punish infractions of sumptuary codes.[68]

But such recommendations were soon abandoned because it was difficult to convince those favouring repression of the suitability of reform of hierarchies based on rank. The effectiveness of earlier experiments had been purely local in character and, hence, not encouraging in the long term. It was difficult to keep tabs on lineages who participated in schemes for reform which were not legally enforceable in courts. Moreover, status itself was a complex and shifting category, almost impossible to regulate and fix conclusively. Indeed, attempts to do so seemed to have little impact on female infanticide. In part due to the influence exercised by theories of 'improvidence', it was assumed that female infanticide was primarily a response to the pressures of poverty by lineages unable to pay large dowries and that the regulation of such expenditure would lead to a decline in the practice. But this did not happen. Officials were unable to grasp that dowries were not the sole cause but a symptom of deeper contradictions within Rajput matrimonial strategies.

As they groped for a solution to the problem of female infanticide in this period, policy-makers concluded that if rules limiting marriage expenses were made legally binding, they would interfere with Rajput cultural sensibilities and customary practice. Given this situation, they argued that the coercive enforcement of sumptuary codes would have been impossible to enforce successfully without 'undue interference' with the 'liberty' of their colonial subjects. Paradoxically, such assertions were followed by the regulation and surveillance of Rajput households and punishment of those suspected of committing female infanticide. Interestingly, efforts to control and 'civilize' Rajput masculinities in the 'domestic space' after 1857 coincided with the promulgation of new laws, the streamlining of the coercive apparatus of the state and the marginalization of the 'dangerous' Rajput in the 'outside world'.

5. The 'Civilizing State': the Female Infanticide Act and the 'Domestic Space'

In the early nineteenth century, despite missionary pressure, the early British impetus, which tended towards reform, was characterized by a reluctance to hurt Rajput sentiment. The prevailing ignorance about the extent of the crime due to the lack of statistics had also constituted a major stumbling block in the path of punitive action.[69] As more data began to be collected on the Rajputs in the aftermath of the administrative reorganization of the 1840s, there were greater possibilities of disciplining these lineages. The timing of the Female Infanticide Act (Act VIII of 1870) was especially significant, given the prevailing climate. Missionary pressure on the colonial state about this issue had been steadily increasing. The Act also derived its inspiration after 1857 from the drive to discipline, regulate and reform 'dangerous' and 'turbulent' communities as diverse as 'criminal tribes' and vagrants, all of which crystallized as legislation in the 1870s.[70] Moreover, the apparent success of early experiments in repression, from the 1850s, in Agra, Mainpuri and Basti promoted the cause of this method of intervention. Using comparative statistics to prove their point, administrators in these areas asserted that the proportion of females had registered an increase after local censuses focused on male:female sex ratios and births and deaths of girls and boys among suspected localized lineages.[71] After Act VIII of 1870 was passed, to lay the groundwork for its proper functioning investigative teams systematically collected exhaustive statistics and qualitative evidence on marriages from the 1860s to 1912, when interest in female infanticide waned.[72] It was on the basis of statistics that it was decided whether to put households under surveillance or not. Therefore, it was vital that the figures amassed were as accurate as possible.

In certain ways, the localized and periodic census operations, conducted by the massive Judicial Infanticide Department, created for this purpose, constituted the most intensive databank collected on the domestic life of Rajput lineages. Censuses before this period had been inaccurate and depended for the most part on guesswork. Now special attention was paid to villages where the proportion of girls to the total minor population was less than 40 per cent. The figures covered the whole adult and non adult population in the villages concerned. Matters recorded in the registers with the help of village officials, such as the *chaukidar*s (or watchmen), included all manner of information, including the names of the head of the household, pregnancies, marriages and their cost, arrivals and departures of all women and children. Most important, the statistics noted information of the sex ratios of all female and male infants born since 1857, especially those under the age of one year.[73] Information regarding girls between the ages of one and twelve was also collected.

The result of the investigations showed that in selected areas the proportion of little girls in relation to the total minor population was often as low as 25 to 30 per cent, if not less. The death rate of girl children under one year was higher than among male children. Over the age of one, 50 per cent of girl children were killed through violence and neglect.[74] The death rates of girls between the ages of one and twelve was double that of boys among the general population.[75] If enough evidence was made available on the basis of the sex ratios, those found 'guilty' by the collective of the anti-infanticide squad and the courts could be imprisoned for life or transported. The very taking of a special census, it was hoped, would stigmatize the clans concerned and force them to abandon female infanticide.[76] The Act also assumed that once male:female sex ratios were regularized female infanticide would be eliminated.

Fast realizing that male:female sex ratios varied from locality to locality, census officials collected statements from each village in areas where female infanticide was supposedly rife.[77] Soon grasping the fact that it was unwise to adhere blindly to statistical data, officials also sought a wealth of qualitative evidence relating to marriage practices and female infanticide.[78] They argued that to understand the causes of infanticide and influence suspected lineages, administrators needed to possess a 'thorough acquaintance' with the history of the concerned village, 'the feuds and friendships, the relationships, legends and traditions'.[79] To this end, members of the anti-infanticide squads interacted with village officials, the headmen of settlements and village *panchayats* to publicize Act VIII of 1870. *Panchayats*, for example, were involved in all investigations, accusations and inquests.[80]

Rajput women played a very important role in the act of female infanticide. Very little, unfortunately, is known about the feelings of these women, except that they were '[. . .] as much parties to the deed, if not more, than their sterner accomplices'.[81] While, in most cases, fathers ordered infants to be put out of the way, most observers agreed that women of the family and midwives carried out the act. In many cases, women killed girl children without being told. This is not to suggest that women did not resist the Rajput paterfamilias. They often saved their daughters on the sly, especially if they gave birth in their parents' house. In other cases, women seem to have refused to be brow-beaten into killing their daughters. For the Act to make an impact, it would have been necessary for local officials to have direct access to Rajput women, who, clearly, were actively involved in the perpetuation of the practice. However, women were bypassed. Keeping in mind the 'delicate' nature of their task, the door-to-door census was conducted in a manner that would 'avoid any offensive interference' with women in Rajput families.[82] This meant relying on the men of the suspected settlements, police officials and other friendly persons for accurate data on women and children.[83] The end result was that the system of information-gathering on events occurring within the 'domestic space' was intensely flawed.

The sources through which information was collected included village accountants, watchmen and midwives. Tabs were kept on these eyes and ears of the colonial state. Midwives were the main sources of information on deliveries, birth and deaths of infants. *Chaukidars*, too, had great responsibilities. They were to keep an eye on pregnant women, especially in 'blood-red' villages, (in which the percentage of girls was less than 25 per cent, where surveillance was designed to be especially vigilant. After the statistics were collected, they were housed in local police stations and officers in charge were to follow up all reports sent in to them.[84]

Another method of collecting information was to note down the number of girl children, but this was not possible in any systematic way. Access to girl children, always a sensitive issue for officials, was regulated by male family members. During the early census operations, enumerators did not insist upon the production of girls, although large numbers were seen casually.[85] To solve the problems of unreliable information, counting was undertaken in front of the whole village and the account of each family head was verified by questions put to the boys and girls belonging to the settlement, neighbours and others.[86] After 1874, when it was made compulsory for the female children of the heads of households to be present at special inspections, their numbers were checked by asking each girl above five how many siblings she had, their names and those of their fathers.[87]

Viewing married girls and children nearing twelve was particularly difficult.[88] Many village officials, of their own accord, struck girls off their lists as soon as they were married, others when they departed for their husband's house, and yet others retained them on their lists until they were twelve. What confused matters was that, while most children were married between the ages of five and ten, they did not join their husbands until they were between ten and thirteen. Girls in Rajput households, therefore, were excluded or included in the census in a haphazard manner. Clearly, much depended on the information of village officials and heads of households.[89]

Heads of all households might have played a pivotal role in the crusade against female infanticide, for they were seen as bridging the gap between the outside and the inside world, by reporting all domestic events to the female infanticide squad. It is worth noting that it was not easy for the colonial state to define the position of the 'head of the household'. According to the census of 1853, the 'family' was defined as a loosely bonded kinship group, comprising those who lived together or who cooked their food at the same hearth.[90] By 1871, every married man who performed the marriage ceremony, called *gauna*, was held to be the head of his own family, and in so far as these rules were applicable to unmarried women and widows, the chief unmarried member residing in the house was held to be the head of the family.[91] Each man within the kinship group was asked how many sons and daughters he had, together with their ages.[92] When doing a head count of the members of Rajput households, officials included every woman related by birth or marriage to the head of the family 'ordinarily resident in his house and every concubine residing in his house or under the protection of any person residing in his house'.[93]

In 1874, the 'head of the household' was further defined as any person with a wife and children, as distinguished from the head of a 'joint family', which included a wider kinship network to avoid all confusion. Proclaimed families were not registered according to the *chula*, or hearth, for several families usually belonged to one house: when registered together it was difficult to learn anything as to their precise character. Now, the category of 'head of the household' was substituted for the old 'head of the family', so that the natural responsibility and interdependence of each family who lived under the same roof was not lost sight of, while at the same time the numbers and status of each were separately recorded.[94]

Ironically, the coercive machinery of the colonial state was dependent upon heads of households and families who had every reason to suppress information. Powerful lineages claiming high status usually controlled all information networks, given their influence with the police, watchmen and *panchayat*s. This was used to good effect to limit the recording and policing of events in the world of women, easily done given the position of men as spokespersons for their families. In this manner, the births and deaths of girl babies were concealed, when they were not misrepresented as boys in the infanticide registers which took note of both male and female birth and mortality rates. Figures relating to boys were neglected; inaccuracies in the registers made it easier to evade surveillance. Pregnant women and young girl children were removed from settlements, while the exact number of removals was imperfectly reported. In many cases, families paraded a neighbour's daughters as their own during inspections to put officials off the scent.[95] Not merely were the anti-infanticide squad unable to keep tabs on women and young girl children, but the continued accuracy of the census figures, on which the Act depended for its success, was threatened.

Additionally, *chaukidar*s, committed to powerful patrilineages, often only reported on Rajput landholders in villages divided by feuds. Likewise, lineages gave information about other villages if a feud had occurred and pretended ignorance otherwise. Problems were compounded because of the refusal of witnesses, usually women, to give evidence in cases dealing with female infanticide. The latter were either accomplices or browbeaten by men, who in most cases mediated between them and the representatives of the state. *Panchayat*s, dominated by high-status or wealthy brotherhoods suspected of female infanticide, also participated in acts of opposition. In many cases, before inquests took place, the bodies of children who had died in 'suspicious circumstances' were first shown to *biradari* councils.[96] The latter usually testified that death had occurred from natural causes. Inquests by civil surgeons, too, were forced to dismiss all but extremely suspicious cases on insufficient grounds.[97] Given this situation, most cases dealing with female infanticide were dismissed from the colonial criminal courts.

The debates surrounding Act VIII of 1870 had envisaged stringent punishments for the heads of households. Thus, the magistrate of Farrukhabad suggested in 1871,

> Let every Rajput be thoroughly convinced that he will go to jail for ten years for every infant girl he murders, with as much certainty as he would feel about being hanged if he were to kill her when grown up, and the crime will be stamped out very effectually; but so long as the Government show any hesitation in dealing rigorously with criminals, so long will the Rajpoot think he has a chance of impunity and will go on killing girls as before.[98]

Any concession to the 'immemorial custom' of the *thakur*s, it was argued, would be bound to entail failure.[99]

In the late nineteenth century, however, these ideas soon ran aground. Although the heads of households were declared personally responsible for the neglect and death of children unless they could prove that the neglect was 'unavoidable' or that the child had died from natural causes,[100] in most cases very few men were hauled over the coals. When those suspected of committing female infanticide were actually punished, the rules were more effective. But more watchmen and midwives were punished in an average year. In most cases, Rajput men were only imprisoned for short periods and almost none were transported. When female infanticide was committed by women in the absence of the husband and other male members of the family, allocating blame was even more difficult. The husband was often employed at a distance from his family and only visited his home at intervals; to attach culpability to him was often impossible, though baby girls were killed with his connivance if not at his command. In fact, the excuse was frequently made that given the absence of the male members of the family and as the women were in *parda* no information was available.[101] Far from gaining access to the domestic arena after the 1870s, the coercive machinery was denied information by Rajput *biradaris* in myriad ways.[102]

The apparent fall in female mortality statistics made officials assert that the practice was extinct by the end of the nineteenth century on the basis of a special census carried out between 1888 and 1889 in the north-western provinces. Subsequently, about nine-tenths of the originally proclaimed villages were released from the Act on the grounds that the proportion of girl children to the total minor population had risen to over 40 per cent. Nonetheless, many villages were 'reproclaimed' soon after being exempted from the rules, while in parts of the Agra and Meerut divisions there were numerous families still on the rolls when the Act was abolished in 1912, indicating that punitive control over the household was unable to contain female infanticide.[103] The Act, which merely scraped over the surface of the problem, had been unable to 'civilize' or bring about social change in a cultural world devaluing girl children.

6. Towards Some Conclusions

The evidence examined above indicates that 'civilizing' Rajput masculinities within the 'domestic space' was a complex and ambivalent process for the colonial state. From the beginning of the nineteenth century, official opinions had been divided on the course of action to be followed regarding female infanticide, a violent act involving the taking of life within the home. As early discussions considered the notion of policing Rajput families 'objectionable',[104] there was an emphasis on appeals to 'reason' and reform of those aspects of Rajput marriages influencing the practice. Encouragement of more equitable marriages between lineages and the regulation of status hierarchies reached its height in the 1850s and thereafter declined because of the problems involved in tampering with the cultural mores of marriage. Gradually these measures gave way to others involving the surveillance and disciplining of the Rajput household, culminating in the Female Infanticide Act of 1870. The latter was one of the most systematic and unequalled efforts by the colonial state to monitor and 'civilize' the Rajput family and household, in an era in which the power of these *biradaris* was increasingly circumscribed in public arenas.

It appears that the expansion of the state coercive and administrative machinery in the late nineteenth century did not put paid to the ambivalence of official attitudes when it came to intervening in the private world of the Rajputs. While the colonial state attempted to tighten surveillance over clans and lineages suspected of female infanticide after 1870, it also simultaneously sought to mitigate the effects of the same so as not to do any unnecessary violence to the 'feelings' of powerful Rajput lineages and to make sure that there was no undue interference in their innermost private lives. Most powerful lineages suspected of female infanticide inhabited, as we have seen, 'scores' of settlements in the same area and had a recent history of rebellion, which the state did not wish to incite, although, as we have seen, the British came down hard on the Rajputs after 1857 in many other respects. Clearly, the tensions evident in the early forays of criminal law into the household had an equally important role to play in the legislation pertaining to female infanticide in the later period. Indeed, the preceding discussion has highlighted how all efforts to reform marriages and implement Act VIII of 1870 largely operated within, and were limited by, the web of rank, gender and kinship hierarchies impelling female infanticide within Rajput families, who successfully resisted the attempt to monitor and control domestic events. For all their persistence, then, official efforts in the second phase of colonial involvement left the deeper contradictions in Rajput marriage practices largely untouched.

The British presumed that once male:female sex ratios were regulated and forcibly 'normalized', female infanticide would be eliminated once and for all. However, sex ratios fluctuated and changed over time as patrilineages shifted and changed their marriage strategies in constant dialogue with the demands of the social, ideological and ritual significance of marriage, in so far as alliances were the determinants of power and gendered identities among martial elites, struggling over and rearticulating their authority, status and identity in colonial India.

In fact, the article has tried to suggest that Rajput marriages responded to the systemic crisis and struggle over the reconstitution of Rajput gendered identities as lineage power, rank and cultural conceptions of honour were separated from the political culture and economy of which they had hitherto formed an integral part. Changes in the nature of state formation and conceptions of sovereignty and power in the public space probably stimulated changes in the nature of Rajput marriages among elite and upwardly mobile lineages, Moreover, it is likely that as individual choices interacted with economic variables, rates of female infanticide intensified among certain families, as the world of martial elites was gradually displaced in our period. The Rajput household was at the centre of these developments.

In the ultimate analysis then, colonial interventions in the household to eradicate female infanticide had little impact on the status of Rajput girl children, who were of little interest to the state once Act VIII of 1870 was abolished. The census figures of 1900 and after indicate that male:female sex ratios continued to remain disparate among certain sections of those claiming Rajput identity. Indeed, recent studies tend to confirm that female infanticide is very much in existence today among a number of social groups, indicating that an investigation into some of the multiple social processes influencing the practice remains a significant task.[105]

6

What Is Your 'Caste'? The Classification of Indian Society as Part of the British Civilizing Mission[1]

MELITTA WALIGORA
Humboldt-University, Berlin

The idea that there is a relationship between colonial rule and the interpretation of Indian society as a fragmented, hierarchical system of numerous 'castes' is not a new one. At the end of the last century, there was a fundamental shift of paradigm, in the course of which the role of so called objective sciences in the process of shaping the image of the Orient (the East or India) became a major topic of research.[2]

A set of new terms and ideas borrowed from post-modern western philosophies such as 'construction', 'invention' and 'discourse', has been used for a new understanding and critique of the colonial approach. An important aspect of the discussion related to the issue of whether, and in what ways, colonial rule might interfere in the course of Indian history. So, for instance, did colonial rule institute a fundamental break? If so, what kind of break? Or, was there continuity, whereby the British could only intervene to make some modifications rather than establish a wholly new direction?

This discussion is not only an academic one: it has important implications for present day India concerning the character of the nation-state and the shaping of modern Indian society. Modern India has to cope with the problems of a 'caste ridden society' and the 'evil of untouchability'. An important question, then, is whether caste is a sign of an eternal unchanging India, an invention of colonial rule, or something between these extreme positions. For instance, did the British use the idea of 'caste' as a tool to legitimate their rule? That is, did they base their legitimacy on the claim that they were civilizing this strange and anarchical form of social organization with the help of law and order?

I shall concentrate on two points in this article. First, I will provide a short survey of the main positions within the literature addressing the questions I have already set out. Second, I will examine reports of two influential colonial ethnographers writing on nineteenth-century Bengal. Here I will focus my remarks on their understanding and description of 'caste' and the 'caste system'.

1. Survey of the Literature

There is a certain deficit of historical research about the phenomenon of 'caste' in India – about the origin and various forms of castes or caste systems in different periods in Indian history, as well as in different geographical areas. There seems also to be a lack of comparative historical approaches, for instance between the structure and ideology of pre-modern societies in Europe and India (as opposed to the comparison of the so called *homo aequalis* of modern western societies and the so-called *Homo hierarchicus* of India – à la Dumont). Many works refer to 'caste' from the perspective of religion, anthropology, sociology or ethnology, but such literature is not within the realm of this paper: authors tend to be more concerned with the description and explanation of 'caste' and the 'caste system' (in terms of mobility, structure, dominance, power, pollution, and kinship, etc.), and take the existence of the phenomenon for granted. They tend to be less interested in its historical and variable aspects.

It is only recently that historians have 'discovered' the topic of caste for themselves. Apart from articles and books dealing with some aspects, we have now two works published in *The New Cambridge History of India* series. These works are: Thomas R Metcalf's *Ideologies of the Raj* (1994) and Susan Bayly's *Caste, Society and Politics in India from the Eighteenth Century to the Modern Age* (1999). 'Caste in the Perception of the Raj' is the title of an article by Shekar Bandyopadhyay in *Bengal Past and Present* (1985); the author has followed it with a huge amount of work about 'castes' in Bengal. There is also some research about the imagining of special social groups as castes by colonial administrators (Kayasthas, Devadasis, Rajbansis, , etc.). Nicholas B Dirks's *Castes of Mind* (2001) is the latest major publication on the subject. 'Imagining India' and the Indian 'caste system' has been the topic of much research, and has not been confined to the work of Ronald Inden.

Some general points have emerged from this literature. 'Caste' is a fact of Indian society, but not in an ahistorical, all-embracing, idealized, brahminical, fixed hierarchical manner. The way that 'caste' and the 'caste system' are conceptualized today is, to a certain extent, the result of colonial ideology and practice. S Bayly summarizes: 'These current manifestations of caste are now far more generalized across the subcontinent than was the case in former times. . . . caste as we now recognize it has been engendered, shaped and perpetuated by comparatively recently political and social developments'.[3]

The British investigation into 'caste' and the 'caste system' began with a scriptural approach, studying classical brahmanical texts with the result that an image of a static Hindu society dominated by *brahmins* took shape. After the revolt of 1857–9 the emphasis shifted increasingly to codifying empirical knowledge about social relations through ethnological research. The different social, ethnic and tribal groups across India were counted, classified and exhibited according to the contemporary European understanding of the principles of scientific inquiry. The last step in the history of colonial western imaginings of 'castes' was to discover an all-India caste system and to identify depressed groups – to protect them as scheduled castes from the evils of the system. In all these areas, the British could rely on Indian informants. The knowledge they gathered from them was coloured by the latter's interests, opinions and status. *Brahmins*, *pandits*, officials like village headmen and newly founded 'caste' associations used the opportunity to raise or lower the position of certain social groups or tribes. Thus, the image of India as dominated by a fixed hierarchical 'caste' society is a product of cooperation between colonial officials and certain Indian social groups.

Several interests underpin colonial ideology. There was, of course, the desire to legitimize the rule of a few British over millions of Indians, drawing on the notion of a 'civilizing mission'. The British set out to discover as much as possible about Indian society and culture in order to rule justly, according to the customs, beliefs and traditions of the people, to bring progress, to encourage social and religious reforms (for women and the depressed classes), and because collecting revenue (*diwani*) was traditionally connected with juris-diction, it required a certain understanding of traditional laws.

A second concern was to secure the empire in as many ways as possible. One such strategy was the idea of *divide et impera*. The religious division between Hindus and Muslims and the fragmentation of Hindu society into thousands of 'castes' was posited as an explanation for why India could never be united as one nation, or launch an effective challenge to foreign rule. James Kerr, the principal of Presidency College at Calcutta, revealed this motive in 1865: 'It may be doubted if the existence of caste is on the whole unfavourable to the permanence of our rule. It may even be considered favourable to it, provided we act with prudence and forbearance. Its spirit is opposed to national union'.[4] A third aim might have been to search for allies in this seem-ingly chaotic social reality, or to identify suitable objects to validate their desire to legitimize (such as 'castes' in need of protection) and secure their rule (with the help of some representatives of the old ruling classes). For these purposes it was crucial to know as much as possible about the different status groups. It was also important to prevent any particular group monopolizing political power – such as the new social elite, the Bengal *bhadralok.*

As far as I can see, these points would be accepted by most historians thinking about caste. What, then, are the points of dissent, and which areas have not been elaborated in any detail, requiring more research? I shall suggest some questions: What does the invention of 'caste' mean? Is it the invention of the institution of 'caste', or the introduction of new meaning, a change in the 'spirit' of 'caste'? Does a study of the ethnographical glossaries and descriptions of the nineteenth century reveal a hegemonic discourse on 'caste' as an essence? Did the British in their accounts of India's people, use only categories intended to denote India's difference? Were concepts familiar to European society such as 'class', nowhere to be found? Or is there any kind of 'analogical sociology', for instance the understanding of British society as hierarchical and, thus, Indian society, too?

Is it necessary to determine one main approach of the colonial administrators, officials or scientists, such as to 'caste' or race, or should we look for the different contexts in which one or another approach became important or suitable? How did the British understand the relationship between race and 'caste'? Did they simply equate high races with high 'castes' and low races with low 'castes'? Or are there different hierarchies of races and 'castes'? There is also disagreement about when the concept of 'caste' came to dominate colonial understanding of Indian society, and also whether this colonial conception is identical to the idea of an overall Indian caste system.

2. The Role of Colonial Ethnographers

This section will explore whether it is possible to find answers to the above-mentioned points of dissent in the works of two prominent amateur scientists, Buchanan Hamilton and Herbert Risley.

I confess that I am one of those scholars who pore over volumes of alphabetized empiricism collected by ethnological hordes as they prepare their research papers – the very scholars of whom Inden makes fun.[5] And I admit that it is stupid to read thousands of pages, with paragraphs from *Abadhut* to *Zatti,* in an attempt to discern valuable information about 'castes' in Bengal. But I did it, with my students, and later I found these consoling words of Susan Bayly:

> No one wishing to write credibly about caste today would accept the colonial ethnographic literature as a source of neutral, 'scientific' observation and fact. Nevertheless, there is much to be gained by

taking a fresh and far from dismissive look at the so-called colonial discourse of caste. This analytical literature from the nineteenth and early twentieth centuries is richer and more diverse than one might expect.[6]

S Bandyopadhyay mentioned four stages in the official ethnological studies of Bengal society, starting at the beginning of the nineteenth century with Buchanan Hamilton's general survey of Bihar and northern Bengal, *The History, Antiquities, Topography and Statistics of Eastern India* (1838) published in three volumes with nearly three thousand pages. In the mid-nineteenth century, especially after 1857, we have more specialized ethnographical descriptions, for instance the work of E Dalton, the *Descriptive Ethnology of Bengal* (1872). In the late nineteenth century, this tradition developed into statistical annals and ethnological glossaries with the new project of census reports. H Risley's *Tribes and Castes of Bengal* (1891) will provide examples of this.

In the first half of the twentieth century, this tradition was completed by listing some social groups and tribes as depressed classes or scheduled 'castes' for special protection. Bandyopadhyay's concern was to show that the colonial government had sponsored these studies for specific political purposes from the second half of the nineteenth century onwards. I will look for some shifts in the approaches of these colonial ethnographers concerning the structure of Bengal society and particularly with regard to the concept of 'caste' during the nineteenth century.

First, there is obviously a shift from Buchanan to Risley. The latter is interested only in counting and classifying people, while Buchanan's survey embraced land and people providing information about nature, climate, industries, trade and business, and included anything that might be useful in understanding a newly conquered territory. The practical advantage of Risley's alphabetical compendium is not so easy to determine. Perhaps the British administration was in need of 'a dictionary of caste and a proper classification of occupations', as Risley quoted the superintendent of census for Bengal, to determine to which main caste each clan or family belonged.[7]

Second, both authors give us a description of the different races, tribes, social groups, classes and 'castes' in the relevant regions in great detail, and attempt to provide accurate figures. Buchanan explains his method of estima-tion: '[. . .] from various statements and considerations I have conjectured the number of men required to cultivate each division, and then made an allowance for the other classes of society according to estimates given by the most intelligent persons that I could procure. In doing this, however, I experienced much difficulty.'[8]

Risley does not give estimates but precise figures – for example of 5,169 Haris in Hazaribagh – and there seems to be progress in counting. Both men try to give an order of precedence for all these different races, tribes, classes and castes. I will return later to this point.

Third, Buchanan always begins his descriptions of the people with the military classes. These are of different race, social background and religion, belonging to the military order either by birth or by their willingness to be employed as soldiers, or by their predatory inclination. He found that all the higher ranks who kept arms at home for their defence, and also the agricultural castes and tribes who carried arms as a defence against robbery or from family habit, considered themselves born soldiers. All in all there was a sizeable section of people who could defend their own interests and possessions. But it is difficult to find in Risley's alphabetical glossary any hint of military, warlike or martial inclinations among the people. According to the brahmanical concept of an ideal society – the theory of the four Varnas – the *kshatriya*s should be the military class, but in Bengal there seems to exist an anomaly. The brahmanical texts, written in the thirteenth and fourteenth centuries, spoke of two Varnas only, the *brahmin*s and the *shudra*s. The Rajputs of Bengal, who claim to be the modern representatives of the *kshatriya*s of the classical tradition, are in Risley's opinion only a pale reflection of the real one in the western and northern parts of India. I was not able to find any professional soldier in Risley's glossary. But even Buchanan had to admit the disuse of arms by the military groups and other inhabitants: 'The custom of going abroad armed, which was lately general among the numerous gentry even of the sacred order, has in a great measure been abandoned; and many of them have disposed their arms, thinking them unnecessary for their domestic security; for the police in that essential point has been much improved since the establishment of the Company's government'.[9] According to Buchanan, the reason for this growing disuse of arms, apart from improvements of police work, was the success of the civilizing mission through British discipline, arms and law. 'The power of European discipline having rendered all resistance to law hopeless. [. . .] since the people were under the protection of the well known, and highly respected bayonet'.[10] He also mentioned the effect of these changes on the military groups: 'The chiefs, and most natives of rank, of the military tribes at least, seem very much to regret this change in the administration of affairs; and it seems in fact to have been much less fatal to their interests, than the endless litigations, in which they are now involved, and in which they vent their mutual heart-burnings and ancient feuds'.[11] This 'was only the beginning of the long and disruptive process of demilitarization which had so much to do with the reshaping of caste in the later colonial period', as Susan Bayly reminds us.[12] At the end of the process we have these 'pale reflections' of the formerly strong and proud *kshatriya*s, Rajputs, military *brahmin*s as well as military peasants and tribes. Buchanan could still observe the habits of some Rajput groups in Bhagulpoor: 'They are considered as peculiarly warlike, and bold, and plough with their own hand; but, owing to their violence, their purity is not disputed.'[13]

The *brahmin*s, once at home in the sacred sphere as well as in worldly affairs of power, economy and war, were now elevated and at the same time reduced to the sacred order alone. Brahmanical ideals and values of spirituality, purity and sacred hierarchy, long existing in the texts and habits of some *pandit*s, *guru*s or *purohit*s (priests), became prominent for the lifestyle of Indians in general, whereas the ideals and values of 'the royal man of prowess' declined.[14]

Fourth, one of the most obvious shifts seems to be in the descriptions of *brahmin*s. The military *brahmin* is, for Buchanan, one of the important figures in the regions in which he travelled. Many *brahmin*s had not only taken over the profession of arms, but also agriculture and even held the plough.[15] For Buchanan their known ferocity secured for them high rank. In a case where a *brahmin* was a *raja* who reared one of his sons in the Muslim faith, he explained: 'If any one may be surprised at this, and ask, why a *Brahman* did not lose caste by such an action, I reply, that a man, who has Raja Mitrajit's power, cannot lose caste'.[16]

Buchanan observed at the beginning of the nineteenth century what Susan Bayly described later as 'synthesis between the three modes of existence'[17]: 'Whatever his birth may be, a Brahman may either become a Pandit, who adheres to the proper duties of his profession, or he may engage in worldly affairs, and take service'.[18]

But even if we look at the *brahmin*s as a sacred order only, we can find within this status group the same hierarchical order as we can see in society as a whole. So there were *brahmin*s degraded below the pure *shudra*s[19] and even impure *brahmin*s. Buchanan described the priestly *brahmin*s of Dinajpoor:

> A most essential difference arises in the rank of the five tribes [of Brahmans], from that of the persons whom they condescend to instruct in religious matters, or for whom they act as priests. The former or teachers, are called Gurus; the priests who read prayers on solemn occasions are called Purohits, and in general are less respected than the former. Those who perform these offices for Brahmans alone are highest in rank; but few of such respected persons belong to the five tribes. Next follow such as perform these offices for the two higher ranks of Sudras, the physicians and scribes. Then follow those who cut for the nine pure castes of tradesmen

(Novosakh), and for a few tribes that are admitted to be of the same rank.[20]

The Brahmans, who condescend to act as Gurus and Purohits for any of the impure tribes, are called Vorno, and occupy the next rank; but differences exist in their rank, according to the various degrees of their disciples' impurity.[21]

It must be observed, that many of the impure tribes of Hindus have Gurus of their own, totally independent of the Brahmans.[22]

It seems to be clear that, to Buchanan, the *brahmins* were far from being a uniform status group occupying an undisputed top position in a sacred hierarchical order. On the contrary, he saw them in all spheres of society and in all possible positions according to the circumstances in which they lived. Sometimes they were learned and sometimes as ignorant as their disciples, sometimes rich and sometimes poor, sometimes living from revenue or other allowances, sometimes begging for alms and sometimes working with their hands, sometimes leading a moral life and sometimes not. He assumed 'that in the early ages the term Brahman would not appear to have been hereditarily annexed to the sacred order'.[23] Instead,

[. . .] a farther examination of the genealogies contained in the writing reckoned sacred, has afforded very numerous instances indeed of the sons of Brahmans being Rajas, of the sons of Rajas being Brahmans, and of intermarriages between the two professions. This examination has also produced some instances of marriages or cohabitations with low, and even barbarous tribes, neither occasioning loss of caste in the parents or children; of the same person at different times having been of different professions; and even an instance of the son of king having been a merchant (Vaisya).[24]

Looking at the entry for *brahmins* in Risley's glossary, we find a lot of traditional and mythological stories about the origins of this group, suggesting they were the highest of the twice-born and originally the priests of the Aryan community. But there is no hint of *brahmins* entering secular professions such as the army, trade or agriculture before the establishment of modern professions through the colonial government. It was only now that they were 'engaged in various professions and following all respectable means of livelihood, except those involving personal or ceremonial pollution'.[25] So we acquire an idea of the *brahmins* as the priestly and always highly respected 'caste' at the top of a caste hierarchy based on some rules of purity and impurity, which are not explained in detail. We get the impression that there was primary a regional difference, as the rules of caste in Bihar were far less stringent and rigid than in Bengal. In Orissa, the *brahmin*s were Dravidians or acquired a considerable infusion of Dravidian blood. So, for Risley this regional difference is basically a difference of race and blood, essentially a racial hierarchy. But there is a problem with the *brahmin*s of Bengal because they lived in a 'country proverbial among Hindus for its ceremonial impurity',[26] where it was difficult for Risley to discover any pure Aryan origin of the group at all. We are informed that the *brahmin*s of Bengal also had, in certain parts, modified the strict rules of caste in accordance with the dictates of social necessity, which involved a serious a departure from orthodox usage. In the long entry of *brahmin*s we learn not so much about the facts of their actual life but more about mythology and marriage rites. Obviously, the brahmanical way of life and value system now dominated Indian society – or, rather, the image of Indian society, western as well as Indian. Anyway, a careful reading of this entry reveals some information contrary to the picture Risley perhaps wanted to give and also to later theories of 'caste'.

> Caste, then, at least in the rigid form in which we now know it, is an institution of comparatively late origin. [. . .] the whole body of Vedic literature as interpreted by modern scholars is adverse to the existence of a clear-defined hierarchy of endogamous castes. Even in the Epic era the system had not hardened into its later form. Brahmanhood is a matter of personal qualities and aptitudes rather than of descent.[27]

Marriages between members of different castes were possible, but this fact contradicts his fundamental view of caste as race and as mainly a matter of marriage, which must be endogamous. This, however, was not always the case and besides hypergamy and dowry the opposite could also take place when bride-prices were payed. For instance, Risley mentioned that 'a girl of a higher class marries a man of lower class'.[28]

The *brahmin*s seemed to be not a purely sacred order, but Risley acknowledged that 'the germ of the Brahman caste [is] in the bards, ministers, and family priests'.[29] The brahmanical ideals and values could be maintained only with the help of secular power. Hindu *raja*s give rules of caste and 'their observance depends upon the maintenance of his supervising authority otherwise breaking up completely'.[30]

In Risley's description of different customs, especially marriage rites, we can read a lot of *stri-archar* or women's customs, which tells us something about the non-brahmanical view of women's behaviour and position. We can also find an astonishing remark on some customs of *brahmin*s, which have the same general character as savages, 'like the Australian blacks and the African bushmen'.[31] Moreover, we get a hint at an interesting historical deal between local chiefs eager to attain the status of *kshatriya*-hood and *brahmins* eager to get a livelihood: a local chief, far removed from the great centres of brahmanical lore, promotes the spread of orthodox Hinduism throughout his realm with the help of grants of land to *brahmins*. In a countermove we have an 'invention of tradition' by the *brahmins*: 'The Brahman find for him [a local chief] a pedigree of respectable antiquity or provide him with a family legend, and in course of time he succeeds in getting himself recognized as a member of some branch of a great Rajput community.'[32]

In these scattered remarks we catch a glimpse of history, change and development within the Indian social structure at large and the *brahmins* in particular. And if we look at the further entries on many groups and tribes of Bengal living on the outskirts of or even outside Hinduism, the idea of an overall brahmanical 'caste society' begins to falter.

Fifth, we now turn to the use of the concepts of race, tribe, class and caste by the two authors. In general, there seems to be no precise definition of these concepts and it is difficult to see any difference in usage. For Buchanan the concept of race was not as prominent as it was for Risley; it explained no social hierarchy. He sometimes used the concept of class to denote a more general division of the people along the lines of gentry, mercantile tribes, artisans and those whose duty it was to plough and reap. Within each class there was a further stratification of social status, according to power, character and the importance of occupation or trade.

For Buchanan there seemed to be no recognizable principle for this order of precedence, neither religious purity nor racial differences. He notes that:

> On such a system no uniformity can be observed, and accordingly in different parts of India the rank of the same tribe or profession varies exceedingly [. . .][33]
>
> The extreme variance that is found in the arrangement of castes in different parts of India, appears to me a pretty convincing proof, that they did not proceed from any original general law.[34]

As far as Bengal was concerned, he found a historical explanation for the ranking of the *shudras* at least in pure and impure groups, stating that 'The list of the professions, which were admitted into the limits of pure Sudras by Bollalsen, seems to me curious; as it probably shows the degree of importance which each possessed in his time.'[35]

Buchanan's description of the people of east India provides us with a varied picture of a society divided into many status groups and occupations, such as aristocrats, merchants, various artisans, palanquin bearers, servants, slaves, beggars, dancing boys, prostitutes and so on, without a strict or clear relation between these occupations and without any recognizable hierarchical order. 'The Sudras here are usually divided into four classes, in the following order, the Satsudra, Sudra, Mahasudra and Antyaja; but the people, who assisted me in making up this account, could not with certainty refer each caste to its class; for they never had bestowed pains to enquire concerning the various claims of such low persons'.[36]

In Risley there is a clear shift in the use of the concept of race as the most important tool in the classification of 'castes'. 'Castes', according to his under-standing, were races that preserved their purity through strict rules on marriage and through a strong feeling of contempt for all those they con-sidered inferior to their own race. But there is no definite difference in the use of the concepts of caste, tribe and class. *Brahmins* are described variably as class, caste or tribe, but always as Aryans – in spite of the dubious origins of the Bengal *brahmins* – except for the poor *brahmins* in the jungle and hill regions of Orissa. Risley applied a theory of race that had nothing to do with research into Indian reality, or with the social and ethnic groups which com-posed Bengali society. However, he had a clear concept in mind about the hierarchy of races as well as of 'castes', which helped him solve some tricky problems in applying his theory to reality.

First, there seemed to be a 'caste system' specific to the Bengal society. As I mentioned above, we have only *brahmins* and *shudras*; as to the precedence of the *brahmins* there is no discussion. But what about the *shudras*, the majority of the people? Risley explained, and sometimes decided, the order of precedence with the help of his racial theory. Of the professional group of writers in Bengal, the *kayasthas*, he wrote that there was much controversy with regard to its origins. He decided the controversy as follows: 'Putting tra-dition aside, and looking on the one hand to the physical type of the Kayasths and on the other to their remarkable intellectual attainment, it would seem that their claim to Aryan descent cannot be wholly rejected'.[37] But because the *kayastha* group was composed of elements drawn from the two lower grades of Aryan society, he decided the controversy between *baidyas* and *kayasthas* regarding their relative rank in favour of the *baidyas* (doctors), who could claim pure Aryan descent.

There is some confusion among ethnographers in regard to the high-'caste' appearance and pride of the *chamars* (tanners) and much speculation about their origin. Risley noted: 'Looking at the evidence as a whole, and allowing that there are points in it which seem to favour the conjecture that the Chamars may be in part a degraded section of a higher race, I do not consider these indications clear enough to override the presumption that a caste engaged in a filthy and menial occupation must on the whole have been recruited from among the non-Aryan races'.[38]

Both examples clearly demonstrate that, for Risley, the racial hierarchy was the same as the social hierarchy, with race being the dominant factor. Race was the main criterion for social hierarchy, therefore the purity of the *brahmin* was much more purity of race than of religion. However, if the concept of race proved wrong, then the remaining concept of an explanation of caste and its ranking might be religion, only because both power and economy did not enter into Risley's considerations.

Sixth, a difficult but crucial point for understanding pre-modern social orders is the ranking of the numerous groups of merchants, peasants, artisans and tradesmen. That there was a troublesome fight over the top position, for power and wealth, in a given community between regal and sacred groups is a well-known fact of history elsewhere. As far as India is concerned, it is increasingly admitted, too: over the years, the balance of power alternated often between the competing status groups of *kshatriyas* and *brahmins*. But what exactly was the position of *vaishyas* and *shudras* in the ideal brahmanical society? Which of the numerous professions mentioned above belonged to which status group and what were the reasons for their classification? In fact, there are no traditional *vaishyas* in Bengal: nearly 90 per cent of the population are *shudras* or belong to tribal groups, which is no classification at all. However, this seems to be an indication that the vast majority of the Bengal people were not in the realm of the classical brahmanical traditions and laws, because these are for the twice born only, the *brahmins*, *kshatriyas* and *vaishyas*. This means Bengal is in general a non-brahmanical land with some pockets of brahmanical learning. Buchanan rightly observed: 'Here a great proportion of the Hindus, among whom are even many of the sacred order, and a large share of the military Brahmans, attach themselves to no sect, do not trouble themselves with daily prayers, and consult no sage to receive a secret form of worship. These are at perfect liberty to apply to any god that comes in their way.'[39] But when they were in need of powerful help they worshipped the ancient *gram-devatas* (village deities): 'The ghosts, in fact, and the others called Gram-devatas, seem to be the gods most usually applied to in all cases of danger by all ranks, and their favour is courted by blood sacrifices and other offerings'.[40]

The majority of the population could live without any concern for brahmanical ideals and values such as purity and pollution, which are the ordering principles of castes according to modern theories. But there was a rough division into pure and impure *shudras* and into pure and impure tribes, while the terms '*shudra*' and 'tribe' were not always clearly distinguished. Buchanan, for instance, spoke of two classes of impure *shudras*, one divided into eleven, the other into ten tribes.[41] Within each division of pure and impure groups there was a further ranking, the principle of which has to be given. As demonstrated above, for Risley this ranking could be explained by race hierarchy. But the different status between certain peasants or artisans did not always derive from racial differences.

Buchanan had no theory of race at hand and frankly admitted: 'The Barhai are carpenters, and few only do any other work. Why both in Bengal and here [Bihar] this profession, perhaps the most cleanly of all handicrafts, should be reckoned impure, it would be difficult to say.'[42] Here, the term 'purity' seems unclear. Did the purity of social groups or tribes depend on the cleanliness of their profession or perhaps on the honesty of the group or tribe? According to Buchanan, the *goyalas* (herdsmen) were regarded as almost impure because they were suspected of being prone to theft.[43] But more convincing to him was the importance of profession in social ranking, as mentioned above, and even more the fact of power. It has already been said that the position of *brahmins* or Rajputs is not disputed because of the power or ferocity of these groups. This was the case for other groups as well, as Buchanan demonstrated:

> The Kurmis here are a numerous tribe of cultivators, and some of them, as usual with the pure agricultural castes, carry arms. Such tribes appear to be aboriginal Hindu nations that were not of sufficient consequence to be admitted into the order of Kshatris; but too powerful to be thrust into the dregs of impurity.[44]
>
> In fact, every military tribe that has sufficient power seems to have been admitted by the Brahmans into the regal caste, as soon as it became subject to their authority, and betook itself to a pure life.[45]

For Buchanan, impure *shudras* were those from whom a pure *brahmin* would not accept water. To me, this seems a banal statement: pure and impure are explained in themselves. What needs clarification is why the *kumbhars* (potters) were reckoned pure in Bengal and impure in Bihar. The same goes for the *telis* (oil-pressers), *napits* (barbers) and *lohars* (blacksmiths) – pure in Bengal but impure in Bihar. Might a religious principle have been responsible for these regional differences in social ranking? Buchanan did not care much about religion: for him social ranking was basically a matter of power and impor-tance. The greatest part of his work is a description of the various trades and professions, their working life and habits in which caste ranking seems to have no special meaning. We are reminded of a European pre-modern market-place where each professional group had its limited function and purpose as well as special rights and privileges, which were jealously guarded.

The so-called *nabasakh* was mainly a group of artisans ranking as pure *shudras* below the *baidyas* and *kayasthas* of Bengal. The group included, among others, the potter, the blacksmith, the barber, the weaver, the confectioner, the sellers of betel nut and of garlands. Not all artisans and not all regional groups of certain artisans were pure *shudras*. For instance, the weavers of Bengal proper, the *tantis*, were pure whereas the weavers of east Bengal, the *jugis* were impure. The *lohar*, blacksmith, and the *kamar*, blacksmith too, did not occupy the same rank. The term *nabasakh* originally means a group of nine, but now this group included many more. This could be read as an indication of social mobility and of an ongoing struggle for social uprising. Buchanan did not use the term distinctively, but Risley did. For all these artisans he mentioned a magical or religious function in special, mostly non-brahmanical rituals.

> Some Kamars, again, are employed to slaughter the animal offered in sacrifice to Sakti.[46]
>
> The village potter occasionally holds chakaran land, on the condition that he supplies the vessel required at all festivals observed by the zamindar or the village community.[47]
>
> Mali, a caste employed in making garlands and providing flowers for the service of Hindu temples.[48]
>
> In the houses of the rich the barbership is often a hereditary post, as is that of the purohit, dhoba, and dai [. . .] his presence is required at all domestic occurrences. [. . .] for some castes he performs the function of a priest.[49]

Furthermore, some had healing abilities that might have derived from their considerable knowledge of nature: 'One of the chief occupations of this caste [*mali*] is inoculating for small-pox and treating individuals attacked by any eruptive fever.'[50] The *teli* and *madhunapit* (confectioner), too, provided necessary items for magical rituals or religious festivals. Thus, these artisans seemed to be priests of an old belief-system with great importance to and the general acceptance of the community that could not be suppressed or replaced by the *brahmins*. This may be the reason why they were placed among the pure *shudras*. But there were other social groups and tribes who performed similar priestly functions for the community and ranked among the impure *shudras* or tribes – for example, the *chamars* and *dhobas*. Both were considered unclean groups and ranked at the bottom of the Hindu social system. Surprisingly, both were involved in religious and domestic festivities of importance, like marriage and childbirth: '[. . .] a household becomes unclean if a Chamar woman has not attended at the birth of any child belonging to it'[51]; '[. . .] and after the bride has been daubed with turmeric the Dhoba must touch her to signify that she is purified'.[52]

This is what Risley tells us about the *dom*s, another 'degraded' group:

> A curious custom followed by all castes throughout Bengal is associated with the Dom, and may perhaps be a survival from times when that caste were the recognized priests of the elemental deities worshipped by the non-Aryan races. Whenever an eclipse of the sun or moon occurs, every Hindu householder places at his door a few copper coins, which, though now claimed by the Acharji Brahman, were until recently regarded as the exclusive perquisite of the Dom.[53]

What do these facts tell us? That an ancient social ranking existed in pre-modern societies according to principles independent of the then dominant social or religious ideals. Generally, artisans were seen as creators of things, as transformers of matter, substance or elements, and that special ability gave them a particular meaning in a community. The Sanskrit term *kamar* means smith, creator and sacrificial priest, and this priestly function did not necessarily imply a low function, as Icke-Schwalbe suggests.[54] The very old artisan professions, like smith, potter and weaver, belonged to a culture that was, in Bengal, pre-brahmanical and remained non-brahmanical, but they still occupied an important position and were proud professional groups. Therefore, there was a ranking according to traditional magical-religious principles that were not rooted in brahmanical values of purity and pollution, which did not rule out the possibility of a later reinterpretation according to those values. At no time in the history of Bengal was the *brahmin* the only sacred person. Risley found that most of these artisans worshipped Vishvakarman, the great architect of the universe known since Vedic times. But we cannot be sure that this had been a long tradition among them, since in Bengal Vedic knowledge was not well disseminated. These groups of artisans were not generally castes in the sense of birth. For some, the following description given by Risley is valid:

> [. . .] and that the name Kamar, so far from indicating a common origin, is merely the functional designation of an extremely hetero-geneous group. In other words, the profession of metal-worker in its various branches has been adopted from time to time by Aryans, non-Aryans, and people of mixed race; but the fact of their following the same occupation, though it has led to their being called by a common name, has not welded them into a uniform group, and the component elements of the caste still remain entirely distinct.

The 'caste', in fact, is a caste only in the loose popular sense of the word.[55]

[. . .] and for the present at any rate all that can be said is that it is probably a functional group evolved under the pressure of social requirements from whatever elements happened to be at hand in any particular locality. The tendency, no doubt, would be to relegate the ceremonially objectionable work of washerman to the non-Aryan races; and in Orissa, it has been pointed out in the article on Dhoba, some evidences has survived to show that this has actually taken place. But it would be hopeless to trace the various elements which may have been combined in a large functional caste.[56]

At times the now low or even impure social groups or tribes were the 'governing tribe' or the chiefs of a certain region with their own culture and religion. Through ousting, adoption or change they acquired a new position, looking for a niche for survival without the destruction of their own culture and religion. And there were also groups living entirely outside the mainstream culture and ruling power, whether this culture be Muslim, Hindu, Buddhist or of any other kind. According to brahmanical values these groups could only be impure, unless they adopted, either by pressure or by their own concern, some of these values. But it is evident from the different entries in Risley's glossary that many groups and tribes had no idea of pure brahmanical ideals or had only recently adopted some, such as dowry, child marriages, prohibition of divorce and remarriage of widows, dietary regulations and contact. Risley often mentions bride-price, divorce and widow-remarriages, festivals of unknown goddesses and gods where meat and spirits were consumed, with priests belonging to the low stratum of society and sometimes, and with *brahmins*, degrading themselves by taking part in these events.

For a better understanding of such a pre-modern social order it seems to be useful to compare it with similar social organizations in Europe. Sometimes Buchanan and Risley also applied this method, though not intentionally. The German scholar Werner Danckert wrote about the professional groups in German society who were sometimes, up to the nineteenth century, classified as 'dishonourable people'. Among them he mentioned, the executioner, court usher, grave-digger, knacker, shepherd, herdsman, miller, linen weaver, potter, barber, tanner, travelling entertainer and prostitute.[57] It is not easy to tell why these very different professional groups were regarded as 'dishonourable' people, like the low and outcast people of India. Their lives featured particular characteristics: they were not allowed to live in the village or town, they had to wear particular dress and colours; they could marry only people of their own group and practise no commensality with others; they were untouchable so nobody would sit with them in public, and they were assigned their own areas; nobody would carry them to a graveyard; they had their own rights and courts – all in all, they had to live on the fringes of society. This was not because they are 'dishonourable' in a legal or moral sense or because they were born not free. Their professions were not generally of a filthy, useless or despised kind, some were even awe-inspiring. On the contrary, all of them were important, inalienable parts of the society. So why are they regarded as 'dishonourable'?

To Danckert, these groups of people bore the traces of ancient pagan taboo, either of death or concerning the magical-sacral character of artisan creativity. Even Mircea Eliade spoke of the demiurgic experiences of the ancient potter who transformed the earthly substance, like the ancient Indian artisans who saw themselves as earthly representatives of the celestial Vishvakarman.[58] Magical power was sometimes associated with sexual power. The magic of eroticism and sexuality was celebrated by some of these groups in orgiastic cults, openly or secretly. Some professions were associated with special knowledge of body, mind and soul: they had healing wisdom and were supposed therefore to have contact with spirits, demons, goddesses or gods. Other professions were typical female and showed something of the feminine power of creation. Finally, some professions were linked with ancient cults of nature, like trees, mountains and rivers, or with special cults of earth-mothers. In one way or another all these different factors could determine a special ranking of certain social groups.

The result of Danckert's research into the so-called 'dishonourable' people within the social structure of pre-modern Germany was that such people existed all over the world, not accidentally but always where different cultures, religions and cults encountered, overlapped and clashed. The 'dishonourable' or 'impure' people were followers of ancient and now displaced religions in which the powers of nature were worshipped. They were closer to these mysterious powers and therefore their ostracism was mixed with fear of the magical prestige peculiar to them. The now disreputable people were once holy men and women.

To illustrate the point made by Danckert we can compare the social position of weavers in Germany and Bengal. The profession of linen weaver was 'dishonourable' in medieval Germany; up to the eighteenth century its practitioners had to fight against others' contempt. The reasons Danckert mentioned were that, first, the weaving of linen was primarily women's work and thus connected to special female custom and sometimes to alliances of women to celebrate the magical and erotic power inherent in the flax plant as well as in women's creativity. Second, weavers were followers of the ancient

Germanic goddess Nehalennia of whom they were the special cult servants, which gave them a respected position. Perhaps they were involved in some rituals of death, and in following this tradition they had to built the gallows for which they were then held in contempt and later called despisingly 'gallows birds'. Third, during the Christian Middle Ages, weavers were often regarded as heretics; their weaving rooms, mostly basements, were considered a refuge for heretics. They resisted Christian influences, held to their old faith and celebrated pagan festivals of a sometimes orgiastic nature, meant also as a subversion and protest against the ruling power and culture.

As described above, the *jugis*, a weaver group of eastern Bengal, held a despised position, unlike the *tantis*, weavers of Bengal proper. Risley found no intelligible reason for 'the existence of a very strong prejudice against the caste'. He could only quote the opinion of some Hindus: it was because they buried their dead; or because they used a kind of starch that was not considered pure.[59] His own theory of race also failed and 'therefore, the problem must be abandoned as insoluble'.[60]

In a text about proletarian cults and rituals of Bengal, N N Bhattacharya mentioned the *jugis* as a name for the lay followers of a special cult known as *natha*. They were also called *natha* yogis and their main occupation was, until very recently, to weave coarse cloth. They form a distinct *jugi* caste, but *jugi* was a term of contempt.[61] Obviously, this is the same group as the one Risley focused on. But now we can see why this social group is generally looked down upon by *brahmins*: they are followers of a non-brahmanical cult and have no *brahmins* who minister to them. Whether they were beyond the brahmanical influence or they resisted such influence has to be yet researched.

The *jugis* were followers of a different religious ideal and practice which, in pre-modern times, was not a simple matter of faith or conscience but also of social behaviour and practice. Perhaps they had their own customs of marriage, rules of contact and diet, festivals and rituals. Perhaps they were a respected social group. And perhaps they had no idea of any brahmanical ideals and values. As soon as these ideals and values became dominant, their social status changed for the worse. Hence, a comparison of pre-modern societies in different regions of the world might lead to the conclusion that there was not very much 'strangeness' in the social organization of pre-modern as well as pre-colonial India as there has been supposed to be to this day. For example Buchanan wondered about the strange social customs and habits:

> All proper Hindus regret that in these days no caste adheres to
> its proper duties, but that many persons, in order to procure a

subsistence, betake themselves to professions, for which there were not originally intended. In fact the compelling a person, for ever, to adhere to the profession of his father is so contrary to justice and human nature, that it has been found impracticable.[62]

Apart from the fact that Buchanan here observed the rules of 'caste' on the wane at the beginning of the nineteenth century (!) he seems to forget that, at the same time, similar social developments and processes were, at least partly, at work within British society based on more or less the same principles. To be convinced of their own advanced civilization and the civilizing mission in India the colonizers and their officials had to forget their own past.

Perhaps the concept of caste and its associations, like unchanged eternity or religious purity, prevent an unbiased and deeper insight into the different, complex and changing structures. It may be worthwhile to attempt to write the social history of India without using the concept of caste, but taking the same concepts applied in describing the social history of European or other regions of the world.

3. Conclusion

The works of Buchanan and Risley are only two in a series of ethnographical works, gazetteers, census reports and other annals. During the nineteenth century there were other approaches to explain the existence of 'castes', for instance by Nesfield, Ibbetson and K M Banerjee, who view caste as a form of social stratification, adapted to the needs of industry and labour. But in the nineteenth century the concept of 'caste' is not a rigid one and only a concept used by others to understand Indian society. Neither Buchanan nor Risley stressed the image of an all-Indian 'caste system' and S Bayly points out that 'The ethnologically-informed 'experts' drew on empirical investigations of south India, the Punjab, Bengal and other key regions of the subcontinent which they recognized as being ethnographically distinctive, and quite unlike all the alleged 'colonial' stereotypes of fixed pan-Indian 'caste' hierarchies and all-pervading Brahmanical value system.'[63]

But what could be the practical advantage of such a lavish and expensive enquiry as Risley's *Ethnographical Glossary* in which, as we have seen, even his own theory of race is not confirmed? Risley claimed:

In Bengal at any rate, next to nothing is known about the system upon which the whole native population regulates its domestic and social relations. If legislation, or even executive action, is ever to touch these relations in a satisfactory manner, an ethnographic

survey of Bengal, and a record of customs of the people, is as necessary an incident of good administration as a cadastral survey of the
land and a record of the rights of its tenants.[64]

There is not as much to be found in his glossary about the rules of 'caste'
and the 'caste system' as Risley seemed to believe. But he did mention an
important fact: caste became the point of reference for most legal proceedings
under colonial administration from the beginning of the nineteenth century,
concerning matters of marriage, divorce, inheritance and adoption. These
issues were simply associated with the British notions of an 'imagined' Hindu
community and closely connected to the British ideas of private property and
taxation with regard to the fiscal income and the financial administration of
British India. A good illustration for this was the process of changing the social
group of *devadasis* (temple dancers) into a special and new 'caste' in the course
of one hundred years through legal proceedings.[65]

The colonial administration did not invent 'caste' or rather the fact of social
ranking and hierarchy, but it changed the 'spirit'[66] of this social structure in
accordance with its self-imposed civilizing mission. The understanding of
how this civilizing mission could be carried out changed in the course of the
century. At the beginning, there was of course the lure of the exotic, the
experience of the different, which the first merchants and officials liked to see
after a long and dangerous voyage in anticipation of adventure and wealth.
Perhaps they felt themselves freed from the bonds of their own society,
becoming the masters of a new conquered territory and population. They
wondered about the strange social customs and habits, and sometimes, as
Buchanan was surprised to hear, that the native informants had no exact
knowledge about the social ranking of the lower groups. But the same held for
their own society, as David Cannadine wrote:

> But for all its popular resonance, this hierarchical picture of
> eighteenth-century England was, like any vernacular model of
> society, both idealized and partial. It sought to fix *everybody* – literally
> everybody – with an assigned place in a single, linear, interconnected
> chain or ladder. This was an appealing image: but it was indeed an
> image. Inevitably, it became less accurate or detailed the lower down
> the social scale it was applied, where minute gradations of status were
> often less apparent, and where it was more difficult to distinguish one
> person from another.[67]

Here the method of 'analogical sociology'[68] or of simple comparison may
be helpful in understanding the subsequent development. At the end of the
century 'the British were developing in India 'a more closely defined honorific

hierarchy' and increasingly projecting an image of their South Asian empire as a 'feudal order'.[69] This is exactly what Risley tried to do with his *Ethnographical Glossary* and later, for the census reports, with his question on the definite 'caste' rank of each person. Apart from the construction of 'otherness' there was also the 'construction of affinities',[70] for which the concept of 'caste' was a suitable means. At first 'instrumentalized by the courts, caste penetrated deep into South Asian society' and the British then looked upon 'caste' 'as the analogue to their own carefully ranked domestic status hierarchy.'[71]

Uma Chakravarti mentioned a second point, besides the 'fact that status distinctions were deeply ingrained in British society': the 'heavy reliance on the conservative indigenous literati, the Brahman *pandits*'.[72]

There is a well known shift to an understanding 'in which caste was constructed as the religious basis of Indian society, a cultural form that became viewed as a specifically Indian form of civil society'.[73] For both Buchanan and Risley there seemed to be no distinctive relation between 'caste' and Hinduism. Even for Risley most of the population of Bengal lived on the edges or fringes of Hinduism or was only recently in contact with this religion and its social customs. The concept of untouchability played no prominent role for either author, the *brahmins* did not really take the top position. But in 1936 we have a list of 'caste' classified as scheduled 'castes' of Bengal, comprising more than seventy groups. Most of these groups are in fact tribes or tribes that recently had been reduced or compelled to take up a special occupation to find a niche in the by-now dominant Hindu society. They had no idea of forming a 'caste' some forty years before, but for the census reports they had to know their 'caste' as well as their ritual precedence. They had to play the game – 'many only after they found they could not get the game cancelled'.[74]

In the last decades of the nineteenth century and thereafter, the notion arose of a special and close connection between 'caste' and Hinduism as an eternal and all-Indian phenomenon in the works of Indologists like Senart, Bouglé and others who took for granted the brahmanical view. In the last decades of the twentieth century some authors began to undermine this position with works about dominant 'castes', the role of kings and renouncers of the world (hermits) in Indian history. However, these attempts too, 'remained bounded by a surprisingly circumscribed notion of Hinduism'.[75] The colonial ethnographers seem to provide some of the material to support this, but careful reading of their works reveals some interesting points, contradicting the twentieth century theories of 'caste', 'caste system' and Hinduism. Descriptions of Bengal tell us that even in the nineteenth century most of the people knew nothing about infant marriages, the dowry system, the ban on widow remarriages or special brahmanical purity rules concerning food or contact – the theme of so many books on 'caste'.

One way to a deeper understanding of the social history of Bengal and India seems to be to include in the research the vast masses of artisans, tradesmen and peasant groups according to their own understanding and their real social position beyond the brahmanical ideas of them.[76] Therefore, a close and fresh look at our own society in former times is a good helpmate.

PART III:

BODY AND MIND

7

Sporting and the 'Civilizing Mission' in India

PAUL DIMEO
University of Stirling

1. Introduction

In his discussion of the relationship of football and the British 'civilizing mission' in India, J A Mangan wrote that the sport:

> was considered by the colonizers to carry with it a series of moral lessons, regarding hard work and perseverance, about team loyalty and obedience to authority and indeed involving concepts of correct physical development and 'manliness'. As such it was used as a key weapon in the battle to win over local populations and indeed to begin transforming them from their 'uncivilized' and 'heathen' state to one where they might be considered 'civilized' and 'Christian'.[1]

Of course, football was only one of a host of sports and games that were considered to fulfil this social function by the colonial elite. By engaging with sport the 'native' body was to be altered, manipulated, disciplined and reshaped in the name of 'civilization'. In this regard, sports were a means of moral training that supposedly brought together and promoted a bundle of ideologies including masculinity, religion, Victorian middle-class manners and western moral ideals. However, the discourses that linked sport to civilization often implied benevolence: they were founded upon assumptions of the inherent and natural inferiority of Indian bodies and Indian cultures.

The basic paradigm of the 'civilizing mission' and sports went as follows: the British propose that Indians are in need of civilization, that they are physically and morally inferior, and that if they are to become dutiful members of the empire they ought to learn the lessons of sport and benefit from its healthiness, manliness and sense of order. The first aim of this chapter is to give some examples to illustrate this paradigm.

Clearly Indians did not become dutiful members of empire even though they played and still play British sports: the project was not entirely successful. The rise of nationalism in the nineteenth century and the eventual success in gaining independence show that, in political terms at least, Indians had escaped the web of colonialism even while the British were still fantasizing about their 'civilizing mission'. The discourses that emerged about sport's function might well have assumed that the British had a higher level of authority and the Indians a higher level of obsequiousness than was actually the case. The second aim of this chapter is to try to understand why and how the civilizing mission failed.

Finally, I want to address the legacy of colonialism, the time after the supposed end of the civilizing mission: the era of Indian nationhood. British sports continued to be played despite their association with the Raj, the ideologies of moral training remained intact, as did the perceived link between sports and political confidence, but so did anxieties over Indian bodies and their capabilities.

2. Sport and the 'civilizing mission'

Allen Guttmann warns historians not to take such 'jingoist' imperialists as the Reverend J E C Welldon 'at their word'.[2] Headmaster of Harrow School from 1881 to 1895, Welldon was inclined towards grand proclamations of the role sport had played in imperial success. To take one example of many,

> Englishmen are not superior to Frenchmen or Germans in brains or industry or the science and apparatus of war; but they are superior in the health and temper which games impart. I do not think I am wrong in saying that the sport, the pluck, the resolution, and the strength which have within the last few weeks animated the little garrison at Chitral and the gallant force that has accomplished their deliverance are effectively acquired in the cricket-fields and football fields of the great public schools, and in the games of which they are the habitual scenes. The pluck, the energy, the perseverance, the good temper, the self-control, the discipline, the co-operation, the *esprit de corps*, which merit success in cricket or football, are the very qualities which win the day in peace or war. The men who possessed these qualities, not sedate and faultless citizens, but men of will, spirit, and chivalry, are the men who conquered at Plassey and Quebec. In the history of the British Empire it is written that England has owed her sovereignty to her sports.[3]

It is no accident that a man in his position should indulge in such language, after all English public schools had been the crucible in which the link between character formation and games had been forged in the early- to mid-nineteenth century. They had produced the men who had gone on to govern at home and abroad, to lead armies, expeditions and scientific projects, to build houses, parliaments, churches, roads, railways and canals, to trade, to put systems of government into place, to teach and to proselytize. While there was, in J A Mangan's term, a 'reductionism' about Welldon's view that the sporting instinct had 'created in large part the British Empire',[4] he certainly was not alone in this view. Guttmann's aversion to accepting the ideologies expressed by Welldon and other voices from the 'imperial chorus'[5] concern the nature of hegemony in colonial power, and he points to deeper social and political processes that underpinned imperialism:

> Political relationships between the rulers and the ruled cannot be characterized as simply the result of absolute domination by the former and absolute submission by the latter. The most stable form of rule is one in which the strong (who are never all-powerful) have their way only after the weak (who are never completely powerless) have their say.[6]

We shall return to such concerns later in this chapter. But perhaps Guttmann's point overlooks the efficacy in such reductionism and simplification for rallying energy towards a cause and for building up the self-confidence of those who set off for unknown territories unsure of what they would find and how to deal with the locals. It was a 'powerful movement', with a 'seductive image of Empire' that 'was projected unremittingly' throughout the British Empire.[7] It was also extremely functional, offering a reference point for those in difficult places and circumstances: by definition almost it had to be reductionist and simplistic – there was nothing to be gained from agonizing over the complex nature of power in society.

For example, when Theodore Leighton Pennell arrived in Bannu in the North-west Frontier in March 1912 he sought to established a medical missionary for the 'benefit' of the local communities, and to 'civilize' them through moral and religious teachings. He was 'a strong believer in the value of athletics in the development of character, the boys of Bannu School . . . obtained a great reputation for athletic prowess'.[8] In common with many of his compatriots in similar situations, Pennell found a flat piece of land and fashioned a pitch for football and cricket. He then took the boys out to teach them sport, with all its moral baggage. This was an opportunity for contact and the development of friendships, but linked physical activities and body disciplines to the purposes of imperialism and civilization:

this is a side of missionary work which is not often known, but it is a worthy of note that some of the most successful educationalists in connexion [sic] with missions have recognized the fact that, especially among the Indian races, the proper use of athletics has served to strengthen moral backbone, which is often conspicuously weak, and has been an important auxiliary to Christian teaching.[9]

Such examples abound in the history of British imperialism, and in colonial India, as the work of J A Mangan testifies.[10] The assumption was that the body of the colonized was inferior. In India, discourses on the inherent and 'natural' 'effeminacy' of the Indian male were very common in the nineteenth century, and these were especially focused on the Bengalis, who were also viewed as disloyal, potential usurpers of British rule.[11] In Calcutta the connection was made clear between sport, education and character formation through various measures.

For instance, as lieutenant governor of Bengal in the 1870s, Sir George Campbell emphasized the importance of sport in the curriculum of the College of Engineering in Calcutta:

I spared nothing to make that college complete, but the Bengalis seemed infinitely to prefer literature, law, and politics to anything that required some physical as well as mental exertion. At the same time I am bound to say that when I introduced gymnastics, riding, and physical training in the colleges, they heartily accepted these things, and seemed quite ready to emulate Europeans in that respect.[12]

Campbell was clear in his intentions. Sport was as valuable for education, for the making of able men, as scholarly activity. His implication that Bengalis embraced these benefits indicates his belief in both the superiority of British ways and his strategy for Bengali improvement. Another Briton resident in Calcutta in 1885 made similar claims:

Many educated Natives, in Bengal specially, have for years past felt the reproach which attaches to their want of courage and corporeal activity and have earnestly set themselves to remedy these defects: hence on all sides we find efforts to follow the example of Europeans among native students. Football and cricket are becoming popular, and gymnasia introduced.[13]

Another example of similar colonial attitudes towards sports comes from a later lieutenant governor of Bengal, Sir Charles Elliot, who in 1892 proposed measures to assist in the improvement of the Bengali 'race' through physical culture:

> For some years past the physical training of schoolboys had been encouraged by the formation of clubs for athletics, by drill and gymnastic exercises, in Collegiate competitions and annual sports. In 1891–92 it was particularly noticed on every hand that there was a great increase of the zeal with which the national English games, especially football, were played. On tour Sir C Elliot constantly watched the performances of the boys with great interest . . . He looked forward to great improvement in the physique of Bengalis in the course of one or two generations from this source . . . Sir C Elliot expressed a hope that some generous and public-spirited individuals would come forward and provide means for the physical improvement of their race: and with the aid of Government and private subscriptions Marcus Square in the centre of the town was cleared and made available for recreation.[14]

Such opinions were supported by the viceroy, Lord Curzon, in his 1902 appeal to the students of the University of Calcutta: 'Above all, do not think that speech is ever a substitute for action.'[15] The Anglo-Indian Presidency College and the British-run Indian Civil Service both imposed standards of physical fitness as entry requirements in the late-nineteenth and early-twentieth centuries. Evidently the assumption was that Indians preferred inertia and serenity over activity and thus when joining important social institutions had to prove their all-round capabilities through physical testing. It was implied that a man who could not prove his corporeal worth could not have his intellectual, administrative, academic or moral worth taken for granted. In this sense, the public-school games ethic became institutionalized, the belief that the Indian body was inherently inferior and required remedial treatment was still present. Arjun Appadurai has referred to this as a 'project of reform [that] involved cleaning up the sleazy, flabby, frail, feminine obsequious bodies of natives into clean, virile, muscular, moral, and loyal bodies that could be moved into the subjectivities proper to colonialism'.[16]

To return to Guttmann's objections, there is a risk that historical analysis stops here, and simply views the ethic of sport's role in the civilizing mission as important, powerful and influential. There was a 'project of reform' that is worthy of much detailed consideration but the outcome was not as predicted: Indians were not 'moved into the subjectivities proper to colonialism'. To illustrate this, and to try to explain why not, I shall use the example of football in colonial Bengal.

3. 'Rice-eating, Malaria-ridden, Bare-footed Bengalis . . .'

The first set of football rules was drawn up in Cambridge in 1848 by ex-pupils of a number of English public schools, including Eton, Harrow, Rugby and Winchester who had played their own localized form of the game.[17] These humble beginnings soon ushered in the creation of the Football Association in England in 1863. It was a middle class, amateur sport at this stage (professionalism in Britain was not legalized until 1888), played by former public-school boys who established the first clubs after graduating from university. Prior to 1863, schools and universities had their own distinctive rules, so various versions of the game existed. The purpose of the new rules was for wider competition to occur based on consensus, but within this process those who preferred kicking the ball made their departure from those who were inclined towards picking the ball up and running with it.

The game spread quickly around the world through the routes of trade and imperialism. According to today's hierarchy of world football, it is perhaps surprising that football was played in India as early as anywhere else, and that it was organized just as quickly. The first match in Calcutta is supposed to have taken place in 1854 between the Calcutta Club of Civilians and the Gentlemen of Barrackpore.[18] These would have been two British sides, the first made up of bureaucrats, missionaries, teachers and traders, the second of officers stationed in the army base at Barrackpore. In 1868 there was a match between the Etonians and the Rest, which the former won 3–0 and included a goal from Lord Vansittart. These games were played on the Calcutta Maidan, and represented one specific form of sport: that which the British played among themselves, for their own amusement, and from which Indians were distinctly prohibited. Men under the command of such middle-class sporting entrepreneurs were also seen to benefit from the moral worth of games. Presenting the Durand Cup, played in Simla, to the King's Own Scottish Borderers in October 1892, Lord Roberts said that 'the same qualities, discipline and combination, were equally necessary in good soldiers and football players'.[19]

The first competitions were created for the benefit of the large garrison of soldiers stationed in the country, and for the enjoyment of British civilian sportsmen: the Durand Cup in 1888, the Trades Cup in 1889, the Rovers Cup in 1891, and the Indian FA Shield in 1893. As noted above, Indians were not invited to participate in these competitions, and indeed a formal rule prohibiting their involvement was established, known as the 'black law' or 'colour ban'. This appears to contradict the sport as civilizing-mission ethic as there was no attempt to 'improve' Indian bodies. However this ethic was still in place in the more obviously pedagogical settings of the Anglo-Indian colleges. Indians began to play the game as early as the 1870s when, so the story goes, one young boy called Nagendraprasad Sarbadhikari accidentally discovered it:

> One morning in 1879, ten-year-old Nagendraprasad Sarbadhikari of Hare School was accompanying his mother on her morning trip to bathe in the Ganga. As their carriage crossed the Maidan, they saw some English soldiers kicking a round object about. The curious boy got down to watch. The ball landed near his feet. He picked it up: it was surprisingly light. A soldier called out, 'Kick it to me.' Nagendraprasad complied.[20]

Whether or not the events actually happened this way it seems the boy had developed a passion. Along with some friends, he purchased a football (though their first ball was a rugby ball) and they were helped by Professor G A Stack of Presidency College and his colleague, J H Gilliland, to learn the rules and techniques of football. Clearly, therefore, the sport was associated with the Anglo-Indian education system. The colleges soon produced teams, beginning with Presidency College in 1879,[20] followed by Sibpur Engineering College, Bishops College, Medical College, St Xavier's College and La Martinière College. Graduates from these colleges were instrumental in the development of the game among those excluded by the British: 'It was these students, after they left college, who founded the first of today's open clubs in the 1880s and 1890s to enable them to go on playing the game. Chief among their number were Nagendraprasad himself, Kalicharan Mitra, Manmatha Ganguli and Haridas Sheel.'[21]

However, there remained a distinctiveness between the sport-as-pedagogy and sport-as-competition approaches. In Anglo-Indian colleges, the Indian players were not allowed to represent the college in team sports; only the British pupils could do so. Once they graduated, the young Indian men found they were rejected from the existing British football teams so had to establish their own clubs. Even once this was accomplished, they were excluded from the competitions, the ban was gradually reduced so that one Indian team could enter each competition, but remained in place until 1925. It is here that we see the beginnings of the problems inherent in the civilizing mission. The sport-as-pedagogy attitude was based on the notion of Indian physical inferiority, if not effeminacy, and as long as that was intact sports could simply be promoted as a means of improvement towards the (unachievable) goal of

British imperial civilization. Indians were allowed to play football as long as they realized their own inferiority and played the sport only to raise their levels of manliness and morality. Such an approach was sustainable in an education setting, and thus muscular missionaries like Pennell and his like-minded ilk could go on playing football and other sports with pupils because the power ratio was stable. As soon as young men were in 'open society' and looking to play the sport, they represented a threat, not just to the hierarchy of club success but to the very idea of the civilizing mission – they had a chance to prove their equality, their manliness, their ability to discipline themselves towards a common goal, their sacrifice for the greater good. But, of course, they were not doing it for the British Empire, they were doing it for them-selves. This was the threat and the source of much anxiety: the imperialist confidence was being undone, the reductionist and simplistic ideology was shown up as flawed and incapable of dealing with the power of colonial subjects.

The first and perhaps most famous occasion of Indian success was in July 1911 when Mohun Bagan became the first Indian team to win the Indian FA Shield. The context for this game highlights the shifting balance of colonial politics. In response to growing Bengali demands for political power Lord Curzon announced a Machiavellian strategy designed to undermine the determination of Indian nationalism. The presidency of Bengal was partitioned in 1905 and separated the largely Hindu west Bengal from the more Muslim districts of east Bengal and Assam. However, the Bengalis were far too suspicious of colonial intentions to accept the lame excuse offered that the pressures inherent in administering such a large region were too great. The partition was perceived as a policy of divide and rule, and across Bengal opposition was expressed through violent attacks on prominent officials, through mass protest, through media criticism and ultimately through the *swadeshi* campaigns.

Indian football clubs came to symbolize the wider protests and, indeed, attracted as much nationalist attention as the overtly political rallies held by political agitators. The Shovazabar Club was the first to beat a British team in 1892, and Mohun Bagan won the Trades Cup (the first 'open' competition) three years in a row, from 1906 to 1908. The club first entered the IFA Shield in 1909, the only Indian club to be allowed such a privilege, only to lose to the Gordon Highlanders in the first round. Representatives of other Indian clubs who watched the match 'smirked in envious glee' at this defeat claiming that Mohun Bagan's place in the IFA Shield was like 'a dwarf . . . reaching for the moon'.[22] Mohun Bagan's run to the final of the Shield just two years later had a rather more unifying impact on local communities.

After seeing off St Xavier's (3–0), Rangers (1–0), the Rifle Brigade (1–0), and the 1st Middlesex Regiment (1–1, 3–0), the Indian club was recognized as having a serious chance of winning the tournament. Described as having 'simply walked over the military defence' in the semi-final, the scene was set for an exciting final against the 'crack' East Yorkshire Regiment.[23] The final had brought a crowd estimated at between sixty and a hundred thousand[24] who had travelled to the ground from as far afield as Patna, Assam and the outlying regions of Bengal. They came by specially arranged trains, steamers and trams to see the game. A temporary telephone was installed at the nearby Calcutta FC (a British club) ground to transmit reports throughout Bengal. Mookerjee sums up the feelings of the day thus: 'Soccer fever had engulfed Calcutta. The IFA Shield final pushed everything else to the background. Hope, once kindled, whatever the odds against be, refuses to be snuffed.'[25] In an exciting match, the Indians came from a goal down to score twice in the last five minutes, 'wild excitement burst out amongst the Indian spectators . . . When the referee blew the long whistle, shirts, hats, handkerchieves, sticks and umbrellas started flying in the air.'[26]

This was a moment to be savoured, a victory that unified Bengalis of different religions against their colonial rulers.[27] One local newspaper, the *Basumati*, emphasized the cohesive nature of this sporting success by claiming that Mohun Bagan had 'held up before the Bengali an ideal of striving in concert. The Bengali must ever remain indebted to those who have, in the dark days of disunion, found the secret of union.'[28]

However, some other responses point to the complexities of the relationship between sport, colonialism and nationalism in Bengal at this time. During the month prior to the final another local newspaper, the *Nayak*, had restated the sense of inferiority and dependency felt by British-educated Bengalis:

> We English-educated Babus are like dolls dancing on the palms of Englishmen. The education which makes Babus of us, and gives us our food whether we are in service or in some profession, is established by the English. Our . . . political efforts and aspirations are all kinds of gifts of the English people . . . English education and the superficial imitation of English habits and manners have made us perfectly worthless, a miserable mixture of Anglicism and *swadeshism*.[29]

In the wake of Mohun Bagan's success, the newspaper's tone altered dramatically:

> Indians can hold their own against Englishmen in every walk of art

and science, in every learned profession, and in the higher grades of the public service . . . It only remained for Indians to beat Englishmen in that peculiarly English sport, the football. It fills every Indian with joy to learn of the victory of the Mohun Bagan team over English soldiers in the Challenge Shield competition. It fills every Indian with joy and pride to know that rice-eating, malaria-ridden, barefooted[30] Bengalis have got the better of beef-eating, Herculean, booted John Bull in the peculiarly English sport. Never before was there witnessed such universal demonstration of joy, men and women alike sharing it and demonstrating it by showering of flowers, embraces, shouts, whoops, screams and even dances.[31]

This exemplifies the type of reaction that gave a sporting moment deeper meaning in Bengali society. It is a victory that continues to be celebrated as a profound moment in the independence struggle:

Barefoot Bengali *babus* had battled with their British 'bosses' on equal terms, and had got the better of them. A subject race, humiliated by hauteur, ridiculed by so-called racial superiors and derided by a discriminating ruling class, had, at last, delivered a fitting reply. In a moment, Mohun Bagan Athletic Club was transformed from a Calcutta football team into a symbol of nationalist aspirations. The Bengalis had found their voice on a football field, and the voice echoed and re-echoed all over India.[32]

This success was the platform for Indian control over football. Confidence grew such that in 1925 the East Bengal club led the way in demanding full participation in the competitions. By the early 1930s Indians had equal representation in the sport's governing bodies. By 1934, when the Muslim club from Calcutta, Mohammedan Sporting, became the first Indian team to win the Calcutta League, holding it for five consecutive years, and then the second team to win the Shield in 1936 (becoming the second team to win the double), it was clear that football was now Indian: 'The sun had set on the British soccer empire.'[33] This was not the expected outcome: Indians did not show the 'subjectivities proper to colonialism', in the sense that sport, the tool of colonialism, had been used against its founders. As Michael Anthony Budd has commented on physical culture in British India: 'Like other implements of colonial rule such as military equipment and transportation technology, it was not considered inherently or uniquely Western, but as separate from its user, and capable of serving any master. The cultivation of physical strength thus offered the attractive promise that the British might be beaten at their own game.'[34]

Perhaps in simple terms this was because sports did have a successful social function: they did promote pluck, energy, perseverance, good temper, self-control, discipline, cooperation and *esprit de corps*. However, the accusations of inferiority and ideas for improvement (in those terms at least) gave Indians a focus for resistance, something obvious to resist against, and a method of resisting that the British understood. The incompleteness of power meant that Indians had the agency to choose their political objectives and to reinterpret colonial sports for their own ends. As James Mills notes in conclusion to his study of nineteenth century asylums in India, the 'colonizers did not dominate but desired to dominate and the instances where their projects were disrupted and contested emphasize that their domination remained fantasy rather than "fact" and remained well short of "hegemonic"'.[35] If we can conclude anything about the 'imperial chorus' led by enthusiasts like Welldon and supported by others such as Curzon, Campbell and Pennell, it is that it was based on the fantasy of colonial domination, a fantasy rudely and soundly challenged by such nonconformists as the Mohun Bagan club.

4. Legacies of the Sporting Civilizing Mission

Just as the analysis of sport cannot end with the triumph of the civilizing mission, nor can it end with the triumph of resistance. The relationship between sporting triumph, nationalism and colonialism centred on a paradox of which Indians were fully conscious even at the time of the game. The 1911 victory was a moment of nationalist resistance when the ideological under-pinnings of colonialism, the belief in innate British superiority and in Indian physical frailty were dramatically and publicly undone. Yet in celebrating the undoing of these stereotypes there was acceptance of the British moral system introduced through the Anglo-Indian colleges in which only success in sport and the demonstration of physical prowess could signal strength and self-reliance. In other words, the culture of colonialism was neither rejected nor overhauled: Indians still wanted to gain the respect of the British, and still respected British means of classifying moral and physical worth.

While the objectives of sport, in terms of culture and politics, had shifted from 'civilization' to nationalism, the belief in the games ethic remained. For example, when helping to celebrate Mohammedan Sporting's 1934 success, the mayor of Calcutta, Nalini Ranjan Sarkar, expressed views that would not have been out of place in nineteenth century English public-school settings:

> Sports and games are fine things. They develop some of the best qualities in the individual . . . apart from the qualities of concentra-tion and single-mindedness of efforts, in a game like football, where

team work in an important thing, a successful team must develop and *esprit de corps* to a high pitch of excellence. The Duke of Wellington after seeing a cricket match observed that Waterloo was won on that field. The same indeed may be said of football, only with greater emphasis. And those who succeed in cultivating the qualities which collectively go by the name of sportsmanship are, I think, well-equipped generally for almost every walk of life.[36]

Once football had become Indian, it came to express Indian sentiments and social relationships. This was another legacy of colonial sporting missionaries: leaving games like cricket and football for future generations. It means that, despite their colonialist intentions, many of these individuals continue to be revered in contemporary India. By the 1940s, cricket and football were playing out communal conflicts between Hindus and Muslims. In Bombay the annual cricket Quadrangular pitched Hindu teams and European, Parsi and, importantly, Muslim teams. As the communal situation worsened, cricket was not exempt from political pressures, prompting Gandhi to assert his own views of what sportsmanship meant:

> I have never understood the reason for having Hindu, Parsi, Muslim and other communal elevens. I should have thought that such unsportsmanlike divisions would be considered taboos in sporting language and sporting manners. Can we not have some field of life which would be untouched by the communal spirit? I should like therefore those who have anything to do with this movement to stop the match, to broaden the issue and take the opportunity of considering it from the highest standpoint and decide once and for all upon banishing communal taints from the sporting world and also deciding upon banishing these sports from our life whilst the 'blood bath' is going on.[37]

Evidently, the ethics implanted by colonial sportsmen were still influential in Indian life, as was the idea that sport was a means of character building. In 1944, Mohammed Ali Jinnah created a football tournament for Muslim youth, and his opening speech was described by a local journalist as follows:

> Mr Jinnah said that he had great pleasure to associate himself with the organizers of the tournament. He remarked that the tournament had its objective and must teach at any rate what was most essential physically, mentally and morally. The Qaid-e-Azam [Jinnah] asked the Muslims to learn discipline and create a habit of team-work. It

was on such occasions, he remarked, that young men would learn the lessons of discipline and team-work, which would help them in every walk of life.[38]

In the post-independence era, sports have continued to play a large part in Indian culture. Despite the fact of football's popularity, and the successes found in the Olympics in the 1950s, the sport faded just as the national cricket team began to win important overseas matches. These legacies of empire became the source of national pride, in the case of cricket, and national disappointment in the case of football.

However, the sense of Indian effeminacy has continued to lurk in the background, and it seems that modern, global India is struggling to cast off that particular stereotype. Ashis Nandy locates ideas of masculinity as central to understanding the passion found in India for that most colonial sport, cricket. The British assumed team sports to be 'manly' in the traditional Victorian sense, and cricket was no exception. However, Nandy revises this point, suggesting that the British unknowingly had 'a rather classical Brahminic concept'[39] of masculinity in mind:

> The good cricketer was masculine because he had control over his impulsive self and symbolized the superiority of form over substance, mind over body, culture over nature. Above all, cricket was masculine because it symbolized serenity in the face of the vagaries of fate and it incorporated the feminine within the game's version of the masculine.[40]

Despite the fact that this was written by an Indian at the end of the twentieth century, it echoes colonial stereotyping of the Indian as effeminate. Some Indian writers have even offered the theory that football has failed in India because it demands too much of a masculine character, whereas cricket is more cerebral. In a June 2002 newspaper article entitled 'Football Isn't In Our Blood', Chandan Mitra argued that, 'Since 1911, Indian football has rarely enjoyed a moment of glory. I believe football is too swift a game for our temperament or stamina. Indians excel when some intellectual input is required in an activity. Also, we are a ritualistic people and take time to warm up to something. That's why cricket fits into our psyche with such ease.'[41] That such a view is common can be illustrated by the Indian FA's argument that there is a 'genetic imperfection of Indian footballers concerning physical fitness'.[42]

The legacies of the civilizing mission are quite complex, but clearly the notion of inferiority and the availability of sports as a means of improvement has had lasting effects upon Indian society and sensibilities of the body. Of course, there are further complexities. Some nationalists in the nineteenth century rejected British physical cultures out of hand; some players were far more collaborative in their dealings with imperial sportsmen. The civilizing mission was not unified, and perhaps the contradictions between sport-as-pedagogy and sport-as-competition lie at the heart of explaining its failings. Like colonial society itself, Indians were encouraged to develop the means of self-reliance and strength, but found themselves restricted in their opportunities to flex their new-found muscles. Just like the bureaucrat held back in the British-dominated Indian Civil Service, or the magistrate confronting colonial prejudice, the football players of India simply wanted to play their game as best they could. When they were not allowed to do so within the existing power hierarchy they revolutionized from within, they changed the hierarchy. The rules, ethics and stereotypes remained. It is also worth noting that the British-inspired amateurish set-up of the Indian football authority has held back the game's progress. Sports, therefore, have been both a metaphor for, and an embodiment of, colonialism itself.

8

'More Important to Civilize Than Subdue'? Lunatic Asylums, Psychiatric Practice and Fantasies of 'the Civilizing Mission' in British India 1858–1900[1]

JAMES H MILLS
University of Strathclyde, Glasgow

> Everything that consitutes a remedial institution on the modern European footing has to be introduced and exercised for the first time. The classification of the insane, the regulation of their common social life under the cottage system, their recreation, their education, their cure, their employment in various descriptions of appropriate labour, all the processes of benevolence and science have to be studied and carried into effect.[2]

When looking at psychiatric regimes in colonial India in the nineteenth century, it is possible to dismiss much of what the British superintendents of the asylums organized in the name of treatment. Many of the interventions were necessities, as those admitted were often vagrants suffering from the rigours of a life of exposure and malnourishment, and the doctors themselves insisted that 'A very large proportion, however, of our patients require no other treatment than good feeding.'[3] Other approaches were simply efforts to impose institutional control on unruly or violent bodies, one superintendent for example declaring darkly in his report of a particularly disruptive inmate that 'it is of the essence of his treatment that he be brought, by resolution of purpose and persistent effort, within the discipline of the place if he do not at once conform to it'.[4] The persistent effort spent on patients could extend to subjecting them to cold water douches, shackling them in irons, tying them into restrictive bags, locking them in solitary confinement and sedating them with a range of drugs.[5]

The fact that so many of the interventions can be described as either necessities or simply as brute acts of control has led observers to conclude that the asylums fulfilled no other function than to revive and to incarcerate those deemed 'mad' in Indian society by the British. The work of Waltraud Ernst, although largely limited to the asylums in British India for European patients, comes to this conclusion. She characterizes these institutions by the middle of the nineteenth century as simply 'refuges or temporary receptacles'.[6] Shridhar Sharma states in a similar vein that in the period 1858 to 1906 'the asylums then constructed were simply places of detention', and points to 'the apathy and indifference on the part of the authorities at that time to the needs of mental patients'.[7]

To settle for such conclusions is to miss, or to misunderstand, many of the key operations of the asylums in this period. As the quote at the start of this chapter suggests, superintendents had more complex aspirations for their hospitals. This chapter will demonstrate that when the records of the asylums are analysed, and when the treatment regimes in those institutions are more carefully investigated, a picture emerges that implicates psychiatry in the broader projects of the colonial 'civilizing mission'. Moreover, the specifics of the mission appear to be to create a self-regulating, obedient and, most importantly, productive, colonial Indian subject.

1. Reading Reform in Psychiatric Records

Heengun Khan. Mania. Mussulman. Cultivator. 26. 30th April 1860. Sept, 60. An inhabitant of Moosalbagh. Is said to have been subject to fits of insanity for 12 or 14 years. During intervals has been able to work. Is of a very restless disposition + much taken up with his personal appearance, decorating himself with whatever in the shape of supposed finery falls in his way, not despising as a necklace an old leather Doomchee. Is occasionally violent + continually begs for release. General health and appetite good.

Oct.24. For the last month has been generally quiet + well conducted, working hard in the garden + greatly pleased at receiving commendation or trifling rewards. Today became unaccountably violent, had to be confined – blister applied.

March 1861. For the last three months, there has been a steady improvement in this patient. He takes his meals well + has done bheestie's work very steadily. For the last month his demeanour has so much improved that on his relatives coming to enquire after him I discharged him on the 24th March, cured.[8]

The case note for Heegun Khan reads as a heartening story of improvement as it seems to tell the tale of a man recovered sufficiently from being fitful and violent to be released to his relatives. Yet when reconsidered it becomes possible to question the type of information recorded on the case note to indicate illness and recovery. Illness is violence and self-absorption. Recovery is obsequious obedience and the desire or ability to work steadily. Pick out the adverbs of illness and recovery: 'unaccountably' as opposed to 'steadily'. The issue here is whether the privileging of the ability to work and to be governable (because obedient and steady) over the need to be expressive of fluctuating inner desires and feelings (which are unpredictable and sometimes violent) is necessarily a natural correspondence to the state of mentally healthy over mentally ill. In other words, rather than simply telling the tale of Heegun Khan, it may be that the case note is relating something different altogether.

The work of feminist scholars is important in this regard as they are keen to point out that asylum regimes in Europe were not concerned with restoring a natural state of mental health when it came to female patients. Yannick Ripa insists that 'the asylum sought to force women back into the mould from which they had just tried to escape',[9] and that in France in the nineteenth-century 'to be cured meant to be submissive. The image of healthy womanhood put forward by the special doctors, those products and exponents of bourgeois society, was of silent women who showed moderation in everything, and who sublimated all their own desires in their role as mothers'.[10]

Elaine Showalter finds this similar to the experience in England in the same period as 'the ladylike values of silence, decorum, taste, service, piety and gratitude . . . were made an integral part of the program of moral management of women in Victorian asylums'.[11] It was not just in the lunatic asylum that 'recovery' was linked to imposed norms. Joanne Monk examines the Magdalen asylum in Australia which was opened and operated for the reform of 'fallen women' in the 1880s. In it she finds that the regime centred around the performance of laundry duty. This was specially chosen as it was seen as an essentially female task and that, therefore, the correct performance was supposedly signified 'reform' or, rather, return to the desired norm of domesticated femininity.[12] Reform or recovery in women was very much judged in these institutions not by reference to some natural standard of health and illness but by reference to a standard of behaviour derived from the social and cultural discourses of patriarchy.

With the idea that recovery from mental illness could be a judgement on an individual's compliance with certain prescribed ways of behaving, the case note of Heengun Khan included above appears to be rather more than a simple record of the patient's behaviour. Neither was such a case note untypical:

> Ramcharum. Acute mania. 25. Hindoo. Beggar. 11th May 1870. Certified by the Magistrate violent.
>
> 11th May. Sent in by the Depy. Commr. of Oonao. It appears to be a case of mania from excessive bhung smoking.
>
> April 4th 1874. For several months Ramchuram has seemed to be in his right mind. He has been useful in helping to cook for the other patients. To be brought before the Committee.
>
> 7th April 1874. Cured, made over to his friends by order of his friends.[13]

This example, from towards the end of the period for which case notes are available, records the direct relationship between the perceived ability to work and the assessment of recovery. The only information included to justify the statement that he seemed to be in his right mind is that he was eventually able to labour and was useful. Indeed, the doctor who composed the following example from the second volume of case notes seems to acknowledge that when he had to comment on whether somebody was mentally 'well' he was actually looking for certain characteristics.

> Wazeeran. f. Mania. 28. Mussul. Beggar. 15 Jany/ 63
>
> 1863. Sent in by City Magistrate found knocking about the City, is very violent and wild in manner and expression.
>
> 1868 May 5. This woman has been five years in the asylum. She seems to be well, at least she works + does what she is told + gives intelligent answers to questions + is quiet, eats and drinks + sleeps properly.
>
> She says she is a prostitute + will return to the exercise of her profession if released.
>
> May 11. Discharged.[14]

He appears to imply, in qualifying his assessment that she was 'well', that the criteria for being judged 'well' were not an esoteric series of standards regarding proper perceptual relations between the inner life and the outer world but merely the requirements he lists. In other words he is saying that he would not put his name to a judgement that she was absolutely 'well' but rather that she was considered 'well' as she appeared to be socially functional. The criteria for 'socially functional' in this example were productivity, obedience, intelligibility and self-regulation.

This version of what is 'well', 'civilized' or 'normal' has quite specific origins in nineteenth-century western culture. Of particular importance here is the concept of political economy that developed throughout the nineteenth century in British thought. The economy was imagined as a set of self-regulating mechanisms that naturally operated in a benign way to produce a wealthy and well-organized society.[15] It followed, therefore, that each individual was expected to earn an independent living by participating in a responsible manner in the labour market. As such, those who chose not to engage in the economic system, typically those who refused to sell their labour, were condemned as flouting the natural and beneficent mechanisms. Such people became the focus of asylums and workhouses, as a belief in the essential morality of man had encouraged the idea that these individuals were in need of reform as within them existed the essence of a moral (industrious, compliant, deferential, modest)[16] person who simply needed encouragement.

The characteristics connected with the virtues of work and the ethics of political economy were certainly valued by the British in India by the 1860s, 'the qualities that were most prized were efficiency, practicality, conformity',[17] as they sought to create 'a socio-economic environment that rewarded hard work, thriftiness, and a desire to get ahead'.[18] This enthusiasm for political economy and the corresponding enthusiasm for the virtues connected with work explains why the ability to labour in an Indian lunatic patient would have featured so heavily in the case note compiled by a British officer. The culture of political economy dictated that industry was good, indeed natural, so the evidence of a previously disruptive individual beginning to work would have been represented in this cultural frame of reference as a 'recovery' of the natural state. Quite simply the case note was a site where the nineteenth-century European conviction that the desire to labour was natural and normal was constructed.

The connection between being 'well' and being able to work recorded on the case notes has origins more specific to the colonial context, however. In the colonies difference was constructed between the Europeans and the locals in terms of their productive capabilities. Racial discourses on the 'lazy native'[19] created images of Africans and Asians in the colonizers' minds as unwilling and inefficient labourers. In South Asia this supposed inability of the local population to work effectively was itself construed by the colonizers as a reflection on Indian society and the Indian psyche. Ronald Inden points out that the Indian mentality was constructed as the opposite of the western one on the basis of discourses on work and productivity: 'That mind is . . . governed by passions rather than will, pulled this way and that by its desire for glory, opulence, and erotic pleasures or total renunciation rather than prompted to build a prosperous economy and orderly state. The Indian mind is, in other words, devoid of 'higher', that is, scientific rationality'.[20]

Crucially, it was exactly this construction that encouraged the British belief that their role in India was necessary: 'It is the supposed absence of these assumed attributes of Western culture – such as advanced rationality, individual discipline, and social habits of obedience – that mark the Indians as childlike creatures in need of paternal oversight.'[21] The British role, moreover, was often conceived as more than simply 'oversight'. The growing influence of Utilitarian ideas in the British administration of India by the 1860s[22] meant that many colonizers believed that 'it was more important to civilize than subdue'[23] and that many intended that 'the whole of Indian society would undergo a vast transformation, setting it on a rapid advance up the scale of civilization'.[24] In other words the British colonials fantasized that they would transform India from 'uncivilized', that is irrational and unproductive, to 'civilized', that is ordered, industrious and regular.

Mukhsoodally Khan was thus transformed according to his case note.

Mukhsoodally Khan. m. amentia. mussul. service. 25. 8 June/61

1861 June. This man was formerly a sowar in the 1st Regt. of Hodson's Horse at Fyzabad. Was admitted into Regl. Hospital on 14th May on account of mania – cause not apparent – He was noisy, violent + abusive, bit himself on legs + arms + required the constant supervision of attendance to prevent his escaping or injuring himself. Subsequently he had an attack of fever. On admission he was very excitable and talked very unnaturally and abusively.

1862 Feb. In several months past this man has improved in health, has been quiet + well conducted and assisted in the garden. He is stout + strong. All bodily functions properly performed + he does not appear to be labouring under any delusion. His relatives are anxious to remove him + I therefore, as he has been well for months, discharge him cured.[25]

Violent, irrational ('talked very unnaturally') and unpredictable ('cause not apparent') he was represented as becoming regulated ('all bodily functions properly performed'), respectful and a good worker. His case note is a narrative of the fantasy of the colonial project where the Indian Other of the rational and productive European is 'civilized', that is made rational and productive, through contact with the benign British institution. A glance back at Heengun Khan's case note suggests that Muksoodally Khan's case note is not unique in reading as such a narrative. Heengun Khan was constructed as narcissistic and violent at the outset of the case note but by the end was represented as self-disciplined and productive after a spell under British control.

The notes, therefore, can read as a narrative of the assumptions and the processes involved in the 'civilizing mission'.[26] The information on work, violence and self-discipline acts to create a world where the Indian is unproductive and irrational and where contact with the British institution has the beneficial effect of rendering him 'well', that is ordered, productive and rational. The complexities of these cases are not important to the superintendents. The possible and particular causes of the inmates' behaviour, interestingly Mukhsoodally Khan, for example, was a sepoy serving in an elite colonial military unit, are ignored.[27] 'Cause not apparent' is entered on his note to erase any specificity and to emphasize that this is not an individual but a generic case that is being written. Read in this way, the information on the case notes is less a set of medical data or a body of observations about Indian individuals and more a record of the British fantasy of the civilizing mission.

2. Organizing Reform in Psychiatric Practice

While the case notes record the fantasy of the civilizing mission, other asylum records detail the ways in which these institutions operated more practically as tools of that civilizing mission. A potent indication of the ambitions of the asylum superintendents is in their conceptualization of the asylum and the inmate. Dr Payne in Bengal conceived of the recovering patient as developing like a child:

> Practically the simplest and most rational plan is to endeavour to revive the brain from decay by imitating the course of nature in its original growth. Habits and associations are the soil in which the ideas of childhood first spring up and in proportion to the care with which the former are regulated will be the soundness of the latter. It is through the discipline and exercise of the body that this end is achieved, and the organic functions of the brain developed, on the perfection of which, after bodily maturity the growth of understanding begins . . . the damaged organ is the last that should be laid under forced requisition during disorder. If this be done there is danger of

imitating the well known results of urging the education of children prematurely.[28]

In a related vein, Dr Wylie at Ahmedabad liked to think of the asylum as a 'well-regulated household' in that 'discipline and order are successfully maintained under a homely system of kindness, blended with firmness as occasion may demand; and, as a rule, the asylum is ordinarily as quiet and orderly as a well-regulated household'.[29]

The asylum was conceived of as a 'home' and those in it a family in which the patients were the 'children' and the colonial representative the 'father'.[30] This construction of the Indian patient is significant because of the colonial setting of the asylum where the 'native' was often construed as a child in relation to the fully developed adult that was the western man.[31] It is also a construction familiar from asylums in the European context, where there was 'the prevailing view of patients as being in a state of childhood dependence'[32] and 'everything at the Retreat is organized so that the insane are transformed into minors'.[33] Quite simply, this positioning of the Indian patients in a relationship of tutelage to the colonial officer in the asylum reports demonstrates the superintendent's perception of his duty. He is not simply a jailer for the patients under his control. Rather, he considers himself fatherlike in as much as he sees it as his role to mould, form and educate those under his control. Having established in their own minds the correct relationship in the asylum between the colonial medical officer and the patient, the medical officers developed a regime to facilitate 'recovery' in the patient based on the performance of productive tasks.

Work was central to the asylum regime and the inmates were put to a range of tasks in the asylums of India, from attending to farms established within the asylum walls, to performing maintenance jobs around the asylum and even to participating in cottage-industry processes such as spinning and weaving. Dr Holmsted insisted that 'our chief means of cure is labour: if we can persuade a lunatic to labour, we have hopes of him'.[34] Through exposure to work it was thought the Indian inmates would become familiar with what were described above as the 'Victorian fetishes', or what one of the superintendents in the Bombay presidency called 'such wholesome influences as obedience, regularity, forbearance, mutual assistance, diligence and industry'.[35] In submitting the patients to labour, 'none are allowed to be idle',[36] insisted the superintendent at Delhi, the medical officers hoped to effect the 'recovery' of the patients, that is, to train them to be ordered and productive individuals.

The asylum reports also indicate that 'improvement' and 'recovery' in a patient were only recognized by the British medical officers when the patient began to work. One medical officer asserted that all the Insanes are encouraged to engage in work as much as possible and they generally do so willingly. On first admission many sit idle but the force of example induces them speedily to join in assisting their brother unfortunates. It is indeed one of the first marked symptoms of improvement when, from sitting in an idle, listless, unobservant mood, they betake themselves to work.[37]

The superintendent at Hyderabad went further than this, stating that 'nothing looks so hopeful as regards recovery as getting them to work'.[38]

In this way work was central to the modes of treating the Indian inmate as it became both the means and the measure of 'recovery' in the patient. The British wanted patients to be reformed into useful and productive individuals by learning the virtues of obedience, regularity, forbearance and so on through constant work. The medical officers also used that constant work as an indicator of a patient's 'recovery' in as much as the individual's progress towards the reformed, 'recovered' state was signified by the frequency with which work was undertaken.

Crucially, though, the superintendents hoped to do more than have the patient submit to their work regimes. The fantasy was that the patient would be, in the words of the superintendent of Dullunda, 'so transformed that industry becomes a pleasure to him'.[39] This fantasy is expressed elsewhere, John Balfour the inspector general of hospitals in the Dinapore Circle deciding that 'I need only add that not only should there be nothing penal in the work undertaken, but the patients should learn to look on it as a privilege.'[40]

It can also be detected in asylum reports that produce images of the patients 'singing blithely at their task',[41] or that exclaim: 'I must say I never saw a more happy or contented looking set of lunatics; they work both in the gardens and at the looms with pleasure to themselves.'[42] To this end,

compulsory efforts and punishment for not working have been studiously avoided; at the same time every inducement by humouring their fancies, and granting them some coveted indulgence in diet, extras etc. have been employed so as to form a habit; sometimes, when other means have failed, they have been kept with the working party unemployed, and have of themselves taken to work from seeing others employed.[43]

In other words the patients were expected not to have to be compelled to work but to wish to work and to learn to want to work. This was to be achieved through the tactics of peer pressure and the offering of incentives. The British hoped to train in the asylums workers able to motivate themselves to be productive and efficient. The ultimate aim was a *self*-disciplined Indian.

Yet systems of labour were designed to do more than simply take those Indians incarcerated in the institution and turn them into willing workers. The allocation of tasks by gender in the asylum underlines this. At Hyderabad in 1875 Dr Holmsted summarized that 'our chief work is employment in the garden for males, and for females grinding the corn required for the asylum',[44] whereas in the previous year he had included more detail: 'The women grind all the grain required in the asylum, they leep and clean their own quarters, fetch their drinking water etc.; the men are employed in cultivation, making drains, turning water-wheels, attending bullocks, levelling ground, working in the cook-room, brick making.'[45] Similarly, at Delhi, 'no manufactures have been attempted, but the males have been employed in gardening, in keeping the ridges and walks neat and trim, and in any other light labour they could be induced to turn their hands to. The women do a little spinning of cotton thread.'[46] A gendered division of labour was being enforced in the asylums by the medical officers. The emphasis was on women performing domestic tasks and men executing outdoor work involving agriculture and rudimentary construction.

It seems then that the gendered division of labour was intended to reinforce sex identities that the British thought proper. This is an idea familiar from the above discussion of asylum regimes in Europe. Indeed, other features of the asylum regime in India served to emphasize gender distinction. It was a matter of course that women's wards were separated from the male ones, as emphasized at Poona where 'the construction of the asylum provides for the complete separation of the female patients in a distinct ward. Three other compartments, communicating with the central hall or keeper's room, are set aside, one for criminals, another for cases of amentia and dementia, and the third is occupied by the stationary and generally quiet class.'[47]

Surgeon Major Taylor at Delhi revealed a further practice that emphasized sexual difference: 'The diet scale is the same as it was last year. I think that the women should have more food. I recommended last year that they should have the same quantity as the males.'[48] A picture emerges then that suggests that the civilizing mission had more complex objectives than simply to produce obedient, self regulating and productive Indians. It carried within it a gendered component that insisted on a 'proper' ordering of society that privileged the male and that organized a distance in relationships between men and women.

The question of dietary practices in the asylum emphasizes, however, that while much that the British doctors did was intended to make patients less 'Indian' and more 'civilized', in other words less 'unruly' and more 'obedient', they were careful to maintain distinctions that emphasized the ultimate difference of the truly 'civilized' from those they were 'civilizing'. Surgeon Major Niven at Colaba included the details that

> the 1st class includes Europeans and Eurasians, and the nature of the diet is the same as that supplied in European regimental hospitals; the 2nd class includes Parsees, native Christians of all sorts, mixed races and a few non-descript people who are fond of changing their character, and wish to be a Christian one day and a native another; the 3rd class consists of Hindus and Mahomedans, and the diet is composed of flour, rice and dhall, and a small quantity of meat and vegetables; the diet of the 2nd class contains baker's bread, tea and sugar, milk and meat, as well as rice and dhall. The native Christians and Parsees are very fond of tea, and it would amount almost to an act of cruelty to deprive them of that article of diet.[49]

In other words the asylum was also arranged to reproduce the British belief in the separateness of the races and to emphasize to the inmates of the asylum that observance of that separation ought to be maintained. Within the walls of the lunatic asylum the message was clear and was being drummed into even those considered 'mad': no matter what effort was made to 'civilize' Asians, European would remain 'first class' and Indian would remain 'third class'.

Indeed, where aspects of India were convenient to colonial objectives they were carefully maintained and reimposed on the 'mad' despite the care taken to 'civilize' them in other respects. Asylum design enforced communal division as plans of the hospitals designated separate Hindu and Muslim sleeping areas and kitchens.[50] The superintendent at Dacca referred to 'cooking, which is carefully done: lunatics assist in both the Hindoo and Mussulman cookrooms'.[51] The attention to communal separation evident in diet and in design reminds the observer of just how selective the urge to 'civilize' the colonized from their 'Indian ways' could be.

3. Conclusion

The asylums were fostered environments where those deemed insane by the British could learn the key elements of the colonial society that the colonizers desired for all of India. In the first place Indians were to be 'civilized'. In the world of the colonizers this meant made less like the 'Indian' of their own imaginations who was lazy, inefficient, unruly and impulsive, and more like the idealized 'European', who was productive, efficient, ordered and rational. However, the asylum regime was also designed to remind the Indian inmates that whatever the efforts made to improve them, they would for ever remain short of the truly civilized European who, even in moments of madness, remained permanently superior. The regime also demonstrates just how limited and specific the civilizing mission could be. While the British desired to remove certain of the characteristics that they imagined to be inherently 'Indian', those of laziness, disobedience, etc., they were careful to preserve those that seemed to suit the purposes of colonial government. As such the attachment to communal identities and the maintenance of religious divisions were encouraged in the asylum as these identities and divisions in the wider community served to drive a wedge between colonized groups that prevented them identifying the British as a common enemy. The asylums show that while the British engaged upon the civilizing mission in these institutions, this was hedged in by other ideas and agendas that checked and limited the grander fantasies of reform.

9

The Sympathizing Heart and the Healing Hand: Smallpox Prevention and Medical Benevolence in Early Colonial South India

NIELS BRIMNES[1]

University of Aarhus

In 1827, Whitelaw Ainslie – a recognized doctor who had served in the medical service of the Madras Presidency for twenty-seven years between 1788 and 1815 – gave a lecture at the Royal Asiatic Society on smallpox prevention in India.[2] Ainslie was, as modern writers have noted,[3] among the most sympathetic commentators on indigenous medicine in early colonial India, and in the lecture he spoke favourably of the indigenous preventive technique of inoculating with live smallpox matter. This was known as variolation and was, to some extent, adopted in Europe in the eighteenth century. Yet Ainslie considered variolation to be far inferior to vaccination with cowpox virus, a technique discovered by the English doctor Edward Jenner in 1798 and introduced into India in 1802. Ainslie praised Jenner's discovery as 'extraordinary' and declared that: 'the world stands indebted to the observations and patient investigation of Dr Jenner, who, prompted by the best feelings of humanity, and supported by the spirit of ingenious research, most happily established one of the greatest blessings that was ever bestowed on man'.[4] Ainslie also believed that the effect of vaccination was instrumental in convincing millions of Indians of the beneficial results of British rule. Thus, he self-confidently ended his lecture by noting 'that if, from a powerful empire in the West came an inordinate thirst for dominion and the sword of the conqueror, thence also came the sympathizing heart and the healing hand'.[5]

Though highly sympathetic towards indigenous medicine, Ainslie clearly conceptualized the vaccination campaign against smallpox as part of the civilizing mission of British colonial rule. This fits well into the general pattern of colonial rhetoric. Ainslie's assessment was roughly contemporaneous with the prohibition of *sati* and Macauley's propagation of western knowledge in the debate on higher education in India. The confidence in western medicine expressed by Ainslie can be seen as part of the general rhetoric accompanying the belief in liberal reform and 'improvement', which is normally associated with Lord William Bentinck's appointment as Governor General in 1828. Moreover, as Michael Adas has shown, achievements in science and technology were key components in the Europeans' understanding of themselves as harbingers of modernity and civilization throughout the nineteenth century.[6] The notion of the civilizing mission is often connected to the late nineteenth century, but it seems to have been more prominent in India in the period from Bentinck's accession to 1857, when the rebellion damped reformist ideologies and promoted the opposing desire to preserve an India cast in the image of feudal Europe.[7] Thus, Ainslie's assessment of western medicine in general and the technique of vaccination in particular was located at the centre of the vision of the British as bearers of a civilizing mission in India.

Campaigns to immunize against smallpox in India began, however, three decades earlier than Ainslie's lecture and this chapter seeks to investigate whether the vision of a civilizing mission can be traced back to the initial stages of the campaigns around 1800. On the basis of material relating to the Madras Presidency, I analyse the earliest efforts to combat smallpox in India and the ideas about humanity, science and progress that accompanied these efforts. Before I examine the south Indian campaign in greater detail, I discuss the general European valuation of indigenous medicine in the decades around 1800 and also point to some peculiar features of smallpox, which made it different from many of the other important diseases confronting the British in India.

1. European and Indian Medicine in the Early Colonial Period

In the attempt to identify the vision of a civilizing mission, the first thing to look for is a sense of superiority. It is not difficult to find texts written before 1800 that see European medicine as superior to Indian medical traditions. Both Michael Adas and M N Pearson have drawn attention to the highly critical attitude towards Indian medicine in the writings of the French traveller François Bernier, who lived in India between 1659 and 1667. Bernier was educated as a medical doctor and Adas finds that he is the best illustration that 'early European ambivalence toward Indian scientific learning had turned decidedly negative by the last half of the seventeenth century'. Pearson similarly sees Bernier as 'the first manifestation of an overt claim to

European advancement'.[8] Bernier's critical assessment can be supplemented with remarks from the British surgeon John Fryer, who travelled in Persia and India in the second half of the seventeenth century, or the French traveller and naturalist Pierre Sonnerat, who visited the Coromandel coast around 1780. Sonnerat, for instance, disparaged indigenous medicine in the following way: 'The Indians are almost all Physicians. From their infancy they are instructed in the knowledge of some simples, and different receipts handed down from father to son. These are for them a resource in their calamity; and they often make a mixture of plants, of whose property they are ignorant and their effect equally unknown'.[9]

Also, commentators from within the British colonial administration commented critically on indigenous medicine. Francis Buchanan Hamilton, who was sent to survey the newly conquered territories of Mysore and Malabar in 1800, laconically remarked that 'medicine, in this country, has indeed fallen into the hands of charlatans equally imprudent and ignorant'.[10] Benjamin Heyne, employed as the East India Company's naturalist in the early nineteenth century, found an Indian treatise on medicine to exhibit 'a banquet of absurdity sufficient to satisfy the most voracious quests'.[11]

Despite these statements of European superiority, a number of modern scholars have argued that the relation between European and indigenous medicine in the first half of the nineteenth century was much more ambiguous. David Arnold finds that indigenous medicine continued to serve as a source of inspiration for colonial medicine until the second half of the nineteenth century, while C A Bayly emphasizes both the fundamental uncertainty of western scientific thought and the complex relations between indigenous and western medical knowledge.[12] Mark Harrison has recently provided a useful and varied picture of the relation between European and indigenous medicine from the fifteenth to the late nineteenth century. According to Harrison, it was only after 1820 that Europeans saw their own medical knowledge as fundamentally different from and indisputably superior to indigenous traditions. Between 1670 and 1750 European medicine began to depart from the Galenic, humoral conception of the human body, which it had previously shared with both Indian and Arabic medical traditions. Yet, this was a slow process and the attitude towards Indian medicine in this period was not uniformly negative. Harrison emphasizes – by contrast to Adas and Pearson – that Bernier was 'not wholly critical of Indian medical systems'.[13] From 1750 to around 1820 ambiguous relations continued. As part of the colonial administration, representatives of European medicine increasingly saw indigenous medical traditions as a source of useful information. In Harrison's own formulation, these medical men saw their task 'as one of extraction and excavation, as befitted their new status as colonial rulers'.[14]

While orientalists like William Jones found useful – if not quite scientific – information on astronomy and medicine in the classical Hindu texts, more practically minded men such as Benjamin Heyne and Whitelaw Ainslie acknowledged the usefulness of specific medical practices.[15] Despite his scorn of the Hindu medical texts, Heyne admitted that Indian medical practitioners knew more about the use of iron and copper than did Europeans.[16] Whitelaw Ainslie, although he criticized indigenous medicine for being muddled with religion and in a state of 'empirical darkness', directly opposed Sonnerat's negative portrayal of Hindu medical practitioners, known as *vythians*:

> I must say that either Monseiur Sonnerat has been a little remiss in his enquiries, or that I have been peculiarly fortunate, in meeting with *Vythian*s of a very different description from those he alludes to . . . Not a few of them I have known, who were not only intimately acquainted with all the medical *Sastrum*s [*shastra*s], great part of which they had by heart; but who, in other respects, were in their lives and manners correct, obliging and communicative.[17]

It seems increasingly difficult to maintain that European medicine by the early nineteenth century saw itself unambiguously as superior to indigenous traditions. It would indeed be a simplification to see the statements of European superiority in medical matters, which undeniably are easy to find in the writings of Bernier, Fryer and Sonnerat, as the beginning of a uniform development of a still harsher valuation of indigenous medical traditions. Instead, we need to distinguish between different layers in the European discourse about non-European medicine. While texts intended to represent 'the other' to a European audience abound with claims to European superiority in medical matters, the issue became much more ambiguous in the texts produced closer to the administrative context in India. As the British presence in India developed into territorial dominion in the first decades of the nineteenth century this ambiguity became highly visible. The employees of the Company's medical service were concerned with the need to devise strategies of specific and sometimes urgent disease management. To them indigenous medicine was not so much a confirmation of European superiority as it was a reservoir of potentially useful knowledge.[18]

The vision of colonial medicine as part of a civilizing mission was further impeded by the environmentalist paradigm, which prevailed well into the nineteenth century. This paradigm saw the human body as universal and explained disease patterns and human 'constitutions' with reference to the climate and the physical environment.[19] It thus explained European superiority – Europeans lived in a more benevolent or stimulating climate –

but offered little prospect that European medical knowledge could be applied in India to the benefit of the Indian population.[20] On the contrary, until at least 1800 European medical men were concerned with the 'seasoning' or 'acclimatization' of Europeans to the Indian climate – partly by recommending indigenous ways of life such as vegetarianism – and to avoid the degenerating effects of the Indian environment.[21] It was not until Utilitarian rhetoric began to explain the Indian constitution with reference to 'ignorance' and 'superstition' rather than climate and environment that colonial medicine could be envisaged as a central part of a civilizing mission. To sum up, then, there is not much merit in the argument that colonial medicine in general was conceptualized as part of a civilizing mission in the first decades of the nineteenth century. The feeling of superiority in medical matters was modified by profound ambiguities, while the environmentalist paradigm saw issues of health and constitution in India as caused by factors beyond the reach of even the most resolute human endeavours.

The discussion might easily end here if smallpox had not in two important respects differed from the other major diseases facing the British in India. But it did. First, smallpox was not seen as a peculiarly Indian or 'tropical' disease. It was well known in Europe in the eighteenth and early nineteenth centuries and became a tropical disease only in the twentieth century, when it had been virtually eliminated in Europe and North America. It presented none of the mysterious qualities of the 'fevers' (malaria, typhoid) or 'fluxes' (cholera, dysentery), which medical writers ascribed to India's particular environment.[22] If smallpox in India presented any particularly Indian features, it was in the cultural practices surrounding it: the devotion to the smallpox goddesses – Sitala in the north and east, Mariamman in the south – and the highly ritualized practice of variolation. By contrast to the physical environment, cultural practice was a field where the notion of a civilizing mission made sense, because such practices could be altered or even abolished through reform and 'progress'. Second, shortly after Jenner's discovery of the cowpox vaccine it became clear that smallpox was – in David Arnold's phrase – an eminently preventable disease.[23] While early-nineteenth-century European doctors were as inefficient in their treatment of cholera and malarial fevers as their Indian counterparts, they arguably possessed a superior preventive against smallpox. For these reasons, smallpox prevention might not be an improbable place to look for the vision of a civilizing mission within the rhetoric of British colonialism in the first decades of the nineteenth century.

Finally, it should be noted that campaigns against smallpox in Europe were also accompanied by a rhetoric touching upon the theme of the civilizing mission. European and Indian peasants were to benefit from immunization in the same way and in the medical discourse they occupied the same position as beneficiaries, who might in varying degrees – according to the level of ignorance and superstition – resist this blessing from established medicine.[24] We might say that the campaigns against smallpox everywhere entailed the opposition between benevolent medicine and popular resistance, or between universal reason and an irrational 'other'. In India, however, this notion of 'otherness' was amplified because the campaigns were launched at a time when the British were gradually coming to an understanding of India as a land dominated by ancient traditions and where progress had been absent for centuries.[25] Thus, the creation of 'otherness' in the medical field intersected with the more general creation of 'difference' inherent in the establishment of British colonial rule. Yet even when colonial power and scientific medicine joined forces to create an ignorant and non-scientific 'other', which could serve as the target of the colonialist's civilizing mission, ambiguity could not – as I hope to demonstrate in the next section – be totally eliminated.

2. Advertising the Campaign against Smallpox

Efforts to combat smallpox in the territories subject to Madras began in earnest in 1800 when the government decided to launch a campaign to encourage variolation among the civil population. Extracts from the colonial records were published in Arab, Tamil and Telugu, medical officers were encouraged to promote variolation, and district collectors were told to assist in convincing the population of the benefits of this practice.[26] According to the admittedly unreliable statistics 475 persons were inoculated in the first 'cold' season between December 1800 and March 1801. A year later the total number of inoculated since 1800 was given as more than 26,000.[27] But the enthusiasm within the colonial administration for variolation was short-lived. In the autumn of 1802 the cowpox vaccine reached Madras and the government immediately redirected the campaign to promote vaccination instead of variolation. Vaccination was considered a superior technique because variolation occasionally caused serious cases of smallpox, which threatened to turn into epidemics. Vaccination was also less dependent on the relatively short 'cold' season. On the other hand, vaccination was less reliable, mainly because the vaccine disease was easily lost and did not exist naturally in India.

The shift towards vaccination clearly intensified the campaign against smallpox and in January 1803 an ambitious plan for the diffusion of vaccination throughout the Madras Presidency was set in motion. Between September 1802 and April 1804 145,000 persons were reported to have been vaccinated. This is a very high – and presumably exaggerated – figure. It is nearly six times higher than in the period when variolation was promoted and much higher than in both contemporary Bengal and Bombay.[28] Despite these impressive figures, the campaign was soon criticized for being inadequate and inefficient. In the spring of 1805 there was a fierce debate within the colonial administration about the best way to promote vaccination. It resulted in a thorough reorganization of the campaign and in the season of 1806–7 the number of reported vaccinations exceeded 240,000.[29] Even these efforts were vastly insufficient and smallpox continued to be a significant and dreaded disease in south India into the twentieth century.[30] Still, the initial stages of the campaign against smallpox represented a significant and early attempt to intervene in the daily life of the indigenous inhabitants at large, and this intervention was based on the assumption that western medicine would bring health and prosperity in its wake.

As long as the campaign promoted variolation it was not, however, possible simply to conceptualize it as part of a civilizing mission. By contrast to Bengal, where variolation was widespread among Indians in the eighteenth century, it was virtually unknown in the Madras presidency and the campaign in south India therefore began as an attempt to introduce and diffuse an 'Indian' practice.[31] Moreover, before 1800 the main promoter of variolation was Vasareddy Vencatadry Naidu, the *zamindar* of Chintapilly in Guntur district. He had been inoculated by an English surgeon in 1793 and he subsequently employed his own indigenous inoculators. Under these circumstances, it was impossible for the colonial authorities to promote variolation without somehow acknowledging its roots within Indian society. Thus, in a public advertisement from November 1800, variolation was promoted exclusively with references to its indigenous roots and indigenous agency:

> The practice of Inoculation has been known from time immemorial in the Northern part of the Circars, and most of the [Woodiah] Zemindars Inoculate their Children; It is well known that it has been introduced, tho' lately in this Circar, by Rajah Vasareddy Vencatadry Naidoo, who first submitted to it himself and who now employs Native Doctors to inoculate such of the Inhabitants of this zemindary as are willing to submit to it.[32]

It is, however, significant to note that the colonial authorities immediately began to question the relation between variolation and indigenous society. This happened in two ways, and first by drawing attention to indigenous 'prejudice' and 'ignorance'. Shortly after the advertisement quoted above, Governor Clive in a letter of recognition to the *zamindar* of Chintapilly declared:

> The only impediment to the successful practice of this part of the

Art of Physic is derived from the prejudices of the Natives which is founded in an Ignorance equally of the beneficial effects of the practice [and] of the principles on which the Objections are grounded, for it is notoriously known that the practice of Inoculation has been and still is familiar to whole Tribes of Hindoos in the Northern Provinces of Hindostan, while the prevailing ignorance in the Deckan annually dooms the greatest portion of the persons affected with this disorder to death.[33]

Although Clive had to exempt the people of north India from his criticism, he was eager to contrast the 'vigour' and 'understanding' of the *zamindar* with 'the obstinate prejudices of the Hindoos' in general.[34] Second, the colonial authorities represented variolation as a technique, which – despite its indigenous roots – had been significantly improved by Europeans. One of the British pioneers of variolation, Surgeon Nicol Mein, noted that he had prepared his patients after 'Baron Dimsdale's method'.[35] In April 1801, the government envisaged that inoculations performed by indigenous agents in the future were to be conducted first according to the practice of the *brahmins* in the northern part of the presidency and then 'gradually according to the improvements which may be suggested by the Medical Gentlemen of the district'.[36] Similarly, the collector of Coimbatore had little doubt that variolation was a technique controlled entirely by Europeans. Thus, he suggested to the Board of Revenue that the 'first introduction of it under the Collectors inspection should of course be done by means of European Surgeon; and Native Doctors – of whom some should be Brahmins – ought to be instructed by the European Surgeon and obliged to perform the operation in his presence'.[37]

There was, no doubt, some justification for distinguishing between the indigenous practice of variolation and the practice advanced by European surgeons. The most obvious was that whereas indigenous inoculators conducted the practice in a ritual context – according to the collector of Vizagapatam it was performed 'with many Superstitions [and] unnecessary Ceremonies' – the 'European method' had been thoroughly de-ritualized.[38] There is no point in denying that the colonial authorities introduced, changed and perhaps even improved the 'Indian' technique of variolation. In the present context, however, it is important to note that – despite attempts to mask the indigenous roots of variolation and take as much credit as possible for the diffusion of the practice – the colonial authorities could not conceptualize the promotion of variolation within a simple dichotomy of western science versus indigenous superstition.

The arrival of the cowpox vaccine in the autumn of 1802 changed this situation. The colonial authorities immediately redirected their campaign to promote vaccination instead of variolation. In this way they substituted a technique that could easily be conceptualized as a pure product of European reasoning for a technique with muddled and hybrid origins. The first task was to advertise the sudden shift. In January 1803 the government published an advertisement that began with an explicit reference to the last advertisement to promote variolation from August 1802. The Governor in Council now declared that he deemed it proper to 'postpone' the measures mentioned in the earlier advertisement and then commenced on a narrative on the efforts of the medical men in Europe to 'ameliorate the condition of Human life'. From a passage on the celebrated transfer of the vaccine from Europe to India, it clearly emerges that the British were acutely aware that they were now benevolently donating their discovery to the rest of the world:

> The same spirit of benevolence which guided the labours of these persons in Europe, led to the adoption of the means best calculated to convey the fruits of the happy discovery to India; and this humane object having been after much care effected the Inhabitants of India may, by following the example of the European Nations be for ever freed from further apprehension or danger from the small pox.[39]

The British now employed an increasingly universalistic language, which permitted them to conceptualize themselves as representatives of universal reason, struggling against a dreadful disease on behalf of mankind. They expressed the hope that 'such inestimable benefit to mankind will be received with equal gratitude by the Inhabitants of India [as] it has been evinced by the Inhabitants of every other part of the World . . .'[40] In October 1804 the collector of Madurai in a locally published proclamation referred to 'The benefit which has been experienced by all the world by an inoculation called the Cow Pox', while the acting collector in Trichinopoly wrote to the Tondaiman *raja* of Pudukkottai:

> You will no doubt have heard of the late important discovery of the vaccine Inoculation or Cow Pox a disease not only mild in its operation but a sure and Certain preventitive [sic] against the dreadful ravages Committed by the Natural small Pox among all Classes of People in every part of the World without distinction [–] but as I am doubtful that the knowledge of the inestimable blessing which mankind may derive from this important discovery has yet come to your knowledge . . .[41]

Finally, when the collector of Madurai in 1806 requested local *zamindar*s to donate a sum of money to Dr Jenner, he referred to 'The benefit which all the world has derived from the human attentions of Doctor Jenner'.[42] It seems clear that the shift to vaccination removed the ambiguity accompanying the earlier rhetoric on variolation. Within a few years the colonial authorities had changed from promoting variolation with reference to its indigenous roots to promoting vaccination with reference to the benevolence and humanity of European medical community. The campaign against smallpox had changed from an ambiguous enterprise at the junction between Indian and European medicine to being part of the civilizing mission of the British in India.

3. Conceptualizing Indigenous Resistance

While the introduction of the cowpox vaccine significantly changed the way in which the campaign against smallpox was advertised, it did not have the same impact on the pattern of indigenous resistance or the way this resistance was conceptualized by the colonial authorities. Basically, the inhabitants of south India resisted variolation and vaccination to the same degree and in similar ways. As immunization was never enforced resistance was overwhelmingly 'passive'. Reluctant Indians could easily reject or ignore the offer of immunization and there were few reports of violent forms of resistance.

The statistics indicate, however, that a shift in the geographical distribution of immunization took place as a consequence of the introduction of vaccination. As long as variolation was promoted, the area around the mouth of the river Krishna (Guntur and Masulipatam districts) was most successful, while the southern part of the presidency was more successful after vaccination was introduced.[43] One might speculate that the success of variolation in Guntur and Masulipatam – no doubt instigated by the efforts of the *zamindar* of Chintapilly – inhibited the introduction of the 'rival' practice of vaccination. In the southern part of the presidency, by contrast, variolation made less impact and thus became less of a rival to vaccination. An alternative or supplementary explanation is that the risk of losing the vaccine disease was greater in the dry and sparsely populated tracts to the north.[44]

There are no clear indications that indigenous resistance can be understood in terms of social stratification or ritual hierarchies. The Mapilla Muslims in Malabar formed perhaps the only larger community that was singled out as particularly hostile towards vaccination, and this hostility does not seem to have applied to Muslims in general.[45] There is contradictory evidence regarding the readiness of the *brahmin*s and other high castes to accept immunization. In 1802 it was reported from the Black Town of Madras that resistance came mainly from 'the higher orders of the Natives'. It was difficult to get access to the houses of these groups and the Medical Board recommended that more *brahmin* inoculators were employed to overcome this problem. Similarly, it was reported from Travancore that it was chiefly Christians and Hindus with low caste status that accepted vaccination.[46] On the other hand, there were also reports of great readiness on the part of the *brahmins* to accept immunization. The collector of Coimbatore explicitly rejected the notion, expressed by Physician General James Anderson, that south Indian *brahmins* were 'prejudiced against inoculation', and from the northernmost part of the Presidency the surgeon in Maddepollam and Ingeram referred to the readiness among *brahmins* to submit their families to inoculation.[47] The statistics also indicate that resistance cannot be attributed to certain social groups. A breakdown of 4,588 persons variolated in the season of 1801–02 in Masulipatam district shows that variolation was accepted by a variety of people ranging from *brahmins* to low-ranking barbers and dancing girls. Less precise is the breakdown of the more than 145,000 persons vaccinated in the Presidency between September 1802 and April 1804, but it does confirm that all major groups in south Indian society from *brahmins* to *paraiyans* were among the vaccinated.[48] This information must, of course, be treated with caution, but it seems substantiated to conclude that social position or ritual prestige was not a crucial factor in determining the extent to which immunization was resisted.

It makes more sense to see indigenous resistance as determined by local conditions. As indicated above, one of the most significant features of the campaign was a remarkable concentration in Guntur and Masulipatam districts until the introduction of vaccination. This was presumably a result of the initiative shown by the *zamindar* of Chintapilly. Similarly, in Ramnad in the southern part of the presidency, where local magnates such as the *rani* of Ramnad and the *zamindar* of Shivagangai supported vaccination, it was reported in 1803 and 1804 that 'the people in general seem perfectly reconciled to the operation'.[49] Not surprisingly, attempts to get leading figures in indigenous society to endorse immunization and submit their own families to the operation was a preferred strategy in the campaign. Thus, in 1801 the collector in Rajahmundry believed he could overcome widespread resistance if he succeeded in inoculating 'the better sort and more enlightened of the inhabitants'. In 1804 Physician General James Anderson noted with satisfaction that not only were the *zamindar* of Chintapilly and the *raja* of Tanjore favourably disposed towards vaccination, but the *diwan* of Travancore had even submitted himself to vaccination.[50]

Local differences in the attitude towards inoculation, of course, could not always be explained with reference to the stance taken by local leaders. In Salem district, Assistant Surgeon Smith found the inhabitants too hesitant and crossed the border to neighbouring Coimbatore district, where the population was much more inclined to accept vaccination. Smith explained this difference as resulting from the efforts of the British officers in Coimbatore to convince the inhabitants of the great benefits deriving from vaccination.[51] While the efforts of colonial officials were probably of less importance than he assumed, a number of other local conditions might have influenced the degree to which the inhabitants accepted vaccination. Among the most obvious are the incidence of smallpox outbreaks in the area and the specific relationship between indigenous inoculators and vaccinators on the one hand and the local population on the other.

We can only guess why Indians resisted the campaign, but two issues are obviously important. First, vaccination was an alien technique, which violated Indian conceptions of the body and notions of ritual pollution.[52] To some extent this was also true of variolation, because the practice had been de-ritualized under British guidance. Second, Indians were suspicious about what motives the distant and unfamiliar ruler had to intervene in their daily life in such an intrusive and unprecedented way. In their understanding of indigenous resistance the colonial authorities occasionally referred to these circumstances. Reflecting the religious perspective on smallpox, a report from Trichinopoly noted that, the Indians saw variolation as 'an unnatural and dangerous Provocation of a disease, with which in the course of Life they may not providentally [sic] be affected'. J A Dubois, who worked for many years as superintendent of vaccination in Mysore and drew up a list of 'objections' to vaccination, also referred to the 'fear of irritating the Goddess of small pox Mariamma, and being exposed to her revenge'. [53] Indigenous mistrust towards the motives of the colonial authorities was reported by Surgeon Dalton – another of the pioneers of vaccination in the Madras presidency – in an account of one of the few instances of violent resistance. In 1804 Dalton was vaccinating in Trivatore near Madras and found himself surrounded by a mob of angry Indians. He eventually had to flee from the scene and leave the duty of vaccination to Sawmy Naik, one of the most successful indigenous vaccinators. Dalton later explained the reaction of the Indians with the widespread belief that the practice of taking down personal details of every vaccinated person was a preparation for either a capitation tax or transportation.[54]

Generally, the British did not seek to understand the specific reasons behind indigenous resistance, but took recourse to the increasingly dominant colonial conceptualization of Indian society as static and traditional; immobilized by an age-old aversion to change and innovation. Moreover, having lived for so long under oppressive and despotic regimes, the Indians were not capable of understanding the benevolent motives of the British regime. Dubois, for instance, included in his list of objections 'distrust about the generous views of government'. This distrust was not, however, understood as a result of specific concerns among indigenous inhabitants but related to the abstract notion of 'Oriental despotism':

> these poor people, to these last times accostomed [sic] to live under a Government, who had recourse to every kind of craft and imposture to oppress them, imagine that so much trouble is taken, and the great expenses gone to by their rulers not to benefit but to injure them; and that their Children when grown up, shall be carried away, or that at least an heavy tax shall be levied as a compensation for the benefit bestowed on them by vaccination.[55]

Dubois also listed the equally abstract notion that Indians were opposed 'to everything which was not transmitted to them by their forefathers' and referred to the *'apathy* and want of forecasting in the Hindoos [emphasis in original]'.[56] Not surprisingly, the most widespread conceptualization of indigenous resistance was by reference to 'prejudice' and 'superstition'. An account from Tanjore opened with an unusually explicit version of this reference:

> this aversion is to be attributed chiefly to religious prejudices and partly to the reluctance with which the Hindoos accept of every innovation and change. In no part of India perhaps are the religious prejudices so strong, nowhere are all the forms and Institutions accumulated by the growing Superstition of Ages so carefully preserved as in Tanjour.[57]

Explaining to London in October 1800 his intention to promote variolation, Governor Clive wrote 'that many thousand Lives would be saved Annually, if the prejudice of the Natives did not so strongly oppose the introduction of the practice of Inoculation'. In 1801 the Board of Revenue referred to efforts of the *zamindar* of Chintapilly as 'an instance of superiority over the prejudices and superstition of the Hindoos in general'. From Rajahmundry the collector reported that not a single case of variolation had taken place 'as the prejudice is so great at present against the practice that no persuasions will induce them to submit to it'.[58] Routinely reducing the diverse and specific reasons Indians had to oppose immunization to abstract notions of indigenous prejudice and superstition helped the British to envisage the campaign against smallpox as a civilizing mission. This decontextualized construction of an irrational, non-scientific 'other' provided the civilizing mission with a target: an extensive population capable of occupying the position of reluctant beneficiaries of the blessings of European medicine.

4. Concluding Remarks

While it would be a simplification to claim that colonial medicine in the first decades of nineteenth century self-confidently saw itself as part of a civilizing mission, it can be argued that the campaigns against smallpox in India from around 1800 represent early and more limited manifestations of this vision. By contrast to diseases such as malaria and cholera, smallpox was not seen as a particularly Indian or 'mysterious' disease, which should be explained with reference to the peculiarities of the Indian climate and physical environment. Instead, smallpox was well known and seen – particularly after the discovery of the cowpox vaccine – as comparatively easy to prevent. Still, the campaigns against smallpox were too ambiguous enterprises to be simply conceptualized as part of a civilizing mission. In this article I have drawn attention to two features of the south Indian campaign, which required some discursive 'tailoring' before the rhetoric of the civilizing mission could be applied without reservations. First, it was only after the introduction of the purely European technique of vaccination that the colonial authorities could eliminate acknowledgement of indigenous techniques of smallpox prevention from their rhetoric. Second, they had to employ a decontextualized understanding of indigenous patterns of resistance in order to create a homogenous superstitious 'other', against whom their medical benevolence could be directed. With these issues settled, however, the colonial perception of smallpox prevention in early colonial south India does indeed qualify as an early instance of the vision of the British civilizing mission in India. This vision might not have been fully developed around 1800, but when the Madras government in 1801 described the work of the medical men campaigning against smallpox as 'insulated efforts in the Cause of Science and Humanity', this statement contained the seeds of what, three decades later, would become Whitelaw Ainslie's vision of sympathizing hearts and healing hands.[59]

10

Perceptions of Sanitation and Medicine in Bombay, 1900–1914

MRIDULA RAMANNA

SIES College, University of Bombay

Indo-British encounters in the field of medicine were characterized by opposition and competition between the western import and the established Indian system at most times, and by limited borrowings at others. For the first half of the nineteenth century, a complexity in the relationship between the two systems of medicine has been perceived, on the basis of an examination of Anglo-Indian debates on medicine, British responses being conditioned by particular local circumstances.[2] But as the century progressed, there was an apparent confidence: the colonial self-assumed mission to 'civilize' and 'sanitize' was based on the conviction of the superiority of western medicine and ideas of sanitation. The high point of confidence in the transforming power of imperial medicine was in the late nineteenth and early twentieth centuries.[3] This chapter focuses on some aspects of sanitary reform, epidemic control and western medicine as perceived by British officials and Indians in Bombay during the years 1900–1914. Were public health measures, promoted in the new century with caution, in view of the vehement opposition to medical intervention during the plague epidemic of 1896–7? While the colonial assumption about Indian habits and customs being the root cause of disease is evident, there was also the view that for sanitary reform to progress, gradual promotion and public cooperation were the keywords. But the schemes stumbled on the issue of who was to meet the expenses. Government reluctance to provide funds is obvious: it wanted local bodies to pay. Though Bombay was considered the 'first' city, and initiated civic changes to benefit public health, vital issues of drainage and overcrowding remained unsolved. These years also saw a shift in policy from curative to preventive medicine, which called for the greater involvement of the public.

This raises the second question: how did Indians respond? The western system of medical education, hospitals and dispensaries, established in Bombay from the mid-nineteenth century, had met with ambivalent reactions. These institutions were endowed by Indian philanthropy in most cities of the presidency. Yet there had been opposition, even from social reformers, to measures aimed at sanitary improvement, like underground drainage, clean tap water (that is, water from taps as opposed to well water that was regarded as pure for ritual purposes) and immunization campaigns.[4] By the turn of the century, there had been some positive results, the smallpox vaccination campaigns reducing smallpox mortality and sanitary improvements decreasing the number of cholera deaths. In the new century, voluntary organizations, spearheaded by perceptive officials and supported by Indians with funds and volunteers, made efforts to tackle these public-health issues. The plague prophylactic was promoted in place of the unpopular steps of evacuation and isolation. Attempts were also made to cope with diseases like tuberculosis and malaria and with the question of high infant-mortality rates. Nevertheless, there was resistance to both the plague prophylactic and the directive issued to close wells in Bombay city to counter malaria. The contemporary Indian press, an important source for gauging public attitudes, commented on various health issues, and raised the question of who was to pay for the campaigns.

While Indian responses thus remained mixed, it is important to examine the perspective of western-educated Indian doctors. Though they were not in the forefront of policy-making, they were the vital intermediaries in the promotion of western medicine, of whose efficacy they were convinced. Some presented papers, based on their practical experience, at the Bombay Medical Congress of 1909, and others campaigned for the dissemination of 'sanitary knowledge'. These doctors supported the Registration of Medical Practitioners Act, passed in 1912, which was seen by other Indians as an attempt to keep out the *vaids* and *hakims*, practitioners respectively of *ayurvedic* and *unani* medicine, who provided the majority of the population with cheaper and culturally more acceptable treatments. The Act did not lead to any drastic improvement in the status of Indian doctors, who still had no access to either the senior positions or the same salaries enjoyed by the Indian Medical Service (IMS), but established the dominant position of western medicine. Nevertheless, the Government of India Resolution on Sanitation of 1914 acknowledged the value of public cooperation in promoting sanitary reform and referred favourably to Bombay's efforts in that direction.

1. J A Turner : 'The Missionary of Sanitary Work'

By the mid-nineteenth century, it was accepted that better sanitation might check the spread of diseases. Hence sanitary reform was promoted with zeal by Bombay's health officers, Thomas Gilham Hewlett (whose tenure lasted from 1865 to 1873) and Thomas Stephenson Weir (who served from 1873 to 1897). Their annual reports speak of the need for cholera hospitals in every locality, cleaning of *gullies* (trenches) and alleys with carbolic acid, removal of tiles from the roofs of houses that sheltered cholera cases, whitewashing of walls and 'sanitary raids'.[5] Florence Nightingale, that ardent sanitarian, hailed the efforts of the able Hewlett, whom she described as the 'best' sanitary officer, for supervising the expensive system of hand labour to remove night soil and thus saving Bombay from cholera.[6] The 'insanitary Indian' and his habits were often criticized. Pilgrimages, whether the annual *jatras* (pilgrimages) to Alandi, Jejuri or Pandharpur or the *haj*, were invariably regarded as the source of epidemics. Indians were also thought of as having poor immunity, which was attributed not only to their customs and religious practices of fasting and feasting but also to their poverty and inadequate diet. 'It is impossible to say upon how little the sepoy manages to exist,' remarked Surgeon Davey. Rice, a little *dal* (pulses) *ghi* (clarified butter) and occasionally fish were all that sepoys in the Twenty-first Regiment Native Infantry ate. 'It is surprising to see how aged some men appear after a short service of fifteen years.'[7]

John Andrew Turner, MD, DPH, health officer of Bombay, from 1901 for nearly two decades, made a distinct contribution to tackling the health problems of the city.[8] He was described as 'the missionary of sanitary work' by Sir Pherozeshah Mehta, the great civic leader. Soon after Turner joined the municipality this 'indefatigable gentleman recognized that we could make sanitary laws and take sanitary measures but if we tried to compel people we would never succeed thoroughly and fully until we had tried and educated them and made them acquainted with sanitary requirements'.[9] Turner's views are to be found both in *Sanitation in India*, and a paper, with the same title, read at the Bombay Medical Congress in 1909. The former included a compilation of lectures and demonstrations given as a course run by the public-health department of Bombay, for trainees for the posts of inspectors or health officers in the mofussil. It seems to have attracted students from all over India and Burma.

In his book, Turner described the 'habits and customs' of Indians relating to health, including the insistence on using well water, the method of keeping and milking cows, the manner of cleaning vessels and the 'primitive preparation' of foodstuffs. He deplored the 'joint family', which led to overcrowding in houses, the custom of early marriages and purdah.[10] In his paper, given at the congress, Turner contended that there was an urgent need in India for the development of sanitation, which was in its infancy. This included not only drainage and water supply, but everything that tended to improve public health and prevent the spread of disease, like investigations into the causes of sickness and death, the provision of hospitals, medical relief, health visitors, instructions in personal hygiene and in the supply of food and milk. He ascribed the introduction of cholera to the water brought from the wells of Mecca and to 'certain habits of the backward classes'; the practice of smear-ing cow dung was 'the medium for diseases such as diarrhoea, tubercle, typhoid etc'.[11] Turner believed that there were also 'suitable conditions' for plague to thrive in Indian habits, like sleeping on the floor, walking barefoot, squatting or eating on the floor and 'native remedies'. Even Indian funeral rites were characterized 'by apathy with regard to life and fatalism regarding death'.[12] He maintained that these problems called for intervention, but recognized that there might be 'resistance to interference', which could be overcome by teaching, educating, gradually adopting modern appliances and steadily enforcing laws and regulations, 'which should be made sufficiently adaptable to the circumstances of the situation'.[13] He endorsed the municipal regulation that required all floors to be of cement and *chunam* (mortar), replacing houses with earth floors that could not be disinfected even with the most potent chemical solutions.

On the other hand, some Indians saw sanitation as a fad of certain adminis-trators rather than as a specific remedy for the low standard of public health and the high rate of mortality. Turner's energy was commended, but it was observed that his enthusiasm for flushing privies had only caused a noxious stench since the water supply in the city was inadequate.[14] *Pickings From The Hindi Punch* referred to Turner as the 'Pied Piper' and commented, 'For his silent quiet, unostentatious work on a bicycle, morning after morning, on the streets, commend me to Dr Turner. Still waters run deep.'[15]

2. Local Organizations

To answer the need felt for disseminating information about sanitary matters, the Bombay Sanitary Association, (BSA) was founded in 1904, at the initiative of Turner, under the patronage of Lord Lamington, the governor of Bombay Presidency from 1903 to 1907. Turner was inspired by the museum of public health in London and envisaged a library, with books on sanitation and hygiene, and a hall for meetings. At the inaugural of the BSA, both Lamington and Turner observed that the poor, who suffered so much from the insanitary condition of Bombay, were, compared to the people of London, not wanting in personal cleanliness. The former pointed out that there was dirt and destitution in London, even in houses that looked respectable from the outside. These officials conceded that the high mortality in Bombay was as much due to poverty as lack of medical aid. With a know-ledge of the laws of health many of the poorer classes, who succumbed to disease, would take better care of themselves and improve their surroundings.[16] Membership of the BSA was open to all medical and public health professionals, and two hundred joined. Its objectives were to deliver public lectures in English and the vernaculars, to appoint paid health visitors, who were to educate the public in their area on personal hygiene and public health.

Dr Nasarvanji Hormusji Choksy, MD, deputy health officer in charge of the Infectious Diseases Hospital, gave the first public lecture titled 'Some Common Sense Views on Plague'.[17] J P Orr, chairman of the City Improvement Trust (CIT), which had been established in 1898 to deal with the city's unhealthy environment, to clear slums, broaden roads and build sanitary *chawls* (tenements), lectured on municipal amendments. His suggestion that power should be given to officers to declare any building insanitary and unfit for habitation was seen by Pherozeshah Mehta as a proposal to legalize confiscation of property.[18] Sir (Dr) Bhalchandra Krishna Bhatavadekar read a paper on 'Overcrowding in Bombay' in which he observed that 'the absence of stringent regulations enabled owners to build houses without adequate provision for air and light; and therefore in spite of our efforts to the contrary slums will continue to grow as steadily as before'.[19] Ten years later Sir George Sydenham Clarke (1908–13), Lamington's successor, referred to this as prophetic, since tenements built in Bombay after turned out to be insanitary. He called for this practice to be stopped, citing the 'medical authority' of Bhatavadekar.

In 1905 the BSA organized a health exhibition, in connection with the industrial and agricultural exhibition, which was well received by the public.[20] A class on sanitation was set up to train a body of men and women to teach elementary hygiene to students of primary schools in the city and elsewhere. Leaflets and brochures were brought out on some diseases, translated into the vernaculars and distributed. In the same year, two health visitors paid 4,519 visits to different houses and reported to the health department on the insanitary condition and overcrowding of houses, and on alleys that needed flushing. Despite the BSA's promising start, the local press questioned what the health department was doing if their work was being done by these 'volunteer' health visitors.[21] While conceding that there had been a reduction in the BSA membership to seventy-one in 1912, Sydenham Clarke explained this away by asserting that it was an educative body, its efforts having 'sown seeds' and stimulated people to acquire some knowledge of sanitary laws.[22] He applauded the BSA's use of teaching aids like magic lanterns and the cinematograph to instruct on sanitation.

An offshoot of the BSA was the King George V Anti-Tuberculosis League (ATL), founded in 1912 through the combined efforts of Turner and N H

Choksy. Though the Compulsory Notification of Tuberculosis Act had been passed in 1903, notification had remained, for all practical purposes, voluntary. The League sought to spread awareness and knowledge of the disease. At a public meeting of doctors, called by the Bombay Medical Union (BMU),[23] the aims of the League were delineated: to spread information about tuberculosis through lectures and distribution of pamphlets; health visitors to conduct visits to and medical inspection of mills, schools and factories; to supervise milk and food supplies; and to set up a special fund to relieve distress. The ATL received a donation of 15,000 rupees from Ratan Tata, the industrialist and 135,000 rupees was subscribed by the public, while the Bombay government and the municipal corporation gave grants of 10,000 rupees each annually, for three years. At the suggestion of Sydenham Clarke, the ATL also managed to secure a promise from mill owners to contribute one rupee per employee per annum.[24] He believed that the success of the ATL depended on the cooperation of Indian medical professionals.

Another issue that attracted frequent comment in the sanitary reports was the high rate of infant mortality. This was invariably attributed to the social environment, child marriages and the economic condition of the parents. Turner held that 'habits' and poverty affected mothers during pregnancy and influenced the health of the child before and after birth; unhygienic conditions swelled the numbers of those who came into the world only to die.[25] The BSA was associated with the Lady Willingdon Scheme (1914), which provided for twelve female health visitors, three maternity homes and an infant milk depot. While admitting that infant mortality could be ascribed partly to early marriage, Indian opinion held that impure milk and high prices were also to be blamed.[26]

The BSA spawned similar bodies in other cities of the presidency: Dharwar (1912) and Broach (1914) established district sanitary associations to educate the public on sanitation and hygiene. Non-official bodies, the Arogya Mandals were set up in Puna, Sangli and Dhulia, to provide medical relief and offer suggestions to the municipalities.

3. Reactions to Epidemic Control Measures

The contradictions in Indian responses are evident in their reactions to epidemic-combating measures. As part of his campaign against smallpox, Turner suggested that aboard infected ships, all *hajis* who had not been previously vaccinated against smallpox, should be compulsorily vaccinated prior to disembarkation, and that they should be housed in temporary camps before their departure on *haj*. While this move was welcomed, the collection of the name and address of every *haji* disembarking was termed 'uncalled-for'.[27] On the other hand, the action of the commissioner of police in taking heed of the objections of *hajis* to the use of western medicines, on the grounds that they contained alcohol, was appreciated.[28]

While the numbers attending hospitals and dispensaries marginally increased, reservations regarding hospital stay persisted. The compulsory removal of smallpox patients to hospitals created panic and led to concealment; hence, it was advocated that everyone living with an infected person should be vaccinated.[29] The forcible segregation of smallpox patients at the infectious diseases hospital during an outbreak in 1905 was condemned even by municipal councillors who were doctors. It was believed that the 'foolish measures' attempted in 1896–7 during the plague epidemic were being tried again because Europeans had a dread of smallpox. The Madanpura riots, it was recalled, had their origin in the exasperation to which desperate masses had been driven.[30] *Victoriawalas* (horse carriage drivers) were hauled up, relatives and friends accompanying helpless patients were marched off to courts of law. *Hindi Punch* commented that people were more troubled by the measures to repress it than the epidemic itself.[31]A lay municipal councillor observed that if this had happened in east London, 'the authorities would have found to their cost how they might have been overwhelmed'.[32] When Turner tried his experiments with tuberculosis, his work was hampered by the unwillingness of cattle owners to either have the animals inoculated during life or subject them to examination after death.[33]

As for plague, the Epidemic Diseases Act of 1897 had been regarded not only as vague but also as harsh and arbitrary in its implementation: travel in remote parts had become impossible. The *Indian Spectator* reported that passengers were made to walk half a mile under police protection, like a gang of criminals, and instead of putting down plague the 'faddists and doctrinaires had disrupted business everywhere'.[34] The government of India's resolution of 1905, explicating the results of the experiences of the plague administration for the previous five years, was hailed by the *Jam-e Jamshed* for having the courage to admit 'the futility of making war on such an enemy without the cooperation of the people'.[35] The *Maratha* saw it as a 'climbing down' from 1897: 'The policy of regarding plague as bound to be amenable to their laws and administrative measures offers a pitiable contrast with the almost fatalistic tone of the present resolution.'[36] *Kaiser-I-Hind* welcomed the resolution, for the government had at last realized that the application of several measures must depend on the circumstances of the locality, the character of the people, the stage the disease had reached and the agency available for dealing with it.[37]

The funding of the campaign was a sore point with Indian opinion. The

Maratha did not mince its words when it remarked that the government, after suspending all local bodies, acted solely on its own discretion as to the fashion and cost of plague measures, yet made demands on municipalities and local boards for contributions towards plague expenditure.[38] Similar sentiments were expressed by *Hindi Punch*, which contended that since containing plague was more to reassure European nations and protect trade, the government should share in the enormous expenditure this entailed.[39] The *Gujarati* felt that the establishment of health camps for the poor during the plague season was the most successful measure in control of the disease, but the government's stinginess had prevented it resorting to this on a large scale. This paper strongly disapproved of the government's directive to collectors in other cities to carry out the extermination of rats, at an incentive of one rupee for every twenty killed, inspired by Turner's success in Bombay.[40] *Jain* maintained that this not only conflicted with religious sensibilities but observed that rats contaminated food grains after consuming the poison.[41]

The pros and cons of Waldemar Mordecai Haffkine's plague prophylactic, developed in 1896, were extensively debated. Endorsement had come from an unlikely quarter: Marishankar Govindji Shastri, a *vaid*, had declared that the vaccine was supported by the 'Aryan system' of medicine.[42] Despite advocacy of its use in *Kesari* in 1899 by Dr Vishram Ghole, assistant surgeon in Puna, the paper contended that people were not convinced of the efficacy, particularly in the light of the Malkowal incident.[43] Colonel W B Bannerman, director of the Bombay Bacteriological Laboratory (BBL), explained its harmlessness at a citizen's meeting in Bombay, while the BMU declared its conviction of the vaccine's efficacy. In answer to Lokamanya Tilak's queries about the effects of the inoculation, Bhatavadekar pointed out that inoculation was unsuitable only in cases of phthisis (pulmonary tuberculosis), rheumatism, kidney diseases and general debility.[44] The paper *Arunodaya* alleged that his endorsement of the prophylactic had earned Bhatavadekar his knighthood.[45] The resumption of its promotion in 1905, after a gap of five years, was ascribed to the influence of the 'class of capitalists', the major employers, as the workers had not the 'least desire' to be inoculated.[46] The Mill-owners' Association passed a resolution in its favour: workers were given day's leave with pay to get themselves inoculated and an insurance policy that would yield fifty rupees to the family of anyone who died from plague. Turner's proposal that the inoculated should be insured for 100 rupees was rejected by the government, much to the disappointment of *The Times of India* but the approval of the *Maratha*.[47] Various suggestions were put forward to make the plan more acceptable: secretariat officials, members of the Bombay municipal corporation and the legislative council, justices of peace and mill-owners would be inoculated, thus setting an example to others. Another idea was to publicize that the serum was a vegetable product. It was regarded as discriminatory that Europeans and 'well-to-do natives' were not required to be inoculated because they lived in ventilated houses, and did not risk infection.[48] In fact the abolition of health camps in Bombay was seen as pandering to the fashionable and influential sections of the city.[49]

Sydenham Clarke invited editors of Gujarati, Marathi, Urdu and Portuguese newspapers to visit the BBL and see for themselves the process of the vaccine's preparation. Fifty editors responded and were shown round by W G Liston, acting director, then presented with a booklet describing the process of manufacture. Sydenham Clarke assured them that inoculation was simple and painless, with discomfort only of short duration; the servants of Government House were frequently inoculated. He appealed to them for constructive criticism.[50] Newspapers associated with social reform, like the *Indian Spectator* and the *Indian Social Reformer* supported the vaccine, and the latter recommended that one way of countering sceptics, because every illness was ascribed to it and used to discredit inoculation, was to maintain a record of the exact condition of an inoculated person's health.[51] It was also suggested that the new discoveries, embodied in the government's despatch to local bodies, should be explained to the people, particularly since villagers were under the impression that the government had caused the plague. The discoveries included the following facts: (a) bubonic plague was spread by infected rats; (b) the medium of contagion between rat and rat, and rat and man was the rat flea, and (c) the life of the plague germ in the soil floors and walls of houses was of short duration.[52] The *Indian Social Reformer* explained the process of the preparation of the anti-plague vaccine and showed that all chances of contamination of the serum were carefully considered and eliminated. [53]

Elsewhere in the presidency, too, there were contrary responses. While the prophylactic was advocated in Broach and Kaira, newspapers from Satara and Belgaum objected to compulsion. Voluntary acceptance should be the keynote, advised *Indu Prakash*.[54] A recent study has shown that evasive tactics were used to counter official regulation in the pilgrim centre of Pandharpur.[55] By the second decade of the twentieth century, opposition seems to have decreased, though there were accounts associating the vaccine with leprosy and continuous fever.[56] *Kesari* dropped its opposition on the grounds that the serum had become pure and claimed that had the press not protested initially the quality of the serum would not have improved.[57] *Indu Prakash* contended that inoculation afforded the poor security, since evacuation was not within the reach of everyone.[58] The success of its promotion in Wai, was attributed to the efforts of Dr D A Turkhud, and it was accepted by mill workers in Nagpur.[59] The positive response by 1908 to the campaign fighting plague in Puna, was particularly commended since that city had been in the forefront of agitation against it in the previous decade. This turn around was ascribed to the autonomy given to the non-official plague-relief committee. Under the leadership of Gopal Krishna Gokhale and his team of volunteers, led by Gopal Krishna Devadhar, the Puna committee cooperated with the municipal authorities not only in propagating inoculation (successfully persuading 15,250 persons to have this done) but also in rat destruction, evacuation and disposal of the dead.[60] They compiled statistics showing 1,250 deaths among the uninoculated and only four among the inoculated, concluding that there had not been a single instance in which 'evil effects' had resulted from inoculation.[61]

4. 'Obstacles to Malaria Prevention'

This was the title of a section of the report written after an investigation into the causes of malaria in Bombay by Charles Bentley, IMS. According to Bentley, the obstinacy of the 'upper classes' was a greater obstacle in the prevention of malaria than 'the ignorance of the masses'. He observed that this 'ignorance' had, however, not prevented the adoption of a pure-water supply once the 'educated had decided that it was necessary'.[62] His conclusion that there was a higher rate of malaria among Parsis was strongly refuted by this community, which had been in the forefront of the acceptance of western medicine. Bentley referred to a particular house owner, who had threatened to take legal proceedings for trespass if any of his properties were visited by inspection staff, and regretted that the many Indian doctors had little influence on their wealthy clients. Even Parsi doctors made a vigorous onslaught on Bentley for holding their private wells to be the cause of the prevalence of infection.[63] Finally, a committee of medical men, subsequently appointed by the Bombay Zoroastrian Association, supported Bentley's conclusions.[64] Three hundred and fifty Parsi priests had petitioned the municipal commissioner in 1910, protesting against the directive to close wells or cover them. They had contended that they could not use water for religious purposes if it was pumped from covered wells, since they believed that it had to be exposed to the sun, a great purifier.[65] K B Shroff, himself a Parsi doctor and special assistant to Turner, referred to the 'sentimental objections' raised by some persons of his community, such as the presence of 'saintly beings' resident in wells. The Jain community objected to the stocking of wells with fish, which had been recommended as a means of reducing mosquito larvae.[66]

While the reformist paper *Rast Goftar* recommended that municipal corporations should help people overcome prejudices rather than just criticize Bentley's report,[67] there were strong objections in other papers: 'Is the campaign to be of the same draconian and oppressive character which drove people mad exasperating them to a boiling point?'[68] A 'house owner' wrote that Turner could instruct all well-owners to empty and clean them, but to seal all wells was 'sheer *zulum* (oppression)'.[69] Closing of wells with gauze was advocated: it would not offend religious scruples, government or the municipality bearing the expenditure.[70] However, most well owners seem ultimately to have borne the expense, and trap-doors were permitted over wells in order 'not to wound religious susceptibilities'.[71] Yet Shroff saw, while inspecting, that in 90 per cent of cases, the trap-doors were left open and larvae were found even in closed wells, indicating that they had been left open at night. To bolster support for the campaign, public lectures were given at different venues by Shroff, Dr C Continho and Dr Hirji Gini. Sir Jamsetjee Jejeebhoy exhorted his coreligionists to cooperate with the authorities. To oppose the closure of wells, he said, 'was as much against the spirit and teaching of religion as against the laws of health'.[72] Pherozeshah Mehta maintained that the objections were more due to an inordinate attachment to custom than to 'a proper appreciation of the spirit which runs through religion'.[73] A weekly report of wells with larvae was even sent to local newspapers like *The Times of India*, *Jam-e Jamshed*, the *Bombay Gazette* and the *Bombay Samachar* in the hope that it would have a salutary effect in convincing the recalcitrant.

Another reason for the dependence on well water was the inadequacy of the water supply; Dr Dinsha Bomanji Master's proposal that wells should not be sealed until adequate supply was provided was rejected by the municipal corporation. There was disappointment that the popular Liston had supported this measure, since he had overlooked the fact that some areas had no water for days.[74] The dismissal of a petition of Narottam Morarji Goculdas and others protesting against the directive was termed 'unstatesmanly' by Mehta.[75] The rejection by the standing committee of the municipal corporation of the petition of 25,000 residents requesting a postponement of the proposed scheme was described as having trampled upon public opinion.[76] Described as a 'cold-bloodedly colourless reply', it was remarked, 'If the answer had come from the executive we could have understood it but the answer comes from the corporation, in theory a body representing the public.'[77] The Bombay government's endorsement of the corporation's decision came six months later.

5. Bureaucratic and Financial Impediments

While the authorities had often criticized the contradictory nationalist stand of calling for the reduction of expenditure and taxation and for an increase in expenditure on welfare, which included sanitary works and medical relief,[78] another factor in understanding the working of colonial health policy was the divergence of views within the establishment. A point of contention had been the extent of the state's financial responsibility for health. When Hewlett had retired from office as sanitary commissioner in 1888, he had made a plea for more governmental involvement. He contended that 'when the annual loss, which our commerce has to meet on account of the imposition of quarantine is calculated it will be evident that the actual loss of money now entailed on the country by disease, the offspring of filth, far outbalances the expense which would be required, if Government were pleased to sanction the cost of the agency necessary to maintain cleanliness in our villages'.[79] Chief Secretary John Nugent, ICS, had dismissed these remarks as 'discursive, controversial, egotistic and objectionable'.[80] Subsequently C W Macrury, Hewlett's successor, recommended the study of sanitation by officers of the civil service as part of their curriculum at home, instruction in hygiene in schools and a scheme for public lectures to sway opinion in favour of it. As for municipalities since they were unwilling and unequal to deal with problems of sanitation, he maintained that responsibility could only rest with the government.[81]

Mark Harrison has pointed out that the Bombay government did assist municipalities in their efforts to combat plague after 1903 when the first allocation was made for plague relief. From 1908, the growing revenue surpluses enabled the government of India to allot annual grants of 3 million rupees to provincial governments for sanitary purposes.[82] This was apparently inadequate. Turner's annual reports show the ramifications of the working relationship between the government, the municipality, and the City Improvement Trust. Dr Jehangir Cursetji and Dr Dinsha Bomanji Master in their paper on 'Defects in the Present Modes of Disposal of Sewage and Town Refuse of Bombay' presented to the Bombay Medical Congress, referred to the efforts of Turner to improve the state of things. They blamed the Great Indian Peninsula (GIP) Railway, the Bombay Baroda and Central Indian (BBCI) Railway authorities for not cooperating with Turner despite his long correspondence with them over five years.[83] Public ignorance, leading to insanitary habits, was ascribed to a half-hearted educational policy.[84] Turner's suggestions for drastic slum clearance were not supported either by the municipality or the CIT. His other proposals for sanitary improvement – though approved later by the corporation – were not implemented owing to financial constraints. The corporation had recognized the necessity for, and freely sanctioned, annual expenditure on medical relief, and control of diseases. Though the question of the inadequate system of drainage had been raised with municipal commissioners for twenty years, it was to no avail. At the end of his eighteen-year tenure, Turner observed that what had 'been done in improving public health had been due to organization and systematic and constant supervision and not to capital expenditure.'[85]

These tensions did not escape the local press. The sanitary commissioner's report of 1903, which recorded the unsanitary conditions in *mofussils* seems to have provoked a government resolution in 'a resentful spirit'.[86] While recognizing the burden placed on local bodies by successive outbreaks of plague, it was held that both the governments of India and Bombay had failed to realize their responsibility. They would not accept that their land-revenue system was defective and that their famine administration might have been more prompt. It was believed that while medical experts had discovered the causes of diseases, the government of India's stinginess had prevented mitigation of the severity of an epidemic if not its elimination. If the government had relieved the municipal bodies and local boards of unnecessary expenditure, it was observed in 1904, they might have concentrated their resources on sanitary improvements.[87] Ten years later, the same refrain was heard: schemes were approved for various cities, but government had no money for their implementation.[88] Clearly, the expectation was that the state should fund sanitary improvements, and economy in sanitation was condemned. Preventive and curative measures in public health were regarded as the 'imperative obligations of the state and local bodies', and such an effort had to be supported by them.[89]

6. Views of Indian Doctors

The conviction of Indian doctors, trained in western medicine, of the benefits of sanitation is apparent in their papers, presented at the Bombay Medical Congress convened at the initiative of Sydenham Clarke in 1909. Among the local doctors, N H Choksy reported on the results of serum treatment in plague cases, he and his colleagues having treated 275 cases with the subcutaneous method of administration, the other method being intravenous. He had observed that meat-eaters seemed to suffer more than vegetarians from the after-effects, with rashes, oedema, joint and muscle pains. Bhatavadekar found similar results in his private practice.[90] In another paper, Choksy showed the negative effects of alcohol, internal antiseptics, anti-pyretics and the use of carbolic acid in the symptomatic treatment of plague.[91] D A Turkhud related the results of a two-year experiment in treating leprosy patients with Röntgen X-rays, at the Acworth leprosy hospital. One of the most interesting papers was entitled 'Unhygienic Bombay' wherein the authors, Dr Jehangir Cursetji and Dr Dinsha Bomanji Master outlined the reasons for this unfortunate title.[92] In addition to an inadequate water supply, overcrowding, an incomplete and imperfect sewage system, pollution of the soil and improper location of cattle sheds, the authors regarded the peculiar customs and prejudices of the people as an important cause. Their recommendation was that the poor, who were ignorant in the principles of hygiene and household sanitation, should be educated, and advocated free primary education at municipal expense. In another paper, on the defects in the disposal of waste (referred to above), the two doctors made a case for more funds for the health department, particularly since the corporation was solvent.[93] Sorab C Hormusji, in his paper on methods of disinfection referred to the use of pesterine (crude petroleum) and emulsions of kerosene oil.[94] An exhibition of surgical, sanitary, building, disinfectant and fumigation appliances, drugs, food and toilet requisites, medical and scientific publications was organized, with magic-lantern slide show to explain types of fever to the public.

There had been high expectations that the congress would provide an opportunity for a closer study of Indian customs from the sanitary point of view, and that Indians would be able to explain to the world theories such as the *tridosha* (the three humours: air, bile and phlegm) and the value of herbs and plants in use since time immemorial.[95] Consequently 'India and Indian problems would receive greater attention in future.'[96] It was also hoped that a joint committee of medical experts from Europe and from the Bombay presidency could be formed to tackle the problems posed by plague, cholera and malaria.[97] However, all the papers presented at the congress were on western medicine. The participants included experts like Ronald Ross, S Kitasato and Leonard Rogers. While Sydenham Clarke was commended for giving this opportunity of reviewing the practice of medicine from the point of view of the latest theories, it was noted that there was not a single exponent of Indian medicine at the congress. To the lay person, the papers seemed lengthy, academic and highly technical.[98] At the end of the congress, a critic concluded that the governor was an idealist, and there was no point in talking about sanitary improvement unless the government was prepared to spend two or three crores of rupees on sanitation.[99]

7. Instruction on Public Health

Both doctors and health officials held that education was invaluable in disseminating knowledge on sanitation. At a conference held in 1910 under the auspices of the director of public instruction, Bhatavadekar delineated the principles of instruction of sanitation. He began with the affirmation that the value of hygiene had been appreciated even in ancient times. The Hindu *shastras* had enjoined scrupulous attention to cleanliness, abstention from unwholesome food, alcoholic liquor and narcotics. In modern times, Hindus had departed from those standards. Applauding the efforts of Turner and the BSA, Bhatavadekar hoped that, with education and the dissemination of hygiene principles, 'the Hindoo will certainly cease to regard smallpox and cholera as divinities and the Musalman will rely more on his own efforts than surrender himself entirely into the hands of providence'.[100] The province of hygiene was to prevent not cure disease. Hence, it had to depend for its advance upon the advances of pathology and aetiology. In promoting this knowledge, Bhatavadekar regarded the schoolmaster as an 'effective and useful agent', who could inspect the children and give directions regarding cleanliness, food and sleep.[101] He advised that in dealing with ignorant parents the schoolmaster would have to use tact and sympathy. He endorsed Sydenham Clarke's comment that the school hygiene primers needed revision. Bhatavadekar ended his lecture by contending that parental responsibility in teaching hygiene was equally important. The spread of education, not just the distribution of quinine, was regarded the key to the solution of the sanitary question. The *Indian Spectator* remarked, 'Every pie spent on the opening of primary schools is so much money devoted to sanitary measures.'[102]

Turner's assistant health officer, Dr D K Goldsmith, collected information and compiled a report on the condition of elementary schools in 1910. It noted that large sums were spent in English schools on imparting the simple fact that cleanliness, proper ventilation and light were the three principal agents in reducing sickness and death rates. Turner held that medical inspection of schoolchildren was the 'duty' of local authorities: 'interference of the state is justified by the large amount of preventive and remediable defects among school children'.[103] The schools committee accepted Turner's other recommendations including the scientific supervision of school methods, baths and douches, physical education, the inspection of school buildings and the teaching of hygiene to teachers.[104] Though these measures would only benefit 38,000 of the 112,000 children of school age in the city who actually went to school, it was a beginning. Liston gave a course of eight lectures to the students of the Secondary Training College, Bombay, on some of the common diseases of India. Another lecture series was delivered to the students of the Puna Training College. Lessons on tuberculosis, malaria and microbes and a pamphlet containing a description of simple precautionary measures to be taken had been circulated in schools. A textbook on sanitation was prescribed for use in Anglo-vernacular secondary and primary schools, while lessons on hygiene were included in the science curriculum at the secondary level.[105]

8. Triumph of Western Medicine: Registration of Medical Practitioners Act, 1912

Poonam Bala has shown that in the early years of colonial rule there had been friendly coexistence between the established Indian and western systems of medicine, but from the 1860s there was increasing criticism of the lack of refinement of indigenous medicine. The third phase, in the late nineteenth century, saw western medicine move away from indigenous medicine, owing to increasing professionalization that led medical practitioners both in Britain and in India to discard the humoural basis of diagnosis.[106] Yet in that period Surgeon General W J Moore, found that only one-tenth of the population of Bombay went to western-educated doctors, and the rest to indigenous practitioners.[107] The move to register medical practitioners was initiated in 1881 by Principal Cook of the Grant Medical College, and endorsed by the Grant College Medical Society.[108] The government had then felt it was premature, since the bulk of the population consulted indigenous practitioners. In 1887, a move to reintroduce the proposal, this time only for the city of Bombay, was also turned down. It would appear that the government, while increasingly confident of western medicine, was reluctant to take on the responsibility of shutting out indigenous practitioners. The suggestion was revived two decades later, and the Bombay presidency became the first to pass the Registration of Medical Practitioners Act (RMP) in 1912. Many people still went to *vaids* and *hakims*, but among them there were a number of charlatans and quacks. The Act was passed to prevent untrained men passing themselves off as qualified. It laid down that state-run and aided dispensaries would employ registered medical practitioners and that no certificate was valid unless signed by a medical practitioner registered under the Act. The recognized qualifications were university degrees, government-school diplomas in medicine, surgery and midwifery, and those possessed by military assistant surgeons or sub-assistant surgeons or hospital assistants.

Though the measure was initiated and supported by Indian doctors, the BMU protested, before it was passed, that the bill equated them with hospital assistants because it included them as registered practitioners. They submitted a petition to the governor, in which they maintained that it had lowered their professional and social status.[109]

The medics did not have many sympathizers in the local press. *Sanj Vartaman* said they had brought the Act on themselves because they had tried to denigrate the indigenous practitioners, and *Bombay Samachar* referred to their selfishness and disregard of the public.[110] *Kesari* remarked, 'They asked for bread and the Government gave them stones.'[111] *Akhbar-e-Saudagar* described the Act as ' one more highly obnoxious measure'.[112] The BMU had also objected to the Bombay Medical Council because it was packed with government nominees. The council, which did not have the power to implement the Act, had authority over curricula and could refuse to register anyone guilty of 'unprofessional conduct'. Pherozeshah Mehta pointed out in the Bombay Legislative Council that this latter clause went beyond the British Act after which it had been modelled. He averred that public opinion in Britain was homogeneous, distinguishing between qualified medical men and quacks, and the qualified medical men themselves were homogeneous. In India the *vaids* and *hakims* were considered quacks by those who were qualified, and there were three bodies of medical men including them, the IMS and Indian doctors.[113] Sydenham Clarke countered this argument by pointing out that there was more homogeneity in Bombay, since all the doctors were from one college, Grant Medical College, while in Britain they were from different colleges; and further there was not even 'racial' homogeneity since there were English, Irish and Scottish practitioners.[114] While describing the prejudice of the 'enormous mass' of the people against western medicine as 'unreasonable', Mehta pointed out that the mass would have nothing to do with it. He further observed that the Act did not affect *vaids* and *hakims* and 'in reality it is an attempt to bring the qualified medical practitioners under their (government's) control'.[115]

The *vaids* and *hakims* registered their protest at a meeting held in Bombay, and submitted a petition to the governor seeking redress of their grievances. They held that 'myriads' of Indian people had unshaken confidence in the healing power of their medicine. They wanted recognition of the death certificates they issued and the right to sue patients for failure to pay bills. By excluding all indigenous practitioners from the right to registration, the government was seen to have cast a slur on them, favouring allopathy. A suggestion was put forth that the government could develop the Indian system of medicine by providing instruction and holding examinations in the *ayurvedic* and *unani* systems. The governor's reply to the petition was a vague assurance that native medicine would be recognized when it improved. *Kesari* asked pertinently what encouragement it had been given to make improvements.[116] The basic issue was that, as the *Jam-e-Jamshed* pointed out, in 'the present state the country was in', the masses could not afford 'qualified medical relief, and for many years to come the number of medical practitioners and hospitals and dispensaries is certainly not going to multiply to justify the belief that they will be able to reach out the hand of relief to the poorer classes now dependent on *vaids* and *hakims*'.[117] Another view was that the masses had a dread of the European physician. 'Most of them have the notion that to go to a hospital is to die, that British doctors mercilessly hack and hew the body instead of treating as the native doctor does, with drugs and balsams. It would not be proper or politic to prohibit them as a class.'[118] Indigenous medicine was considered best suited to the Indian climate and constitution,[119] and diseases incurable in the western system had been 'miraculously' cured by *ayurveda* or *unani*.[120] While the supporters of indigenous practitioners conceded that there were many pretenders, who claimed to cure by incantations and magic, the truth was that the poor could not afford the 'doctor'. *Kesari*, doubting the good results that were expected from the Act, contended that doctors starved, while *vaids* and *hakims* prospered.[121] There were also objections in the Legislative Council, because of the suspicion that the powerful IMS would use the Act to the detriment of the Indian medical graduates. It was passed in the face of opposition from independent medical practitioners.[122] In this, 'The partisan attitude of the state was thus unambiguously articulated,' as K N Panikkar has observed.[123]

9. 'Knowledge of the People'

This was the theme of the Indian Sanitary Conference held in Bombay in 1911 and presided over by S Harcourt Butler, the education adviser on the viceroy's Council. Bombay was lauded as a model for other cities to emulate. Butler held that 'living knowledge' not 'paper knowledge' of Indian ways of life would form the basis of understanding on sanitation. He was consequently hailed by reformist opinion: 'There is not a more enlightened and sympathetic Englishman in India.'[124] He also recognized that measures possible and effective in the West could not in every case produce identical results in India. The papers at the conference covered a wide range of subjects, the call to government to ensure the purity of food supplies being of particular public interest.[125]

Sydenham Clarke had noted that 'legal measures for the enforcement of sanitation were becoming the key feature in the civic life of Western countries'.[126] But here they had to proceed slowly. He claimed that 'the people were learning that *kismet* [fate] will admit of some amendment'.[127] At fairs and large gatherings, it was found that there was an increasing readiness to accept and act on arrangements made for them. 'All this is encouraging in a country where we have to try to lead the people quietly and gradually into compliance with natural laws vital to their well being and where strong sanitary measures elsewhere enforced are not possible.'[128]

The Government of India Resolution on Sanitation (1914) emphasized three cardinal principles to be borne in mind in sanitary reform, while handling the 'labyrinth of difficulties': a knowledge of the people, their social customs, habits and prejudices, the diversity of local conditions and the fact that reform should be preceded by surveys.[129] Though the resolution acknowledged the value of cooperation with the public, Indian reformers felt that the government's primary motivation was a disproportionate concern with epidemics, and that it failed to visualize the problem as a connected whole. Even if plague, cholera and phthisis were stamped out, the pressing problem of high infant mortality would remain.[130] The *Prajabandhu*, of

Ahmedabad, agreed with the observation that there was little hope of improving sanitary conditions permanently unless the congestion in cities was relieved and the streets broadened.[131] It was posited that if the people were to cooperate Indians should be trained for superior positions.[132] In *Kesari* the issue was linked to the neglect of Indian medicine, since the majority of the population consulted its practitioners. Besides, the government might state that doctors should know the customs and habits of the people but how many of them were Indian? Even women doctors were imported from Britain. The GOI resolution commended various initiatives of Bombay officials, including many of Turner's and the survey conducted by Bentley. It also referred to the Bombay government's publication of 1914, and mentioned the efforts made to date in line with it. The latter had concluded with the assertion that the boundaries of the field of 'sanitary endeavour' would be expanded with public cooperation. [133]

10. Conclusion

Preventive medicine had been perceived as 'a factor' in empire building. Speaking at the Royal Institute of Public Health in 1904, the British prime minister, Arthur J Balfour, contended that it touched the greatest internal and external problems. The internal problem, he said, referred to the dangers from the inevitable increase of the urban population, and the external to 'the necessity for rendering the conditions of life in the Colonies such as to mitigate the dangers which threaten the Europeans, whose presence is necessary for the development of those countries'.[134] Thus the agenda was clear: the risks to Europeans' health had to be reduced, particularly since their presence in the colonies was considered essential. But the new era of preventive medicine prevailed in Britain, because of a large commitment of public funds, as Ira Klein has pointed out in a recent paper.[135]

The above analysis, focusing on Bombay, has shown that there appears to have been a paucity of finances, and an underlying tension between the government and the municipality, notwithstanding Turner's enthusiastic plans. The Bombay Municipal Corporation, despite an increased income, found that they did not have adequate means to undertake works of permanent utility. But Turner, the man on the spot, pressed ahead with his schemes, garnering public support. He regretted that while efforts were made by the health department, it could not grapple with socio-economic factors and, therefore, voluntary agencies should be encouraged in their efforts. He achieved some success in this direction during the influenza epidemic in 1918, when his appeal for assistance from the voluntary organizations was responded to handsomely.[136] Even as Sydenham Clarke spoke of the 'tyranny' of custom, and perceived the task to be gigantic, he recognised the need to proceed gradually since public health was intimately connected with the habits of the people.

Indian responses to Turner's initiatives were both appreciative and resistant, as could be seen in the reactions to the anti-malaria campaign in Bombay. Generally, there was a greater assertiveness in Indian opinion, reflecting the growing national consciousness, and there was clearly the expectation that the government had the responsibility to fund public health. The fatalistic and heartfelt reaction of *Kal* is significant: 'We are unable to fathom the ground of their [people's] opposition [to plague control measures].' The slave's body belonged, after all, to the master. 'As we must die one day or the other of starvation or some other disease why should we hesitate to submit to inoculation?'[137] Change in the opposition towards the plague vaccine was attributed to the fact that Indian vigilance had made the medical researcher improve the quality of the serum. There was also the assertion of self-pride: 'The people have their own ideas of cleanliness which they scrupulously carry out according to their lights.'[138] Pherozeshah Mehta regretted that the East was so backward in sanitation, 'when it is remembered that in the days of our ancestors it was the people of the East who were so remarkable for sanitary progress and sanitary improvement'.[139]

The dominance of western medicine had been established, by the Registration of Medical Practitioners Act, as has been shown above. While Indian medicine was effectively sidelined, it remained popular. Hence the Bombay government's proposal in 1915 to shut down in Puna an *ayurvedic* dispensary, maintained by the municipality for the previous twenty years, was not only strongly resisted but had to be dropped. This move was made as a consequence of the Act, which required that the physician in charge of even an aided dispensary should possess recognized qualifications. The important fact was that the average attendance here was larger than it was for two other dispensaries providing western medicine. Other dimensions of the tension between the two systems of medicine could be further explored.

Solutions to tackle health problems were put forward. The development of Indian industry might reduce the number of half-starving people, who were prone to diseases. Another voice called for greater involvement of the masses, who evinced little interest in civic affairs since the nominated members in the legislative councils invariably sided with the officials and were thus more representative of the government by whom they were appointed. To Indian reformers, including doctors, poor health was caused by the ignorance of the masses, and the spread of education for a better understanding of the value of sanitation was seen as the remedy. Doctors were not only vital in making western medicine more acceptable, but also in disseminating information on sanitation and on precautions to be taken against disease. This study has shown through the varied perspectives of British officials and Indians that complexity and ambivalence marked this facet of the Indo-British encounter.

PART IV:

THE CIVILIZING MISSION INTERNALIZED

11

National Education, Pulp Fiction and the Contradictions of Colonialism: Perceptions of an Educational Experiment in Early-Twentieth-Century India[1]

HARALD FISCHER-TINÉ
Humboldt-University, Berlin

> That the Gurukula is calculated to produce healthy, clean-living, disciplined, patriotic and enthusiastic exponents of Aryaism is obvious! The question that arises is whether it will produce open-minded, loyal, practical and useful citizens of the British Empire.[2]

1. Introduction

In nineteenth-century British India, the notion of the civilizing project of the colonial state grew in popularity. Increasingly, an influential school of official opinion came to believe that the colonial enterprise entailed the responsibility of improving the lot of a people steeped in despotism and ignorance and enslaved by irrational social institutions. The British argued that the 'childlike natives' in the Indian colony would have to be trained to become active citizens, capable of acting in a responsible manner. In this regard, the educational system created by the colonial state was perceived as the backbone of a consistent policy of 'improvement',[3] which coupled the desire to bring about the material betterment of its subjects with more ambitious goals that were shaped by strong moral overtones. Moreover, as policymakers in British India assumed that Indians suffered from serious 'defects of character'[4] the provision of education to eliminate these imperfections seemed all the more necessary. Hence, 'character formation', the teaching of 'right conduct' and the 'progressive and orderly development of the mind' were regarded as more important aims than the mere transmission of knowledge.[5] However, as Thomas Metcalf has recently reminded us, 'the ideals sustaining the imperial enterprise in India were always shot through with contradiction and inconsistency'.[6] In the field of education such contradictions and inconsistencies are fairly obvious. The success of an educational policy seeking to transform natives into 'brown Englishmen' threatened to render the British presence altogether unnecessary and was difficult to combine with the pragmatic everyday need to legitimate and exercise power. This is in line with Homi Bhaba's argument that mimicry – a complete assimilation of the indigenous population to the culture of their colonial masters in dress, behaviour, language and ways of thinking – was regarded as the most dangerous threat to colonial rule since it blurred the line separating the colonizers from the colonized.[7]

The friction between civilizing aspirations on the one hand and concerns about governance on the other became evident when Indians with a nationalistic bias – echoing colonial objectives – established their own educational institutions to promote 'self betterment' and 'national regeneration'. While some British officials welcomed these efforts as fulfilling the colonial *mission civilisatrice*, another strand of opinion condemned such ideas as heralding the prelude to open sedition. The ambivalence of the British position towards 'national education' is explored in this chapter by analysing the discourse that emerged around the Gurukul Kangri, one of the most original experiments in education in twentieth-century India. It is argued that until 1912 an attitude, which may be labelled as 'conservative imperialist', prevailed among British officials, whose firm belief in the 'illusion of permanence' made them perceive the Gurukul's ambitions to promote 'national self-respect' as a potential threat to colonial rule. In subsequent years things changed dramatically when 'liberal imperialists',[8] who viewed the British Raj much more as a trusteeship that was limited in time, gained in influence. Paradoxically, an outspokenly 'national' institution like the Gurukul, which had been conceived by its founders as a 'living and concrete protest against foreign innovation',[9] increasingly came to be regarded as a useful agency in fulfilling the imperial educational mission.

That such paradoxical positions were not confined to the colonizers alone is demonstrated in the final section of the chapter dealing with the self-perception of the Gurukul authorities and their assessment of the Raj. It seems clear that the 'civilizing values' of the British had been internalized by the school's founders to a remarkable degree for, in spite of their nationalistic rhetoric, they shared the view that British rule was necessary (if not providential) for the time being. Apart from dissecting the various and partly antagonistic voices within British imperialism itself, a study of the various perceptions of the Gurukul experiment thus also provides an excellent example of a phenomenon Ashis Nandy defines as 'colonial consensus'. As Nandy convincingly argues, colonialism – or at least its non-material dimension – has to be understood as a 'shared culture' in which 'the ruled are constantly tempted to fight their rulers within the psychological limits set by the latter'.[10] Thus, the Gurukul authorities accepted many British presuppositions, especially the idea that Indians would remain unfit for self-rule unless they were thoroughly (re-)educated to become loyal and manly citizens. As a result, the Gurukul became instrumental in perpetuating an imperialist myth sustaining the ideological basis of the Raj rather than contesting its legitimacy.

Before concluding this introductory section with a brief overview of the historical context in which the Gurukul emerged, a word on the sources used for this study might be appropriate to shed some light on the rather cryptic title of this chapter. Besides police reports, other official records and the writings and speeches of the Gurukul teachers, one of the most important sources to elucidate this complex bundle of imperial perceptions and schemes is a widely read (though rather trashy) novel entitled *Siri Ram Revolutionist*, published in 1912 and written by an employee of the Indian Civil Service. It offers remarkable insights into the imperial reading of early Indian nationalism and will be used extensively in the argument spelt out below.

The Gurukul Kangri and the Quest for National Education

The deficiencies of the colonial educational system, the perceived threat of cultural alienation and the fear of a possible infiltration by Christianity provoked a growing disaffection among the Indian public in the latter half of the nineteenth century.[11] Among educated Hindu elites, particularly, this led to a quest for 'national education'. It was evident for the newly emerging middle classes familiar with the colonial milieu[12] that religious education of the traditional type was not a viable alternative to the education imparted in high schools and colleges run by the British. Thus, from the 1870s, countless educational institutions were founded throughout the country with the aim of combining the 'best of both worlds' and providing students with western education that would qualify them for a career in the colonial apparatus and imbue them with a strong sense of 'national pride', as well as a profound knowledge of the 'essentials of national culture and religion'. It hardly needs to be stressed that the opinions on what exactly represented these essentials were as diverse as the various social, political and religious reform movements that were the main carriers of these educational endeavours.

The Gurukul Kangri, which is the focus of this paper, reflected the social and political visions of the Arya Samaj, the most influential Hindu reform movement in northern India.[13] It would not be an exaggeration to claim that it was among the more radical of the many educational experiments launched in late nineteenth- and early-twentieth-century India.[14] Munshiram (1857–1926), the leader of the so-called 'militant faction' of the Samaj founded the school in 1902. Munshiram, who became better known as Swami Shraddhanand after he had taken *sannyas* in 1917, was a major figure in the Hindu reform movement and widely respected as a 'Mahatma' (great soul) even outside Arya circles years before such a title was conferred on Gandhi by public opinion.[15] He had conceived the school as the reformers' 'testing ground and showcase'[16] to articulate the newly constructed national culture and disseminate it to a wider Hindu public. In the vision of its founders, the institution was to become the blueprint for a whole network of schools and colleges modelled in its image, which, it was hoped, would finally replace the colonial system of education. In spite of its relative insignificance in terms of the number and direct influence of its graduates, the school soon became an icon of early Hindu nationalism and its history is highly relevant for an understanding of the Hindu middle classes' strategies of intellectual decolonization. As the name indicates, the school's founders claimed continuity with the ancient Hindu seats of learning,[17] and one of the main motives for its foundation was the desire to provide an institution at which an intensive study of Sanskrit and the Vedas was combined with a 'modern' curriculum. At first glance, the institution indeed brought to mind a traditional Sanskrit *pathshala*: the students had to shave their heads and wear traditional clothes (*kurta* and *dhoti*), and at least some of the classes were held outside the buildings under the trees. Moreover, religious rites (for instance the Vedic fire sacrifice, *havan*, conducted according to the Arya Samaj practices) formed a compulsory part of the daily routine. These features misled some scholars to believe that the Gurukul was only concerned with 'building up the religious character of the students'.[18]

Nonetheless, this educational experiment also had an overtly political dimension. Among the measures undertaken in Kangri that were supposed to foster a national identity, the spread of Arya Bhasha (a 'purified' style of Hindi) as a national language, the rewriting of Indian history and the reorganization of society on the basis of equality and social mobility were prominent.[19] The most important goal, however, was to promote 'national regeneration' by completely reshaping the mind and body of the individual. This included a stress on physical culture (even eugenics theories found their way into the Gurukul ideology)[20] and the transmission of ideals of manliness and discipline. The extraordinary emphasis placed on 'character-formation' is certainly the most striking feature of the school. From the outset, physical training, fencing, horseback riding and drill formed an important part of the daily programme for the 'Brahmacharies', as the students were called, in allusion to ancient educational practices. The similarities between the 'revivalist seminary' of the Aryas and English elite schools did not stop there: the Gurukul had one hockey and two cricket teams, and football was played on a regular basis. Nonetheless, the Gurukul authorities saw their institution as perfectly in line with ancient traditions and constantly stressed its authentic 'Indianness'.[21]

How, then, did British administrators perceive and deal with a Hindu nationalist educational institution that was ostensibly different yet similar in many ways to their own public schools?

2. Grappling with 'Uncompromising Hostility to British Rule': the Conservative Imperialist Discourse

The Arya Samaj had been the subject of official distrust ever since the mid-1880s when it was increasingly held responsible for the growing tension between Hindus and Muslims in its regional strongholds in the Punjab and the United Provinces.[22] Since one of the main objectives of the Samaj was to check Christian conversion, western missionaries left no stone unturned to further discredit this 'most hostile body to Christ and Britain in India'.[23] The Arya commitment to cow protection and reconversion, as well as the prominent role played by leading Arya Samajis like Lala Lajpat Ray and Ajit Singh during the so-called Punjab disturbances in 1907, added to the growing suspicion of the colonial authorities who seriously considered prohibiting the organization.[24]

As expected, the official assessment of the Arya Samaj had an impact on the perception of the Gurukul, considered by many to be the movement's premier institution. By this point, the school founder Munshiram's fund-raising tours had been closely followed by police informers.[25] The fact that the school was situated in the jungle, miles away from the city of Hardwar seemed to prove its doubtful character in the eyes of the authorities and the annual festivals attracted dozens of informers and undercover agents, often disguised as *sadhus* and *babas*.[26]

The British distrust of the Gurukul reached its peak in the wake of the Punjab disturbances.[27] In 1908 police officers and other officials speculated that the school was actually used as a training camp for terrorists. The students, they suspected, would be ideologically equipped and physically prepared to take up arms against the British because of the emphasis placed by the institution on rigid physical exercise and paramilitary training. There were even rumours about an alleged subterranean bomb-factory supposedly situated under the *yagyashala*, the central building where students and teachers gathered twice a day to perform a fire sacrifice according to Vedic rites.[28] Official anxieties were fed to a large extent by the traumatic experience of revolutionary terrorism in Bengal. In particular the stress on physical culture and paramilitary exercise reminded the authorities of the secret societies formed by Bengali 'terrorists'.[29] Even the fact that the students of the Gurukul were not allowed to wear shoes or caps throughout the year, regardless of the weather, was interpreted as being inspired by the 'hardening exercises' of Bengali revolutionaries and further evidence of the institution's 'seditious' outlook.[30]

The fact that representatives of the extremist wing of the Indian National Congress had made the foundation of 'national schools' an important part of their 'revolutionary' agenda exacerberated the government's reservations towards Munshiram's Gurukul. This becomes clear from a confidential report by the Criminal Investigation Department (CID), in which the author first denounces the 'seditious' activities of the National schools in Calcutta and the Maharashtra Vidyalay in Poona, then suggests 'that a similar danger exists in the Gurukul at Kangri, near Hardwar, [. . .] where youths are said to be trained from an early age in principles of uncompromising hostility to British rule'.[31]

The drastic increase in secret police reports between 1909 and 1912 indicates that colonial suspicion of the institution was continually growing. One of the factors responsible for this development was the publication of a highly influential book by *Times* correspondent Valentine Chirol. In *Indian Unrest* (1910), Chirol tries to reconstruct the causes that led to the terrorist outbreaks and disturbances of 1907 and 1908 and concludes that the Arya Samaj played a decisive role.[32] The Gurukul, once again, seems to deserve special attention and the author leaves no doubt that he considers the school a serious menace to British rule.[33] However, when reading between the lines of Chirol's argument, one can also detect a certain respect and admiration for the institution, particularly when he describes the elements of Gurukul education, which were simultaneously responsible for the school's efficiency and for the threat emanating from it:

> Life in the *gurukuls* is simple and even austere, the discipline rigorous, the diet plainest and a great deal of time is given to physical training. As the *chelas*[34] after 16 years of this monastic training at the hands of their *gurus* are to be sent out as missionaries to propagate the Arya doctrines throughout India, the influence of these institutions in the moulding of Indian character and Indian opinion in the future cannot fail to be considerable.[35]

However, in contradistinction to the ambiguity in this account by Sir Valentine Chirol, most British officials of the 'conservative imperialist' type quite frankly condemn the notion of education for pride and self-respect as imparted in the Gurukul Kangri. This becomes apparent in another CID report written in the same year as Chirol's book:

> It is reported that with this object the boys are taught always to address each other as 'Ap' [sic!][36] and to do so even when they quarrel. The result of this kind of teaching was illustrated by an incident which occurred some months ago, where a party of Brahmacharis and Masters of the Kangri *gurukula*, parading their new-found 'nationality' and independence, succeeded in coming into collision with two Europeans on two separate occasions in one day.[37]

Such incidents occurred frequently in this period. In November 1911, Principal Munshiram took to court two Englishmen who had insulted him during a railway journey.[38] A few months earlier, his son Indra – who was later among the first graduates of the institution – was insulted by a British cavalry officer while on an excursion with some fellow students and teachers of the Gurukul.[39] This so-called '*salam*-incident' was hailed by nationalists as an act of bold protest against the rulers' racial arrogance and discussed even outside Arya newspapers.[40] Interestingly, the officer called the Gurukul student 'son of a Bengali swine' when he refused to salute him. This apparently insignificant detail indicates once more that everything 'seditious and revolutionary' was associated with Bengal by large numbers of British military and administrative officials.[41]

Thus we can conclude that until 1912 a negative assessment of the Arya's educational experiment prevailed in the official discourse. Initially, the cultural and political self-assertion embodied by the Gurukul was seen as the preliminary stage of overtly political self-assertion jeopardizing British rule. The degree of 'efficiency' and 'discipline' with which the institution was run, and hitherto rarely encountered, made the Gurukul appear all the more dangerous. Such perceptions were responsible for the government's policy of utmost caution and control. Subsequently there was a shift in colonial attitudes towards the Gurukul, which was now regarded as a potential agent in the fulfilment of the colonizer's civilizing mission.

3. In Search of the Loyal Native: the 'Liberal Imperialist' Discourse

As we have noticed, early official discourse dealing with the Gurukul could be ambiguous in its assessment of the institution. Alongside the serious concern policymakers expressed about the political role Gurukul graduates might potentially play in the future, there was also a barely concealed admiration for the commitment of both teachers and students and the 'discipline' that so conspicuously prevailed on the school's premises. A predominantly positive view of the institution was particularly pronounced among the 'liberal imperialists', whose position has already been briefly outlined above. As they were part of the colonial administrative apparatus, the liberal imperialists had a direct impact on the school's fate. Although they were not completely free of the deep-rooted suspicion of the political ambitions of the Arya Samajis, such officials were extremely receptive to the emphasis the founders of the Gurukul had placed on qualities like honesty, obedience, self-control and frugality – all of which were compatible with 'Victorian values', the spread of which formed an important part of their civilizing programme.

This becomes particularly obvious in the case of Sir James Meston, the first and arguably the most important agent among the liberal imperialists. He replaced John Hewett as lieutenant governor of the United Provinces in 1912 and left no doubt about his liberal outlook right from the outset; it soon found expression in the provincial government's attitude towards the Arya Samaj. According to Meston, the most efficient way of preventing seditious activities among Hindu reformers was not by a further tightening of the existing measures of surveillance and suppression but rather an open cooperation with the more moderate elements within the Samaj – namely the faction associated with the Gurukul Kangri. Such a strategy, his argument ran, would eventually lead to the isolation of the movement's radicals and at the same time 'win over the more moderate elements to our side and induce them to discourage violence in speech or teaching'.[42]

However, the interest in the educational experiment shown by the new lieutenant governor cannot be placed exclusively in the context of this strategic manoeuvre, but was to some extent also due to a fresh approach towards matters of education on the part of the government. In a speech held at Calcutta University in 1911, George V had announced that he wanted to build a network of schools and colleges all over India with the avowed aim of educating 'loyal, manly and useful citizens'.[43] The initiatives in reforming the educational system following the king's declaration were accompanied by reappraisal of the so-called 'oriental education'.[44] British officials announced their intention to place a stronger emphasis on promoting institutions that spread traditional religious education. It is obvious that the Gurukul Kangri was an ideal object for cooperation as it stood not only for the above-mentioned values but also for a thorough training in Sanskrit and Hindi, promising, as one of the English admirers of the school put it, that '[h]ere character would be formed in harmony with the genius of the country and not against it'.[45]

Meston toured the United Provinces in March 1913 to gather support for his proposed educational reforms. In the course of his campaign he gave speeches in Meerut,[46] at the Central Hindu College in Benares [47]and at the Muhammadan Anglo-Oriental College in Aligarh.[48] Thanks to the mediation of John Ford, the deputy collector of Saharanpur district,[49] he also paid a visit to the Gurukul. The lieutenant governor's arrival in Kangri proved a turning point in the school's history. It was not merely the first visit of a senior government official to the Gurukul but it also marked the end of a six-year period of suspicion and close surveillance by the police. The impending danger of the school being closed down no longer loomed large on the horizon after Meston's short stay.[50]

The Gurukul authorities, fully aware of how important it was to win over Meston to their cause, did their utmost to leave a positive impression on him. The report on his visit, in an in-house school publication, is worth quoting at some length:

> The institution presented a gay and festive appearance. Triumphal arches were erected and the school and the Boarding House were profusely decorated with Veda Mantras, Slokas [sic!] from ancient Sanskrit classics, evergreens, buntings, mottos in Sanskrit and English, flags bearing the sacred symbol *Om* and Union Jacks. [. . .] On alighting from the elephant, His Honour was greeted with tremendous cheering from the yellow-robed Brahmacharies who lined both sides of the route and presented a picturesque, magnificent appearance. [. . .]
>
> After his Honour and Party had partaken of refreshments [. . .] and refreshing decoction prepared out of the leaves of the sacred 'Tulsi' plant, they adjourned to the reception Pandal where an address of welcome was presented to His Honour. The address was in Sanskrit and was artistically written on art paper by the calligraphy expert of the Gurukula staff. It was enclosed in a casket exhibiting artistic swadeshi engraving work in ivory.[51]

The account beautifully illustrates the hybrid character of the institution. The ceremony seems to have been somewhat artificial and contrived. The Brahmacharies dressed in their yellow uniforms and waiting in line to salute the representative of the imperial power riding on an elephant[52] seem perfect embodiments of King George's vision of 'loyal, manly and useful' and yet unequivocally 'different' citizens. The slightly bizarre combination of saffron flags and Union Jacks might be read as a metaphor for the synthetic goal underlying the Arya educational experiment.

The self-portrayal of the Gurukul as a model institution for 'oriental learning' did not fail to impress Meston who later described the institution as 'one of the most original and most interesting educational experiments in British India' and hailed it as a 'wonderful and stimulating institution'.[53] It is interesting to note which features he mentions as particularly praiseworthy in his address to the audience gathered in Kangri:

> Here we have a band of ascetics [the teachers of the Gurukul], devoted to their duty and working in the wilderness, following the traditions of the ancient Rishis combined with the most modern scientific methods and working practically for nothing and a set of students of strong physique, obedient, loyal, truthful and devoted, extraordinarily happy and extraordinarily well fed.[54]

This observation is typical of the liberal-imperialist position. The central features in his appraisal are physical prowess and bodily strength due to regular exercise, loyalty and obedience. These seemingly disjointed qualities were regarded as being closely interconnected in Edwardian Britain: the former were seen as indispensable prerequisites for the latter.[55] It is well known that discipline and education for obedience played an even more crucial role in colonial educational institutions than they did in Britain itself. Within the British Empire the high schools and colleges 'run on western lines' were supposed to serve as 'character factories'[56] to transform a small native elite into useful subjects by inculcating in them the necessary 'grit' as well as the moral values prevalent in late-nineteenth- and early-twentieth-century Britain.[57] The ideal of a 'public spirit', of selflessly fulfilling one's duty in the service of a larger community, is most important in this regard.[58] A quality Meston fails to mention in his speech was noted by other European visitors to the school. The first westerner who came to Kangri, the missionary W E S Holland, who was not sympathetic towards the Arya Samaj project, nevertheless admitted '[that] the whole thing showed a capacity for organization with which the Indian is usually not credited'.[59] This capacity was demonstrated every year in a striking manner on the occasion of the school's annual festival, celebrated with scholarly symposiums and learned speeches, cultural events and competitions in sports and games. These *varshikotsav*s attracted up to seventy thousand people and were organized solely by the Gurukul staff and students without any external help,[60] a fact mentioned approvingly in various official or semi-official accounts of these events.[61]

Meston's pioneering visit prepared the ground for other top officials. Lord Islington[62] and Viceroy Chelmsford[63] were among others who made their way to Kangri in the years that followed. Official acclaim was clearly expressed shortly after Meston's departure when 'a high Government official'[64] offered officially to acknowledge both the high school and the college section of the institution and to recognize the degrees they awarded. It was further suggested that the Gurukul be put on a sound financial basis by including it in the government's grants-in-aid scheme. In return for this generosity, compromises regarding the curriculum were expected.[65] Munshiram did not accept this tempting offer, but the mere fact that it was made clearly indicates a general shift towards the liberal-imperialist position in the 1910s.

The main reason for the strong appeal of the Arya's educational experiment among 'enlightened' British administrators is all too obvious: these liberal imperialists perceived the Gurukul as an institution that shared, to a large extent, 'British values' and yet was deeply rooted in the ancient traditions and culture of the people. It was, therefore, a welcome alternative to the attempts at educational reform undertaken by 'seditious and westernized' nationalists in Bengal. British administrators felt much more at ease with '*pukka* natives'. Keeping these observations in mind, it is not surprising that the 'arcadian academy' of the Aryas was seen as the expression of a variety of nationalism that was acceptable to a certain degree. It was a nationalism that did not radically question the legitimacy of the British presence. For the advocates of the Gurukul system of education, political sovereignty was the reward of a long and arduous learning process and not a 'birthright' which could be taken for granted. It was not very difficult to reconcile such views with the liberal imperialist notions of trusteeship. This 'elective affinity' becomes even more pronounced when we turn to a literary expression of the liberal imperialist creed in improvement.

Siri Ram Revolutionist

Official acclaim for the Gurukul had been anticipated in *Siri Ram Revolutionist* – a popular novel published anonymously in 1912[66] and widely read among the British in India.[67] The book was written by Edmund Candler (1874–1926),[68] an English educationist, novelist and civil servant, who spent most of his life in Asia. After graduating from Emmanuel College, Cambridge, in 1895, Candler started his career as a teacher in a college for Anglo-Indians and lower-middle-class whites in Darjeeling,[69] remaining there from 1896 to1898.[70] Subsequently he worked as private tutor to the *raja* of Parlakimedi and taught at a 'native' college in Bengal, but soon became disgusted with the 'soft college-bred lads'[71] he regarded as typical of this province and even more so with their political aspirations. Frustrated by the omnipresence of politics in Bengal and convinced that 'liberty is not intended for all sorts and conditions of men but only for those who deserve it',[72] in 1906 he jumped at the opportunity of becoming the principal of a small college in the princely state of Patiala in the Punjab.[73] It is this personal experience that forms the basis for his novel,[74] whose subtitle, *A Transcript From Life 1907–1910*, lays claim to historical authenticity. From the detailed account he gives in his book, it appears likely that he knew the Gurukul Kangri from first hand experience.[75]

The novel with its 'flat' characters and its action-packed but predictable plot is of rather doubtful literary value. As a historical source, however, it is highly interesting as its represents a literary expression of the critique of the British-Indian educational system as formulated in Valentine Chirol's *Indian Unrest* in 1910. Chirol had pointed at the 'estrangement of the young Hindu' in the government schools and colleges as 'the most alarming phenomenon of the day'.[76] In a similar vein, Candler's novel relates the story of the fatal meta-morphosis of Siri Ram, a young Punjabi college student who strays from the path of righteousness, becomes a terrorist against the Raj and finally dies by his own hand while serving a prison sentence for having assassinated a British officer. The two final chapters are, doubtless, the most dramatic in the book; for our purposes, however, the first part of the story, which deals with the protagonist's gradual infection with the 'poison of seditious nationalism', is of greater relevance.

The story is told from the perspective of the Englishman Skene – the principal of Siri Ram's college – who can quite easily be identified as the *alter ego* of the author. Significantly, it is in the environment of Gandehshwar College, a westernized educational institution, that the hero's career as a 'revolutionist' starts. In his mind, envy and the underlying self-perception of being inferior and defective mix with fragments of 'western ideas' that are only half understood, as well as the propaganda of the Arya Samaj[77] and the inflammatory agitation of a political *sannyasin* (who comes, predictably enough, from Bengal).[78] Siri Ram is depicted as morally underdeveloped and, hence, receptive to various types of negative influence. An explanation for this deplorable 'weakness of character' is also provided by the narrator. We learn '[that] no coercing had seduced him into cricket, which might have brought him into contact with the more healthier minded of his companions'.[79] Besides being a perfect illustration for the omnipresence of the Victorian/Edwardian notion that physical exercise was the remedy for 'unruliness' and disobedience, which is explored in greater detail in Paul Dimeo's contribution to this volume (see page 000), this statement also helps to explain the author's positive assessment of the Gurukul experiment. The affinity appears to be even more logical when one takes into account Candler's personal 'fondness for sports and games'.[80]

The spirit of sedition becomes manifest for the first time when Siri Ram and his friend Lachmi Chand organize a conspiratorial meeting in the college to recruit their fellow-students to the national cause. Principal Skene discovers the conspiracy and the two ringleaders are expelled from the institution. The negative protagonist Siri Ram subsequently comes completely under the sway of the demonic *sannyasin*. He becomes a terrorist and undergoes a quasi-military training conducted by reckless Bengali revolutionaries. Lachmi Chand, on the other hand, is obviously constructed as a positive foil to Siri Ram. He learns his lesson and opts for the correct solution: he becomes a teacher in the Gurukul Kangri.

> Skene was relieved to hear the news [. . .]. The Gurukul at Hardwar was perhaps the best melting pot for him, if he had the patience to endure it. The school is the nursery of the Arya Samaj and its aim is the realisation in modern life of the 'Back to the Vedas' cry. [. . .] The only way to recapture the lost heritage was a return to the discipline of life which made it possible. That was the truest and sanest form of patriotism [and] the only sure road to political independence [. . .]. The wiser half of the Samaj – even the Aryas were divided – had the courage to face the fact which Skene had explained to his students, that you must be the thing, before you enjoy its privileges.[81]

This motive is elaborated further in the following chapter. When Siri Ram visits his old companion several months later in Kangri, Lachmi Chand recounts the speech of a *pandit* he had the chance to hear during a *varshikotsav* in Kangri and which finally brought him to the right path:

> The gist of his dismal creed had been, that the Indians had lost their country because they were not worthy of it. They had no character. [. . .] they had no sense of duty, responsibility, discipline and organi-zation. And until they had developed these characteristics in the way Englishmen have done, they could not hope to do anything. They must wait for a new generation – a distant generation, when the system of Brahmacharya which was being taught at the Gurukul had leavened the whole nation and recaptured its past glories, before they could even dream of swaraj. In the meantime, they must serve the British Government faithfully, and they must imitate the good qualities of the Englishmen.[82]

It is hard to find a more concise abstract of the trusteeship theory than is given in this short passage. There is strong evidence that these lines were not merely conceived as the utterings of a fictitious literary character but also reflect Candler's personal view. Following the protest aroused by his novel, which represented the Arya Samaj as partly responsible for sedition, Candler decided to add an afterword[83] to the second edition to prevent all possible misunderstandings. He used the occasion for a reappraisal of the Gurukul at the expense of colonial educational institutions:

> As for the Gurukul at Kangri [. . .] I am ready to believe that it is the best educational institution in the country. It certainly ought to be as it is of the soil and is bound up with the traditions of the people. [. . .] Possibly if there were no English schools and colleges, but only Gurukuls in the country, there would be no Siri Rams. The reader should remember that Gandeshwar, Skene's College, was responsible for Siri Ram [. . . not] the Gurukul whose honourable aim is the attainment of independence not by bombs or Browning automatic pistols, but by strengthening of character. Siri Ram was not worthy of the Gurukul: he did not attain it.[84]

The most interesting part of this quote is the well-known theme of distrust towards those Indian reformers who are not 'bound up with the traditions of the people' and adopt completely modern methods of the regeneration of the colonized self. Once again, it is the Indian who has completely lost his 'difference', the English-educated and westernized *babu* who can do the greatest harm to the British Raj.[85] One is reminded, again, of Valentine Chirol arguments.[86] The *Times* correspondent had drawn similar conclusions regarding the role of Indian students in the *swadeshi* movement in Bengal in 1905, stating that 'picketing of the most aggressive character was conducted by bands of young Hindus who ought to have been doing their lessons'.[87]

Having thus outlined the discourse on the national school in Kangri as produced by representatives of both the 'harder' and 'softer' varieties of British imperialism at work in India, we may now address the pivotal questions as to how the founders of the institution understood their own 'educational mission' and, even more importantly, how they saw their position *vis-à-vis* British rule. The analysis will focus on Mahatma Munshiram, the 'founding father' of the Gurukul and the most eloquent advocate of its cause.

4. 'Colonial Consenters'? – Self-perception of the Gurukul Spokesmen

On account of the continuing attacks in the government press following the outbreaks of 1907–09, the leaders of the Arya Samaj were compelled to react in some way or other. The founder of the Gurukul, Munshiram, was especially under pressure since his school, as we have seen, was one of the main targets of official suspicion.[88] The 'Mahatma' used the thirtieth anniversary celebrations of the Lahore Arya Samaj in November 1908[89] as a platform to define the position of his institution towards the British.[90] It was an excellent occasion to address the colonial officials almost directly, for he was perfectly aware that such a huge *mela* would be witnessed by scores of informers and policemen, and expressed his desire that what he had to say that night 'may reach every corner of India and England – that Lord Minto and John Morley and even [the] gracious Emperor may learn from authentic sources'.[91]

In the first part of his speech, the Arya leader tackled the problem as to whether the Samaj really deserved the label 'political society' given to it by the authorities. He observed that in the Indian context 'political' was almost exclusively used as a synonym for 'anti-government' and hence a pejorative term. There were only three political parties in India according to this narrow definition: the moderates and the extremists within the Indian National Congress, and the 'terrorists' acting outside the framework of parliamentary politics.[92] The Arya Samaj had nothing in common with either of these factions, quite the reverse: it was a completely apolitical body. The fact that it was regarded as seditious by the government was explained as the result of a conspiracy by the 'forces of pig-headed conservatism and religious bigotry'.[93]

After dwelling at great length on the various instances of injustice suffered by innocent Arya Samajis through government agencies, Munshiram turned to more general statements about the outlook of the Arya Samaj in general and the Gurukul Kangri in particular. It is remarkable that he constantly stressed the loyalty of the school's teachers and students towards British rule and left no stone unturned to emphasize their admiration for 'British values':

> It is said, that the Arya Samaj is a political body and that it breeds disloyalty to the present Government. But I say if you ever come across a student of a European school and talk to him and then talk to a student of the Gurukula you will find out the difference in training. If the Arya Samaj is hostile to law and order, how is it that the students trained under its guardianship are so well-behaved, so respectful to constituted authority and so anxious to oblige one and all.[94]

Once again he underscored the importance of self-control and obedience towards authorities. That there was a 'colonial consensus' behind such an uttering became even more explicit when the Gurukul founder proceeded to argue that a true Arya Samaji would prefer the enlightened and tolerant rule of the British to the 'despotism of idol worshipping Hindus and cow slaughter-ing Muslims'.[95] There can be hardly a doubt that, in spite of the claims of the Gurukul to genuine 'Indianness' and the extensive use of religious symbols, it was western values to a large extent that served as a point of reference for the Mahatma and his Gurukul project. The concept of *swaraj*, very much in fashion at the time, was thus modified by the Gurukul faction of the Arya Samaj in a way that differed fundamentally from the understanding of, say, Aurobindo Ghose or B G Tilak. It was made compatible with the tacit accept-ance of the notion of British moral superiority and – perhaps not surprisingly – quite close to the position of M K Gandhi:[96]

> [. . .] we advocate Swraj [*sic!*] or self-Government but not in the lower sense. True Swraj is dominion over the self, self conquest, the thorough control of concupiscence and the lower passions. If the individuals composing a nation are devoid of this kind of Swraj, political swraj becomes a curse instead of a blessing and brings in its train widespread misery and corruption instead of social happiness, material gains and intellectual tranquillity.[97]

Munshiram returned to this line of argument exactly one year later at the 1909 anniversary gathering in Lahore. Here we may trace a trifle more bitter-ness in his words – he was obviously upset by the continuing repression by the government and particularly by the witch-hunting that had occurred in the wake of the 'Patiala conspiracy case'.[98] However, regardless of his disappoint-ment with official policy he appealed to his 'dharmic brethren' to refrain from 'evil thoughts and deeds',[99] in other words, direct political agitation against the Raj. He reiterated once more the universalist claim of the *arya dharm*, the ultimate goal of which was – in contradistinction to that pursued by Islam – not the achievement of 'worldly power and temporal sovereignty'. For this very reason, no adherent of the Arya faith could even 'think for a moment that the British should go away and their *raj* be replaced by the *raj* of some barbarian from the frontier'.[100] It is interesting to note how his declarations of loyalty were combined with an anti-Islamic rhetoric. His anti-Islamic stance, however, did not hinder him from commenting on the terrorist attacks perpetrated by fellow Hindus in Bengal. He left his audience in no doubt about the disgust he felt for this type of violent action and condemned terrorism in the strongest terms:

> [. . .] our nation has reached depths of moral degradation which it is difficult to fathom. How utterly unfit are we for Swarajya just at present! [. . .] Recent events have disclosed plague spots and revealed

leprous sores in the body politic, the existence of which I had never so much as suspected before. I believe, now, that for another three hundred years British supremacy alone can ensure peace and order in this land and that if this guarantee of peace was taken away all facilities of advancement on evolutionary lines would vanish.[101]

Gradual long-term development and advancement 'on evolutionary lines', he suggested, were the only way to earn the right even to think of political independence. In this struggle the British were not regarded as enemies. Instead, they were perceived as indispensable brothers in arms though only on a temporary basis. Their task was to guarantee the political stability necessary for a 'nation of slaves'[102] to undergo the arduous process of learning. The alumni of the Gurukul Kangri were trained to become the first representatives of this new species of disciplined and mature Indian citizens, the avantgarde who could set an example for the masses. Countless writings by other advocates of the Gurukul prove that these statements did not merely reflect the personal opinion of Munshiram but were part of the dominant ideology within the so-called 'radical' faction of the Samaj. Two of the more original statements of loyalty uttered by members of this faction to defend the Gurukul deserve to be mentioned in this context. The first was brought forward by M M Seth[103] in an open letter to the viceroy. Seth not only refused to accept any of the accusations of seditiousness spread by government officials and the loyalist press – he went a step further by claiming that the Gurukul was an important ally of the British since hundreds of youths were confined in its premises, pursuing intellectual and physical refinement and thus not able to attend political gatherings and demonstrations.[104] The second example is a poem written in a style reminiscent of English translations of the Bible current in late-nineteenth-century India. The text in which the anonymous author reproduced a fictitious address by Swami Dayanand to 'John Bull' was published in the *Vedic Magazine*, the Gurukul's English monthly, in the summer of 1909. Once again, the grudging admiration for the British 'civilization' is quite striking:

John! John! Why persecutest thou me? Thou art a noble fellow at heart but thy intellect is sluggish. Be true to thy higher self and thy history. And learn to judge for thyself. Listen not to calumnies and vile misrepresentations. I have always praised thy beneficent work in Aryavarata. [*Sic!*] Open thine eyes and earn the blessings of a Sanyasin.[105]

Given the political circumstances of the time, one certainly has to ask to what extent such utterings reflected the opinions of the Gurukul spokesmen. Is it not more likely that these were either cases of a particular caustic irony or simply rather naive attempts at flattering the colonial authorities to distract the attention of the CID from the 'seditious' political ends of the institution? Admittedly, the particular situation in which the texts emerged has to be taken into account but nonetheless the reader does not get the impression that the Arya leaders were paying merely lip service to the British. This is particularly evident in Munshiram's Lahore speeches. He was much too frank in his critique of the arrogance of the British to be misunderstood as a flatterer. Moreover, the Mahatma was one of the few who had the courage to vindicate Lala Lajpat Rai at a time when the latter was regarded by the government as a rebellious agitator. [106] Further, even in Seth's article there is no evidence that he wanted his comments to be read as irony. No doubt both authors were quite serious in their assessment of British rule as 'beneficent'. This perception is underscored by the reaction of the representatives of a more radical strand of nationalism. While the Gurukul had been hailed as a national icon even by the 'extremists' almost from the outset, the distance was now growing. The declarations of solidarity uttered by the Arya leaders were condemned as cowardly opportunism by 'extremists'. Referring explicitly to Munshiram's speeches the Bengali newspaper *Swarajya*, for example, warned the Arya Samajis that 'the world no longer requires societies [. . .] which seek certificates for the propagation of truth and *dharma* and are ready to deny their religion on account of cowardice.'[107]

5. Summing up

The aim of this chapter has been two-fold. By analysing the perceptions of an educational institution in early-twentieth-century northern India, it hoped to highlight some basic contradictions in the British colonial project and identify diverse, even antagonistic, voices within official imperial discourse. The findings of the case study of the United Provinces seem to indicate that, at the provincial and all-India level, there was a shift of paradigms regarding the self-understanding of the administrative elite on the eve of the First World War. The idea of a civilizing mission based on the idea of trusteeship and the assimilation of 'moderate elements' within the spectre of emerging Indian nationalism gained ground at the expense of an imperial ideology of 'benevolent despotism' advocating harsh measures against 'seditious activities' or 'hostility towards British rule'. This led to the paradoxical situation that an allegedly 'traditionalist' and nationalistic institution like the Gurukul Kangri increasingly became attractive to the British as a potential partner in the civilizing project, since it appeared apt at fulfilling the educational needs of the country by strengthening the 'native character'. The stress here lies on 'native', for even this liberal brand of imperialism was based on a 'rule of difference'. It has become abundantly clear that it was its 'native' outlook and its perceived authentic 'Indianness' that made the education imparted in the school preferable to an entirely 'modern' college education, which would result in a superficial westernization of the students and possibly produce 'revolutionists'.

At another level, the paper has attempted to analyse the ways in which the Gurukul authorities viewed themselves. It demonstrates that the colonial civilizing mission was internalized by the school's spokesmen to an astonishing degree. This is not to say that they were *completely* submissive to 'colonial discourse(s)' for we have also detected signs of outspoken criticism and resistance. The famous '*salam*-incident', for instance, illustrates that the Gurukulis felt loyalty not so much to British authorities as to what were perceived as 'British values'. Likewise, Munshirams refusal to accept the government's offer of grants-in-aid indicates that the Gurukul founders were well aware of the potential danger of their institution being subverted to suit British designs and ends. Nonetheless, they seem to have shared the colonial assumption that Indians were not yet ready for political self-rule, that they had to earn independence by undergoing an arduous educational process which would transform them into useful and 'manly' citizens of a future India. These findings not only corroborate Ashis Nandy's theory of an overarching 'colonial consensus', they also suggest that the ideals which sustained an important strand of Indian nationalism (the one that has often been labelled as 'Hindu revivalist') were as shot through with contradiction as those underpinning the imperial civilizing mission itself.

Abbreviations

IES	Indian Educational Service
IOR	India Office Records
MAS	*Modern Asian Studies*
NAI	National Archives of India
NCHI	New Cambridge History of India
NMML	Nehru Memorial Museum and Library
OIOC	Oriental and India Office Collection
SNNUP	*Selections from the Native Newspapers Published in the United Provinces*
VM&GS	*Vedic Magazine & Gurukula Samachar*
VS	Vikrami Samvat (roughly corresponding to AD +57 years)

12

In Search of the Indigenous: J C Kumarappa and the Philosophy of 'Gandhian Economics'

BENJAMIN ZACHARIAH
University of Sheffield

1

This chapter examines the problems of persuading an educated middle-class audience of the intellectual validity of Gandhi's economic ideas for India. I shall examine this through the interpretation of Gandhi's ideas provided by J C Kumarappa, his deputy in the All-India Village Industries Association, the organization that was intended to promote and actualize Gandhi's economic ideas; and shall deal with the strategies adopted by Kumarappa to clear a discursive space to secure a hearing for these ideas. In dealing with the arguments thus put forth as 'strategies' I do not mean to suggest that these were merely strategic ploys; most of them were part of a larger world-view, to which Kumarappa was committed, whose rationale and philosophical underpinnings needed to be explained before the more specific ideas that followed could persuasively be put forth. Personal conviction being taken for granted, how best could the ground be laid for the communication of ideas of which the intellectual environment of the time was sceptical, if not downright hostile?

The debates in which Kumarappa involved himself were embedded in other debates with a longer genealogy in various versions of the imperial civilizing mission and opposition to it. Kumarappa attempted two crucial manoeuvres in the oppositional version he presented: the detachment of the idea of 'civilization' from the West and its attachment instead to the East; the imposition of these allegedly indigenized standards of civilization on the Indian 'masses'. What is curious is that certain aspects of that imperial mission remain crucial to the anti-colonialism expressed in such debates, in particular the coupling of moral and material progress, and the attempted appropriation by anti-colonial nationalists of the imperialists' right to be considered agents of positive change.

This cannot properly be understood without reference to the general context of the debates on 'development' within which the arguments fell. The following section attempts to provide an outline of these debates.

2

The term 'development' caught on in liberal usage after the Second World War, largely in the context of Cold War thinking, in which well-meaning desires to raise standards of living and incomes in the 'Third World' merged with the need for containing Communism by ensuring that poor countries felt they had a stake in the economy of the 'free world'.[1] As an idea, however, it had a richer history: it had long been a crucial part of contending world views. Development had, of course, long been a part of the Marxist tradition. The word was also widely used in British colonial discourse.[2] In the last years of British colonial rule – and in the context of the rising strength of anti-colonial movements and sentiment in the dependent world, the metropole, and out-side – Britain's claim to furthering the development of the colonies provided the basis of her defence of empire before home and world public opinion.[3]

In India development was an idea around which converged opposition to colonial ideas of the 'backwardness' of the subject people – racial, social, political and economic – as a justification of the metropolitan country's right to rule. By the 1920s and 1930s the idea of backwardness was framed in pre-dominantly economic terms, in British colonial as well as nationalist argu-ments. The 'difference' between British standards of political behaviour and those of the Indians had also to be underplayed if an increasingly difficult-to-govern India had to be convinced of the sincerity of Britain's claim of the pro-gressive grant of self-government to Indians.[4]

Arguments regarding specifically economic backwardness, however, could be based on more 'objective' and supposedly impartial criteria; and eco-nomics was ideally suited as an arena for such debate between imperialism and nationalism, there being a general level of agreement regarding its terms. The signs of economic backwardness were agreed upon, according to terms laid down by the discipline of economics, by British and Indian alike: regard-ing the causes of and the ways of emergence from this backwardness, there were of course strong disagreements, but this particular form of backwardness was acknowledged by Indians themselves. On the imperial side, on the other hand, there was also recognition that British rule in India had a strongly eco-nomic dimension: after all, the economic advancement of India was professed to be one of the constituent goals of British imperialism in India – though this seldom led to a willingness to acknowledge that its purposes were primarily economic.

The strategies of argument adopted in such debates are well known. The official British argument in India, as elsewhere, was centred on the beneficial nature of the colonial connection for finance, trade and commerce, its 'modernizing' role through contact with the scientific and developed West and its crucial role in preserving internal peace and law and order, these being used as justification for colonial rule's continuance. The subject people responded by attributing backwardness to the effects of colonial rule itself; in this scheme of things, economic backwardness, which was a consequence of colonial rule, was itself the cause of other forms of backwardness, social and economic.[5] In addition to combating colonial claims to 'good government', economic and otherwise, India had also to come up with schemes for development. This was more than a search for a model economic plan (though there were many of those), not just a question of material betterment: it was also one of the 'moral health' of the nation[6] – here again one may note the convenience of economic development as an arena for debate between imperialism and nationalism: the assumption that 'Moral and Material Progress' go together is not lost either on imperialists and nationalists. Economic development became a sort of synecdoche for the more general problem of the search for a framework within which to conceptualize the Indian nation, discussions thereon incorporating and informing discussions on 'nation-building', 'national discipline', forms of government and more.[7]

Consequently, there emerged around and alongside the idea of development strong debates among Indians on matters such as 'westernization', 'eastern' culture, civilization and values, 'indigenous' practices, tradition and culture – debates that were perhaps reminiscent of an earlier era in which British administrators and thinkers tried to work out the differences between the Orient and the Occident, similarly to work out the principles on which to order the economy and society they sought to control. Such debates were not subordinate to the apparently more practical matters at hand regarding economic development: on the contrary, they were considered essential questions that must be resolved to clear the way for practical constructive programmes and developmental plans.

The coming together of all these ideas can be traced to the impact of the Great Depression and the emergence of economic planning as a visible alternative to the largely non-interventionist liberal economics of the pre-1914 era. There had long been a tendency for the bits and pieces of economic nationalist arguments against colonialism to merge into a critique of colonial rule.[8] Yet for this to coalesce into a recognizable nationalist discourse on development took some time. The pattern of economic discourse in British India – committees and commissions of enquiry, notes of dissent, minority reports and then the slow bureaucratic process through which it went – was strongly geared towards the existence of precedents to justify an idea or policy initiative. The justification of Indian economic nationalism had similarly to be through precedents – earlier nationalists had appealed to Friedrich List and Germany; in the 1930s the appeal was to the Soviet Union and planning. This was not the only example: the economic successes of Japan, the USA through the New Deal, of Fascist Italy or Nazi Germany were commonly cited as examples worthy of emulation in some of their aspects, with the emphasis varying according to political orientation. It became necessary at times to separate the economic achievements of some of these countries from their political behaviour: thus, from about 1937, Nazi Germany and Fascist Italy are less well-quoted examples; praise for Japan's economic success is explicitly stated not to imply support either for her aggression in China or her behaviour during the Second World War. The Soviet example remained the most-cited one, if only by virtue of being the most successful, its influence therefore cutting across the political spectrum; but the goals of most of those citing that example were quite un-Soviet, seeking only to try to emulate its material successes.[9]

However, while such dissociations as were necessary between the economic and non-economic aspects of the ideas and examples under discussion were being made, it was impossible to make the dissociation without being aware of the conflicting philosophies and world-views of which they were a part; and in the context of the need to anticipate a framework for the desired independent Indian state, they could in turn build up associations of ideas. 'Economic development' set off a chain of thought on various matters thought to be related to it. It was thought necessary and desirable to make explicit certain connections between projects of economic regeneration and development and the wider process of 'nation-building': 'Along with economic planning, sooner or later, questions will also come to the front of reforms and recon-struction in other spheres of national life – political, social, intellectual and spiritual. These are all interconnected and changes in them, fast or slow, will be inevitable. Planning under all these heads will come under the comprehensive title of Nation Building.'[10]

Such connections were explored in the writings and speeches of several men who came to be closely associated with ideas of development in India: this period saw the rise of a significant band of proselytizers for various models of development, concerned with putting into ideas of economic development the social philosophies they contained, or ought to contain.

3

Gandhi, apparently, stood apart from these trends in nationalist thinking. He refused to join a debate with the colonial government on terms he understood to be its own. The solution to problems of backwardness was to reject definitions that depended on a conception of 'civilization' based on making 'bodily welfare the object of life',[11] founded on material rather than spiritual values. The Gandhian opposition to development through industrialization was dependent on an equation of industrial modernity (a convenient abbreviation we can use for the purpose of this article) with 'westernization', which by implication or by direct accusation could be considered alien, immoral and culturally disruptive.

It has been said of Gandhi's writings and statements that they were essentially moral in character; though Gandhi was capable of putting forward arguments in which his idea of the village as economic unit was defended on essentially economic grounds – the wisdom of village industries in a large agrarian economy with an abundance of under-employed labour – this was not his main argument. According to this view, it was only reluctantly that Gandhi expressed himself in terms of capitalism, socialism, law and so on, but the terms of the debates on development that emerged strongly from the 1930s forced him occasionally to do so. Here, this was in terms of the possibility of applying 'our own distinct Eastern traditions' in finding a 'solution to the question of capital and labour',[12] or to the organization of the national economy around village-centred production by self-sufficient small producers. Otherwise, Gandhi might be said to have conducted a 'total moral critique of the fundamental aspects of civil society' of the 'dubious virtues of modern civilization', without an appeal to history or precedent, outside 'the bounds of post-Enlightenment thought'.[13]

Starting from this point, Gandhian ideas, economic or otherwise, can be seen as a more authentic articulation of the Indian situation; this is done through a critique of 'post-Enlightenment modernity' and its socio-cultural standards, and the reading of Gandhian ideas as 'cultural resistance',[14] an 'alternative vision'. They may also be seen as emanating from the debate within 'Hindu' tradition regarding the need to revitalize Hindu society and to defend it against colonial assaults;[15] or as a necessary stage in nationalist thought, its 'moment of manoeuvre', in which decrying the 'modern' (colonial capitalism) serves to consolidate the 'national' and pave the way for (Indian) expanded capitalist production, in Gramscian terms 'the development of the thesis by incorporating a part of the antithesis'.[16]

Gandhian ideas could indeed have served any or all these purposes, though whether he stood outside 'the bounds of post-Enlightenment thought' or appealed to history and precedent only in exceptional circumstances seems more doubtful. There are other interpretations as well, matters not being made much easier by his refusal to be consistent in his 'aphoristic' language. Perhaps the strength of Gandhi's language is that it could acquire different meanings to different audiences – the Gorakhpur peasantry, Marwari businessmen or militant Chitpavan *brahmins*.[17] Many of the later interpretations of Gandhi emanate from readings of him in new contexts, for which he can only be held responsible by a severe stretching of arguments.[18] There have been attempts to read consistency into 'Gandhian economic thought', either in terms of criteria externally defined and therefore relatively unconcerned with Gandhi's own lack of consistency and coherence (separating the valid and the invalid aspects of his economic ideas on the basis of such criteria);[19] or by imposing consistency through a chronological reading of Gandhi's economic ideas, pointing to their 'development', and analysing them according to standards validated by philosophical, ethical and economic debates conducted in academia long after Gandhi's death.[20] It seems unproductive to quibble about the essential character of Gandhian thought; nor does it seem possible to arrive at a consensual description of Gandhism; instead, an attempt to unravel its specific meanings in relation to different contexts and audiences might prove to be more meaningful.[21]

It is well known now that, Gandhi's successes in turning the Congress into a mass movement notwithstanding, his political associates accepted many of his ideas as expedient rather than out of conviction. His economic ideas seemed particularly clouded in moral rhetoric and were regarded as far from practicable as the basis of national economic policy, although a 'constructive programme' of spinning and weaving *khadi* could be accommodated without much trouble. With the advent of a strong school of thought that regarded planning for industrialization as the basis for national development, opposition to Gandhi's economic ideas grew more explicit. This coincided, from the mid-1930s, with Gandhi's own relative eclipse in national politics: although he remained the most effective link between the Congress and the masses and the single most effective mass leader, there were now a number of political voices opposed to his ideas and to the class alliance he led, and Gandhi's control over the masses began to look less effective.[22]

The connection between this school of thought's concern with economic development, more specifically with industrialization, and the desire for modernity was self-evident to those concerned with the project: 'Industrial life connotes production, wealth, power and modernity',[23] all these being both necessary and desirable. In this scheme of things, the Gandhian dissenting voice seemed to represent an unfortunate commitment to backwardness – it was admitted by 'modernizers' that village industries might have a place in a scheme to provide employment at the local level, and for this purpose might even be worthy of government protection, but to place a commitment to 'the philosophy of spinning wheel and bullock cart' at the centre of national economic life could only be a denial of the progress of science, of the 'techniques of modern civilization'.[24] There was room for dissent among committed 'modernizers' on the best route to industrialization, but not for dissent on its desirability. Their response to accusations of 'westernization' or a lack of respect for 'tradition' was based on the claim that the principles of science and the benefits of technology on which industrialization was based were universally valid. In their arguments, it was the misuse of science and technology by imperialism (or capitalism, for those further to the left) that had distorted the results obtained. In the hands of a nationalist government with due regard for Indian conditions they could be put to the best possible use.

This point of view could be expressed rather forcefully by the Indian left, certainly, but also by others nearer the centre. Scientists, for instance, were increasingly being cast as the most potentially influential group in the new India; they were included in discussions on developmental matters as 'experts'; and a number of them had already begun to take this role extremely seriously, carrying the message of the importance of science to a wide and constantly increasing readership among the educated middle classes. It was felt that an emphasis on agriculture, rural life and village crafts demonstrated an incapacity to understand 'the way in which the world progresses'. Industry was necessary for political as well as, in the last analysis, military power, which was necessary for the survival of a 'nation' (here the state and the nation were unproblematically elided).[25] It was conceded that 'the genius of the people' must be taken into account in discussing development ('By the genius of the people is meant their origin, custom and faith').[26] But certain aspects of 'culture', according to this view, needed to be jettisoned: 'many medieval ideas and traditions which are instilled into their minds in the name of religion, philosophy, custom, tradition or history'. This could be achieved through 'a good dose of scientific education'.[27]

All this clearly and explicitly set itself up in opposition to Gandhian ideas. Yet in such an attack the main target was not Gandhi's search for an 'Indian' solution, but his ideas' lack of 'modernity'. Science itself was not to be regarded as outside the 'indigenous' framework:

> It is probably not so well known that the East has originated all those arts and crafts which are responsible for the greatness of the present European civilization. It was in the East that copper was first discovered from its ores and used to replace tools made from stones. The East has used bronze which is far superior to copper for offence,

defence, and work, up to 1200 BC. It was again the East which first showed that iron by special treatment could be converted into steel, a product far superior to bronze for fighting and tool making. Even the use of mineral coal originated in the East.[28]

This rather ingenious reversal of arguments turns the problem on its head: European civilization having borrowed from the East, the East is entitled to reclaim the fruits of its own achievements. Science thereby performs its rightful duty in developing a modern India whose modernity is her own, not plagiarized.

We must note here, of course, that the need to legitimize a potential direction of national policy as 'indigenous' is an inescapable one. The big question then was the criteria by which 'indigenism' could be identified.

4

If Gandhism had a weakness, it was that its appeal to the urban professional middle classes and intelligentsia was limited. A philosophy that consciously depended on anti-intellectualism was not particularly influential for the Indian intellectual elite. When dealing with matters of 'development', such ideas were at their weakest: it was important to convince the main protagonists in the debate – intellectuals – that Gandhian ideas deserved a hearing. But the moral rhetoric used by Gandhi was not particularly useful in this regard; although, of course, the ideas of the 'modernizers' also drew on moral principles, the rhetoric was predominantly that of Economics, Science and Rationality, moral principles being regarded as secondary, merely reinforcing arguments whose validity had already been established. Consequently, in order effectively to join this debate, Gandhism required translators who could dress Gandhian ideas in appropriate form. Gandhi himself was not particularly well suited to the task; by his own admission, he knew little about economics, and it was felt that he was rather too dependent on G D Birla in this regard.[29] It may be suspected that he knew more than he was willing to let on; nonetheless, he preferred to allow his disciples to interpret his economic ideas on his behalf; at any rate, he was prepared to endorse these views as compatible with his own.[30] In 1944, that *annus mirabilis* of the production of paper plans for India, Shriman Narayan Agarwal published a Gandhian Plan for the economic development of India;[31] for some years before that, J C Kumarappa had been addressing economic problems and advocating Gandhian solutions.

J C Kumarappa was the most original and interesting of Gandhi's authorized interpreters. Born in 1892, the ninth of ten children, the grandson of a priest, he was himself a devout Christian.[32] He wanted to be an engineer, but ended up as an accountant, completing his training in chartered accountancy in London. Then, in 1927, he was invited by his elder brother J M Kumarappa (then known as John J Cornelius) to come to New York. Having arrived in the United States, he obtained a BSc from Syracuse University in business administration, and then an MA in public finance from Columbia University in 1927–8, under the supervision of Professor E R A Seligman.[33] He was a late convert to nationalism, apparently arriving at his views on British exploitation of India in the course of his study of Indian public finance. Thereafter he turned his back on his 'upbringing on English model', as one of his biographers puts it,[34] met Gandhi (on 9 May 1929), by which time he had already written a pamphlet entitled *Public Finance and Indian Poverty* based on his MA thesis, began to wear *khadi* and, along with his brothers, adopted the Hindu family name 'Kumarappa', changing his name from Joseph Chelladurai to Joseph Cornelius Kumarappa on 10 May 1929. He remained a bachelor all his life. From 1935 till his death in 1955 he was at the head of Gandhi's All-India Village Industries Association; in 1938–9 he was involved in conducting an industrial survey of the North-west Frontier Province and the Central Province and Berar. As member of the Nehru Committee in 1947–8 he helped formulate the 'Economic Policy of the Congress in Free India'; and was chairman of the Agrarian Reforms Committee of the All-India Congress Committee from 1948–50. He had also been a member of the Congress's National Planning Committee, which came into being in 1938, but resigned soon after as he felt nothing in particular could be gained by remaining a member of a body committed to large-scale industrialization.[35]

Kumarappa's major statement of Gandhism's economic philosophy was formulated in a book entitled *Why the Village Movement?*.[36] According to Kumarappa this was meant to clarify the ideals of the All-India Spinners' Association and the All-India Village Industries Association;[37] the book grew nonetheless with each subsequent edition, addressing wider debates on socialism and capitalism, nation-building, centralization, development and planning as they emerged.[38] This book largely succeeds in being an annotated commentary, from a Gandhian perspective, on debates on development in India in the 1930s and 1940s; and it may be said that Kumarappa is the best possible such commentator, given his early training. But it is a lot more than that as well: in it, Kumarappa undertakes the rather ambitious project of enunciating an entire social philosophy on which his economic arguments are to be based. *Why the Village Movement?* is, after *Hind Swaraj*, the closest we have to a manifesto of Gandhism. Kumarappa could be expected to interpret Gandhi to middle-class audiences and seek to persuade them with intellectual tools readily assimilable to mundane, rational thinking; he elaborates a series of arguments with a keen sense of the specifics of the arguments with which he has to contend, centralizing, Communist, socialist or capitalist. Unlike much of Gandhian discourse, *Why the Village Movement?* is direct and unequivocal; Kumarappa's interpretation of Gandhi, though authorized, is far less bounded by Gandhi's compromises and, among other things, by the latter's gentle treatment of capitalists. Kumarappa's classificatory system of West and East is also particularly interesting; although it draws on Gandhi's ideas, they are more clearly worked out. In the sections that follow I shall try to outline the basis of this rather elaborate classificatory system.

The Evolution of the Species and of Man

The book opens with a section entitled 'Historical Background' in which Kumarappa elaborates his version of the course of human history. He begins with the familiar premise that for men and animals alike, 'in the most primitive stages', economic activity is the result of an urge to satisfy three primary needs: hunger, protection against the natural elements and pro-tection against outside attack. Thereupon, he builds his philosophy of the evolution of species. Animals demonstrate the predatory instinct when gather-ing food – 'in this activity the animal is highly self-centred and individualistic'; even gregarious species who hunt in herds 'are only interested in their group, and unite mainly for aggression', the group thereby behaving collectively as the self-centred individual. In protecting themselves from the elements, how-ever, there is 'not much predatory activity' because 'the creature makes its own contribution towards the creation of the needed supply' – the distinction here is somewhat unclear; for some reason Kumarappa was unwilling to acknowledge this contribution in hunting and gathering. Finally, safety from attack is often obtained by herding together for safety. This creates strong feelings of social dependence; and such animals (sheep, cattle, elephants) 'are generally passive and peaceful and not aggressive and ferocious like wolves'. And they are generally 'vegetarian'. Kumarappa thus sought to establish the basis for two 'types' that are crucial to the arguments that follow: the 'pack type', who 'unite for aggression' (and are usually 'carnivores'); and the 'herd type' who gather together for safety.[39]

Within this framework is now placed the specific history of mankind. Man evolved, we are told, from gatherer and hunter ('primitive savage') through nomad (characterized by the capture and domestication of animals) to one who 'began to control his environment' – having reached 'the agricultural stage of civilization'. Beyond this stage, '[a]s civilization advanced, the need for a greater division of labour was felt. Industrialization began in various forms according to the genius of the people in different places'[40] Civilized man's economic organizations still bear marks of earlier forms – the 'herd type' and the 'pack type'. The latter is characterized by a short-term outlook; central control and the concentration of power 'in the hands of individuals or small groups in a personal way' (presumably as opposed to the impersonal); rigorous discipline; 'disregard of the welfare of the actual workers or contributors to the success of the organization'; the '[s]uppression of individuality of the worker and a spirit of intolerance either in competition or in rivalry'; concentration of benefits among a limited few 'without reference to the altruistic value of service rendered'. Its motive force is 'the prospect of obtaining gains' and its activities 'generally radiate from a limited geographical area such as cities'.[41]

The drift of these arguments is quite visible already: having proceeded to set up the 'pack type' as particularly unpleasant and undesirable, Kumarappa needs only to characterize the forms of economic organization he was opposed to as pack-type organizations. Despite the jagged edges and lack of clarity of a number of these arguments, which were probably obvious to contemporary readers, their strategy was clear. Kumarappa was perfectly aware that he was engaged in defending an extremely difficult position which, by the generally held standards set by 'economics' and 'science' (the two terms considered to be intimately linked), was highly suspect. He had thus to come up with an argument that undermined the sanctity of these standards. Some of the images called upon to describe pack-type organizations were reminiscent of existing socialist and Communist ideas: capitalism having reduced social relations to a cash nexus, the idea of alienated labour, and the ideal of individual freedom within a consensual community.[42] At the same time, as becomes clear as one reads further, Kumarappa intended these remarks to be a prelude to his attack on the Soviet system, which he also classified as pack-type, and bracketed in the same category as capitalism – for Kumarappa, as for many contemporaries whose ideas he opposed, an attack on the Soviet system constituted an attack on socialism. Kumarappa probably deliberately played on the similarities to make more of an impact with his divergence from them; and he deliberately avoided sharing socialist or Communist terminology in his own arguments until the basic premises of the Kumarappa argument were established on their own terms. Above all, the concentration on material conditions on which socialism relied was to be avoided if the battle with materialism was not to be lost – the accusation of materialism being one of Gandhians' main arguments in the struggle against Communist ideas.

This becomes clearer as Kumarappa outlines the advantages of the 'herd type': long-term outlook; social control, decentralization and distribution of power being 'impersonal'; '[a]ctivity steered into desired channels by rules of conduct and social regulatory machinery' with attempts being made to safeguard the weak and the helpless; encouragement to individual growth, a considerable amount of tolerance; 'distribution of gains as wide as possible according to the needs of individuals', with activities 'directed by a consideration of certain set ideals and social movements'. The object of all this is 'to satisfy needs judged from an altruistic point of view' (the community being, presumably, the custodian of the 'altruistic point of view').[43] The herd type meets Kumarappa's 'test of civilization': 'We must bear in mind that the true test of civilization is not our material possessions or our manner or mode of life but the thought we bestow on the well-being of others. In predation, which is really barbarism, we cannot expect to find any civilization, for true culture shifts the emphasis from "rights" to "duties".'[44]

On this basis, Kumarappa proceeds to approach the description of 'western' and 'eastern' economic organizations. Here, for the first time, the author takes us to the fringes of the field of battle, for it is on this distinction that the crucial question of the direction to be taken by Indian national development, economic and otherwise, hinged: 'the ostensible object of this book is to enable us to lay a foundation for the proper evolution of the future economic organization of our own country'[45] – the ostensible object, because the project under discussion is, of course, a much larger one. Western economic organizations are of the pack type: westerners were agriculturists for too short a time before 'industrialization overtook them'. There follows a bit of European history, in which western economic organizations are classified, 'according to the personnel of the central controlling group', into five groups: 'the dynasty of might, the dynasty of finance, the dynasty of the machine, the dynasty of labour, the dynasty of the middle classes'. The 'masses, whether of the West or of the East, are of much the same kind' and are therefore not a basis for classification.[46] Kumarappa's classificatory system is based on the assumption that the economically dominant group controls military and political power – a familiar and unobjectionable assumption to his audiences. Yet given that his arguments hinge on a distinction between the West and the East, it is strangely elitist that he does not attribute to the 'masses' any capacity for cultural or other differences based on their 'easternness'.[47]

A History of Western Civilization:

The first dynasty, that of might, 'is represented by the feudal organization in which the feudal baron with his retinue under military discipline descended on the villages from his castle and compelled the producing masses to surrender part of the fruits of their labour to him for no conceivable reason beyond the doubtful protection afforded by him from the attacks of marauders other than himself'. (His description of feudalism is rather spoiled by the example he selects: 'what did Napoleon care how many of his soldiers he left dead on the way so long as he could get to Moscow?')[48] The dynasty of finance came into being 'with the commercial exploitation of inventions and the accumulation of capital secured through centuries of economic activities'. This process began in Britain: religious persecution brought 'men with original thinking powers' from middle western Europe to Britain, then a poor country without the required capital to make use of this 'imported brain power'. This problem was solved 'by Empire Builders directing the flow of gold from the Ganges to the Thames. With the rise of financial power the feudal baron found it to his advantage to join hands with the financier. This combination of might and finance led to what is called in modern times "Imperialism".'[49] The dynasty of the machine is exemplified by America. Control of machines being restricted to a few, 'the interests of those who contributed to the production were ignored . . . Under this dynasty, discipline took the form of a speeding process and standardization of the article.'[50] Kumarappa considers these first three dynasties, taken together, 'capitalist'. The middle classes' struggle to seize power, epitomized according to Kumarappa by Nazism and Fascism, is also described as being 'based on much the same lines as capitalism'.[51]

The classification of Communism or the dynasty of labour as pack type seems not to be quite so self-evident, so Kumarappa explains:

> Most of the characteristics of the other organizations are represented, *viz.* centralization of control and power, rigid discipline and suppression of the individual in regard to production and distribution. Whatever good may have been obtained or envisaged by the directing body giving primary consideration to the needs of the community and not so much to the amount of profit obtained, yet the organization too is a sectarian or class organization run by the proletariat with special privileges attached to the sect in power.[52]

There are certain features common to all these pack-type organizations that Kumarappa has tarred with the same brush. All of them are 'city-centred' and will lead to the 'degeneration of the producing masses because no initiative is left to them, their functions being merely one of carrying out higher orders'. Kumarappa sees symptoms of this degeneration in the high incidence of 'nervous diseases' in the USA and the consequent 'clamour for "leisure" . . . under their system, leisure is a necessity as their organization is unnatural'. Thus, the worker is led to 'resort to drink and other vices'.[53] Leisure, according to Kumarappa, is unnecessary if the worker has a rewarding life; all that is needed is a 'rest period' between spells of work.[54]

Under capitalism, 'every individual gets an opportunity to exercise his talent and energy as he likes', though this may be 'at the cost of injuring society'. Communism takes things to the other extreme: the profit motive is done away with, individualism is suppressed, and 'a small idealistic group plans the work for the nation'. Under both systems 'human values are not fully taken into account . . . We have no right to look upon the common run of human beings, as either gun-fodder as under capitalism, or a cogwheel in a machine as under communism.' Both systems have failed to bring out the best in individuals, and both have led to 'group violence'; while under imperialism this violence is 'directed towards foreigners and strangers', Communism directs it internally 'in order to suppress the bourgeois class'.[55] He accepts that:

> a certain amount of violence will always be involved in any state control, but what matters is the degree and the spirit behind what appears to be violence. Even a loving father chastises his child . . . If the Government is truly democratic the Government will represent the people. In such a Government any regulatory functions that require violence, will be self-inflicted and so it is nothing more than self-discipline.[56]

Economics and the Wisdom of the East

It is in the eastern civilizations, such as India, China, and Japan before she chose to imitate the West, that one finds 'agricultural civilization influencing economic organization'. 'Such civilizations are the results of philosophical and conscious social planning. The . . . West can hardly be said to have a civilization at all. It is more a refined barbarism.' The only exception to this in the western world is Soviet Russia, 'the first attempt at a well-planned society in the West with a sociological philosophy, good or bad, behind it'. But this shares with other western pack-type forms of social organization the common characteristic of 'aggression for economic purposes'.[57] In the political sphere, too, this is reflected in the West's lack of 'true democracy': what exists is a system that 'masquerades under the cloak of parliamentary organization in which real power is vested in a group or in a single dominating personality'; and in religion, even a tolerant religion such as Christianity came to vest power and authority in a single person or institution. By contrast, in India 'village republics managed their own affairs', which continued undisturbed 'even when foreign invaders came'; and in religious life a 'tendency to decentralize the form of worship and views in regard to the Godhead' resulted in 'extreme tolerance'.[58]

Oriental systems achieve regulation and decentralization of power by 'hitching the economic machinery either to civil laws or religion or super-stition'. Kumarappa conducts a defence of the joint-family system, the 'division of labour by caste', and the 'method of distribution to artisans of a share in the products of agriculture'. In the joint family, competition is con-trolled and the weak protected through the 'equitable' sharing of the income of the earning members with non-earning members. The caste system 'aimed at directing the various units of economic activity in consonance with one another and safeguarding the community from overproduction', and pay-ment in kind to artisans such as the carpenter, blacksmith or *chamar* ensured everyone a 'minimum subsistence allowance', the underlying principles being 'the conception that work itself is a method of distribution of wealth', and that the community as a whole was 'a corporate unit', its parts akin to organs of the same body.[59]

'Exploitation,' Kumarappa accepts, 'was not altogether absent' in these 'old systems'; but 'the purpose of the organization' was to minimize such exploitation by erecting 'social barriers' to it. And although they were admitted to be incapable of 'bearing the strain put on them by the tremendous expansion in the field of economic activity', and are now 'decadent', Kumarappa stresses the necessity of modelling 'present-day pro-duction' on similar principles: 'a system of economic production best suited to modern conditions and capable of working satisfactorily in India, if indus-trialization is not to bring with it all the evils attendant on its development in the West', for '[i]f we attempt to superimpose a foreign structure on our ancient foundation, the edifice will certainly tumble like a pack of cards'.[60]

Kumarappa has an ingenious interpretation of the *varnashrama*. People in society can be divided into four groups: the idealistic, taking a 'long-range view of life'; the altruistic, whose somewhat narrower view 'is still beyond the span of their own life'; the materialistic; and finally 'those who follow in a rut without much imagination'. These correspond, respectively, to the *brahmin*, *kshratriya*, *vaisya* and *sudra* respectively. These categories are therefore not dependent on birth; nor, indeed on occupation, but on motives:

> For example an electrician who lives to explore the possibilities of the science without any regard to personal gain is a Brahmin. One who learns the science with the object of helping to industrialize his country and thereby raise the economic standards of his people is a Kshatriya. He who takes contracts or deals in electric supply or goods in consideration of material gain is a Vaisya. But the man who wants to enter the Government electrical department because of the permanency of tenure, economic security and a pension is a Sudra.[61]

In much the same manner, a *brahmin* or *kshratriya* by birth can degrade himself by acting contrary to the principles of his caste. The caste system, therefore, '[p]runed of all extraneous growth', is 'graded on a cultural standard of values almost unknown to money economy. Material considerations sink into insignificance when human needs claim our attention. Duty and not our rights determines our position in society.'[62]

Similarly, 'forms of human activity' can be classified, according to dominant motive forces, into four schools: the first, the economy of predation, is the 'lowest type', with life being 'on an animal plane'. The next, the economy of enterprise ('*laissez-faire*' and the 'capitalist mentality'), stresses the exercise of the rights of the individual in a 'self-centred' manner. The 'economy of gregarianism' acknowledges certain ties between man and man, but includes imperialism, Fascism, Nazism, Communism and socialism, in that '[t]he higher cultural values are forgotten and man is to live by bread alone'. All these are based on short-term interests: that of the individual's life-span or that of a group or nation, therefore are 'Economies of Transience' and are correspondingly characterized as *sudra* (predation); *vaisya* (the economy of enterprise and imperialism); and *kshatriya* (Nazism and Communism), where 'individual interests are sacrificed on the altar of altruism'.[63]

The fourth school, the economy of permanence, is, however, '*Brahmanical* in its idealism and conception. It is an attempt to get into alignment with the order that prevails in the universe and work in unison and in tune with the Infinite. It is the highest evolution man is capable of.' The emphasis is on 'actions founded on eternal principles', duties and a 'belief in the Divine ordering of the universe', as Gandhi does. Principles of economics framed therein are framed 'in the perspective of eternity': a sparing use of natural resources, the consumption of labour and materials readily creatable by man rather than the drawing on exhaustible resources and, consequently, an emphasis on distribution.[64]

Science, Economics, and the Eastern Modern

These ideas are the basis for all the distinctions, definitions and characterizations that the author seeks to make in the rest of the book. It is significant that Kumarappa finds it necessary to set up this elaborate structure on which to build his arguments. That he is not merely tilting at windmills is evident when his seemingly abstract polemic is viewed against the backdrop of the arguments he sought to oppose.

Apart from positioning his arguments as a better alternative to Communism or socialism, and consequently as an 'Indian', 'non-violent' socialism – which was arguably the only available space for the arguments in the political discourse of the time – Kumarappa was also involved in addressing the arguments of science. Kumarappa's principles were far from self-evident, given the prevailing intellectual and economic environment. The desirability of industrialization did not need to be established on theoretical grounds, the possession of power and affluence being so clearly with the industrialized nations. Kumarappa could not, however, be seen to draw merely on extra-economic or moral arguments, given the 'technical' or 'scientific' terms of the debates he sought to enter. He had the dual task of establishing that what he believed was morally correct was also economically rational. Conceptions of science were therefore brought in to reinforce ideas of the wisdom of the East and the need to 'regain the principles that guided our forefathers'.[65]

Thus, principles of economics framed 'in the perspective of eternity' alone can 'lead to the peace and prosperity of the human race and to a life of peace and goodwill based on culture and refinement'. It is because of this that the 'science' of economics must be studied 'from objective standards' and its application approached 'in relation to laws that govern the universe' rather than to 'man's needs of the moment'. This will

> give expression to a mode of life very different from what is con-
> sidered 'modern' in the West . . . The 'Modern' world is of Iron and
> Steel. We cannot afford to draw on our inheritance too freely and
> extravagantly . . . Strange as it may seem the mud huts of India
> belong to the Economy of Permanence while the steel and concrete
> sky scrapers of New York are symbols of the Economy of
> Transience.[66]

Kumarappa thus seeks to establish the practicability of the village-based economy on the basis of the scientific wisdom of the principles of economics on which it rests. This is not a rejection of 'modernity' altogether; Kumarappa challenges the basis of generally accepted yardsticks of 'modernity', claiming to establish a case for a better yardstick in the consideration of a longer time-frame: 'the perspective of eternity'. Far from rejecting conceptions of 'modernity', and consequently of 'science' or 'economics', Kumarappa therefore seeks to persuade his readers that his standards of 'modernity', 'science' and 'economics' were better than those that had currency.

5

There are many discrepancies, inconsistencies and incoherent passages in Kumarappa's arguments, which are not even internally consistent. One of the main opponents in this text is an imagined Communism, which Kumarappa seems to have read a little about – in Columbia as part of his MA course, as well as afterwards – but of which he had little direct experience.⁶⁷ The ideal state, in his view, would inflict 'discipline' on itself. This self-disciplinary 'violence' is acceptable, he writes, because if a government is 'truly democratic', it 'will represent the people'; this violence is as a 'loving father chastises his child'. Kumarappa stops short of saying that the state will be the people: at best, it can be a sort of extended patriarchal family. He also frankly admits that existing ('western') states are characterized by the nature of their leadership, and do not in any sense arise organically from society: the 'masses' are the same, eastern or western. But his envisaged alternative can think no further than a loving, decentralized patriarchy. This might even be read as a pre-conscious Fascist argument, though Kumarappa would probably have been horrified by such a reading. His defence of caste in terms of its 'directing the various units of economic activity' – as a mechanism for redistributing wealth, preventing falling prices, as a guarantor of subsistence and an obstacle to exploitation – is vulgar economism of a kind most 'western' by his standards. Again, Kumarappa's (and Gandhi's) argument about the spiritual basis of caste was not particularly appealing at the time. A *brahmin* might degrade himself, but no one had any difficulty distinguishing the spiritually poor *brahmin* from the spiritually rich *sudra*, the consequences for acting contrary to one's caste being quite different in the two cases. Kumarappa's claim to study economics 'in relation to laws that govern the universe' is strongly reminiscent of Stalinist dialectics – history and society follow universal laws that cannot be influenced by human beings or their conscious behaviour. Kumarappa therefore gets entangled in the positions he seeks to oppose.

But the defects in his arguments are not the point of this essay. How, if at all, was his persuasive strategy meant to work? What ideas did it link up with? The main link in Kumarappa's assimilation of the Gandhian, moral, discourse with the developmentalist, modern, one, was the distinction between East and West. This distinction had been used in various ways in constructing a rationale of 'difference' in both colonial and nationalist arguments. In nationalist versions, the West is generally spiritually inferior though materially superior (an argument with which not all colonialists were uncomfortable); in the Gandhian version material superiority is devalued by an assault conducted on the basis of that spiritual inferiority, enabling the East to claim an overall superiority. Gandhi, of course, claimed that his was not a critique of western culture or religion, 'only a critique of the "modern philosophy of life"; it is called "Western" only because it originated in the West'.⁶⁸ Kumarappa maintains this distinction; yet he goes a step further, using Gandhi's ideas in seeking to detach modernity from the West and claim it for the East: the latter's 'modernity' is only apparently so, as he seeks to demonstrate in his descriptions of the 'transience' of Western economic organizations or of the 'barbarism' of western civilization.

Kumarappa's strategies of argument were substantially different from Gandhi's. He made a very definite appeal to history and the process of evolution of human societies – although there wasn't much historical evidence in it that would be accepted according to the contemporary standards of the discipline, and some of it was very bad history. Although in a number of his other writings he also claimed a more spiritual and religious sanction for this 'Gandhian' order in the Christian scriptures, this was largely before Christian audiences, who Kumarappa had made it his personal task to wean away from collaboration with British rule in India.[69] For general audiences, while discussing the desirability of contending visions of the future development of India, he stuck to less directly religious arguments.

In doing so he was less mystical than Gandhi. Those attracted by Gandhi's moral ideas were often frustrated by the 'exceedingly elusive' nature of his economics,[70] and were constrained to sift through his numerous writings and statements to put together a coherent version. Kumarappa's success lay in his preserving a strong moral content – which though possibly as much Kumarappa's own as Gandhi's was compatible with the latter's – while presenting economic matters in such a way as to bring Gandhian ideas into the field of everyday rational discourse, as well as to attempt to fit this moral and economic world view into 'modern' clothes. But Gandhi's own mysticism on the subject has often been taken as a mysticism of approach rather than of rhetoric. Gandhi was fully aware of the need for such 'modern' clothes; and although he did not take such a line himself (perhaps he felt this would undermine his position as a spiritual leader), he believed it was important that somebody did. Kumarappa, his authorized interpreter, was the logical choice; and Gandhi, consequently, made certain demands on him. Dissatisfied with one of his efforts, Gandhi wrote sternly to Kumarappa in 1941,

> Your article on industrialization I consider weak. You have flogged a dead horse. What we have to combat is socialization of industrialism. They instance the Soviet exploits in proof of their proposition. You have to show, if you can, *by working out figures* that handicrafts are better than power driven machinery products. You have almost allowed in the concluding paragraphs the validity of that claim.[71]

This rather empiricist approach to the problems of persuasion is quite 'post-enlightenment', coming from Gandhi. Perhaps, however, Gandhi also gives some of his game away by suggesting that 'socialization of industrialism' rather than 'industrialism' itself was the enemy position.

Kumarappa's (and Gandhi's) project was in this regard not fundamentally different from that of the 'modernizers': both were engaged in contesting the link between the West and the 'modern'. The latter, as I have said before, stressed the universal character of the 'modern' – and/or, in the version provided by *Science and Culture*, the connection, albeit indirect, of that modernity to the East, where originated 'all those arts and crafts which are responsible for the greatness of the present European civilization'. Kumarappa, similarly, claimed that a 'science of economics' based on 'eastern' principles was better deserving of the term 'modern'. Kumarappa's was, of course, still the more ambitious project, conducted in terms of the defence of principles, institutions and customs especially considered opposed to the 'modern', rather than following the simpler path.

6

It should be clear by now that the terms which keep cropping up in these debates – the modern, modernizers, modernity; the western, westernization, and so on – were not used with any precision or intellectual rigour; they were generally assumed to be intelligible in similar terms to the audiences before whom they were placed. In the political discourse of the time, their emotive significance had already been well established. They did not need to be defined; precision might perhaps weaken their effectiveness. The untestability and shakiness of many of the arguments are also evident; but they seem to have met a need.[72]

At the same time, it is now easy to see why Kumarappa's version of Gandhism fits more easily into the political discourse of the time. Given the fundamental importance to nationalists of the project of 'modernizing' India through economic development, while at the same time appearing to be carving out a path different from that prescribed by colonialism,[73] there was a need to break the link between 'westernization' and 'modernity'.[74] It was not desirable to claim that the principles on which Indian development was to be based, despite their 'western' origins, were perfectly relevant to India – nationalists could not afford to be seen as plagiarist.[75] This would have been a surrender to the British imperialist view of Indian nationalism: nationalists belonged to a tiny elite of westernized, English-educated urban professionals and intellectuals cut off from the 'real' India, creatures of Macaulay's Minute.

This, it may be said, was one of the vital points regarding Indian nationalist thought: 'derivative' or not, whether it succeeded in being different or not, it sought to be different.[76] But it had to seek to be so without seeming to fit

British descriptions of backwardness. The search by Indian nationalism for resources of resistance to British rule had long included claims to a better, more civilized, glorious past before British rule. The sources of these claims are uncertain; perhaps they leaned on early British and European scholarship on the Indian past.[77] Kumarappa's appeals to 'regain the principles that guided our forefathers', to 'the perspective of eternity' and to rather selective 'Eastern principles' are not incompatible with his claims to defending a 'modern' position. Kumarappa was therefore drawing on a long-standing conventional framework of argument in which nationalist thought sought to be different by claiming a longer tradition: counterpoising Indian antiquity to that of Europe's classical antiquity; recovering the original nature of a now decadent *varnashrama*; or claiming that eastern civilizations were 'the result of philosophical and conscious social planning' as opposed to western systems' 'haphazard growths', were all ways to claim that India was modern before anyone else. This was not a unique claim, but one he shared with predecessors (in, for instance, the Arya Samajists' 'back to the Vedas' ideology, or Rammohun Roy's quest for a more rational religious faith in the ancient scriptures) as well as contemporaries and near-contemporaries.[78] Kumarappa's version of 'Indianness' or, 'eastern wisdom', as opposed to 'westernization' thus had something in common with other arguments which similarly looked for solutions to economic or social problems that could either be regarded as 'Indian' or, at any rate, not un-Indian.

This indicates not a separate trajectory but a similarity in strategies of argument and possibly also similar anxieties shared by Indians under colonial rule. For some, the modern was more appealing for its being universal, fears regarding 'culture' or 'Indianness' being secondary; for others, modernity was more comforting if it could be Indian. This provides a reminder of the dual purpose that nationalist developmental ideas had to serve: to be modern, not backward (in answer to colonial claims) as well as to be Indian, not western (in answer, once again, to colonial claims of the progressive aspects of colonial thought, as well as in response to Indian accusations or fears of loss of 'culture').

Instead of treating Kumarappa as a visionary who anticipated pro-environment or anti-Enlightenment positions well before their time, therefore, it is more suitable to treat him within the context of his time and its concerns, nationalist and developmental. The question as to his success or failure in communicating and propagating his ideas therefore rests on the persuasive capacity of his ideas within their time, as possible resolutions to the given problems, at a time when more philosophically satisfying resolutions were available elsewhere, which were also backed by the endorsement of present successes and the prospect of similar success in India. Part of this was due a conjunctural situation: for instance, the 'socialist' arguments that came to be accepted as part of the conventional rhetoric of post-independent India relied on a confusion inherent in seeing a planned economy as somehow socialist in itself, separate from questions of the ownership and control of technology, or the nature of the state which claimed to control technology and development on behalf of the nation. But this is part of a longer history that the present paper does not claim to deal with.[79]

Practical and conjunctural issues notwithstanding, it is also possible to suggest that Kumarappa's lack of success as the interpreter of Gandhism as a philosophy for the development of independent India was the result of a slight disjuncture in the timing of his intervention. Although Kumarappa, as I have argued, was within the parameters of conventional nationalist thinking in arguing as he did, he was actually stuck within slightly older debates that had been resolved and were therefore considered relatively uninteresting: this was in part a consequence of his Gandhian training and his role as Gandhi's spokesman. The debates around *swadeshi* in the period after the first partition of Bengal had led to heated and intense debates on 'constructive Swadeshi', and the desirability and extent to which borrowings from the 'West', intellectual or material, were desirable.[80] It was these debates that Gandhi must have been aware of as the immediate background to his intervention, with *Hind Swaraj* attempting to define the parameters of *swaraj* and *swadeshi*.[81] By the 1930s, when Kumarappa was writing, these questions had been resolved, at least temporarily: science and technology, though at present a 'western' import, were universal achievements, worthy of emulation.[82] Once this resolution had been achieved, even given the fact that the anxieties and concerns that had generated these debates still existed, turning the clock back was extremely difficult.

13

The Civilizational Obsessions of Ghulam Jilani Barq

MARKUS DAECHSEL

University of Edinburgh

The mission to civilize played a central part in Ghulam Jilani Barq's (1901–85) life. As an educationist and publicist he strove tirelessly to persuade the Muslims of Punjab to recognize what he saw as the many shortcomings of their religious tradition. He urged them to adopt an Islam that incorporated all the hallmarks of western modernity. While Barq's relationship with his own inherited identity frequently descended into hatred and disgust, his adulation of western ways went far beyond what could be expected from a self-reflexive and critical writer. It is not difficult to link some of the major themes in Barq's oeuvre – the Protestant work ethic, his obsession with hygiene, an almost blind faith in education and science – to the kind of discourses that British colonial rule employed to argue its own civilizing mission. But – as the following chapter is meant to demonstrate – it would be insufficient to understand Barq and his work exclusively in terms of colonial discourses colonizing or extirpating pre-existing thought structures and identities. Barq operated in a variety of discourses – Islamic and western – without managing to integrate them into a coherent whole. His work is characterized by many contradictions and inconsistencies, which fuel an unusual emotional intensity. Ghulam Jilani Barq did not embark on a civilizing mission, he suffered from civilizational obsessions. The contradictions he could not resolve were not the shortcomings of a weak mind. They pointed to fundamental problems that many human beings both in the West and the non-West encountered when they tried to make sense of the twentieth-century universe.

1. The Mullah 'Turned Inside Out'

Ghulam Jilani Barq is not a well-known figure in the historiography of South Asia. This necessitates a few remarks about who he was and why he has been selected for study in this context. As far as can be ascertained from his own writings, he belonged to a family of small landowners in central Punjab that had a long-standing connection with religious learning. He himself was sent to Madrasah to become an *alim*. But after a good decade within the system the young *tālib* developed a deep and lifelong antipathy towards traditional Islamic learning and all it stood for. As a result he opted for western education in local missionary colleges and later used his knowledge to pursue a career as a teacher and educationist. He became particularly interested in sciences, eventually acquiring an MA and a Ph D degree, which he proudly attached to his name whenever he wrote. His subsequent teaching appointments took him to Rawalpindi and Campbellpur (present-day Attock). Both places were provincial backwaters or, in Anglo-Indian terminology, *mufassil* towns. Although Ghulam Jilani did travel to the West on a couple of occasions,[1] he remained essentially a South Asian provincial intellectual. His literary output from the late 1930s to the 1970s consists of at least thirty-five books and many articles.[2] With one exception in English all of Barq's publications are in Urdu, although *Eik Islam* – one of his more influential books – has been translated into English by Fazl-i-Ahmad Kuraishi shortly after its original appearance.

Judging by his work, Barq was as much influenced by what he rejected as by what he endorsed. He found it difficult or impossible to establish an emotional distance to the world of the *madrasah* that had dominated his youth. Personal insecurities clearly had their role to play in this obsessive relationship as the following indictment suggests. For Barq his fellow *madrasah* students were '. . .a class of people sunk in homo-sexuality, masturbation and other unmentionable methods of sexual satisfaction'.[3] This passage is much more than a simple description of some of the experiences that Barq might or might not have had in his youth. What matters here is that traditional Islam was not simply something that other, lesser-educated people practised and which the reformer could criticize from the safe distance of his westernized upbringing and learning. Traditional Islam remained an enemy within, a constant temptation and a source of self-hatred. Despite the harsh and very partisan rhetoric that he adopted throughout his work, there was something fundamentally unresolved in Barq's stance. He was a mullah 'turned inside out', a phrase Roy Mottahedeh used to describe the somewhat similar figure of Ayatollah Sayyid Ahmad Kasravi in Iran.[4] Although traditional Islamic learning is rejected, this rejection takes place within the mindset of the *madrasah*.

For both Kasravi and Barq the trigger for their 'conversion' was the confrontation with western science in its most vulgar and positivist form.[5] Out of the twenty-four publications mentioned in the bibliography of *Do Qur'an* – Barq's first book – twenty-one are popular science manuals of questionable quality in both Urdu and English.[6] Scientific illustrations and anatomical cross-sections are used to argue the basic idea that the Holy Scriptures and the natural world are equally important manifestations of God's Law. This was neither a new nor a particularly anti-Islamic idea. The great figures of Muslim reform in Egypt had said very much the same several decades earlier.[7] But in Barq's hands the equation of science and 'true' Islam quickly led to a principled and dogmatic rejection of Islam as most Muslims understood it.

Barq saw himself as a preacher and philosopher of epochal importance. In the preface of *Eik Islam* he described his own role as the 'revolutionary thinker' of the East who would continue the work of great Enlightenment figures such as Montesquieu, Voltaire, Diderot and Rousseau.[8] He frequently chose the tone of a prophetic figure, at one point starting his elaborations in *Eik Islam* with the exclamation 'O People of the World!'.[9] The world could be saved, he believed, if his opinions were transmitted by radio and the press to all four corners of the globe.[10] In other publications, he adopted a different but no less ambitious persona – that of the Socratic thinker who brings out the falsehood in other people's opinions by engaging them in seemingly innocent conversations. But, unlike Socrates, Barq did this without humility and clearly enjoyed having exposed some of his interlocutors' follies.[11]

According to a footnote in Aziz Ahmad's *Islamic Modernism in India and Pakistan*, Barq was a thinker of lesser originality whose appeal was limited to some members of the Urdu-reading *petit bourgeoisie*.[12] Ahmad was not too far off the mark in regard to the quality of Barq's writing. Especially in his earlier work there is hardly an important argument that has not been made before and better by more illustrious thinkers such as Muhammad Iqbal or Inayatullah Khan 'Mashriqi'. Liberal references to Muslim intellectual history are combined with an equally eclectic use of western sources ranging from Enlightenment thinkers to Hitler and Mussolini. But Barq – the mullah 'turned inside out' – was remarkable for the emotional intensity with which he produced his diatribes against traditional Islam. His work stands out by virtue of his readiness to reach extreme conclusions. Barq offered caricatures of some of the most fundamental questions afflicting Muslim identity in the modern world – caricatures that bring out the central problems in the starkest possible way. Barq voiced opinions that many people might have held secretly, but felt too insecure to express openly. To be more precise, opinions that most people would not allow themselves to think to their logical conclusion because this would have plunged them into desperation and insecurity.

To make painful intellectual journeys on other people's behalf gave and still gives Barq a certain popularity. He remains a remarkably familiar topic in dinner-party conversations in present-day Pakistan, not only among the English-speaking elite but also among the Urdu-speaking intelligentsia and professional class. Some of his students from pre-Partition days are still alive today. One particularly striking example is Mian Nizam Din, an octogenarian with cult status among the Pakistani Left, who was at some point the private tutor of the well-known broadcaster and writer Tariq Ali. In striking similarity to his old mentor Barq, Nizam Din was also a mufassilite of modest background who was once drawn to Islamic learning. He later turned his identity inside out by pledging total allegiance to atheism and socialism. Like Barq, whom he still admires, Nizam Din is an outspoken and sometimes stubborn disciplinarian. But unlike Barq, Nizam was a ferocious opponent of colonialism and remains a staunch critic of westernization – in many ways a further inversion of the original converted mullah. Although Barq never became an atheist himself, there can be no better encapsulation of the Barqian spirit than the following statement that Nizam Din made in an interview: 'You should never greet me with assalamu alaikum! How do you dare invoke God's blessing on me? I am a communist, and when I am called before God's throne on the Day of Judgement, I will proudly say in His face: I don't care about Your laws. I don't believe in You. I am a communist. Send me to Hell if You like, I am prepared to suffer for my beliefs'.[13]

Barq deserves study, but not because he was typical in the sense of representing an average: he was typical because he represented the extreme, which – according to the German-Jewish sociologist Siegfried Kracauer – offers the best access point to understanding social and cultural realities.[14]

2. Islam and History

As a first step it is necessary to sketch Barq's problematic and to locate it within the framework of Indian Muslim thought of the colonial period. Barq's great concern is how objective historical experience can be reconciled with the promises of Islamic *heilsgeschichte*. It is not an exaggeration to say that this problem remains at the core of the Muslim experience. Right from the beginning the Prophet's mission was fraught with the fundamental contradiction between its claim to absolute truth and its often precarious existence in the temporal world. The first Muslim community faced constant threats to its existence from both within and without. In order to offer solace to a beleaguered *ummah* the Qur'an proclaimed in Surah 3 (Al Imran):

O ye who believe! (. . .) hold fast all together (. . .) and be not divided
amongst yourselves; and remember with gratitude Allah's favour on
you. (102–103) (. . .) Allah means no injustice to any of his creatures.
To Allah belongs all that is in heavens and on earth: to Him do all
questions go back for decision. (108–109) Ye are the best of peoples
(khaira ummatin), evolved for mankind, enjoining what is right and
forbidding what is wrong, and believing in Allah. If only the People
of the Book (Ahl ul-Kitab) had faith, it were best for them (. . .) but
most of them are perverted transgressors. They will do you no harm,
barring a trifling annoyance; if they come to fight you, they will show
you their backs, and no help shall they get. Shame is pitched over
them (like a tent) wherever they are found (. . .) they draw on themselves wrath from Allah and pitched over them is (the tent of) destitution. (110–112)[15]

In short, Muslims are promised that they will be the best community on
earth, recipients of God Almighty's favour, inherently superior to all of their
enemies, as long as they remain united and bound by the injunctions of their
religion. The crux about this equation of actual history (defeat of enemies)
and *heilsgeschichte* (rallying around God's messenger) is that it can be read back-
wards. If the enemies of Islam gain the upper hand and manage to subdue
Muslims, this can only mean that the Muslim community has failed to live up
to this fundamental promise, and that God in His infinite justice has punished
them either for disunity or for straying from the path of true Islam.

Historical failures such as the catastrophic collapse of the Abbasid
Caliphate in the thirteenth century or the Crusades have always provoked
attempts to purify Islam from allegedly harmful innovations and from intellectual discourses believed to contribute to disunity. But never was historical
failure so fundamental than at the time of colonial occupation, and nowhere
were the results of this failure so visible as in India, previously a Muslim
empire and now directly ruled by the allegedly destitute and shamefaced
People of the Book. As is well known from the literature, Indian Muslim
responses of the nineteenth century followed two lines of argument: some
tried to purify the existing religious orthodoxy along the lines of the
thirteenth-century thinker Ibn Taimiyya hoping for a relatively swift recovery
of political power,[16] while others maintained that the entire Islamic tradition
needed a complete overhaul, which would ensure political success only in the
distant and unforeseeable future. Sir Saiyid Ahmad Khan – foremost proponent of the latter position – argued that Islam had become perverted in its
very essence by its unwillingness to adapt to the changing needs of the times.
Military, technological and political inferiority in the present were indeed

God's wake-up call to the *ummah*, exhorting them to break the encrustations of tradition. Muslims could be saved only by combining a reappropriation of the pioneering spirit of early Islam with an openness to learn the new sciences and technologies of the West. This position was painful, but ultimately supremely optimistic, because Islamic reform charted a clear and reliable path to regaining God's favour. With the right kind of commitment, one hoped, *heils-geschichte* and history could be made congruent again.

The twentieth century saw this optimism dashed and produced far more radical responses to the promise laid out in Surah Al Imran. History was put into a position where it came dangerously close to devalidating the Islamic *heilsgeschichte* altogether. The two most important proponents of this new radicalism were Muhammad Iqbal and Inayatullah Khan 'Mashriqi' – both major influences on Ghulam Jilani Barq.

Iqbal's clearest and most striking response to the problematic is his celebrated long poem 'Shikwa (Complaint)' of 1909.[17] Adopting a radical ethics of intent and emotional authenticity, Iqbal turns the tables on God Himself. He argues that despite their weakness the Muslim *ummah* had always stood faithfully by their Messenger and God. Their current state of political crisis was not a justified divine punishment, but an incomprehensible divine let-down. God is equated with the figure of the capricious and unresponsive lover, which plays an important role in the *ghazal* tradition. The passionate accusations of infidelity that are hurled against God remain far removed from a lapse into atheism, however. Precisely by complaining so bitterly, Muslims unequivocally affirm their unconditional love for God and His Messenger. In fact, the deeply moving and strangely satisfying experience of unrequited love is turned into a central pillar of Islamic identity itself – a move that represents the delight in strong emotions and romantic self-pity prevalent at the time. Rather than to make *heilsgeschichte* and history congruent through a project of reform, emotionalism and will-power are held up as a shield against the ordeals of actual historical experience. Following a Nietzschean agenda, Iqbal suggests that the creation and cultivation of an uncompromising heroic self could act as the starting point for eventual recovery and salvation.

Inayatullah Khan 'Mashriqi' – a political and religious theorist rather than a poet – was prepared to steer much closer to a complete rejection of Islam as it existed. Mashriqi's rereading of the Qur'an – especially of the passage from Surah Al Imran – was coloured by Nazi *lebensphilosophie* and the Fascist insistence that might was right. God's infinite justice was seen as naturally favouring the strong.[18] The Supreme Being of Islam became equated with what Adolf Hitler called 'Providence' – actual history as metaphysical authority.[19] In other words, whereas traditionally *heilsgeschichte* had been regarded as more fundamental – more real – than actual history, actual history was now elevated to the status of a new positivist *heilsgeschichte*. Turning the Qur'an upside down, Mashriqi questioned whether the promise of Al Imran was aimed at the manifestly destitute and defeated real-existing Muslims at all.[20] Was it not more convincing, he asked, to regard those who were actually successful – the peoples of the West – as the true Muslims, rather than those who called themselves Muslims? As some of Mashriqi's student admirers proclaimed, the real 'God-men' (*khuda mard* – a term taken from Iqbal) of history were Hitler and Napoleon.[21] The real existing Muslim community had no right to survive on this earth, unless they could prove in actual history that they could be victorious in the struggle for political survival. The apocalyptic mood associated with the Second World War gave the real-existing *ummah* no second chances. Mashriqi's call was their last opportunity to rustle up the strength to become true Muslims again. If they failed, their permanent demise from world history would be entirely justified, in the same way that Hitler saw Germany's destruction as justified because the Germans had proved incapable of fulfilling their historical mission. Muslims could no longer rely on the long-winded process of internal reform that Sir Saiyid and others had proposed before. What was needed now was primarily military strength. In order to achieve this aim, Mashriqi founded a paramilitary organization, the Khaksar Tahrik. Although much of the movement's programme was targeted at resolving individual character flaws – weakness, laziness, lack of cleanliness and punctuality, etc. – great emphasis was placed on drill and physical training.

Ghulam Jilani Barq was strongly indebted to Iqbal and especially to Mashriqi. Over long stretches, *Eik Islam* or *Do Quran* read like Khaksar publications.[22] Most importantly, Barq maintained and elaborated the basic distinction between true Muslims – those who make history – and those who simply profess to be Muslims on the basis of their religious observance. As Barq put in one of dozens of similar passages in *Eik Islam*: 'The non-Namaz offering people of Britain, Russia and America have in their grips 60.000 000 namaz-offering people'.[23]

But Barq's frequent invocations of giant battles and martiality sat uneasily with his own personal mission. He was an educationist and publicist, not the self-styled military man and party-leader that Mashriqi had been. Blood and soil had to be transferred from the training pitch and the street battle to the classroom and the scholarly publication. Most of Barq's books appeared after the apocalyptic mood surrounding the Second World War and Partition had begun to wane. As a consequence, Barq was often thrown back to a more long term approach to the problem of God's promise to the *ummah*, which led him to a revised restatement of Sir Saiyid's old position recommending improvement through educational reform. But in Barq's hands the liberal-reformist project took on the character of a civilizing crusade.

By the time *Eik Islam* was published (1953), the Khaksar movement had all but disappeared and Mashriqi's ideas had been transformed from a living political possibility to an underground intellectual stance. This gave Barq both the opportunity and the obligation to dwell on some of the theoretical and theological implications of Mashriqi's thought that had gone largely unnoticed in the preceding period of hectic political activity. The move to elevate positive history to be the new *heilsgeschichte* turned the Islamic message upside down. The prophets of the Qur'an were no longer the sole nodal points of world history. They had to share this role with other great men who claimed their special status not on the basis of God's grace but by virtue of their actions. The only way of keeping Islam at least nominally intact was to stress its nature as the universally valid and· meta-historical religion of mankind as a whole. On its own, this claim was still recognizable to established Islam. But Barq widened it far beyond its traditional scope by arguing that true Islam had been the religion that any successful political leader or outstanding intellectual anywhere and at any age had been following, even if unwittingly. To put it differently, Islam was the religion of Reason with a capital R. God's message to humankind – the true Qur'an – was equally universal and unchanging. It represented what Barq believed to be the universal standard of morality and right action that could be observed in all history. All religious and political leaders of great importance, the Buddha, Jesus, even the Hindu deities Rama and Krishna or the founder of the Sikh community Guru Nanak, were in reality exponents of true Islam.[24] Real-existing Islam as it was founded by the Prophet Muhammad and expressed by the real-existing Qur'an was only one historical manifestation of universal Islam, albeit one with special importance and resonance.

Barq's oeuvre was thus firmly located within an old and well-worked Islamic problematic. But it is impossible to separate this framework from the Muslim encounter with the West. Both the fundamental question and many of the answers in contemporary Muslim thought would be unthinkable without the European presence. Barq's main intellectual masters Mashriqi and Iqbal belonged to the English-speaking elite of colonial India and had received substantial portions of their education from European universities. As a consequence, their own intellectual stimuli lay in the European intellectual and political tradition – influences Barq absorbed despite his own confinement to the *mufassil*. More importantly, it was the experience of colonial rule that constituted the immediate challenge to Muslim identity for most of Barq's formative years. It was British rule that seemed to prove at every step that Muslims had failed.

3. *Gharbzadegi*

When formulating his response to the problem of Islam and history, Barq went further in his adulation of western ways than most other Muslim intellectuals. He never made more than a half-hearted attempt to salvage a Muslim identity that could be juxtaposed to westernization. For him, the obvious answer for Muslims in their contemporary predicament was to follow European models hook, line and sinker. The move of equating the 'successful' peoples of this world with true Islam and his simultaneous denigration of the existing Muslim tradition as false and misguided provided an easy philosophical basis for this move. Pious, but idle nations, Barq argued, 'have no clever technicians, real scholars or gifted artists. Their countries are deserts without roads or other means of communication. They have no industries, laboratories or observatories and their raw materials enrich other nations. [. . .] God rewards sweat and toil without distinction of external appearance or religious beliefs'.[25]

A similar textual strategy – first separating traditional Islamic practice from the 'true' spirit of Islam and then to identify the latter with Western values and achievements – was adopted in an article entitled '*Islami Gadagarun se Mulaqatein*' ('Encounters with Islamic beggars'), which is interesting because it represents a step-by-step rejection of all the main institutions of Muslim tradition. Barq as the author-narrator described his encounters with a range of figures from the Islamic establishment, who all turned out to have a sole interest: the collection of money for established Islamic causes that Barq demonstrated were unproductive and therefore unworthy. The Muslim orphanage, the charitable foundation, the society for the protection of the Qur'an, the village committee to build a mosque, the Sufis – were all rejected because they focused on empty rituals and outward symbols of the faith. They all relied on a somewhat hypocritical air of piety, but did nothing to improve the lives of Muslims. What was needed in their place were practical initiatives modelled on western examples – employment and development projects, technical education, literacy campaigns, political mobilization.

The following passage from *Eik Islam* about which kind of dress Muslims should adopt is a good example of how far Barq's preference for western ways went and how he argued their superiority. After pointing out that Muslim forms of dress – invariably including long and flowing garments – was a sign of inferiority and shame, Barq asserted:

> [the Muslim] personality has fallen lower than that of a grass cutter and other people cannot bear his presence. The best form of dress in modern times is Western dress. It was invented by a Muslim scholar

– Zaryab of Spain. According to the 'survival of the fittest' all other forms of dress are falling into disuse, and the Western coat and trousers are being adopted by the people of all the countries.[26]

The stern rejection of all garments hitherto worn by Muslims reminds us of Mustafa Kemal Atatürk's well-known cultural revolution. Such a position was extremely rare among Muslim South Asians, however, because it could all too easily endanger Muslim claims for a separate national identity. Barq himself is a case in point because he felt compelled to mix his Kemalistic pro-westernism with a much more conventional Indian Muslim argument. Trousers and coat should be adopted – not only because they represented a superior form of culture but also because they were ultimately more truly Islamic than conventional Islamic dress. After all, coat and trousers were invented by a Muslim from Andalucia, the wonderland of the Indo-Muslim imagination. This is a classic example of the kind of Islamic apologetics that Sir Saiyid had made the staple of the Muslim western-educated classes. The invocation of social Darwinism in matters of dress is not as innocently simplistic as it looks. It was not so much coat and trousers by themselves that were 'more fitting' than Islamic forms of dress, but the wearers of coats and trousers, who were 'more fitting' than the wearers of Islamic dress – a point which should be noted for later.

Barq's forceful advocacy of copying the West is a particularly striking form of what the Iranian polemicist Jalal Al-e-Ahmad has called '*gharbzadegi*' ('westoxification')[27] – an obsessive and, in his mind, pathological admiration of anything western. But in Barq's case this was never simply a mindless adoption of the dazzling and easy ways of an alien culture backed up by superior political power. As already mentioned, his *gharbzadegi* was primarily driven by the rejection of a cultural milieu that he knew only too well.

The intention to offend the Islamic establishment appears to have been one of Barq's driving forces. He wanted his writings to hurt in order to shake up Muslim complacency. A good example of his spirit was a daring pro-Christian intervention in the dispute about the so-called Gospel of Barnabas, a topic that had preoccupied Christian-Muslim controversies for several centuries. St Barnabas, an early missionary associate of St Paul, is believed to have produced a version of the Gospel that predicts the coming of Muhammad as the True Prophet. Islam had always seen itself as the legitimate successor of Christianity, which had become necessary because Christians had perverted their original revelation. For most Muslim authors, the existence of the Gospel of Barnabas was the ultimate proof of how the Church hierarchy had maliciously falsified and suppressed parts of the original New Testament. Ever since the text of the Barnabas manuscript was published in Muslim languages (including Urdu) at the beginning of the twentieth century, Muslim authors had used it to denounce Christianity.[28] Missionaries countered by dismissing the text as a medieval fabrication. Barq was one of the few Muslim intellectuals who defended the missionary line and demanded to see physical evidence of the Gospel's existence prior to Muhammad's mission[29] – a position that was explicitly designed to destroy any notion that Muslims might enjoy an essential superiority over non-Muslims: 'To say that the earlier scriptures are distorted and adulterated is neither a remedy for any of your ills, nor a solution of any political and economic problem. It can neither bring you any good nor make you superior to others'.[30]

The West was best for the sole reason that it was successful in this world. Whether the Holy Scriptures worshipped by the West were true or false did not matter. Barq's entire project was nothing but a desperate attempt to appropriate the secret of western strength, even if it meant rejection of everything Muslims had held dear for centuries.

4. Weakness and Strength

Barq expressed his hatred for traditional Islam with diabolical disdain. Consider the following passage which appears in proximity to the ones about homosexuality and the merits of western dress. Once again, Barq described the Muslims of India and conjured up a disgusting image: 'Generally there is a crust of dirt on their foul-smelling bodies, which they scratch like monkeys every few minutes, thus getting sores and other skin disease all over.'[31]

Unsurprisingly, he then pointed to the Europeans as epigones of a hygienic and healthy lifestyle. According to the Wesleyan motto 'Cleanliness is next to Godliness' their superior living habits were interpreted as moral and religious superiority.[32] Barq's description is much more than a simple invocation of the virtues of hygiene and cleanliness which belonged to the stock-in-trade of most social reformers both inside and outside Europe. As with his remarks about homosexuality, this statement speaks of an obsessive aversion to the Muslim body – which is ultimately his own body. Although the disgusting details of Barq's imagery might have been influenced by the intent to shock and denigrate, something more disturbing lurks behind the equation of Muslims with dirty wild animals. It is very plausible that Barq made a subconscious statement about his own perceived racial inferiority. The 'crust of dirt' that needs to be washed off is a well-known symptom of African-American racial insecurities, which are fuelled by the tacit acceptance of white supremacy.

But there is another complementary explanation, which integrates the aforementioned passages into Barq's larger theoretical framework. The main reason behind his rejection of traditional Muslim identities was that they represented weakness. To be more specific, traditional Islamic ways did not produce the ideal of male strength that Barq regarded as necessary in the global battle for survival. As he put it succinctly: 'Throw away the sword and you will be crushed to powder. Your national life will come to an ignoble end and the relentless pen of History will bury you in the grave of extinction.'[33] Or paraphrasing Mussolini in a later chapter: 'The young men of a nation who do not have a taste of war at least once every year become ease-loving and consequently wash their hands of life.'[34] And again, now focusing on private careers: 'Success in life is a perpendicular rock to climb which one has to strain every nerve and use one's utmost endeavour. Lily-livered shirkers and chicken-hearted cowards can never achieve success.'[35] Needless to say, he included most of his compatriots in this category, particularly the young men who suffered from 'listless indifference'[36] – presumably the state of torpor following sexual over-indulgence or excessive religious observance. (It is interesting that Barq does not comment on women and their role in history at any point in the literature under review.)

Weakness appeared in the same context as dirt, homosexuality and the shameful outward appearance of Muslims. The underlying connection is most obvious in the case of homosexuality: a man having sex with another man supposedly denigrates his masculinity and as a result fails to live up to the demands of History. Traditional Muslims cease to be men, they become females or eunuchs – an accusation that was openly made by Barq's great mentor Inayatullah Khan 'Mashriqi'.[37] Barq's disgust with weakness and emasculation is then expressed in terms of dirt. The weak human being is as repulsive as a filthy animal. Traditional clothes invoke both weakness and filth. They look so untidy and undignified that 'other people cannot bear [a traditional Muslim's] presence'. And in contrast to trousers and coat, long-flowing garments do not accentuate masculinity. They are – from a westernized point of view – androgynous, somewhat akin to the practice of homosexuality itself.

Barq did not simply think that weakness was a problem in need of a remedy. He hated and despised weakness, and the intensity of his emotions suggested that they were, at least in part, directed against himself. His project was not reform but the desperate quest to re-establish self-respect through success – a project that was continuously undermined by insinuations of failure.

Barq was hardly unique in making a fetish of strength. Many, if not most, figures in Indian politics of the early twentieth century shared his obsessions – most prominent of all, perhaps, Mohandas Karamchand Gandhi, who believed as a young man that he had to eat meat in order to ingest the miraculous powers that the British colonizers possessed, and who later in his life adopted ascetic practices to become the wielder of spiritual super-power.[38] Others – like the educationists of the Arya Samaj studied by Harald Fischer-Tine – combined rigorous physical education with *brahmacharya* – the idea that the retention of semen could increase a man's physical and mental prowess. It is now often taken for granted that this obsession with strength was a simultaneous internalization and rejection of colonial discourses that constructed the colonized as weaker beings.[39] It is unquestionable that the colonial identity of British India relied on an image of male strength – the long horse-rides, the tiger-hunts, the homoerotic fascination with the strong warriors of the North-west Frontier[40] – and that some Indians were perceived as effeminate weaklings, particularly the proverbial Bengali *babu*. The distinction between self and other on the basis of strength was a logical component of the colonial civilizing mission, because the British had to explain why they were better suited to rule India than the people of India themselves. In order to be legitimate colonizers, the people of the West had to believe that the sub-jugated people of the world had failed *sub specie aeternitatis* and that they required outside assistance to survive the onward march of history. This was also, of course, the belief and life-project of Ghulam Jilani Barq.

But to interpret Barq's obsessions exclusively in terms of an internalization of colonial discourses is a simplification and an explanatory short-circuit. Unless one takes discourse to be the subject of history and unless one analyses its working at a very high level of abstraction, the *parallels* between a colonial fetishisation of strength and Barq's own fetishization of strength do not *explain* anything. In order to understand Barq's entanglement with colonial ideas, we have to identify which particular ideas he was exposed to and *in which way* and, more importantly, why they made sense – to him.

It can be taken for granted that Barq was well acquainted with the colonialist outlook of early-twentieth-century Punjab. He attended and taught at missionary colleges and regularly conversed with colonial officials posted in his area. Some of Barq's motifs – particularly sexual over-indulgence and dirt – are infamous ingredients of general Orientalist images of 'the East'. But colonial ideology was not a homogenous edifice, and Barq consciously adopted some aspects of it but rejected others. The discourses most prevalent in Punjab emphasized rather than denied masculine strength in a select group of subject peoples. This was particularly the case in the North-west where Barq lived for most of his life. These were army recruiting grounds populated by the proverbial 'martial races' whose leaders had been co-opted into the colonial elite. As a Punjabi Muslim, Barq would have had no reason to feel particularly affected by colonial caricatures of the weak Indian, which were most commonly applied to Hindus in other regions of India. He could easily have invoked the prowess of the meat-eating 'Punjabi Musalman' who was supposedly so much stronger than the vegetarian Hindu. But Barq never did so. In fact, the only relevant reference to martial-race theories to be found in *Eïk Islam* briskly dismissed Muslim claims of physical superiority as unproductive and irrelevant.[41] Clearly, Barq felt that the theme of the decrepit Orient with all its subsidiary motifs was a more appropriate description of the *ummah*'s state than the colonial martial-races theory. The discourse of decay was well suited to insult – always one of Barq's intentions – precisely because it identified Muslims with images that Barq's communalized readership would have liked to be identified exclusively with Hindus.

Selective parallels with colonial discourses apart, Barq's ruminations about strength and weakness need to be placed in the wider cultural context of twentieth-century north India. A complex and still under-researched process of social transformation produced its own notions of well-being and disease.[42] The key ingredients were the emergence of a sizeable literate lower middle class in the cities and the corresponding introduction of consumption as a social form. People began to be deeply influenced by the compulsion to acquire objects of desire or, more precisely, to associate themselves with the identities and dream-worlds that consumer products carried with them. One of the most noticeable features of the time was the commercialization of medicines of all kinds and their dominant position on the consumer-goods market. At least from the late nineteenth century onwards, newspaper and magazine readers and, presumably, shoppers in urban markets were bombarded with advertisements selling patent medicines and drugs of any conceivable description. Western biomedicine and colonial 'quacks' were as much present in this medical pandemonium as *unani tibb* and *ayurveda*. All tried to attract customers by promising to alleviate relatively unspecific ailments such as general fatigue, lack of concentration, and lack of sexual performance – usually described with the blanket-term 'weakness' (*kamzuri*). These products were not straightforward medicines prescribed by doctors, but branded commodities available over the counter or through mail order. In order to compete, they had to carry advertising messages designed to invoke dreams and pleasant emotions originally unconnected with their actual product nature.

The dominant advertising message of the interwar period established a direct link between social, political and personal problems and physical ill-health. Whatever the problem at hand – even if it was strictly connected to the mind or soul – it could be remedied by the ingestion of a magic substance affecting the body. Exam performance was to be enhanced by Andrew's Liver Salts. The manifold pressures faced by a middle-class woman would disappear with the help of Horlick's Hot Energy Drink.[43] Social pressures of all kinds were embodied – experienced and conceptualized as unspecific physical ailments – and then approached through physical remedies. The threat of unemployment during the Great Depression, a tightening of work discipline, growing competition for academic excellence, a general feeling of insecurity in a complex and threatening political climate, all fed into an extremely wide-spread hypochondria that simultaneously sustained and was sustained by the booming market in medical commodities. *Kamzuri* was nothing other than a generalized performance *Angst* – the fear of failing in the arduous struggle for success that Barq had identified as the key element of a life worth living. It is the hypochondria associated with the patent drug that Barq had in mind when he spoke of the 'listlessness' of the contemporary young men.

Exactly like medical advertising discourse, Barq's understanding of strength moved between different registers. The passages about war, sexuality and dirt focused on the body as the main location of strength/weakness. But equally important was Barq's association of strength with brain-power and an unrelenting will. He was a dyed-in-the-wool social Darwinist[44] and believed that all that counted was success per se. As evolution progressed from animals to humans, methods of success grew ever more sophisticated and shifted from the body to the brain – hence Barq's adulation of scientific discovery, artistic creativity and technical development. Despite his love for fascist machismo Barq was the opposite of a cultural pessimist. He might have admired Mussolini a great deal, but he also admired Einstein, Spencer, Goethe, Ibn Sina and Homer for what they had achieved in their respective fields. Even captains of industry – unlikely examples of physical prowess – deserved praise as model human beings because they represented success.[45]

5. Taming an Apocalyptic Universe

Despite his occasional strong words Barq's recipe for gaining strength was always bookish – scientific education, literary sophistication and technical development. In his ultimate analysis the mind and the soul counted for more than the body. What, then, was the secret behind mental strength? The conventional and moralistic Islamic answer – spiritual purity through minute observance of religious obligations – was as much rejected as the more complex association of power with Sufi practices.[46] For Barq, the ability to survive in the evolutionary battlefield came primarily from what Weber has called '*methodische Lebensführung*'[47] – a constant and never-ending compulsion to systematize and rationalize daily life in order to maximize practical life achievement. Consider Barq's description of a typical day of the Prophet – the ideal for all of mankind: he gets up at sunrise and prays until nine a.m., proceeds with housework including sweeping, cleaning his shoes and washing his clothes. Between one p.m. and evening prayers he decides court cases, receives reports from his provincial governors and fills in the account books of the Bait ul-Mal, the state treasury. After the evening prayer, the Prophet again spends long hours on meditation and communication with God, to retire long after midnight for a meagre two hours' sleep until the next day.[48] There are two points to notice in this description: first, the Prophet does not shy away from manual labour, even in its inferior manifestations. He strives to do everything by himself and does not employ servants. Second, no minute of the Prophet's life is spent on any activity that is not immediately and exclusively oriented towards practical purpose or achievement. The biggest source of weakness is the unproductive pursuit of pleasure.

This was precisely the problem with the 'listless' young men of the day. Barq accused them: 'You need all sorts of trash . . . tales of fairies and demons, detective novels and books on sex.'[49] Apart from presenting a list of the most successful genres of popular fiction in mid-twentieth-century Punjab, this sounds very similar to the exhortations found in Islamic instruction literature. Ever since the emergence of a large middle-class readership in the colonial cities religious publicists had striven to make a living out of the compilation of moralistic tracts for the faithful, particularly for devout and relatively well-to-do women who observed purdah and had plenty of time at their hands.[50] The biggest competitors of religious literature of this type were precisely the popular romances, detective stories and compilations of film songs that came in for specific criticism by the religious authorities.[51] But despite similarities between Barq and other more conventional religious commentators, there is a fundamental difference in the interpretation of the sin of reading for pleasure. For most Islamic publicists, reading pulp fiction led to 'unclean thoughts'[52] and thereby endangered the smooth progress of an individual Muslim towards Paradise. For Barq, the same sin led to weakness and 'listlessness' which was a crime not because it contravened an individual moral code, but because it rendered a people unfit in the global battle of survival.

The core of Barq's world-view is the direct link between the collective battle for survival in a Darwinist universe and individual weakness and strength, which is the result of the individual conduct of life. It is this association that elevates success in one's career to a matter of life and death for the community. Failure is not simply inadequacy, but treason. The weak are no longer the recipients of pity and the theologically necessary beneficiaries of charitable activity – as in the world of traditional Islam – but a disgrace to History, associated with the most disgusting practices (for example, filth, homosexuality), little better than animals.

The association of individual failings with historical failure could only make sense in a universe that was perceived as a giant interconnected structure where every minute change had an impact on the structure as a whole – the kind of universe in which the proverbial flick of a butterfly's wing at one end of the world could cause a hurricane at the other. Barq used a different metaphor to describe the same idea. Having asserted the Qur'anic dictum that 'the deeds of none are wasted',[53] he introduced an image of God that is clearly reminiscent of European Enlightenment thought. God is the workman who keeps 'the human machine ticking'[54] – a machine that is but a small part in a giant workshop. When discussing the role of angels in the universe Barq wrote:

> If you go down to the railway workshops at Lahore, you will find a hundred thousand workmen employed at various kinds of jobs. Now the universe is infinitely bigger than this workshop. Is there no labourer or worker in this vast workshop of God? Is God doing every job with his own hands? Has God so many hands that at one and the same time he is able to create, pull and rotate and make every one of the immovable planets in the solar system run its course?[55]

This image is the direct outgrowth of the argument made in *Do Qur'an* – Barq's first book – that there is no difference between God's law and natural law. This is the universe of popular science with all its schemes, tables and diagrams translated into God's giant machine.[56] The main difference to more conventional Islamic perspectives is not so much that even small deeds may be important but – as mentioned already – that small deeds do not only affect individual salvation but the equilibrium of the whole system. If even a small lever in one of the many machines of the universe fails, the overall functioning of the universe suffers.

The equation of individual action and history has other conceptual roots – in themselves embedded in processes of social transformation – that identify Barq as a product of the interwar period. Both poles of the equation – the autonomous individual and history as a structured universe moving through homogenous time – are eminently modern concepts which emerged in late-eighteenth-century Europe. The idea that linked the individual so closely to history was the concept of the nation. While the nation was the subject of history par excellence, its members were perceived – at least in theory – as equals as far as their membership in the nation was concerned. As a result, every member of the nation – not just exalted institutions such as the Church or the monarchy – became responsible for the historical fate of the nation. It is a well-known fact that the preferred literary genre of nationalists was the autobiography, because it expressed the link between the development of a person at the micro-level and the development of the nation at the meta-historical level.

The ideas of nation, autonomous self and history had already been well established in Indian intellectual circles before Barq started to write. What was new during his formative years between 1920 and the late 1930s was that a political culture exclusively based on the individual on one side and world history on the other took hold of the imagination of large sections of the Indian population – particularly among the new literate middle-class in the cities. The rise to eminence of this socio-political formation was a complex process, which I have analysed in detail elsewhere.[57] Its main cause was a paradoxical refashioning of imaginary time/space: while the world that people actually experienced in their day-to-day lives shrank more and more to the domestic spaces in newly established middle-class housing societies and suburbs, the spaces that people could imagine expanded far beyond their normal radius of interaction. Illustrated newspapers and magazines, radio and the newsreel brought the entire world to people's doorsteps.[58] The rapid expansion of print entertainment – particularly historical romances and detective stories – enabled even the most lethargic and home-based person to experience wild adventures in far-off areas of world history. The encounter between the individual reader and the fictional world had only to be transposed to the 'real' world to produce the impression that world history was all about individual action. What was entirely lost in this perspective was a multi-layered and complex understanding of collaboration and negotiations at the level of associations and groups. Like most of his contemporaries Barq only addressed human activity at two extreme levels: nations and religious civilizations working in History, and individuals determining the actions of these meta-entities with their individual actions. No matter how much Barq disliked the 'listless' young men absorbed in their fictional universe, one could argue that his meta-historical viewpoint would not have made much sense to anybody else.

The intensity of condemnation that Barq heaped on anybody who could be seen as letting his side down in the fight for survival was directly linked to the eschatological way in which he perceived the world around him. Total catastrophe was imagined side by side with final salvation. Today's universe was eternal darkness, 'a Stygian pit', humanity 'blundering about in utter gloom', with weapons of mass destruction ready to eradicate the world, Barq observed. But, he added: 'I can even now perceive the first flush of a radiant dawn where the cavalcade of Humanity will enter that glorious stage of its long journey, where the milk of human kindness will enrich social relationships and the radiance of Universal love illuminate Man's path to progress in an atmosphere of amity and concord'.[59]

Elsewhere he exclaimed: 'Let us carry Man to the gloriously radiant world where . . . the high and the low, the rich and the poor, the lion and the lamb and the mighty and the weak breathe in an atmosphere of freedom and fraternity, so that even the stars tremble in the sky with the fear of Man becoming their master.'[60]

This is a remarkable ideological hotchpotch mixing biblical and Qur'anic imagery with the ideals of the French revolution and Iqbal's celebration of Man the master. But what is most striking about this passage (and the one quoted before) is that it represents a significant change in ideological register. The glorious future that Barq wanted to achieve is precisely the opposite of the social Darwinist universe that he associated with the present. His ideal world is far from Fascist. It is an ordered cosmos where might is *not* right, where weakness does *not* lead to annihilation and where there is no never-ending compulsion to be successful.

Barq hated weakness because it forestalled the luxury of being weak. He denied the existence of any moral principles apart from success in the present, so that a morality of unalienable human dignity might reign supreme in the future. This is a deeply troubled consciousness wanting to believe that the world is good – a moral ordered whole – but being confronted with the fact that it is not. Barq lamented: 'In this world of ours, which is in fact the domain of infinite caprice, one man's meat has become another man's poison . . . the worst enemy of man is man itself.'[61]

This is the very heart of the civilizational obsessions of Ghulam Jilani Barq. When he looked around him, he saw a world that was either completely unpredictable – 'infinite caprice' – or an amoral mechanism that mercilessly selected the fittest. Both rebelled against the kind of moral universe that religion was all about and that he desired so badly to preserve. If he had fully subscribed to social Darwinism, what was the point in writing thirty-five lengthy books on religion? Without God, Barq argued, there could be no universe, without God's law there could be no living space for the helpless:[62] 'The Day of Judgement is the most heartening hope of the poor. If the conception of the Day of Judgement were not there, all the poor will have to commit suicide and thus put an end to their wretchedness.'[63]

Nowhere does the desire to salvage a moral cosmos from the clutches of nihilism come out more clearly than in the following three passages, which revealingly are also among Barq's most obsessive:

> When I was young, a sin was committed inadvertently, committed by me, as a result of which I suffered from terrible nightmares of handcuffs, police and jail. For many weeks I wept, repented and begged for God's mercy . . .[64]

> Take [. . .] the little matter of truthfulness and spread out the scroll of

your life. Now try to find a single day in your past when you could manage without telling a lie. Be truthful at least now and say that you cannot find any such day.[65]

Thirty years ago, I lost the bicycle of a friend through my negligence. My friend pardoned me, but God did not. In 1947, I was invited to tea at the bungalow of a Lieut. Colonel. It put my bicycle in the compound. [. . .] When I came out after tea, I found only my bicycle missing, whereas those of all other guests were there. In 1920 when I was a raw youth, I gave a slap on the face of a hostel cook. [. .] A few days after that I was travelling by train without ticket and was caught [. . .] The ticket collector gave such an explosive slap on my face that it turned a beautiful blue . . .[66]

Barq examined his life in a fashion closely following Weber's famous Protestant methodology of constant introspection. No deed – however trivial – is forgotten or goes unpunished. But unlike his Protestant precursors Barq was not primarily interested in securing divine election. What Barq was desperately trying to prove in his stories of sin and retribution was that there was a moral universe at all. The historical events he lived through while working on *Eik Islam* suggested that the world was nothing but caprice – a battlefield where the weak annihilated the strong: the Second World War and its million dead, the horrors of Partition, the collapse of a democratic system in Pakistan, the loss of Kashmir, the humiliation of the people of Egypt under Khedive rule, the return of Dutch colonial rule to Indonesia, the creation of Israel. There could be hardly any better evidence that God's promise to the Muslim *ummah* was null and void, that the long encounter of Islam and History had finally been decided in favour of the latter. In a world where there did not seem to be any morality (recognizable to a Muslim), Barq was struggling to unearth hidden connections – no matter how spurious or ridiculous – in order to prove that this morality still existed. The very obsessiveness of this search indicates that – despite his own assertions to the contrary – Barq did not fully believe in the existence of a moral cosmos any longer. Why else would he endorse doctrines of social Darwinism with such ferocity? Barq's attempts at taming the twentieth-century universe from a Muslim point of view led him to adopt contradictory positions that find their unity only in the exaggerated and obsessive ways in which they were proposed.

6. Conclusion

In laying out Barq's arguments, I have tried to show how his ideas of Islam, of western technology and science, of strength and weakness and of the relationship between individual and universe connect within an overarching problematic. Barq's main question was defined by the collision of two discourses, which posed similar yet opposing claims. On the one hand there was a discourse of European civilizational superiority, which Barq encountered not only in the form of the colonial civilizing mission with all its subsidiary arguments, but also in the form of fascist and national socialist ideas of social Darwinism. On the other hand, there was the claim of Islam to be the universally true religion, which was promised global dominance by God the Creator Himself. In the end, Barq failed to offer a convincing defence of the latter against the former. He had to concede that might was right and that Islam was doomed to failure unless it merged with social Darwinism. But Barq was clearly uncomfortable with this conclusion. He retained the idea of a moral universe in his vision for the future and tormented himself in search of clues that would enable him to suggest the existence of such a universe in the present. His obsessive hatred of weakness and failure had a double edge: it stemmed both from the acceptance of the norms of social Darwinism and from the compulsion of having to accept these norms in the first place.

Barq was a product of his time, which means much more than that he was a product of colonial education and a human carrier of colonial discourses. Colonial rule was certainly an important presence in his life, because it offered the most painful manifestation of western superiority. But it did not exhaust the modern universe, with which Barq tried to come to terms. Global processes of transformation – for instance, the global spread of consumption, the availability of certain literary genres and the impact of new news media – changed the way in which the people of India looked at the world. The experience of the Second World War and subsequent events imposed new challenges. The enterprise to come to terms with new situations was certainly determined by whatever structures of thought people had at their disposal, but they often exhausted these structures or made them crack – as Barq's own idiosyncrasies demonstrate.

Put in the broadest possible terms, Barq's writings have been understood as an attempt to make sense of a changing world in which pre-existing discourses pose certain questions but do not provide any easy answers. A person like Barq is not seen as the embodiment of a pre-existing discourse – an internalized civilizing mission – which acts as a history-making force on its own. Such an approach would fail to explain the most important and most puzzling element in Barq's work: his obsessions born out of human struggle and despair.

NOTES

'Torchbearers Upon the Path of Progress'

1. Many thanks to Harald for improving the introduction.
2. Charles Grant, 'Observations on the State of Society among the Asiatic Subjects of Great Britain, particularly in respect to Morals; and on the means of improving it', written chiefly in 1792, first published 1797, *Parliamentary Papers*. Report from the Select Committee on the Affairs of the East India Company, vol. VIII, 1831–32; Colonies East India, vol. 5, Shannon: Irish University Press, 1970, General Appendix, no. I , p. 63.
3. For the impact of the First World War on Britain's imperial mission in India see also Margaret Macmillan, 'Anglo Indians and the Civilizing Mission, 1880–1914', in Krishna Gopal (ed.), *Contributions to South Asian Studies 2*, Delhi, Oxford University Press, 1982, pp. 73–109. Also of interest is Michael Adas, 'The Great War and the Decline of the Civilizing Mission', in Laurie J Sears (ed.), *Autonomous Histories, Particular Truths: Essays in Honor of John R. W. Smail*, Madison, University of Wisconsin, Center for Southeast Asian Studies, Monograph, no. 11, pp. 101–121. Gyan Prakash, *Another Reason. Science and the imagination of modern India*, Princeton, Princeton University Press, 1999.
4. On the ambivalence of Anglicist paternalism and liberal friendship of the Indian Civil Service's members see Clive Dewey, *Anglo-Indian Attitudes. The mind of the Indian Civil Service*, London and Rio Grande, Hambledon Press, 1993.
5. George Orwell, *Burmese Days*, Harmondsworth, Penguin Books, 1967, pp. 36–7.
6. *Ibid.*, p. 40.
7. *Ibid.*, p. 41
8. *Ibid.*
9. Michael Adas, *Machines and the Measure of Men: Science, technology and ideologies of Western Dominance*, Ithaca, Cornell University Press, 1989. For the role of science in the French Empire see Lewis Pyenson, *Civilizing Mission: Exact Sciences and French Overseas Expansion, 1830–1940*, Baltimore, Johns Hopkins University Press, 1993.
10. Alice L Conklin, *A Mission to Civilize. The republican idea of empire in France and West Africa, 1895–1930*, Stanford, Stanford University Press, 1997, pp. 5–6.
11. For the background of an Indian concept of legitimate rule, see the various chapters in the volume edited by John F Richards, *Kingship and Authority in South Asia*, Delhi, Oxford University Press, 1998.
12. See also Homi K Bhaba, *The Location of Culture*, London, Routledge, 1994, pp. 66–84.
13. See, for instance, Robert Orme, *Historical Fragments of the Mogul Empire of the Morattoes and of the English Concerns in Idostan from the Year M.DC.LIX etc.*, New Delhi, Associated Publishing House 1974, pp. 280–91.
14. *Ibid.*, p. 291.
15. See Ashis Nandy, *The Intimate Enemy. Loss and recovery of self under colonialism*, Delhi, Oxford University Press, 1996, pp. 4–11.
16. Paul Langford, *A Polite and Commercial People. England 1727–1783*, Oxford, Clarendon Press, 1989, pp. 235–88. *Cf* Eric Stokes, *The British Utilitarians and India*, Oxford, Oxford University Press, 1959, pp. 27–8.
17. Boyd Hilton, *The Age of Atonement. The influence of Evangelicalism on social and economic thought, 1785–1865*, Oxford, Clarendon Press, 1988, pp. 7–35. Eric. J Evans, *The Forging of the*

Modern State. Early Industrial Britain, 1783–1870, London and New York, Longman, 1983, pp. 45–55.

18. Thomas Babington married the daughter of a Scottish Presbyterian. Her brother, Zachary Macaulay, made a fortune in the West Indies and later on, with profound insider knowledge, became most influential in the slavery abolition campaign. His son, named Thomas Babington after his uncle, was brought up and privately educated with Wilberforce's son. See E J Evans, *Forging of the Modern State*, pp. 45–6.

19. See, for example, James Bryce, *A Sketch of the State of British India, with a view of pointing out the best means of civilizing its inhabitants, and diffusing the knowledge of Christianity throughout the Eastern world, etc.*, Edinburgh, G. Ramsay, 1810. William Cockburn, *A Dissertation on the Best Means of Civilizing the Subjects of the British Empire of India, and of diffusing the Light of the Christian Religion throughout the Eastern world, etc.*, Cambridge: Deighton, 1805.

20. James Bryce, *A Sketch of the State of British India*, pp. 112–4.

21. Francis Hutchins, *The Illusion of Permanence. British imperialism in India*, Princeton, Princeton University Press, 1967, p. 18.

22. Margret Frenz, ' "A Race of Monsters": South India and the British "Civilizing Mission" in the Later Eighteenth Century', in Harald Fischer-Tiné and Michael Mann, *Colonialism as Civilizing Mission*, London, Anthem Press, 2003, pp. 46–64.

23. Radhika Singha, *A Despotism of Law. Crime & justice in early colonial India*, Delhi, Oxford University Press, 1998, pp. 3–4, 26.

24. For a comprehensive discussion of the colonial perception of and the ensuing fight against 'thugee' see Martine Van Woerkens, *Le Voyageur étranglé. L'Inde des Thugs, Le Colonialisme et L'imaginaire'*, Paris 1995.

25. Sandra B Freitag, 'Crime in the social order of Colonial North India', in *Modern Asian Studies*, 25 (2), 1991, pp. 227–61; and S Nigam, 'Disciplining and Policing the Criminals by Birth', in *Indian Economic and Social History Review*, XXVII (2), 1990, pp. 131–64 and XXVII (3), 1990, pp. 257–87.

26. *Ibid.*, chapter 3, 'The Privilege of taking Life: "Anomalies" in the Law of Homicide', pp. 80–120.

27. Michael Mann, 'Dealing with Oriental Despotism: British Jurisdiction in Bengal, 1772–1793', Harald Fischer-Tiné and Michael Mann, *Colonialism as Civilising Mission*, London, Anthem Press, 2003, pp. 27–45.

28. Thomas R Metcalf, *Ideologies of the Raj*, Cambridge, Cambridge University Press, 1994; *New Cambridge History of India* III (4), pp. 37–9. See also K K Raman, 'Utilitarianism and the Criminal Law in Colonial India; A study of the practical limits of utilitarian jurisprudence'; in *Modern Asian Studies*, 28 (4), 1994, pp. 739–91.

29. Ainslie T. Embree, *Charles Grant and British Rule in India*, London, Allen & Unwin, 1962, pp. 141–57. Grant's 'Observations' circulated among the directors of the East India Company, but, subsequently, also among 'Evangelicals' and, of course, Members of Parliament after 1797, yet his pamphlet only became widely known after it had been printed in 1813, in preparation of the Company's charter renewal.

30. Charles Grant, 'Observations on the State of Society', 1813, pp. 59–72.

31. *Ibid.*, pp. 76, 79.

32. *Ibid.*, pp. 72–82, quotes pp. 81, 82.

33. *Ibid.*, p. 84.

34. Eric Stokes, *English Utilitarians and India*, pp. 52–8.

35. Charles Grant did not only influence the writings of James Mill but also the politics of William Bentinck which can be observed in the Governor General's reforms with regard to the abolition of *sati* and the remarriage of Hindu widows.

36. James Mill, *The History of British India*, 3 vols, London 1819, reprinted Delhi, Atlantic Publishers, 1990, vol. 1, p. 24.

37. For an insightful discussion of their respective readings of Indian society see also Thomas R Trautmann, *Aryans and British India*, New Delhi, Vistaar, 1997, pp. 101–24.

38. George D Bearce, *British Attitudes towards India, 1784–1858*, Oxford, Oxford University Press, 1961, pp. 65–78.

39. Eric Stokes, *English Utilitarians and India*, chapter 1, pp. 1–80.

40. John William Kaye, *The Administration of the East India Company. A history of Indian progress*, London, 1854, reprinted Allahabad: Kitab Mahal, n.d., *passim*.

41. *Moral and Material Progress and Condition of India* 1 (1859/60)–70 (1934/35) Oriental and India Office Collection OIH330.954. British Library, London. Many thanks, again, to Harald for this information.

42. Zaheer Barber, *The Science of Empire. Scientific knowledge, civilization, and colonial rule in India*, Delhi, Oxford University Press, 1998. Deepak Kumar, *Science and the Raj, 1857–1905*, Delhi, Sangam Books, 1995. Satpal Sangwan, *Science, Technology and Colonisation, 1757–1857*, Delhi, Anamika Prakashan, 1991.

43. Henry T Bernstein, *Steamboats on the Ganges. An exploration in the history of India's modernization through science and technology*, Hyderabad, Orient Longman, 1960. Ian J Kerr, *Building the Railways of the Raj, 1850–1900*, Delhi, Oxford University Press, 1997. Ian Stone, *Canal Irrigation in British India: Perspectives on technology change in a peasant society*, Cambridge, Cambridge University Press, 1984.

44. Ravi Ahuja, '"The Bridge-Builders". Some Notes on Railways, Pilgrimage and the British "Civilizing Mission" in Colonial India', Harald Fischer-Tiné and Michael Mann, *Colonialism as Civilising Mission*, London, Anthem Press, 2003, pp. 89–110.

45. David Arnold, *Science, Technology and Medicine in Colonial India*, Cambridge, Cambridge University Press, 2000; *New Cambridge History of India*, III (5), pp. 57–86.

46. See on this aspect the latest publication of essays by Biswamoy Pati and Mark Harrison (eds), *Health, Medicine and Empire. Perspectives on colonial India*, New Delhi, Orient Longman, 2001. *New Perspectives in South Asian History*, vol. 1.

47. David Arnold, *Colonizing the Body: State medicine and epidemic disease in nineteenth-century India*, Berkeley, Los Angeles and London, University of California Press, 1993.

48. Neil Brimnes, 'The Sympathizing Heart and the Healing Hand. Smallpox Prevention and Medical Benevolence in Early Colonial South India', Harald Fischer-Tiné and Michael Mann, *Colonialism as Civilising Mission*, London, Anthem Press, 2003, pp. 183–196.

49. Helen E Meller, *Patrick Geddes. Social evolutionist and city planner*, London and New York, Routledge 1990. Mariam Dossal, *Imperial Designs and Indian Realities. The planning of Bombay city 1845–1875*, Delhi, Oxford University Press, 1991.

50. Mridula Ramanna, 'Perceptions of Sanitation and Medicine in Bombay, 1900–1914', Harald Fischer-Tiné and Michael Mann, *Colonialism as Civilising Mission*, London, Anthem Press, 2003, pp. 197–217.

51. For a more general background see Mark Harrison, *Public Health in British India: Anglo-Indian preventive medicine 1859–1914*, Cambridge, Cambridge University Press, 1994. Roger Jeffrey, *The Politics of Health in India*, Berkeley, Los Angeles and London, University of California Press, 1988. Anil Kumar, *Medicine and the Raj: British medical policy 1835–1911*, New Delhi, Sage, 1998.

52. James H Mills, '"More Important to Civilize than Subdue"? Lunatic Asylums Psychiatric Practice and Fantasies of the "Civilizing Mission" in British India 1858–1875', Harald Fischer-Tiné and Michael Mann, *Colonialism as Civilising Mission*, London, Anthem Press, 2003, pp. 171–182.

53. Vinay Bahl, *The Making of the Indian Working Class. The case of the Tata Iron and Steel Company, 1880–1946*, New Delhi/Thousand Oaks/London, Sage, 1995. Samita Sen, *Women and Labour in late Colonial India. The Begal Jute Industry*, Cambridge, Cambridge University Press, 1999.

54. Dietmar Rothermund, *India in the Great Depression, 1929–1939*, Delhi, Manohar Publishers 1992.

55. Dietmar Rothermund, *An Economic History of India from Pre-colonial Times to 1986*, London,

Routledge, 1988, pp. 76–117. See also Dharma Kumar and Tapan Raychaudhuri (eds), *The Cambridge Economic History of India*, 2 vols, Cambridge, Cambridge University Press, 1982, vol. 2: *c*.1757–1970, pp. 553–675.

56. Partha S Gupta, *Imperialism and the British Labour Movement*, London, Macmillan, 1975.

57. Stephen Constantine, *The Making of British Colonial Development Policy, 1914–1940*, London, Cass, 1984. B R Tomlinson, *The Economy of Modern India, 1860–1970*, Cambridge, Cambridge University Press, 1993. *New Cambridge History of India*, III (3), pp. 1–29, 101–68.

58. B P Pandey, *Gandhi and Economic Development*, New Delhi, Sangam Books, 1991. Ajit K Dasgupta, *Gandhi's Economic Thought*, London/New York, Longman, 1996).

59. Benjamin Zachariah, 'In Search of the Indigenous. J C Kumarappa and the Philosophy of "Gandhian economics"', Harald Fischer-Tiné and Michael Mann, *Colonialism as Civilizing Mission*, London, Anthem Press, 2003, pp. 248–69.

60. Jana Tschurenev, 'Between Non-interference in Matters of Religion and the Civilizing Mission: The Prohibition of "*sati*" in 1829', Harald Fischer-Tiné and Michael Mann, *Colonialism as Civilizing Mission*, London, Anthem Press, 2003, pp. 68–91.

61. Ajay Skaria, *Hybrid Histories. Forests, frontiers and wilderness in Western India*, Delhi, Oxford University Press, 1999.

62. See the recent study of Nonica Datta, *Forming an Identity. A social history of the Jats*, Delhi, Oxford University Press, 1999.

63. The latest book on this subject is Ramachandra Guha, *Savaging the Civilized. Verrier Elvin, his tribals, and India*, Chicago and London, University of Chicago Press, 1999.

64. Malavika Kasturi, 'Taming the "Dangerous" Rajput: Family, Marriage and Female Infanticide in Nineteenth-century Colonial North India', Harald Fischer-Tiné and Michael Mann, *Colonialism as Civilizing Mission*, London, Anthem Press, 2003, pp. 117–141.

65. Lynn Zastoupil and Martin Moir (eds), *The Great Indian Education Debate. Documents relating to the Orientalist-Anglicist Controversy, 1781–1843*, Richmond, Curzon Press, 1999, introduction, pp. 1–72.

66. '"English in Taste, in opinions, in words and intellect". Indoctrinating the Indian through textbook, curriculum and education' in J A Mangan (ed.), *The Imperial Curriculum. Racial images and education in the British colonial experience*, London/New York, 1993, pp. 175–93.

67. Minute recorded in the General Department by Thomas Babington Macaulay, law member of the Governor General's council, dated 2 February 1835, in ibid., pp. 161–73.

68. K Kumar, *A Political Agenda of Education. A study of colonialist and nationalist ideas*, New Delhi, Sage, 1991. Kenneth W Jones, *Socio-religious Reform Movements in British India*, Cambridge, Cambridge University Press, 1989. *New Cambridge History of India* III (1).

69. Harald Fischer-Tiné, 'National Education, Pulp Fiction and the Contradictions of Colonialism. Perceptions of an Educational Experiment in the Early Twentieth-century India', Harald Fischer-Tiné and Michael Mann, *Colonialism as Civilizing Mission*, London, Anthem Press, 2003, pp. 229–47.

70. See J A Mangan, *The Games Ethic and Imperialism: Aspects of the diffusion of an ideal*, London, Cass, 2000.

71. Paul Dimeo, 'Sport and the "civilizing mission" in India', Harald Fischer-Tiné and Michael Mann, *Colonialism as Civilizing Mission*, London, Anthem Press, 2003, pp. 165–78.

72. See the latest book on this subject by Ramachandra Guha, *A Corner of a Foreign Field. The Indian History of a British Sport*, London, Picador, 2002.

73. Markus Daechsel, 'The Civilizational Obsessions of Ghulam Jilani Barq', Harald Fischer-Tiné and Michael Mann, *Colonialism as Civilizing Mission*, London, Anthem Press, 2003, pp. 270–90.

74. Macmillan, 'Anglo-Indians', p. 82–3.

75. Peter Robb (ed.), *The Concept of Race in South Asia*, New Delhi, Oxford University Press, 1995. David Omissi, *The Sepoy and the Raj: The Indian Army, 1880–1940*, London, Macmillan, 1994.

76. Mrinalini Sinha, *Colonial Masculinity. The 'manly Englishman' and the 'effeminate Bengali' in the late nineteenth century*, Manchester/New York, Longman, 1995.

77. Metcalf, *Ideologies of the Raj*, pp. 83–6.

78. For a general background see Susan Bayly, *Caste, Society and Politics in India from the Eighteenth Century to the Modern Age*, Cambridge, Cambridge University Press, 1999. *New Cambridge History of India* IV (3).

79. Melitta Waligora, 'What Is Your Caste? The Classification System of Indian Society as Part of the British "civilizing mission"', Harald Fischer-Tiné and Michael Mann, *Colonialism as Civilizing Mission*, London, Anthem Press, 2003, pp. 143–64.

80. Gyan Prakash (ed.), *After Colonialism. Imperial histories and postcolonial displacements*, Princeton, Princeton University Press, 1994), introduction, p. 1.

81. Conklin, *Mission to Civilize*.

82. Singha, *Despotism of Law*, pp. xvii. Michael Mann, *Bengalen im Umbruch. Die Herausbildung des britischen Kolonialstaates 1754–1793*, Stuttgart, Franz Steiner Verlag, 2000 (literal translation of the title, *Bengal in Transition. The emergence of the British colonial state, 1754–1793*), pp. 144–54, 340–3.

83. Carl Bridge, *Holding India to the Empire (The British Conservative Party and the 1935 Constitution)*, London, Oriental University Press, 1986. R J More, *Endgames of Empire. Studies in Britain's Indian problem*, Delhi, Oxford University Press, 1988.

84. Lord Curzon, speech at the Byculla Club, Bombay, 16 November 1905, quoted in Metcalf, *Ideologies of the Raj*, p. 168.

85. The most notable exception is Macmillan, 'Anglo-Indians'.

1. Dealing with Oriental Despotism

1. This article is based on parts of chapter III (3) and chapter VII (1) of my book *Bengalen im Umbruch. Die Herausbildung des britischen Kolonialstaates, 1754–1793*, Stuttgart: Steiner Verlag 2000. I owe many thanks to Harald Fischer-Tiné and Ben Baron for critical comments.

2. Charles Grant, 'Observations on the State of Society among the Asiatic Subjects of Great Britain, particularly in respect to Morals; and on the means of improving it', (written chiefly in 1792, first published 1797), *Parliamentary Papers*. Report from the Select Committee on the Affairs of the East India Company, vol. VIII, 1831–2, Colonies East India, vol. 5, Shannon, Irish University Press, 1970, General Appendix, No. 1, p. 17.

3. Paul Langford, *A Polite and Commercial People. England 1727–1783*, Oxford, Clarendon Press, 1989, pp. 484–5.

4. *Vide* the introductory essay of this volume.

5. Alexander Dow, *The History of Hindostan*, 3 vols, London 1772, vol. 1, p. xi; quoted in Bernard S Cohn, 'Law and the colonial state in India', in *idem*, *Colonialism and Its Forms of Knowledge. The British in India*, Delhi, Oxford University Press, 1997, p. 62–3.

6. Michael H Fisher (ed.), *The Politics of the British Annexation of India*, Delhi, Oxford University Press, 1993, pp. 4–6, 16–33. Thomas R Metcalf, *Ideologies of the Raj*, Cambridge, Cambridge University Press, 1994. *The New Cambridge History of India*, III (4), chapters 3–4, pp. 66–159.

7. Court of Appeal, Quarter Sessions, Mayor's Court, Court of Requests, three *zamindari-*courts; see Charles Fawcett, *The First Century of British Justice in India*, Oxford, Oxford University Press, 1934, pp. 208–11, 216–7. B B Misra, *The Judicial Administration of the East India Company, 1773–1783*, Delhi/Varanasi/Patna, Motilal Banarsidas Publishers, 1961, pp. 134–5. The Mayor's Court was set up in 1726, privileged by a royal charter and

reorganized after 1753. On the charter of 1753 and its regulations, see M Rama Jois, *Legal and Constitutional History of India*, 2 vols, Bombay, Tripathi Private, 1984, vol. II, pp. 119–22.

8. Public Letter from Court, 28 August 1771, para. 21, in *Fort William – India House Correspondence*, vol. VI, Indian Record Series, edited by N K Sinha, New Delh, 1965 (henceforth *FWIHC*), p. 123.

9. Public Letter to Court, 3 November 1772, paras 31–6 in *ibid.*, pp. 426–7.

10. Though the fiscal and the judicial administration were intertwined, this is not the place to deal with the fiscal administration of Bengal after 1765 and the way the British muddled through, since this has been done elsewhere. There are plenty of detailed studies on the revenue administration of Bengal. Contributions providing a more general overview are Richard B Ramsbotham, *Studies in the Land Revenue History of Bengal 1769–1787*, Oxford, Oxford University Press, 1926; Sophia Weitzman, *Warren Hastings and Philip Francis*, Manchester, Manchester University Press, 1929, pp. 68–83; Michael Mann, *Bengalen im Umbruch*, pp. 175–201.

11. Eric Stokes, *The British Utilitarians and India*, Oxford, Oxford University Press, 1959.

12. See below, Jana Tschurenev, 'Between Non-interference in Matters of Religion and the Civilizing Mission: The Prohibition of "Suttee" in 1829', pp. 65.

13. On the Law Commission see M P Jain, *Outlines of Indian Legal History*, Bombay, Tripathi Private, 1966, pp. 615–36. On the Orientalist–Anglicist debate, see Lynn Zastoupil and Martin Moir (eds), *The Great Indian Education Debate. Documents relating to the Orientalist-Anglicist Controversy, 1781–1843*, Richmond, Curzon Press, 1999, pp. 31–54.

14. Charles U Aitchison, *Collection of Treaties, Engagements and Sanads Relating to India and Neighbouring Countries*, vol. 2, reprinted Delhi, Mittal Publishers, 198), no. X, Firmaund from the King Shah Aalum, granting the Dewanny of Bengal, Behar, and Orissa to the Company, 12 August 1765, pp. 241–3.

15. George D Bearce, *British Attitudes Towards India, 1784–1858*, Oxford, Oxford University Press, 1961.

16. B B Misra, *Judicial Administration*, pp. 168–74; N Majumdar, *Justice and Police in Bengal, 1765–1793. A Study of the Nizamat in Decline*, Calcutta, K L Mukhopadhyay, 1960, pp. 96–101 and M P Jain, *Indian Legal History*, pp. 89–98.

17. Copy of a letter from the Committee of Circuit to the Council at Fort William, Cossimbuzar, 15 August, 1772, in George W Forrest (ed.), *Selections from the State Papers of the Governors-General of India: Warren Hastings*, 2 vols, Oxford, Blackwell Publishers, 1910, vol. II, Appendix Papers, Warren Hastings, vol. II, Appendix B, p. 300.

18. The British always regarded a 'benevolent despotism' or 'paternalism' as the most appropriate form of government for the people of India and this policy always determined the political agenda when dealing with India, as can still be observed in the king's proclamation in 1919 passing the Montagu-Chelmsford reform act; see H H Dodwell, *The Shorter Cambridge History of India*, Cambridge, Cambridge University Press, 1934, p. 908.

19. See the Committee of Circuit's plan for the administration of justice in Bengal, dated 15 August 1772, in D N Banerjee, *The Administrative System of the East India Company in Bengal, 1765–1774*, London: Longman, Green, 1943, Appendix 16, paras 1–4, p. 663.

20. *Ibid.*, paras 5–6, p. 663.

21. Although Radhika Singha deals with the problem of capital punishment, she does not analyse the usurpation of this right by the colonial state and its supreme representatives, the Governor Generals Warren Hastings and Charles Cornwallis. In regard to the central quest of the colonial state's legitimacy and 'sovereign power', capital punishment became the core legislative and executive issue of the British in India when establishing the colonial regime. Radhika Singha, *A Despotism of Law. Crime and justice in early colonial India* (Delhi etc.: Oxford University Pres, 1998), ch. 3, The Privilege of taking Life: 'Anomalies' in the Law of Homicide', pp. 80–120.

22. Jörg Fisch, *Cheap Lives and Dear Limbs. The British Transformation of the Bengal Criminal Law*

1769–1817, Wiesbaden, Franz Steiner Verlag, 1983, pp. 24–30.

23. D N Banerjee, *Administrative System*, Appendix 16, para. 4, p. 668.

24. Extract of the Proceedings of the Committee at Kissen Nagar, 28 June, 1772, in G W Forrest, *Selections from the State Papers*, vol. II, Appendix B, p. 289.

25. Radhika Singha, *A Despotism of Law. Crime and Justice in Early Colonial India*, Delhi, Oxford University Press, 1998, p. 28. T K Banerjee, *Background to Indian Criminal Law*, Calcutta, 1963, p. 6. B B Misra, *Judicial Administration*, p. 281–4, 287.

26. J Fisch, *Cheap Lives and Dear Limbs*, pp. 32–4. B B Misra, *Judicial Administration*, pp. 284–6. The fact that no member of the family was necessarily forced to execute father or son, mother or niece, but that the right to pardon was still applicable is typical of Hastings's misunderstanding. No cases of an actual execution by family members in Bengal have come down to us. The legal practice was quite different from the claims made in normative texts.

27. See M R Jois, *Legal and Constitutional History*, pp. 9–10, 14 and T K Banerjee, *Background to Indian Criminal Law*, p. 35. Hastings was categorically opposed to the Hanafi school of Islamic legal tradition when discussing the legal reforms. This school, established by Abu Hanafi (AD 699–767) was only one of four law schools that interpreted the Qur'an from a legal point of view, albeit the most prevalent. Two of Abu Hanafi's students, Yusuf und Imam Muhammad, doubted his opinion that the methods of killing used were a criterion to distinguish between murder and manslaughter and emphasized the criminal intention instead.

28. D Hay, 'Property, authority and the criminal law' in *idem et al.*, *Albion's Fatal Tree. Crime and Society in Eighteenth-century England*, New York, Pantheon, 1975, pp. 17–26, 35–9.

29. For the criminalization of whole groups during British colonial rule – in the case of the 'thugs' they could and also had to be 'invented' – instead of individual criminal prosecution, see R Singha, *Despotism of Law*, pp. 169–228; Sandra Freitag, 'Crime in the social order of colonial North India', in *Modern Asian Studies* 25 (1991), pp. 227–31.

30. *Vide*, for example, the cases of James Biron, master in the pilot service. Letter dated 16 June 1808, Blaquier, Police Magistrate Calcutta, to Secr. to the Government and Peter Hay, James Reiley, John Reid, privates in the Corps of European Artillery, Oriental and Inda Office Collection, British Library (henceforth OIOC, BL) India Office Records: Misconduct of illegal Europeans in India, 1766–1824. O/5/25 year 1808. I owe this information to Harald.

31. T K Banerjee, *Background to Indian Criminal Law*, pp. 8–9.

32. J Fisch, *Cheap Lives and Dear Limbs*, p. 34. The (Muslim) ruler was entitled to the privilege of *siyasa* in cases when no unambiguous legal formula existed in the *sharia* and, therefore, he was consequently acting in public interest; see *ibid.*, p. 20.

33. Proceedings of Fort William (Revenue Department), 3 August 1773, in D N Banerjee, *Administrative System*, pp. 495–500, quote on p. 496.

34. Consultation, Revenue Department, Fort William, of Tuesday, 31 August 1773, in ibid., pp. 500–502.

35. Despatches to Bengal, vol. 7 (1775), 3 March 1775, paras 39–46, pp. 413–26, OIOC, BL.

36. Khan H Mohsin, *A Bengal District in Transition. Murshidabad 1765–1793*, Dacca, Asiatic Society of Bangladesh, 1973, pp. 167–8.

37. On the emerging contemporary idea of 'humanity', see P Langford, *Polite and Commercial People*, pp. 483–5.

38. T K Banerjee, *Background to Indian Criminal Law*, pp. 69–70.

39. J Fisch, *Cheap Lives and Dear Limbs*, pp. 37–8.

40. Vishu A Narain, *Jonathan Duncan and Varanasi*, Calcutta, Mukhopadhyay, 1959), p. 158–61.

41. K M Mohsin, *A Bengal District in Transition*, p. 169.

42. Lord Cornwallis to Rgt Hnble Henry Dundas (Private), dated 8 March 1789, Calcutta,

Cornwallis Papers (1786–1789), PRO 30/11/150, Public Record Office, London.

43. The questionnaires were sent out on 19 November 1789, Bengal Revenue Council, 3 December 1790 only; the collector's answers in the appendix, ibid., ff. 304–905 (OIOC, BL). J. Fisch, *Cheap Lives and Dear Limbs*, p. 38; M P Jain, *Indian Legal History*, pp. 202–3; B B Misra, *The Central Administration of the East India Company, 1773–1784*, Manchester, Manchester University Press, 1959, pp. 322–3.

44. Bengal Revenue Council, 3 December 1790 only, ff. 304–905 *passim*.

45. Bengal Revenue Council, 3 December 1790 only, Governor General's Minute, para. 4, ff. 194v–195r and para. 20, ff. 213v–216v.

46. Cornwallis regarded Muhammad Reza Khan as the prime source of Bengal's criminal judiciary evils, especially because the latter made decisions on personnel without referring back to the Supreme Council, which, according to Cornwallis, was the main reason for the lack of ethic of the *faujdari adalats*; see ibid., paras. 24–46, ff. 225v–247v.

47. Regulation, for the administration of justice, in the Foujderry or Criminal Courts, in Bengal, Bihar and Orissa, passed by the Right Hon. the Governor General in Council, on 3 of December 1790, in James E Colebrooke, *Supplement to the Digest and Laws enacted by the Governor General in Council for the Civil Government of the Territories under the Presidency of Bengal, containing a Collection of the Regulations enacted anterior to the Year 1793*, Calcutta 1807, pp. 141–59.

48. Regulation 3 December 1790, para. 33, *ibid.*, pp. 154–5.

49. J Fisch, *Cheap Lives and Dear Limbs*, p. 45.

50. Regulation 3 December 1790, in J E Colebrooke, *Supplement to the Digest of the Regulations*, para. 34, p. 155.

51. Extract from Proceedings of the Governor General in Council, 9 October 1791, para. 2, *ibid.*, p. 159.

52. Extract from the Resolutions of the Governor General in Council, passed on 9 October 1791, para. 3, *ibid.*, p. 160.

53. Fisch mentions the change in the right to pardon, but misses the point of the legislation from 9 October 1791; see his *Cheap Lives and Dear Limbs*, p. 45, fn. 128.

54. Extract from the Proceedings of the Governor General in Council in the Revenue Department, 13 April 1792, paras 1 and 3, in J E Colebrooke, *Supplement to the Digest of the Regulations*, p. 161.

55. *Ibid.*, para. 1.

56. J. Fisch, *Cheap Lives and Dear Limbs*, p. 46. On the fictional *fatwa* see Regulation IX of 1793, sec. lvi; Richard Clarke (ed.), *The Regulations of the Government of Fort William in Bengal, in Force at the End of 1853*, 3 vols, London 1854, vol. I, p. 96.

57. J Duncan, M Derret, *Religion, Law and the State in India*, London, Faber and Faber, 1968, pp. 239–41.

58. The British had doubts about the validity of Turkish or, more general, Muslim evidence of witnesses; see K N Chaudhuri, *The Trading World of Asia and the English East India Company, 1660–1760*, Cambridge, Cambridge University Press, 1978, p. 112. Warren Hastings basically doubted Bengali witnesses in the Nandakumar case; see Letter to Laurence Sulivan, Fort William, 20 March 1774, in George R Gleig, *Memoirs of the Life of the Right Honourable Warren Hastings*, 3 vols, London 1841, vol. I, p. 391. The inferiority of Indian witnesses in comparison to the British at the beginning of the twentieth century is dealt with in E M Forster's novel *A Passage to India*.

59. Regulation IX of 1793, sec. lvi; see R Clarke, *Regulations of the Government*, vol. I, p. 96.

60. Regulation 10 October 1791, in J E Colebrooke, *Supplement to the Digest of the Regulations*, p. 165.

61. A Aspinall, *Cornwallis in Bengal. The administrative and judicial reforms of Lord Cornwallis in Bengal*, Manchester, Manchester University Press, 1931, pp. 74–6. M P Jain, *Indian Legal History*, pp. 207–11. B B Misra, *Central Administration*, pp. 320–21.

62. David Arnold, 'The Colonial Prison: power, knowledge and penology in nineteenth-

century India, in *idem* and David Hardiman (eds), *Subaltern Studies*, vol. VIII, Delhi, Oxford University Press, 1994, pp. 148–87, especially pp. 160–61.

63. Bengal Revenue Council, 3 December 1790 only, Governor General's Minute, para. 95, f. 298.

64. Bengal Public Letter to Court, letter dated 10 August 1791, *FWIHC*, vol. XXII, pp. 424–5.

65. Robert Orme, 'General Idea of the Government and People of Indostan' in *Historical Fragments of the Mogul Empire*, 1792, London 1805, as quoted in B S Cohn, 'Law and the colonial State', pp. 64.

66. The plan was implemented on 11 April 1780; B B Misra, *Judicial Administration*, p. 263, fn. 1 refers to the plan in the Revenue Proceedings, dated 28 March, but there is a another version, dated 20 March; see Extract from the Proceedings of the Governor General and Council in their Revenue Department 20 March 1780, Home Misc. Series 155 (OIOC, BL).

67. Extract from the Proceedings of the Governor General and Council in their Revenue Department, 20 March 1780, paras 6th–11th, *ibid.*

68. B B Misra, *Central Administration*, p. 237.

69. Regulations for the Administration of Justice in the Courts of Mofussil Dewannee Adauluts, and in the Sudder Dewannee Adaulut, passed in Council 5 July 1781, in J E Colebrooke, *Supplement to the Digest of the Regulations*, pp. 37–86.

70. William Chambers translated the code into Persian, completing in February 1783. Jonathan Duncan did the Bengali translation, which was completed in the same month, V A Narain, *Jonathan Duncan and Varanasi* , pp. 13–15.

71. Regulations for the Administration of Justice in the Courts, in J E Colebrooke, *Supplement to the Digest of the Regulations*, paras v–viii, pp. 41–3, para. xiii, pp. 44–5, para. xxv, pp. 52–6, para. xxx, p. 59.

72. Ibid., para. li, p. 68.

73. Ibid., paras lviii und lix, p. 74.

74. Ibid., para. xlvi, p. 67 and para. l, p. 68.

75. The Committee of Circuit's plan for the administration of justice in Bengal, dated 15 August 1772, in D N Banerjee, *Administrative System*, p. 665, Appendix 16, paras 13–14.

76. *Ibid.*, para. 12.

77. J D M Derrett, 'Sanskrit legal treatises compiled at the instance of the British', *Zeitschrift für vergleichende Rechtswissenschaft* 63 (1961), p. 75, fn. 6.

78. Bernard S Cohn, 'From Indian status to British contract', in *idem, An Anthropologist among the Historians and other Essays*, Delhi, Oxford University Press, 1987, pp. 474–7.

79. Calcutta High Court Record Room, Sadr Diwani Adulat Proceedings, [1796–1797], quoted in *ibid.*, p. 478, fn. 42.

80. David A Washbrook, 'Law, state and agrarian society in colonial India', *Modern Asian Studies* 15 (1981), p. 659.

81. See, for example, Court of Directors to the Governor General and Council, 12 April 1786, para. 85, Walter K Firminger (ed.), *The Fifth Report from the Select Committee of the House of Commons on the Affairs of the East India Company, 1812*, 3 vols, Calcutta, R Cambray & Co., 1917/18, reprint New York, Augustus M Kelley Publishers, 1969, vol. I, p. 53.

82. Regulation XLI of 1793, secs iii–vii and secs xix–xxi; R Clarke, *Regulations of the Government*, vol. II, pp. 232–4, 243.

83. Ibid., sec. vii, p. 233.

84. Ibid., sec. xii, p. 234.

85. Ibid., sec. x.

86. Ibid., sec. xi.

87. Ibid., secs i and ii, p. 323.

88. W K Firminger, *Fifth Report*, vol. I, p. 42.

89. Regulation II of 1793, sec. iii; R Clarke, *Regulations of the Government*, vol. I, p. 11: oaths for

collectors. Regulation III of 1793, sec. iii, p. 21: oath for judges at the Zilla and City Courts. Regulation IX of 1793, sec. ii, p. 87: oath for magistrates; sec. xxxiv, pp. 93–4: oath for judges; sec. xxxv, p. 94: oath for registrars; sec. xxxvii: oath for *mufti*s und *qazi*s at the Court of Circuit; secs lxx und lxxi, p. 98: oath of the registrar and of the supreme *qazi* as well as for the two *mufti*s at the *nizamat adalat*s. Regulation XII of 1793, sec. v, p. 112: oath for *qazi*s and *mufti*s at the *sadr diwani adalat*, sec. vii, p. 113: oath for *pandit*s. Regulation XIII of 1793, sec. iii, cl. 1, p. 115: oath for all covenanted servants; sec. iv, p. 116: for every native officer.

90. Regulation for the Administration of Justice [. . .] 5 July 1781, para. vii, in J E Colebrooke, *Supplement to the Digest of Regulations*, p. 42.

91. R. Singha, *Despotism of Law*, pp. 46–8.

92. To Charles Wilkins, Court House, 6 June 1785, in Garland Cannon (ed.), *The Letters of Sir William Jones*, 2 vols, Oxford, Clarendon Press, 1970, vol. 2, no. 411, pp. 677–8; To Charles Chapman, [Krishnagar] 28 September 1785, *ibid.*, no. 418, pp. 683–4; to Thomas Law, Crishnagar, 28 September 1785, ibid., no. 419, p. 685; to John Shore, [Krishnagar, autumn] 1785, ibid., no. 519, pp. 837–8.

93. Regulation XIII of 1793, sec. ix, cl. 1, in R Clarke, *Regulations of the Government*, vol. I, p. 117.

94. Ronald Inden, *Imagining India*, Cambridge MA/Oxford, Blackwell Publishers, 1990, pp. 36–48, 85–97. C A Bayly, *Empire and Information. Intelligence gathering and social communication in India, 1780–1870*, Cambridge, Cambridge University Press, 1997, pp. 56–96.

95. O P Kejarival, *The Asiatic Society of Bengal and the Discovery of India's Past, 1784–1838*, Delhi, Oxford University Press, 1988, *passim*.

96. The Governor General in Council to the Court of Directors, Fort William, 6 March, 1793, in Charles Ross, *Correspondence of Charles, First Marquis Cornwallis*, 2 vols, London, 1859, vol. II, Appendix LXII, p. 554.

97. Governor General's Minute, 18 September 1789, in W K Firminger, *Fifth Report*, vol. II, appendix no. 5, pp. 510–5 and Minute of Governor General, 3 February 1793, *ibid.*, pp. 527–43. Ranajit Guha points out the frequently mentioned term 'improvement'; see Ranajit Guha, *Dominance without Hegemony. History and power in colonial India*, Cambridge, Mass./London, Harvard University Press, 1997, pp. 32–3. Additionally, the verb 'to improve' turns up another three times.

98. Governor General's Minute, 18 September 1789, W K Firminger, *Fifth Report*, vol. II, appendix no. 5, pp. 511, 514, 512.

99. Minute of Governor General, 3 February 1793, *ibid.*, p. 532.

2. 'A Race of Monsters'

1. Minute on the Situation of the British, Bombay, 19 April 1798, para. 6, Walker of Bowland Papers MS 13621 (National Library of Scotland).

2. Letter probably by A Walker to Wellesley, Calicut 12 July 1800, Walker of Bowland Papers MS 13602 (National Library of Scotland). See also Thomas R Metcalf, *Ideologies of the Raj, The New Cambridge History of India* III (4), Cambridge, Cambridge University Press, 1995, p. 4; Amal Chatterjee, *Representations of India, 1740–1840. The Creation of India in the Colonial Imagination*, London/New York, Palgrave Macmillan, 1998, p. 202; Nicholas B Dirks, *Castes of Mind. Colonialism and the Making of Modern India*, Princeton, Princeton University Press, 2001, especially p. 5.

3. For the timber trade see Michael Mann, 'Timber Trade on the Malabar Coast, c. 1780–1840', *Environment and History* 7 (2001), p. 403–25.

4. Sovereignty today is defined as the highest independent power of a state to rule and decide state affairs. Sovereignty has to be distinguished between the external sovereignty of a state with regard to other states and the internal sovereignty within a state. The latter

includes a defined state territory, the people within and the authority of the state. *Cf* Ludger Kühnhardt, *Stufen der Souveränität. Staatsverständnis und Selbstbestimmung in der 'Dritten Welt'*, Bonn, Bouvier, 1992, p. 9 f.; Helmut Quaritsch, *Souveränität. Entstehung und Entwicklung des Begriffs in Frankreich und Deutschland vom 13. Jh. bis 1806*, Berlin, Duncker & Humblot, 1986.

5. Niklas Luhmann, *Legitimation durch Verfahren*, Frankfurt/Main, Suhrkamp, 1997, p. vii f.

6. *Cf. ibid.*, pp. 12, 23, 25.

7. *Cf* George D Bearce, *British Attitudes Towards India 1784–1858*, London, Oxford University Press, 1961, p. 40 f.

8. *Cf* Wolfgang Reinhard, *Geschichte der Staatsgewalt. Eine vergleichende Verfassungsgeschichte Europas von den Anfängen bis zur Gegenwart*, München, C H Beck, 2000, p. 17.

9. For a more detailed analysis see Stig Förster, *Die mächtigen Diener der East India Company. Ursachen und Hintergründe der britischen Expansionspolitik in Südasien, 1793–1819*, Stuttgart, Steiner Verlag, 1992.

10. In H Sharp, *Selections from Educational Records, 1789–1839*, Calcutta, 1920, pp. 107–17, p. 116.

11. A detailed study is Mrinalini Sinha, *Colonial Masculinity. The 'Manly Englishman' and the 'Effeminate Bengali' in the Late Nineteenth Century*, Manchester/New York, Manchester University Press, 1995.

12. Malabar was seen as a 'market of opportunites'. See Pamela Nightingale, *Trade and Empire in Western India 1785–1806*, Cambridge, Cambridge University Press, 1970, p. 80f., 113.

13. The commission comprised of the following people: Alexander Dow had been military commander in Talasseri since 1789. W G Farmer had served almost thirty years in the Bombay presidency, during which time he had been resident of Fort Victoria. Dow and Farmer had been in Malabar since April 1792. Charles Boddam and William Page had been in Malabar since September and December 1792.

14. *Reports of a Joint Commission from Bengal and Bombay, Appointed to Inspect into the State and Condition of the Province of Malabar, in the Years 1792 and 1793. With the Regulations thereon Established for the Administration of that Province*, 3 vols, Bombay, no date, reprinted Madras 1862, para. II. In spite of the relatively wide-ranging report by the commissioners, which was concluded in October 1793, there were still some points, such as the procurement of geographical data, that never found their way into the report – they remained a *desideratum* until the late nineteenth century. After the Joint Commission had completed its work, it dissolved itself in October 1793, following the model of their report. In February 1794 a supplementary volume was added to the original report by Messrs Boddam and Duncan.

15. Robert Abercromby (1740–1827) was the supreme commander of the British in Bombay and in this capacity he led troops from Bombay against Tipu Sultan.

16. *Reports of a Joint Commission*, para. LXXXI.

17. Quote from Abercromby's instruction to the Joint Commissioners dated 20 April 1792 in *Reports of a Joint Commission*, para. LXXXI.

18. *Ibid.*

19. *Ibid.*, para. LXXXIII.

20. *Ibid.*, paras. CCLVII, CCLXII; William Logan, *A Collection of Treaties, Engagements and Other Papers of Importance Relating to British Affairs in Malabar*, reprinted New Delhi/Madras, AES, 1989, ii, XXV, p. 173.

21. *Ibid.*, para. CCCVIII.

22. *Ibid.*, para. CCCIX.

23. The treaties are printed in Logan, *Treaties*, ii, V, VI, XIII, XV–XVI, and mentioned in *Reports of a Joint Commission*, paras. LXXXIV–LXXXVI.

24. *Reports of a Joint Commission*, para. CCXII; *cf* also C U Aitchison, *Collection of Treaties, Engagements and Sanads Relating to India and Neighbouring Countries (revised and continued up to*

1929), 14 vols, Calcutta, Kingham, 1929–1932, vol. 10, p. 150.

25. The following districts belonged to the area of the northern superintendency: Cirakkal, Kannur, Kottayam, Iruvathinatu, Katattanatu, Kurumpranatu, Kurg; and the following to the southern superintendency: Ramnatu, Parappanatu, Vettattanatu, Erarnatu, Carakkatu, Sananganatu, Palakkatu. The supravisor's headquarters, Kozkikkodu, formed, with its surrounding suburbs, its own sub-unit. *Reports of a Joint Commission*, para. CCXII. Additional instructions for supravisor and superintendents can be found in paras. CCCLXIV–CCCLXXI.

26. *Cf Reports of a Joint Commission*, para. CCXI; William Logan, *Malabar*, 2 vols, Madras, ??? 1887, reprint New Delhi/Madras, AES, 1989, vol. 1, p. 489; T K Ravindran, *Malabar under Bombay Presidency*, Calicut, ???1979, p. 7. This refers to *tahsildars, kanungos* and *parapatti*s. *Cf Reports of a Joint Commission*, para. CCCXVI. So as not to give preference to any one religious group, the Canongo offices were each occupied somewhat later by a Hindu and a Mappiëëa. *Reports of a Joint Commission*, para. CCCCLVI.

27. Hermann Gundert, *A Malayalam and English Dictionary*, Mangalore, Basel Mission Press, 1872, reprint Kottayam, D C Books, 1992, p. 513, col. 1: *amsam* is defined as the largest administrative unit of the *desam*s. This reflects the situation in the mid-nineteenth century. Between the levels of district and *amsam* the land was split up into *hôbalis* (Gundert, *Dictionary*, p. 1081, col. 2: sub-division of a district, also *hôvali*). For this the old *tara*s had been enlarged, something which caused displeasure among the local people and which, as a result, was undone shortly after it was introduced. In restructuring the administrative units the figure of just over two thousand *desam*s was reduced to 429 *amsam*s by the middle of the nineteenth century. The traditional barriers between the former units were thus no longer there. The development was a long process, which meant that in the early stages several old *desavzhi*s were responsible for an *amsam*. The objective however was the abolition of the *desam* as an administrative unit. *Cf* Logan, *Malabar*, vol. 1, p. 89. Eric J Miller, 'Caste and Territory in Malabar', in *American Anthropologist* 56,1 (1954), p. 410–420, p. 418.

28. Gundert, *Dictionary*, p. 24, col. 1: official, magistrate.

29. E K Santha, *Local Self-Government in Malabar (1800–1960)*, New Delhi, Institute for Social Sciences, 1986, p. 6. Yet besides *natuvazhi*s and *desavahi*s, other qualified people were also employed. *Cf* Adrian C Mayer, *Land and Society in Malabar*, Oxford, 1952, p. 33.

30. This measure was a reaction to a decision by the Governor General in Council. Extract from a political letter from Fort St George to the Bombay presidency dated 9 October 1800, in OIOC F/4/117; correspondence between Henry Dundas and Arthur Wellesley, in Edward Ingram (ed.), *Two Views of British India. The Private Correspondence of Mr Dundas and Lord Wellesley, 1798–1801*, Somerset, Adams & Dart 1970, p. 292; Logan, *Malabar*, vol. 1, p. 528 f.

31. Extract from a political letter from Fort St George to the Bombay presidency dated 15 October1800, in BC, OIOC F/4/117; Logan, *Malabar*, vol. 1, p. 534.

32. *Cf* T K Ravindran, *Cornwallis System in Malabar*, Calicut, 1969, p. ii f.; T K Ravindran, *Institutions and Movements in Kerala History*, Trivandrum, Charithram Publications, 1978, p. 87.

33. Letter from the government in Fort St George dated 11 April 1801, in BC, OIOC F/4/119. The most commonly used weapons produced domestically were swords, pikes and Naya knives. In contrast firearms were generally made in England. *Cf* letter by the commissioners J Spencer and J Smee to Fort St George dated 30 April 1801, in BC, OIOC F/4/120.

34. Proclamation of 30 January 1802/M.E., nineteenth Makaram 977, in BC, OIOC F/4/156. For example, the British had collected in 1801, among other things, 11 iron canons, 7872 swords and 9784 stone catapults in Malabar, in BC, OIOC F/4/121.

35. *Cf* G Arunima, 'Multiple Meanings: Changing Conceptions of Matrilineal Kinship in Nineteenth- and Twentieth-century Malabar', *IESHR* 33.3 (1996), pp. 283–307, p. 298.

36. Statement by judge Herbert Wigram (in the civil court) on the case A.S. 434 1878 (South Malabar), cited in Lewis Moore, *Malabar Law and Custom*, Madras, Higginbotham & Co., 1905) p. 121.

37. *Cf* Melinda A Moore, 'A New Look at the Nayar Taravad', in *Man* (n.s.) 20 (1985), p. 523–41, p. 538. The question of language caused further problems, *cf* letter by W G Farmer to the Joint Commissioners dated 22 June 1793, in BRP, OIOC P/366/15, as did the system of time. The Malabar calendar was structured in a completely different way from that of the western calendar, *cf* letter by W G Farmer to James Stevens dated 9 September 1793, in BRP, OIOC P/366/15. See also Christopher A Bayly, *Empire and Information. Intelligence Gathering and Social Communication in India, 1780–1870*, Cambridge, Cambridge University Press, 1996, p. 6 f.

38. *Cf* Peter J Marshall, 'British Expansion in India in the Eighteenth Century. A Historical Revision', in *History* 60, 198 (1975), pp. 28–43, p. 43.

39. The establishment of the court was resolved on 31 December 1792. *Reports of a Joint Commission*, para. CLVI.

40. *Ibid.*, para. CXCII.

41. *Ibid.*, paras CCCLXXIV, CCCLXXXII, CCCLXXXIV, CCCLXXXV.

42. *Ibid.*, para. CCCLXIII. This oath was known as *muchalka* and contained, among other things, the promise not to accept any bribes or gifts from clients. *Cf* Henry Yule and A C Burnell *Hobson-Jobson, A Glossary of Anglo-Indian Words and Phrases, and of Kindred Terms, Etymological, Historical, Geographical and Discoursive*, London, Murray, 1903, reprint New Delhi/Madras, AES, 1995, p. 578, col. 2.

43. *Cf* T K Ravindran, *Malabar under Bombay Presidency*, Calicut, 1979) p. 38–41.

44. *Cf* Logan, *Malabar*, vol. 1, p. 522.

45. *Cf* Ravindran, *Malabar under Bombay*, p. 24f., 62; Ravindran, *Institutions*, p. 85.

46. *Reports of a Joint Commission*, paras CCCCLXIX–CCCCLXXII, CCCCLIII.

47. Logan, *Treaties*, ii, IV–VII, pp. 147–151.

48. The Nambyars appear to have fallen under the protection of Pazhassi *Raja*: letter by Jonathan Duncan dated 2 March 1797, in BC, OIOC F/4/32; letter by James Stevens to John Spencer dated 6 March 1800, in HMS, OIOC H/471.

49. Letter by W G Farmer to A W Handley dated 30 December 1794, in BRP, OIOC P/366/16.

50. *Reports of a Joint Commission*, paras CXXXII–CXXXVII; Logan, *Treaties*, ii, XVIII–XX, pp. 166–170.

51. *Reports of a Joint Commission*, para. CXXXVI.

52. Indication of weight, between 500 and 560 pounds.

53. Spencer, Smee and Walker, however, speak of 25,000 rupees. J Spencer/J Smee/A Walker, *A Report on the Administration of Malabar. Dated 28th July 1801*, Calicut, Collectorate Press 1910, p. 19. See also Logan, *Treaties*, ii, XX, p. 169f.

54. *Reports of a Joint Commission*, para. CCLXII.

55. Logan, *Treaties*, ii, XLII, p. 188f.

56. *Cf* K Rajayyan, 'Kerala Varma and Malabar Rebellion', in *Journal of Indian History* 47,1 (1969), pp. 549–557, p. 549.

57. *Cf* Pamela Nightingale, *Trade and Empire in Western India 1785–1806*, Cambridge, Cambridge University Press, 1970), p. 106.

58. Logan, *Treaties*, ii, LXXIV–LXXV, p. 215f.

59. Complaints by the noblemen of Kottayam dated 10 November 1796, PR 57 B; *cf* also *arjí* (Petition) of the noblemen of Kottayam dated 19 November 1796, in BRP, OIOC P/366/19: 'In the year 970 Malabar Style or 1794 of the Christian Era Chundoo [Pazhavittil Cantu] collected more from us than what had been usual and in the same year [. . .] Chundoo took from us four times the quantity of pepper which we had agreed to give the Company [. . .].'

60. PR 57B.

61. Letter by James Stevens to Alexander Dow dated 21 August 1798, in MCR 1715 (TNSA).
62. Letter by James Stevens to John Spencer dated 1 March 1799, in MCR 1716 (TNSA).
63. Letter by Governor in Council to the Malabar Commission dated 29 August 1799, in OIOC F/4/62.
64. Report by John Smee dated 16 October 1799, as an enclosure to the letter by John Spencer to Jonathan Duncan dated 24 October 1799 and consultation of the *parapattis* in mid-October 1799, in BC, OIOC F/4/62.
65. Logan, *Treaties*, ii, CCXIX, p. 338. In spite of these difficulties, Duncan reported a growth in tax revenue in Malabar: in 1793 it amounted to 334,000 rupees, in 1800 484,058 rupees. Letter by Jonathan Duncan to the Court of Directors dated 28 April 1800, in BC, OIOC F/4/90.
66. In the Bombay presidency the exchange rate came to 7 gold fanams for a Star Pagoda, 15 silver annas for a rupee, while in the province of Malabar a Star Pagoda cost 5⅞ gold fanams and a rupee cost only 5 silver fanams or 14 annas. Thus the exchange rate was to be adjusted. A rupee should cost around 4⁷⁄₃₂ gold fanams or 5½ silver fanams, a Star Pagoda 14⁴⁹⁄₆₄ gold fanams or 19¼ silver fanams. Logan, *Treaties*, ii, CCXXXVI, p. 350; Logan, *Malabar*, vol. 1, p. 534.
67. *Cf* Logan, *Malabar*, vol. 1, p. 535.
68. *Cf* Kumar, Dharma, *Land and Caste in South India: Agricultural Labour in the Madras Presidency During the 19th Century*, Cambridge, Cambridge University Press, 1965, p. 88; A P Abdurahiman, 'Macleod's Paimash and the Malabar Rebellion of 1803', in *Journal of Kerala Studies* 4,1 (1977), pp. 65–71, p. 66.
69. Letter by William Macleod to Fort St George dated 15 July 1802, in BC, OIOC F/4/156.
70. Georg Berkemer, *Little Kingdoms in Kalinga. Ideologie, Legitimation und Politik regionaler Eliten*, Stuttgart, Steiner, 1993, p. 10.
71. *Cf* Kautilya, *The Arthashastra*, ed. L N Rangarajan, New Delhi, 1992, book VI, chapter 1.
72. *Cf* T V Mahalingam, *South Indian Polity*, Madras, University of Madras, 1967, p. 18.
73. *Cf* Pamela G Price, *Kingship and Political Practice in Colonial India*, Cambridge, Cambridge University Press, 1996, p. 17.
74. *Cf* Robert Lingat, *The Classical Law of India*, California, 1973, reprint Delhi, Oxford University Press, 1998, p. 211; Ronald Inden, 'Ritual, Authority, and Cyclic Time in Hindu Kingship', in John F Richards (ed.), *Kingship and Authority in South Asia*, Delhi, Oxford University Press, 1998), pp. 41–91, p. 50 f.
75. These activities are specified in Kautilya, *Arthashastra*, book II, chapter 1.
76. *Cf* Pamela G Price, 'Raja-dharma in 19th Century South India: Land, Litigation and Largess in Ramnad Zamindari', in *Contributions to Indian Sociology* 13, 2 (1979), pp. 207–239, p. 209. Fuller stresses that the protection of a kingdom required the king to have had a respective relationship with the gods and to have taken responsibility for the correct adherence to the rituals. The role of the king in the temple was a constitutive element of his rule. Christopher J Fuller, 'The Hindu Temple and Indian Society', in Michael V Fox (ed.), *Temple in Society*, Winona Lake, Eisenbrauns, 1988, pp. 49–66, p. 57, 59.
77. Price, *Kingship*, p. 15 f. Appadurai and Breckenridge go so far as to describe the deity as a sovereign ruler – not one who rules over a territory, more one who rules over the whole redistributive process. Arjun Appadurai, and Carol A Breckenridge, 'The South Indian Temple: Authority, Honour and Redistribution', in *Contributions to Indian Sociology* 10, 2 (1976), pp. 187–211, p. 195.
78. For detailed analyses on the *little kingdom* see Georg Berkemer, *Little Kingdoms in Kalinga. Ideologie, Legitimation und Politik regionaler Eliten*, Stuttgart, Steiner Verlag, 1993; Nicholas Dirks, *The Hollow Crown. Ethnohistory of an Indian Kingdom*, Ann Arbor, Michigan University Press, 1993; Margret Frenz, *Vom Herrscher zum Untertan. Spannungsverhältnis zwischen lokaer*

Herrschaftsstruktur und der Kolonialverwaltung in Malabar zu Beginn der britischen Herrschaft (1790–1805), Stuttgart, Steiner Verlag, 2000; Burkhard Schnepel, *Die Dschungelkönige. Ethnohistorische Aspekte von Politik und Ritual in Südorissa/Indien*, Stuttgart, Steiner Verlag, 1997.

79. He described his 'younger brother' as 'misguided' but did not do anything to make Pazhassi *Raja* change his course, which Vira Varmma considered to be the wrong one. PR 16 B.

80. Logan, *Treaties*, comment on ii, VII, p. 150f.

81. For example, in PR 19 A&B: '[. . .] I shall inform the Company accordingly and then act according to the act of the Company – this is my decision and practice. [. . .] I request your kind consideration and patronage for everything concerning me', and 21 B: 'Further, I shall be bound by your orders.' *Cf* PR 121 A&B.

82. A brief recapitulation: Vira Varmma had originally grown up in the Kottayam dynasty but had been adopted into the family of the Kurumpranatu *Raja*s, because they (presumably) did not have any successors who were fit to govern. As a result, however, he was excluded from the line of succession in Kottayam. Yet he was able to pass over the old conventions in the treaties he made with the British once they had arrived and changed the situation in Malabar accordingly – this was thanks to the loyalty which he had showed towards the British.

83. Edward Ingram, *Empire-Building and Empire-Builders. Twelve Studies*, London, Cass, 1995, p. 9.

84. *Clash of sovereignty* is to be understood as a collision of differing conceptions of sovereignty. See Margret Frenz, *Vom Herrscher zum Untertan*, p. 68.

85. *Cf* C A Innes, and F B Evans, *Malabar and Anjengo*, Madras, Government Press, 1908), p. 426.

86. Proclamation by Thomas Warden dated 8 December 1805, in BC, OIOC F/4/191.

87. *Census of India 1961*, Census District Handbook 1 Cannanore, p. 77, col.1. You can still visit his gravestone to this day. The inscription on the gravestone reads: 'Vira Kerala Pazhassirajavu ivite antyavisraman kollunu. Manantavati 1805 November 30.' roughly translated as 'Vira Kerala Pazhassi *Raja* found here his last resting-place. Manantavati 30.11.1805.'

88. Letter by Harvey to the principal collector of Malabar dated 27 June 1803, in MCR 2158 (KSA).

89. Report by William Bentinck dated 22 April 1804, in MCR 2384 (KSA).

90. Regarding the concept of the *contact zone* see Mary L Pratt, *Imperial Eyes. Travel Writing and Transculturation*, London/New York, Routledge, 1992), p. 6f.; Margret Frenz, *Vom Herrscher zum Untertan*, p. 60–62.

91. *Cf* Nightingale, *Trade and Empire*, p. 111.

92. *Cf* Pran N Chopra, (T K Ravindran and N Subrahmaniam), *History of South India*, 3 vols, New Delhi, S. Chand, 1979, vol. 3, p. 177.

93. *Cf* M Moore, 'A New Look', p. 525. What is meant by 'establishing laws' is the enactment of regulations in Malabar by the *men on the spot*, in that case by the commissioners, the trusted administrators of Malabars from 1792–1800. Contrarily, the legislation represents the departure from laws made by the government in Bombay or London.

94. Only in 1907 did the governor of Madras officially admit that the British interpretation of the land laws in Malabar had been incorrect. *Cf* Vannarth Veettil Kunhikrishnan, *Tenancy Legislation in Malabar (1880–1970). An Historical Analysis*, New Delhi, Northern Book Centre, 1993), p. 10.

95. The British 'mission' to the world, which they want to liberate from its chains, became the transfer of their parliamentary system characterized by freedom and progress. Clive Dewey, 'Images of the Village Community: A Study in Anglo-Indian Ideology', in *Modern Asian Studies* 6 (1972), pp. 291–328, p. 300.

3. Between Non-interference in Matters of Religion and the Civilizing Mission

1. Government Circular on suttee addressed to military officers (10 November, 1828), no. 50 in Cyril Henry Philips (ed.), *The correspondence of Lord William Cavendish Bentinck, Governor-General of India, 1828–1835*, vol. 1, London, Oxford University Press, 1977, p. 90n.

2. For the 'Idea of Reform' see Michael Mann, 'Dealing with Oriental Despotism', in this volume.

3. Recent scholars prefer the word *sati*, to overcome the colonial terminology. However, I decided to use the term *suttee*, exactly because it refers to the colonial root of the current image of the practice. I understand *suttee* as a modern tradition, defined (or 'invented' during the last 200 years: see *The Invention of Tradition*, Cambridge: Cambridge University Press, 1996, pp.1–4).

   Originally the good woman, the devoted wife was called a *suttee*. From the fifteenth/sixteenth centuries on, when the practice of burning wives after the death of their husbands spread the word *suttee* was used in a more specific sense, denoting the women that followed this practice. The British then chose to call the practice *suttee*, describing the act and not the person. For a short but perceptive overview about the development and the different meanings of the practice see: Romila Thapar, 'In History', in *Seminar* 342, February 1988, pp. 14–19; Shakuntala Narasimhan, *Sati: a study of widow burning in India*, Delhi, Penguin, 1990; A S Altekar, 'The Position of the Widow, Part I', chapter 4 in his *The Position and Status of Women in Hindu Civilisation*, Banaras, Banarsidass, 1956, pp. 115–142; and Jörg Fisch, *Tödliche Rituale: die indische Witwenverbrennung und andere Formen der Totenfolge*, Frankfurt am Main, Campus-Verlag 1998, also follow a historical approach.

   Another advantage of the word *suttee* is just that other terms are even more misleading. To speak about *widow burning* denies the free will of the *suttee*. Even the term 'widow' may not be correct due to the philosophical conceptions of the widow and the *suttee*. Through the practice of *anumarana* (or *anugamana*), as the 'shastras' and Bengal social reformers put it, a wife can avoid reaching the inauspicious state of widowhood. See Julia Leslie, 'Suttee or *Sati*: Victim or Victor?' chapter 8 in Julia Leslie (ed.), *Roles and Rituals for Hindu Women*, Delhi, Motilal Banarsidass, 1992, pp. 175–192. She focused on the religious/philosophical concepts of the *suttee* and the widow. See also Alaka Hejib and Katherine Young, 'Sati, Widowhood and Yoga', in Arvind Sharma, *Sati. Historical and Phenomenological Essays*, Delhi, Motilal Banarsidass, 1988, pp. 73–84.

4. 'Orientalists' has a double meaning here: it refers to the generation of British judges and researchers who – fascinated by the Sanskrit language and texts – established the ideal of the golden Vedic past. So the term differentiates them from the later utilitaristic social reformers of India. They are early 'Orientalists' in the Saidian manner as they collected and transformed knowledge about Indian past and society according to western ideological frames. For a critical 'Saidian' approach to the Indian context see for instance David Ludden, 'Empiricism: Transformation of Colonial Knowledge', in Carol A Breckenridge and Peter van der Veer (eds), *Orientalism and the Postcolonial Predicament. Perspectives on South Asia*, University of Pennsylvania Press 1993, pp. 250–78. See also Ronald Inden, 'Orientalist Constructions of India', in *Modern Asian Studies* 20 (3), 1986, pp. 401–46.

5. See Frederick G Whelan, *Edmund Burke and India. Political Morality and Empire*, Pittsburgh, Pittsburgh University Press 1996.

6. For this process of establishing legal institutions and codes see Michael Mann 'Dealing with Oriental Despotism'.

7. As for the legal practice of the castes see S N Mukherjee, 'Class, Caste and Politics in Calcutta, 1815–1838', in Edmund Leach and S N Mukherjee (eds), *Elites in South Asia*, Cambridge, Cambridge University Press, 1970, pp. 33–78, as well as Sekhar Bandyopadhyay, 'Caste, Widow-remarriage and the Reform of Popular Culture in

Colonial Bengal', in Bharati Ray (ed.), *From the Seams of History: Essays on Indian Women*, Delhi, Oxford University Press 1995, pp. 9–36, especially p. 22.

8. See Ludden, *Orientalist Empiricism*, pp. 255–57.

9. See Melitta Waligora, 'Sie änderten den Geist des ganzen Systems. Zum Beginn der britischen Herrschaft in Indien', in *Beiträge des Südasien-Instituts der Humboldt-Universität zu Berlin*, 10 (1998), pp. 107–37, especially p. 125n.

10. For a description of the *bhadralok* as middle class in a colonial context see Partha Chatterjee, *The Nation and Its Fragments: Colonial and Postcolonial Histories*, Princeton, Princeton University Press, 1993. The *bhadralok* are described in chapter 3: 'The Nationalist Elite', pp. 35–75.

11. Several writers interpret the statistics between 1815 and 1829 by claiming that *suttee* was concentrated in Calcutta and practised mainly by the elites. See, for example, Ashis Nandy, 'Sati. A Nineteenth Century Tale of Women, Violence and Protest', in J C Joshi (ed.), *R M Roy and the Process of Modernisation in India*, Delhi, Vikas, 1975, pp. 168–95; Lata Mani, *Contentious Traditions: The Debate on Sati in Colonial India*, Berkeley, Los Angeles, London, University of California Press, 1998; Benoy Busan Roy, *Socioeconomic Impact on Sati in Bengal and the Role of Raja Rammohun Roy*, Calcutta, Oxford University Press, 1987. Anand Yang, 'Whose Sati? Widow burning in Early Nineteenth Century India', in *Journal of Women's History* 1–2/1990, pp. 8–33, refuses this idea of *suttee* concentrated in Calcutta and its surroundings: '. . . to consider sati as an urban-based phenomenon centred on Calcutta ignores the sizeable territorial dimensions of Calcutta Division', (p. 20.)

12. For the developing media, the *sabhas* and *samitis* and their activities see for instance Mukherjee, 'Class, Caste and Politics in Calcutta', pp. 33–78; Shashi Ahluwalia and Meenakshi Ahluwalia, *Raja Rammohun Roy and the Indian Renaissance*, Delhi, Mittal, 1991; Bruce Carlisle Robertson (ed.), *The essential Writings of Raja Rammohan Roy*, Delhi, Oxford University Press 1999; Sophia Dobson Collet, *Life and Letters of Rammohan Roy*, ed. D K Biswas, P C Ganguli, 3rd edn, Calcutta, Sadharan Brahmo Samaj, 1962.

13. See Janaki Nair, *Women and Law in Colonial India: A Social History*, Delhi, Kali for Women 1996, Nirmala Banerjee, 'Working Women in Colonial Bengal: Modernization and Marginalization'; Sumanta Banerjee, 'Women's Popular Culture in Nineteenth Century Bengal', both in Kumkum Sangari and Sudesh Vaid (eds), *Recasting Women. Essays in Colonial History*, Delhi, Kali for Women, 1989, pp. 9–36, 269–301; Chatterjee, *The Nation and its Fragments*; Bharati Ray (ed.), *From the Seams of History*.

14. Mani, *Contentious Traditions* 1998. Mani had published her basic argument earlier: 'The Production of an Official Discourse in Sati in Early Nineteenth Century Bengal', in *Economic and Political Weekly, Review on Women's Studies*, April 26/1986, pp. 32–40, and 'Contentious Traditions: the Debate on *Sati* in Colonial India', in Sangari and Vaid, *Recasting Women*, pp. 88–124. Mani describes the colonial discourse as an interpretation tool to categorize and define both society and social practices.

15. Since remarkable research about *suttee* in nineteenth century Bengal has been done I want to reassess the broad literature on the topic and some contemporary materials under the aspect of the civilizing mission.

16. See Veena Oldenburg, 'The Continuing Invention of Sati Tradition', in John Stratton Hawley (ed.), *Sati, the Blessing and the Curse: the Burning of Wives in India*, New York, Oxford, Oxford University Press, 1994, pp. 159–173.

17. Edward John Thompso, *Suttee. A Historical and Philosophical Enquiry into the Hindu Rite of Widow-burning*, London, Allen & Unwin, 1928; Ananda Coomaraswamy, 'Status of Indian Women', in Ananda Coomaraswamy, *The Dance of Shiva*, New York, Sunwise Turn, 1924, pp. 82–102.

18. Quoted in Robert L Hardgrave, Jr, *The Representation of Sati: Four Eighteenth Century Etchings by Baltazard Solvyns*, http://reenic.utexas.edu/asnic/cas/Satiart.rft.html, 5 November, 2000, p. 2.

19. The pictures and commentaries have been published and analysed by Hardgrave, *The Representation of Sati*. For the quoted phrase, see p. 15.
20. Quoted in Arvind Sharma, 'Suttee: A Study in Western Reactions', in Arvind Sharma, *Sati. Historical and Phenomenological Essays*, Delhi, Motilal Banarsidass, 1988, pp. 5–13, p. 5.
21. Francois Bernier, *Travels in the Mogul Empire*, trans. A. Constable, Westminster, 1891.
22. De Grandpré, travelling through India 1789–90, tried to rescue a young *suttee* in Bengal without success. The same happened to Thomas Twinning, also in Bengal in 1790; see Hardgrave, *The Representation of Sati*, p. 1.
23. This was told about Job Charnock, the founder of Calcutta (see Arvind Sharma, 'Suttee', p. 4). Also Nicotao Manucci rescued a woman from burning and married her; see Narasimhan, *Sati*, p. 66.
24. William Ward, *A View of the History, Literature, and Mythology of the Hindoos*, vol. 3, London, Kingsbury, Parbury & Allen, 1822.
25. *Ibid.*, p. 326.
26. *Ibid.*, p. 343.
27. *Ibid.*, p. 327.
28. Balthazard Solvyns had a similar argument: '[. . .] every widow is obliged to burn herself, unless she prefers to live as a slave in her own house, to perform the meanest offices, or to become a prostitute in the public places, an outcast from all respectable society, and abandoned by her family. They have but one way to escape such a situation [. . .].' Quoted in Hardgrave, *Representation of Sati*, p. 10.
29. See Mani, *Contentious Traditions*, pp. 25–32.
30. In 1803 officials were send to the villages thirty miles around Calcutta to ask the people how many cases of *suttee* had happened during the last year. In total 438 incidents were counted. In 1804 another research was done in an area of the same size. The estimate was about 250 cases per year, (Ward, *A View on the Hindoos*, pp. 308–41).
31. To this procedure see letter from the Nizamut Adawlut to Government, communicating their required opinion re: prohibition of suttees, and suggesting some instructions that may be issued to the magistrates for preventing any illegal practice (5 June 1805), no. 47, in Jatindra Kumar Majumdar (ed.), *Raja Rammohun Roy and Progressive Movements in India*, vol.1, a selection from records, 1775–1845, Calcutta, Brahmo Mission Press, 1983, p. 97: '2. For the purpose of obtaining the information required by his Excellency the most noble Governor General in Council, the nizamut adawlut proposed a question to the pundits of the court; and subsequently made a further reference to them; the answers to which, together with translations, are submitted for the information of his Excellency the governor General in Council.'
32. Parliamentary Papers on Hindoo Widows, 1821, 18, p. 23.
33. Quoted in Letter of Nizamut Adawlut to Bengal government, 3 September 1812, no. 48 in Majumdar, *Raja Rammohun Roy*, pp. 99–100.
34. *Ibid.*
35. Parliamentary Papers on Hindoo Widows, 1821, 18, p. 28.
36. See *ibid.*
37. No. 47 in Majumdar, *Raja Rammohun Roy*, p. 97n.
38. See also Mani, *Contentious Traditions*, pp. 32–41.
39. No. 47 in Majumdar, *Raja Rammohun Roy*, p. 97n.
40. *Ibid.*
41. '[. . .] that all castes of the Hindoos would be extremely tenacious of its continuance.' (*ibid.*) From the words of the pandit 'every women of the four castes [. . .] is permitted to burn herself with the body of her husband' it was concluded that *suttee* is deeply rooted as a practice of all the castes.
42. *Ibid.*
43. 5 December 1812, no. 49 in Majumdar, *Raja Rammohun Roy*, p. 101n.
44. *Ibid.*

45. No. 50 in Majumdar, *Raja Rammohun Roy*, p. 104n.

46. Claudius Buchanan, *An Apology for Promoting Christianity in India*, London, Cadell & Davies, 1813.

47. *Ibid.*, Appendix IX: 'Report of the Immolation of Females, between Cossimbazar, in Bengal, and the Mouth of the Hooghly, in the Month of May and June, 1812'. The figures rely on the data collected by the Serampur missionaries.

48. Letter from Nizamut Adawlut to several magistrates issuing additional instructions re *suttee* practice, 4 January 1815, no. 54 in Majumdar, *Raja Rammohun Roy*, p. 109n.

49. See letter from Governor General in Council to the Court of Directors re Suttees, 1 February, 1820, no. 61 in Majumdar, *Raja Rammohun Roy*, p. 118n.

50. Benoy Busan Roy's *Socioeconomic Impact on Sati in Bengal* is a study in the cases of *suttee* in nineteenth-century Bengal. He relies on the correspondence of the EIC, Bentinck's letters, the parliamentary papers and contemporary journals such as *Asiatic Journal and the Friend of India*. Based upon his figures he counted 5,388 *suttees* in Bengal between 1815 and 1827. He also analysed the regional origins as well as the caste representation of the *suttees*.

51. See Yang, 'Whose Sati', p.21: 'Reporting was only as good as the administrative infra-structure.' See also V N Datta, *Sati. A Historical, Social and Philosophical Inquiry into the Hindu Rite of Widow burning*, Delhi, Manohar, 1988.

52. See Nandy, 'Sati. A Nineteenth Century Tale of Women, Violence and Protest', p. 170: 'It was only towards the end of the eighteenth century and in Bengal that the rite suddenly came to acquire the popularity of a legitimate orgy.' See also Mani, *Contentious Traditions*; and Thapar, 'In History', p. 18.

53. Parliamentary Papers on Hindoo Widows, 1821, 18, pp. 227–29.

54. No. 61, in Majumdar, *Raja Rammohun Roy*, p. 118n.

55. No. 62, in *ibid.*, p. 120n.

56. Letter from Mr H Wilson to military secretary to government, communicating his required sentiments on suttee (25 November 1828), no. 75, in *ibid.*, p. 133n. Wilson characterized the Hindus as an 'intelligent and inquisitive people, willing to receive infor-mation'. They only needed time and positive conditions to learn.

57. See Clare Midgley, 'Female Emancipation in an Imperial Frame: English women and the campaign against sati (widow-burning) in India', in *Women's History Review*, 9 (1) 2000, pp. 95–122.

58. See petition of the missionaries to Bentinck, May 1829), no. 100 in Philips, *The Correspondence of Lord William Cavendish Bentinck*, p. 191n.

59. See Mani, *Contentious Traditions*, p. 51.

60. Sophie Gilmartin, 'The Sati, the Bride and the Widow: Sacrificial Woman in the Nineteenth Century', in *Victorian Literature and Culture* 25 (1), 1997, pp. 141–58, analysed the representation of *suttee* in the media in England before and after prohibition in 1829.

61. Quoted in Gilmartin, 'The Sati, the Bride and the Widow', p. 142.

62. No. 75, in Majumdar, *Raja Rammohun Roy*, p. 133n.

63. *Ibid.*

64. No. 77, in *ibid.*, p. 139n.

65. Government circular on *suttee* addressed to military officers (10 November 1828), no. 50 in Philips, *The Correspondence of Lord William Cavendish Bentinck*, p. 90n.

66. 25 November 1828, no. 56, in *ibid.*, p. 101n.

67. 16 December 1828, no. 66, in *ibid.*, p. 119n.

68. 1 March 1829, no. 90, in *ibid.*, p.171n.

69. Sati: Regulation XVII, AD 1829 of the Bengal Code, no. 164 in *ibid.*, p. 360n.

70. Rammohan Roy translated *anumarana/anugamana* (dying with/going with) as con-cremation.

71. Nos 102, 103, 104, 112, in Majumdar, *Raja Rammohun Roy*, pp. 179–81, 186.

72. An appeal to orthodox Hindus on the necessity of establishing the Dhurma Subha (6 February 1830), no. 87, in *ibid.*, p. 163n.

73. Sarcastic letter on begging on the *suttee* account (9 August 1830), no. 300, in *ibid.*, p. 177n.
74. Accounts on the hearing of the suttee appeal before the Privy Council (10 November 1832), no. 116, in *ibid.*, p. 194n.
75. Appendix 3 in Mulk Raj Anand (ed.), *Sati. A Writeup of Raja Ram Mohan Roy About Burning Widows Alive*, Delhi, B R Publishing, 1989, p. 71n.
76. Notice of a meeting in the Brahmo Samaj to congratulate the authorities on the rejection of the *suttee* appeal by the Privy Council (6 and 10 November 1832), no. 117 in Majumdar, *Raja Rammohun Roy*, p. 199n.
77. Lamentation of the 'Samachar Chundrika' on the suttee appeal by the Privy Council (14 November 1832), no. 118, in *ibid.*, p. 205n.
78. 'Conference between an Advocate for and an Opponent of the Practice of Burning Widows alive', in Anand, *Writeup of Raja Ram Mohan Roy*, pp. 20–30, and 'A Second Conference between an Advocate for and an Opponent of the Practice of Burning Widows Alive', in Robertson, *The Essential Writings of Raja Rammohan Roy*, pp. 123–46.
79. Anand, *Writeup of Raja Ram Mohan Roy*, p. 23; see also a pamphlet of Rammohun Roy 'containing some remarks in vindication of the resolution passed by the Government of Bengal in 1829 abolishing the practice of female sacrifices in India', 1831, no. 112, in Majumdar, *Raja Rammohan Roy*, p. 189.
80. Anand, *Writeup of Raja Ram Mohan Roy*, p. 22.
81. Pamphlet of Rammohun Roy, no. 112, in Majumdar, *Raja Rammohan Roy*, p. 189.
82. Anand, *Writeup of Raja Ram Mohan Roy*, p. 24.
83. *Ibid.*, p. 25.
84. *Ibid.*, p. 28.
85. *Ibid.*
86. *Ibid.*, p. 29.
87. See the petition of the orthodox Hindu community of Calcutta against the Suttee Regulation, together with a paper of Authorities, and the reply of the Governor General thereto (14 January 1830), no. 86 in Majumdar, *Raja Rammohun Roy*, p. 156n.
88. Anand, *Writeup of Raja Ram Mohan Roy*. pp. 51–8.
89. *Ibid.*, p. 30.
90. No. 77, in Majumdar, *Raja Rammohun Roy* p. 139n.
91. See: The Counter-Petition of some Hindoo inhabitants of Calcutta re: Suttee orders of Government (July 1819), no. 59 in *ibid.*, p. 155n. An appeal to ban *suttee* is also reflected in a letter to the *India Gazette* by Hurriharanand, a *brahmin*. He calls for the humanity and the moral standards of the 'European Gentlemen' and proposes to punish *suttee* as murder, no. 56 in *ibid.*, p. 113.
92. No. 86, in *ibid.*, p. 156n.
93. Particularly the question of competence in matters of religion is addressed elsewhere as well. A letter dated 25 May 1822, written by an orthodox Hindu, accuses the *suttee* opponents of denouncing true religion and misinterpreting the scriptures. The discussion about the contents of the *shastras*, it is claimed, is conducted by non-expert Hindus and proponents of a different religion who had no right to interfere. This is allowed only to learned *brahmins*. The letter mentions Angira to show that the practice of widow burning was sanctioned by the *shastras*. It is the goal of the *suttee* 'to obtain final happiness' (no. 67, in *ibid.*, p. 125).
94. It is not for me to decide whether or not *suttee* is indeed sanctioned by the legal texts, but I would like to remark that the above mentioned quotation in the *Rgveda* was seen by Max Müller as a later misinterpretation or even as a conscious forgery. Historical scholarship, however, reached the consensus that the burning of widows is not mentioned in the Vedas.
95. No. 86, in Majumdar, *Raja Rammohun Roy*, p. 156n.
96. See Monika Horstmann, 'Die Sati-Debatte im Rajasthan des 19.Jahrhunderts', in Ulrike

Roesler (ed.), *Aspekte des Weiblichen in der indischen Kultur*, Swisttal-Odendorf, Indica-et-Tibetica-Verlag, 2000, pp. 1–23.

97. Gayatri Chakravorti Spivak, 'Can the Subaltern Speak?' in Cary Nelson and Lawrence Grossberg (eds), *Marxism and the Interpretation of Cultures*, Urbana, University of Illinois Press, 1988, pp. 271–311.

98. Mani, *Contentious Traditions*, 1998, p. 2.

99. *Ibid.*

100. Sumit Sarkar, 'Orientalism Revisited: Saidian Frameworks in the Writing of Modern Indian History', in *On India. Writing History – Culture – Post-Coloniality*, ed. Ania Loomba, Suvir Kaul, *Oxford Literary Review* 16 (1–2), 1994, pp. 204–27, see p. 215.

101. See Gilmartin, 'The Sati, the Bride and the Widow'.

102. Thompson, *Suttee*, p. 77.

103. *Ibid.*, pp. 130–31.

104. *Ibid.*, p. 48.

105. *Ibid.*, p. 45.

106. *Ibid.*, p. 143.

107. See Ashis Nandy, 'Sati as Profit vs. Sati as a spectacle: The Public Debate on Roop Kanwar's Death', in Hawley, *Sati, the Blessing and the Curse*, pp. 131–49.

108. See Oldenburg, *Continuing Invention of Sati Tradition*.

109. Coomaraswamy, *The Dance of Shiva*, p. 91

110. *Ibid.*, p. 100

111. *Ibid.*, p. 94

112. *Ibid.*, p. 98

113. See Mani, *Contentious Traditions*, Thapar, 'In History'.

114. Nandy, 'Sati. A Nineteenth Century Tale of Women, Violence and Protest'.

115. See, for example, Mark Tully, 'The Deorala Sati', in Tully, *No Full Stops in India*, London, Viking, 1991, pp. 210–36; Sudesh Vaid, 'Politics of Widow Immolation', in *Seminar* 342, February 1988, pp. 20–23; Veena Oldenburg, 'The Roop Kanwar Case: Feminist Responses', in Hawley, *Sati, the Blessing and the Curse*, pp. 101–30; Radha Kumar, 'Gender, Politics and Identity at Times of Crisis: the Agitations around Sati-Daha in India', *Institute of Development Studies Discussion Paper Nr. 309*, August 1992.

116. See Imrana Qadeer, 'Roop Kanwar and Shah Bano', in *Seminar* 342, February 1988, pp. 31–3; Anne Hardgrove, 'Sati Worship and Marwari Public Identity in India', in *Journal of Asian Studies*, 58 (3), 1999, pp. 723–52.

117. Madhu Kishwar, 'Murder vs. Sati', in *The Hindu*, 1 December 1999.

118. Nandy, 'Sati as Profit vs. Sati as a spectacle', p. 141

119. C K Vishwanath, 'Sati, Anti-Modernists and Sangh Parivar, in *Economic and Political Weekly* 25, December 1999.

120. Narasimhan, *Sati*, p. 149.

121. Sangari, 'Perpetuating the Myth', p. 28.

122. Thapar, 'In History', p. 19.

4. 'The Bridge-Builders

1. Ian J Kerr, *Building the Railways of the Raj, 1850–1900*, Delhi, OUP, 1997, p. 212.

2. That 'organizational efficiency' ('*Organisationsmacht*') was one of the main sources from which the colonial state derived 'basic legitimacy' ('*Basislegitimität*') has been argued convincingly by Trutz von Trotha for the West African context. He has also drawn attention to 'public works' as main expressions of this 'organizational efficiency'. Trutz von Trotha, 'Über den Erfolg und die Brüchigkeit der Utopie staatlicher Herrschaft. Herrschaftssoziologische Beobachtungen über den kolonialen und nachkolonialen Staat in Westafrika', in W Reinhard (ed.), *Verstaatlichung der Welt? Europäische Staatsmodelle und*

außereuropäische Machtprozesse, Munich, Oldenbourg, 1999, pp. 235–7.

3. *Cf* Mike Chrimes, *Civil Engineering 1839–1889. A Photographic History*, Stroud, Budding, 1991, pp. 119–21; Kerr, *Building the Railways*, p. 135.

4. R A Buchanan, 'The Diaspora of British Engineering', in *Technology and Culture* 27 (July 1986), p. 513.

5. *Cf* David Arnold, *Science, Technology and Medicine in Colonial India* (New Cambridge History of India III.5), Cambridge, Cambridge University Press, 2000, p. 121–2.

6. This is, for instance, indicated by the fact that the most comprehensive (and still useful) history of British 'public works' in India was published only one year later: G.W. MacGeorge, *Ways and Works in India. Being an Account of the Public Works in that Country from the Earliest Times up to the Present Day*, Westminster, Archibald Constable & Co, 1894.

7. *Rudyard Kipling* (ed. and introduced by D. Karlin), Oxford, OUP, 1999, p. 576.

8. *Cf* Buchanan, 'The Diaspora of British Engineering', pp. 513–7.

9. Michael Adas, *Machines as the Measure of Men. Science, Technology and Ideologies of Western Dominance*, Ithaca/London, Cornell University Press, 1989, p. 200.

10. The following discussion is based on the 1899 edition: *The Writings in Prose and Verse of Rudyard Kipling*, vol. XIII, New York, Charles Scribner's Sons, 1899, pp. 3–56.

11. 'Fictitious' because the bridge of the story is not solely modelled on 'Dufferin Bridge', which crossed the Ganga south of Varanasi and had been opened to traffic in 1887.

12. *The Writings in Prose*, p. 40.

13. Ibid., p. 47.

14. Gyan Prakash, *Another Reason. Science and the Imagination of Modern India*, Delhi, OUP, 2000, p. 167.

15. For a comprehensive analysis of the labour processes on railway construction sites see Kerr, *Building the Railways*, especially chapter 5.

16. 'Christ's warning in John 9:4: "I must work the works of him that sent me, while it is day: the night cometh, when no man can work" ', *Rudyard Kipling*, p. 577.

17. Joseph Conrad, *The Nigger of the 'Narcissus'* (ed. and introduced by C Watts), London, Penguin, 1989, pp. 17–8.

18. David Cannadine, *Ornamentalism. How the British Saw their Empire*, London, Allen Lane, 2001.

19. Edward Said, *Culture and Imperialism*, London, Vintage, 1993, pp. 186–7; see also Cannadine, *Ornamentalism*, p. 43.

20. Rudyard Kipling, 'The Bold 'Prentice' (first published in 1923), in R Bond (ed.), *The Penguin Book of Indian Railway Stories*, New Delhi, Penguin India, 1994, p. 56.

21. Thomas R Metcalf, *Ideologies of the Raj* (New Cambridge History of India III.4), Cambridge, Cambridge University Press, 1995, pp. 28–43.

22. *Cf* Eric Hobsbawm, *The Age of Empire: 1875–1914*, London, Weidenfeld and Nicolson, 1987, p. 188.

23. *Cf* Adas, *Machines as the Measure of Men*, pp. 200–205. The concept of 'practical illusion', which I found helpful in this context, was developed by Marx and Engels in their early writings. See, e.g., Karl Marx and Friedrich Engels, *Werke*, Berlin, Dietz, 1957, vol. 1, p. 248; vol. 2, p. 86.

24. MacGeorge, *Ways and Works*, p. 294.

25. *Ibid.*, pp. 220–21, 293.

26. *Cf* Adas, *Machines as the Measure of Men*, p. 224; see also Arnold, *Science, Technology and Medicine*, pp. 109-10.

27. *The Writings in Prose*, p. 46–7.

28. *Ibid.*, p. 49.

29. 'The White Man's Burden' (1899), in *Rudyard Kipling*, p. 479–80.

30. *Cf* David Arnold, *Colonizing the Body. State Medicine and Epidemic Disease in Nineteenth-Century India*, Berkeley, California University Press, 1993, pp. 183–9; Ira Klein, 'Imperialism, Ecology and Disease: Cholera in India, 1850–1950', in *Indian Economic and Social History*

Review 31, 4 (1994), pp. 500–505. See also Government of India (hereafter: GoI), Central Advisory Board of Health, *Report of the Sub-Committee appointed by the Central Advisory Board of Health to examine the possibility of introducing a system of compulsory inoculation of pilgrims against cholera*, Simla, GoI Press, 1940, p. 2.

31. *Report of the Pilgrim Committee, Bihar and Orissa*, Simla, Government Central Branch Press, 1913, p. 4.
32. Arnold, *Science, Technology and Medicine*, p. 119.
33. Jakob Rösel, 'The Evolution and Organization of Pilgrimage to Jagannatha at Puri', in D P Dubey and L Gopal (eds.), *Pilgrimage Studies: Text and Context* (Sri Phalahari Baba Commemoration Volume), Allahabad, Society of Pilgrimage Studies, 1990, pp. 95–104. For a contemporary report on the organization of pilgrimage at the onset of British rule see OSA, Cuttack District Records, Board of Revenue Proceedings, Accession No. 2c: C Groeme, collector, to T Fortescue, secretary to the Commissioner for the affairs of the Province Cuttack, 10 June 1805.
34. *Cf* Prabhat Mukherjee, *History of the Jagannath Temple in the 19th Century*, Calcutta, KLM, 1977, pp. 203–16.
35. Biswamoy Pati, *Situating Social History. Orissa (1800–1997)*, Hyderabad (AP), Orient Longman, 2001, p. 19. See also Arnold, *Colonizing the Body*, p. 185–9.
36. David B. Smith, *Report on Pilgrimage to Juggernauth in 1868*, Calcutta, E.M. Lewis, Calcutta Central Press, 1868, part V, p. 20 ('Baboo Degumber Mitter's' statement).
37. OIOC: Bengal Public Works Proceedings (hereafter BPWP) August 1882 (P/1831), Railway, no. 4, p. 4.
38. *Report of the Pilgrim Committee, Bihar and Orissa*, p. 2.
39. Pati, *Situating Social History*, p. 19.
40. William Wilson Hunter, *Annals of Rural Bengal* (vol. 2: Orissa), London: Smith, Elder & Co., 1872, p. 155–6.
41. For a discussion of medical regulation in Puri see Biswamoy Pati, ' "Ordering" "Disorder" in a Holy City: Colonial Health Interventions in Puri During the Nineteenth Century', in B Pati and M Harrison (eds.), *Health, Medicine and Empire. Perspectives on Colonial India*, London, Sangam, 2001.
42. Smith, *Report on Pilgrimage*, part II, p. 5.
43. A translation of a lengthy article on this subject from the Bengali newspaper Som Prakash (8 May 1868, 'A True Account of the Pilgrimage to Pooree') can be found in Smith, *Report on Pilgrimage*, part IV, pp. 2–5. For the very similar views of a British gentleman on this subject see John Beames, *Memoirs of a Bengal Civilian*, London, Chatto & Windus, 1961, p. 196. Note that these (and numerous other) reports on strong female participation in pilgrimage were written *before* the introduction of railways, which has been considered, by some historians, as a precondition for a 'gender shift', an increased women ratio among Hindu pilgrims. *Cf* Ian J. Kerr, 'Reworking a Popular Religious Practice: The Effects of Railways on Pilgrimage in 19th and 20th Century South Asia', in idem (ed.), *Railways in Modern India* (Oxford in India Readings: Themes in Indian History), Delhi, OUP, 2001, p. 312, 324.
44. And, one unfortunately needs to add nowadays, there cannot be any justification for violently suppressing debates on such phenomena as elements of the Hindu right have recently done in the case of Deepa Mehta's film *Water*. See also Malini Bhattacharya, 'The Hidden Violence of Faith: The Widows of Vrindaban' in *Social Scientist* 332–3, vol. 29/1–2, 2001, pp. 75–83.
45. Smith, *Report on Pilgrimage*, part IV, pp. 2, 5.
46. OSA: Board of Revenue, Loose Records (hereafter: BoRLR), 18,692 Bd.Doc (J Thomason, Deputy Secretary to Government of Bengal (hereafter: GoB), to R D Mangles, Acting Secretary to the Sudder Board of Revenue, 4 September 1832), p. 11–12.
47. The history of the 'New Jagannath Road' will be discussed in greater detail in another

article, which is presently in preparation: 'Opening up the Country? Orissan Society and Early Colonial Communications Policies (1803–1866)'.

48. K E Verghese, *The Development and Significance of Transport in India 1834–1882*, New Delhi, NV Publications, 1976, p. 23.

49. See, e.g., Richard Temple, *Report on the Mahanuddy and its Tributaries; the Resources and Trade of the Adjacent Countries and the Proposed Works for the Improvement of Navigation and Irrigation* (= Selections from the Records of the GoI, in the Public Works Department XLIII), Calcutta, John G. Hirons, Public Works Department Press, 1864, p. 40.

50. Minute by Lord Dalhousie to the Court of Directors, 20 April 1853, in S Settar and B Misra (eds.), *Railway Construction in India. Select Documents*, New Delhi, Northern Book Centre/Indian Council of Historical Research, 1999, vol. II (1853–73), item 174, pp. 23–57; for the low priority given to the Calcutta–Madras line through Orissa, see pp. 42–3.

51. P W O'Gorman, *Puri Pilgrim Canal Traffic* (OIOC: P/T514; no location and date of publication given for this pamphlet, probably written in the mid-1890s), p. 5.

52. Rohan D'Souza, 'Flood, Embankments and Canals: The Colonial Experience in Orissa (1803–1928) ', *Occasional Papers on History and Society* (Nehru Memorial Library), Third Series, vol. VI.

53. The issue looms large in the Oriya section of the colonial 'Native Newspaper Reports' for Bengal. An early critique that formulated a preference for railways over canals was published in Utkal Dipika of 5 December 1874: 'The imperfect results of the irrigation system initiated in the Province of Orissa suggest the advisability of establishing railways – a project which would accomplish far better results than what canals have hitherto done.' NMM&L Microfilm Acc. No. 139: *Native Newspaper Reports, Bengal*, (hereafter NNRB) Report [. . .] for the Week Ending 6 February 1875, p. 7. Peasant protest was mentioned, for instance, in Utkal Dipika of 7 April 1883 (according to *ibid.*, 17 April 1883). See also 'The Orissa Irrigation Project' in *The Statesman and Friend of India*, 22 June 1882 (NMM&L: Microfilm Acc. No. 1255, Statesman 1882).

54. D'Souza, 'Flood, Embankments and Canals'.

55. Numerous articles on this issue can be culled from the NNRB. See, e.g., 2 February 1884 (Utkal Dipika, 12 January 1884), p. 133; 7 August 1886 (Utkal Dipika, 24 July 1886), p. 895; 25 June 1887 (Bharatbasi, 13 June 1887), p. 652; 3 December 1887 (Sanskaraka, 10 November 1887), p. 1206; 25 May 1889 (Utkal Dipika, 4 May 1889), p. 437–8; 26 April 1890 (Utkal Dipika, 5 April 1890), p. 409; 9 May 1896 (Samvadvahika, 12 March 1896), p. 461. See also: O'Gorman, *Puri Pilgrim Canal Traffic*, pp. 5–7.

56. *Report of the Orissa Flood Committee*, Patna: Superintendent of Government Printing, Bihar and Orissa, 1928, p. 25.

57. OSA: BoRLR, 26,568 Bd.Doc (H Dixon, Officiating Executive Engineer, Cuttack Division, to H Goodwyn, Chief Engineer, Lower Provinces, 14 June 1855); OSA: BoRLR 27,532 Bd.Doc (V H Schalch, Officiating Magistrate of Balasore, to G F Cockburn, Commissioner of Cuttack Division, 8 June 1857); OIOC: BPWP October 1865 (P/16/72), no. 24–27, pp. 14–16.

58. OIOC: BPWP March 1866 (P/432/38), no. 16, p. 10 (Petition of the Inhabitants of Cuttack to C Beadon, Lieutenant Governor of Bengal, 13 February 1866); OSA: BoRLR 14,368 Bd.Doc (T E Ravenshaw, Commissioner of Cuttack Division, to Secretary to GoB, Judicial Department, 27 April 1868).

59. Ganeswar Nayak, *Development of Transport and Communication. A Case Study*, New Delhi, Anmol, 2000, pp. 74–5.

60. OIOC: BPWP August 1882 (P/1831), Railway, no. 4, pp. 3–7: 'An Appeal for a Light Passenger Railroad from Ranigunge to Pooree through Bankoora, Midnapore, Balasore, Cuttack, and Khorda'.

61. See NNRB for: 17 September 1881 (Balasore Sambad Bahika, 4 August 1881), p. 11; 1 October 1881 (Balasore Sambad Bahika, 1 September 1881), pp. 6–7; 3 December 1881

(Utkal Dipika, 12 November 1881), p. 7; 18 February 1882 (Balasore Sambad Bahika, 2 February 1882), p. 58; 22 July 1882 (Utkal Dipika, 9 July 1882), p. 254; 29 July 1882 (Utkal Dipika, 22 July 1882), pp. 270–71; 12/8/1882 (Utkal Dipika, 5 August 1882), p. 293; 19 August 1882 (Medini, 14 August 1882); 9 September 1882 (Utkal Dipika, 26 August 1882); 23 December 1882 (Utkal Dipika, 16 December 1882), p. 471; 17 February 1883 (Utkal Dipika, 3 February 1883), p. 74; 4 August 1883 (Utkal Darpan, 15 July 1883), p. 474; 5 January 1884 (Utkal Dipika, 15 December 1883), p. 23; 12 January 1884 (Utkal Dipika, 22 December 1883), p. 52; 19 January 1884 (Purusottam Patrika, 31 December 1883), p. 76; 2 February 1884 (Utkal Dipika, 12 January 1884), p. 133; 1 March 1884 (Samvad Bahika, 7 February 1884), p. 252; 15 March 1884 (Samvad Bahika, 21 February 1884), p. 312; 20 September 1884 (Utkal Darpan, 2 September 1884), p. 1209; 1 November 1884 (Samvad Bahika, 16 October 1884), p. 1343; 16 January 1886 (Utkal Dipika, 2 January 1886), p. 92; 14 August 1886 (Sebaka, 31 July 1886), pp. 922–3; 23 October 1886 (Utkal Dipika, 25 September 1886), p. 1157; 23 April 1887 (Sanskaraka, 7/4/1887), p. 441.

62. OIOC: BPWP August 1882 (P/1831), Railway, no. 3, Commissioner of Orissa Division to Secretary to GoB, PWD, 15 October 1881, pp. 2–3.

63. OIOC: BPWP March 1888 (P/3170), Railway, no. 45, Appendix A, pp. 1–125: GoB, PWD, 'Railway Branch: Benares–Cuttack–Puri Railway, vol. I: Reports, Estimates, and Correspondence from the Commencement up to the End of 1883–84, Calcutta: Bengal Secretariat Press, 1886'; OIOC: BPWP March 1888 (P/3170), Railway, no. 46, Appendix B, pp. 1–250: GoB, PWD, 'Railway Branch: Benares–Cuttack–Puri Railway, vol. II: Reports of the Engineers upon the Work of 1883–84, 1884–85 and 1885–86, and Estimates and Correspondence up to the Closure of the Work in November 1886, Calcutta: Bengal Secretariat Press, 1887'; OIOC: BPWP October 1890 (P/3632), Railway, no. 38, Note by Mr. Bestic, Under-Secretary to GoB, PWD, 21 February 1889, pp. 51–53.

64. Lord Ripon, Governor General, to Secretary of State for India, 29 September 1884, in Settar and Misra, *Railway Construction in India*, vol. III, item 321, p. 218; OIOC: BPWP December 1884 (P/2235), Railway, no. 30, Appendix B, Cuttack, A Smith, Commissioner of Orissa Division, to Secretary to GoB, PWD, 14 August 1883, p. 13; 'Railway Communications in Orissa' in *The Indian Engineer: An Illustrated Weekly Journal for Engineers in India and the East*, 21/382 (4 August 1894), pp. 421–2.

65. *The Indian & Eastern Engineer: An Illustrated Weekly Journal for Engineers in India and the East*, 24/440 (14 September 1895), p. 555 (report on extraordinary meeting of the BNR Company in London).

66. 'A Great Disaster in Bengal – Loss of the Sir John Lawrence' in *Indian Mirror*, 5 June 1887 (NMM&L: Microfilm Acc. No. 140, *Indian Mirror* 1887).

67. NNRB 18 June 1887 (Bangabasi, 11 June 1887), pp. 621–2.

68. NNRB 11 June 1887 (Dainik, 9 June 1887), p. 595. For further relevant summaries of articles see *ibid.*, 18 June 1887 (Sahachar, 8 June 1887), p. 621; 18 June 1887 (Som Prakash, 13 June 1887), p. 622; 18 June 1887 (Dacca Gazette, 13 June 1887), p. 622; 25 June 1887 (Charu Varta, 13 June 1887), p. 651; 25 June 1887), (Burdwan Sanjiwani, 11 June 1887) p. 651; 25 June 1887 (Navasamvad, 11 June 1887) p. 651; 16 July 1887 (Sahachar, 6 July 1887), p. 723; 16 July 1887 (Samvad Bahika, 6 June 1887, p. 737; 22 October 1887 (Sanskaraka, 8 September 1887), p. 1037; 22 October 1887 (Navasamvad, 15 September 1887), p. 1038; 3 December 1887 (Sanskaraka, 10 November 1887), p. 1206; 21 April 1888 (Utkal Dipika and Samvadbahika, 31 March 1888), p. 430; 30 June 1888 (Utkal Dipika, 26 May 1888), p. 647; 4 August 1888 (Utkal Dipika, 30 June 1888), p. 779; 25 August 1888 (Utkal Dipika, 4 August 1888), p. 857; 17 November 1888 (Sahachar, 7 November 1888), p. 1129; 8 December 1888 (Sahachar, 28 November 1888), p. 1189; 29 June 1889 (Dipaka and Utkal Dipika, 15 June 1889), p. 576; 17 January 1891 (Bengal Exchange Gazette, 12 January 1891), pp. 82–83; 28 March 1891

(Sahachar, 18 March 1891), p. 373.

69. *The Indian & Eastern Engineer* 24/433 (27 July 1895), p. 449.

70. *The Indian & Eastern Engineer* (new series) 4/3 (March 1899), p. 77.

71. *Summary of the Administration of Indian Railways during the Viceroyalty of Lord Curzon of Kedleston*, Calcutta, Office of the Superintendent of Government Printing, 1906, part II, p. 30.

72. OIOC: BPWP August 1882 (P/1831), Railway, no. 4, p. 4.

73. See, e.g., NNRB 29 July 1882 (Utkal Dipika, 22 July 1882), p. 270: 'From Bombay, the Punjab, from east and west, and from Bengal, pilgrims come by rail to Calcutta, and thence by steamer to Cuttack.' The conclusion that Jagannath pilgrimage increased from the 1880s can be drawn from the available figures though they are far from reliable. Yet even contemporaries sensed this increase. See, e.g., *ibid.*, 12 July 1884 (Samvad Bahika, 19 June 1884), p. 844.

74. For a discussion of qualitative changes in pilgrimage patterns on an all-India level see Kerr, 'Reworking a Popular Religious Practice', pp. 313–7.

75. OIOC: BPWP August 1882 (P/1831), Railway, no. 4, p. 4.

76. W Wesley Clemesha, *37th Annual Report of the Sanitary Commissioner for Bengal (1904)*, Calcutta, Bengal Secretariat Press, 1905, p. 12.

77. *Report of the Pilgrim Committee*, pp. 4–5. See also Kerr, 'Reworking a Popular Religious Practice', p. 315.

78. Rösel, 'The Evolution and Organization of Pilgrimage', p. 112.

79. *Hind Swaraj* (1909), in *Collected Works of Mahatma Gandhi*, (1939 edn), vol. 10, p. 267.

80. NNRB 9 November 1895 (Dainik-o-Samachar Chandrika, 31 October 1895), p. 983.

81. Romesh Chandra Dutt, *The Lake of Palms*, London, Fisher Unwin, 1902, especially pp. 154–55, 189–90.

82. Such changes in the practices of pilgrimage seem rarely to have attracted the interest of social historians. I am here drawing mainly on the following excellent article: Rösel, 'The Evolution and Organization of Pilgrimage', especially pp. 110–3. Rösel, however, assumes a steady growth of the Jagannath pilgrimage during the whole of the nineteenth century, while I could not find any evidence for a substantial increase prior to the 1880s.

83. See, e.g., OIOC: BPWP December 1884 (P/2235), Railway, no. 30, Appendix B, Cuttack, A Smith, Commissioner of Orissa Division, to Secretary to GoB, PWD, 14 August 1883, p. 13; W H Gregg, *27th Annual Report of the Sanitary Commissioner for Bengal* (1894), Calcutta, Bengal Secretariat Press, 1895, p. 29; H J Dyson, *31st Annual Report of the Sanitary Commissioner for Bengal* (1898), Calcutta, Bengal Secretariat Press, 1899, p. 24.

84. *Report of the Pilgrim Committee*, p. 4.

85. *Ibid.*, p. 3. On the role of railways (and not only of pilgrim rail traffic) in spreading cholera, see Klein, 'Imperialism, Ecology and Disease', pp. 505-10 and *idem*, 'Death in India, 1871–1921', in *Journal of Asian Studies* 32, 4 (1973), p. 649.

86. *Report of the Pilgrim Committee*, p. 31.

87. *Ibid.*, p. 36.

88. *Ibid.*, p. 51. For the frequency of such complaints see also Kerr, 'Reworking a Popular Religious Practice', pp. 316–19.

89. John W Mitchell, *Wheels of India. Autobiographical Reminiscences of a Railway Official in India*, London: Thornton Butterworth, 1934, pp. 268–9.

90. *Ibid.*, p. 306.

91. *The Writings in Prose*, p. 15.

92. Mitchell, *Wheels of India*, p. 313.

5. Taming the 'Dangerous' Rajput

1. An earlier version of this paper was presented at seminars at Delhi University and the Centre for Contemporary Studies, Teenmurti House, Delhi in March/April 1999 and

was published as 'State, Lineage and 'Domestic Space'; Marriage and Female Infanticide Amongst the Rajput *Biradaris* in 19th Century North India' (Occasional Papers on History and Society, Nehru Memorial Museum and Library, Teenmurti, Delhi, 2000). For a detailed discussion of Rajput marriage strategies and their relationship with hierarchies of status and power, see M Kasturi, *Embattled Identities: Rajput Lineages and the Colonial State in 19th Century North India*, Delhi, Oxford University Press, September 2002.

2. The literature on the family and gender is varied and vast. Among others see K Leonard, *The Social History of an Indian Caste, Kayasthas of Hyderabad*, Berkeley, University of California Press, 1978; K Sangari and S Vaid, 'Recasting Women, An Introduction', *Recasting Women, Essays in Colonial History*, Delhi, Kali for Women, 1989, 1–26; U Chakravarti, *Rewriting History, The Life and Times of Pandita Ramabai*, Delhi, Kali for Women in association with the Book Review Literary Trust, 1998; P Chatterjee, *The Nation and Its Fragments: Colonial and Post Colonial Discourses*, Delhi, Oxford University Press, 1994; R O'Hanlon, *A Comparison Between Women and Men, Tarabai Shinde and the Critique of Gender Relations in Colonial India*, Madras, New York, Oxford University Press, 1994; P Chowdry, *The Veiled Woman*, Shifting Gender Equations in Rural Haryana 1880–1990, Delhi, Oxford University Press, 1994; Arunima, 'Multiple Meanings, Changing Conceptions of Matrilineal Kinship', *Indian Economic and Social History Review* (IESHR), 33, 3 (1996), pp. 283–307; T Sarkar, 'Colonial Lawmaking and Lives/Deaths of Indian Women: Different Readings of Law and Community', in R Kapur (ed.), *Feminist Terrains in Legal Domains, Interdisciplinary Essays on Women and Law in India*, Delhi, Kali for Women, 1996; R Singha, 'Making the Domestic More Domestic': 'Criminal Law and the Head of the Household, 1772–1843', *IESHR*, 33: 3 (1996), pp, 309–43; I Chatterjee, *Gender, Law and Slavery in Colonial India*, Delhi, Oxford University Press, 1999).

3. There is a large clutch of material on the groups under study in Rajasthan. Among others see N P Ziegler, 'Some Notes on Rajput Loyalties During the Mughal Period', in J F Richards (ed.), *Kingship and Authority in South Asia*, Delhi, Oxford University Press, 1998, pp. 215–40; H Rudolph and L I Rudolph, *Essays on Rajputana, Reflections on History, Culture and Administration*, Delhi: Concept, 1984); N Peabody, ' "*Kota Mahajagat*" or the Great Universe of Kota: Sovereignty and Territory in 18th Century Rajasthan', *Contributions to Indian Sociology* (henceforth *CIS*), NS, 25: 1 (1991); V Joshi, *Polygamy and Purdah, Women and Society Amongst the Rajputs*, Jaipur, Rawat Publications, 1995; D Vidal, *Violence and Truth, A Rajasthani Kingdom Confronts Colonial Authority*, Delhi, Oxford University Press, 1997; and M Unnithan-Kumar, *Identity, Gender and Poverty, Perspectives on Caste and Tribe in Rajasthan*, Providence, Berghahn, 1997) and H Singh, *Colonial Hegemony and Popular Resistance, Princes, Peasants and Popular Resistance*, Delhi, London, Sage Publications, 1998. For work on the Rajputs of Uttar Pradesh, see, among others R Fox, *Kin, Clan, Raja and Rule, State-Hinterland Relations in Pre-industrial India* (Berkeley, London, University of California Press, 1971; E Stokes, *The Peasant and the Raj: Studies in Agrarian Society and Peasant Rebellion in Colonial India*, Cambridge, Cambridge University Press, 1978; M Alam, *The Crisis of Empire in North India; Punjab and Awadh 1707–48*, Delhi, Oxford University Press, 1985; and B S Cohn, *An Anthropologist Among the Historians and Other Essays*, Delhi, Oxford University Press, 1987.

4. See, for example, Alam, *The Crisis of Empire in North India*, and select essays in Cohn, *An Anthropologist*.

5. Sarkar, 'Colonial Lawmaking', Kapur (ed.), *Feminist Terrains*, pp. 215–16; Chatterjee, *The Nation and its Fragments*: pp. 116–57. For a critique of Chatterjee's position, see H Banerjee, 'Projects of Hegemony: Towards a Critique of Subaltern Studies' 'Resolution of the Women's Question', *Economic and Political Weekly*, vol. 35, no. 11, March 2000, pp. 902–20.

6. The induction of Rajput notions of patriarchy, protection and power into the world-view of their women has been studied in L Harlan, *Religion and Rajput Women: the Ethic of*

Protection in Contemporary Narratives, Berkeley, University of California Press 1992. Harlan's study seeks to find how and when the foremost Rajput duty, one to protect a community, and the female one to protect a husband take cognizance of each other. Women were responsible for protecting the health and respect of their husbands by serving both them and their families, worshipping their gods and in general avoiding any actions that would lead to the shame of the lineage. Ibid., p. 36. Also see V Joshi, *Polygamy and Purdah*.

7. R Singha, *A Despotism of Law, Crime and Justice in Early Colonial India*, Calcutta, Oxford, Oxford University Press, 1998, pp. 121–67. Also see 'introduction', M Sinha, *Colonial Masculinity: The 'Manly Englishman' and the 'Effeminate Bengali' in the Late Nineteenth Century*, Manchester, Manchester University Press, 1995, reprint, Delhi, 1996.

8. S Freitag, 'Collective Crime and Authority in North India', in A Yang (ed.), *Crime and Criminality in British India*, Tucson, University of Arizona Press, 1985, pp. 141–2; Singha, *A Despotism of Law*, p. 122.

9. H Cowell, *The Hindu Law Being a Treatise of the Law Administered Exclusively to Hindus by the British Courts in India*, Calcutta, Thacker, Spink, 1870, p. 51.

10. Singha, *A Despotism of Law*, p. 122. As with criminal law, civil law also sought in the main to uphold the perceived status quo in issues such as family property, kinship relationships and religion. Nevertheless, the colonial codification of the 'personal laws' of various communities, subjected 'custom' and 'tradition' to unforeseen changes, while civil law was selectively appropriated and manipulated by both the colonial state and its subjects. In this context, see N. Bhattacharya, ' "Remaking Custom", The Discourse and Practice of Colonial Codification', in R Champakalakshmi and S Gopal (eds), *Tradition, Dissent and Ideology, Essays in Honour of Romila Thapar*, Delhi, Oxford University Press, 1996, p. 48. It is clear that the sum total of the colonial codification of personal law buttressed patriarchal power within the 'joint' family as defined by Anglo-Hindu civil code. Thus, those sections of the Anglo-Hindu law-code dealing with inheritance and family property strengthened the rights of men vis-à-vis women. T Sarkar, 'Colonial Lawmaking and the Lives/Deaths of Indian Women, Different Readings of Law and Community, in R Kapur, *Feminist Terrains in Legal Domains*, pp. 210–42; Chatterjee, *Gender, Slavery and Law*, pp. 78–275. In the case of the Rajputs, these lineages benefited from the colonial focus on those aspects of 'brahmanical' 'tradition' revolving around inheritance which emphasized the primacy of transmission of property through male heirs, however distant. Litigation was increasingly used to good effect by male claimants to land within *biradaris* in an era of extended conflict over economic resources, once they realized that Anglo-Hindu law was disposed in their favour and worked against women and 'outsiders' in *sadar nizamat adalats*. Kasturi, *Embattled Identities*, chapter 4, pp. 137–71.

11. Singha, *A Despotism of Law*, pp. 311–18. In other instances, early nineteenth-century legislation dealing with the abolition of slavery and conjugal rights was often ignored in the breach or interpreted in ways benefiting heads of households, not women in court. *Ibid.*, pp. 121–67.

12. For example, as widow burning (*sati*) seemed to be sanctioned by the Hindu scriptures, officials used coercive legislation to outlaw the practice only in those instances in which it contravened 'tradition'. In other words, they differentiated between instances in which *sati* was 'allowed' by *shastraic* tradition, when the women supposedly practiced it of their own 'free will', banning it in all other instances. L Mani, *Contentious Traditions, The Debate on Sati in Colonial India*, Berkeley, Los Angeles, London, University of California Press, 1998, pp. 14–41. For a critique of Mani see Singha, *A Despotism of Law*, pp. 83–5.

13. The British remained at once enraptured and threatened by a group they viewed as a warlike and romantic band of adventurers, reminiscent in some ways of the Highland clans in Scotland because of their 'clanship' and their 'intense love and admiration' for the 'blood feud'. See, for example, District Superintendent of Police, DSP), Hamirpur, to Personal Assistant, Inspector General of Police (IGP), North–Western Provinces (NWP), 9 February 1869, NWP Police Proceedings (NWPPP), 13 November 1869, vol. 50, index

185, progs. 37, Uttar Pradesh State Archives (hereafter UPSA).

14. The cultural identity of a 'Rajput' was an 'attributional' or 'relational' one, revolving around kingship, power and military entrepreneurship, to which numerous social lineages of varied social origins subscribed. 'Martial culture' fed into codes of kingship in the subcontinent in three distinct zones of 'military entrepreneurship', marked by cultural rather than military differences. Rajputhood, therefore, was a collective identity, applied to members of open status groups in a world where jobber commanders gathered groups in search of patronage all over the subcontinent making it possible for a variety of social groups to trace symbolic ties of kinship to clans of high ritual status. The cultural codes of military entrepreneurship available in the pre-colonial arms-bearing cultural milieu, along with kinship and identity were also inextricably linked to elite definitions of martial masculinity. D H A Kolff, *Naukar, Rajput and Sepoy, the Evolution of the Military Labour Market in Hindustan, 1450–1850*, Cambridge, Cambridge University Press, 1990, pp. 59–64.

15. R O'Hanlon, 'Issues of Masculinity in North Indian History, the Bangash Nawabs of Farrukhabad', *Indian Journal of Gender Studies* (henceforth *IJGS*), 4, 1, 1997, p. 16.

16. W R Pinch, *Peasants and Monks in British India*, Delhi, Oxford University Press, 1996), pp. 84–6.

17. M Kasturi, 'Rajput Lineages, Banditry and the Colonial State in British Bundelkhand', in *Studies in History*, 15: 1 (1999), pp. 87–9.

18. *Ibid.*, pp. 90–91. Also see Kasturi, *Embattled Identities*, chapters 5 and 6, pp. 172–228.

19. S Gordon, *Marathas, Marauders and State Formation in Eighteenth Century India*, Delhi, Oxford University Press, 1994, pp. 182–92.

20. On the notion of improvement, see N Bhattacharya, 'Pastoralists in a Colonial World', in D Arnold and R Guha (eds), *Nature, Culture and Imperialism, Essays on the Environmental History of South Asia*, Delhi, Oxford University Press, 1995), pp. 72–4; R Guha, 'Dominance without Hegemony and its Historiography', R Guha (ed.), *Subaltern Studies VI : Writings on South Asian History and Society*, Delhi, Oxford University Press, 1989), pp. 240–42.

21. Settlement report of Pargana Amorha sent by collector, Gorukhpur, to commissioner, Fifth Division, 1 May 1840, GCO/Pre–Mr, Gorukhpur/Rev., Basta 13, vol. 105, F/144, Uttar Pradesh Regional Archives, Allahabad (henceforth UPRAA).

22. S Alavi, *The Sepoys and the Company: Tradition and Transition in Northern India, 1770–1830*, Delhi, Oxford University Press, 1995), pp. 39–55.

23. Ibid., pp. 33–41, 57–67.

24. Ibid., pp. 39–55.

25. M A Sherring, *Hindu Castes and Tribes as Represented in Benares*, London, 1872, reprint, Delhi, 1974, vol. 1, 119. For a discussion of specific Rajput clans vaunted for their 'valour', see A H Bingley, *Handbook on Rajputs*, London, 1899, reprint, Delhi, 1986, pp. 51–101.

26. The resonance of such ideas is still felt in contemporary research, which often unwittingly simplifies the nature of community bonds and identities by reducing them to their 'primordial' essences. H Alavi, 'Peasant Classes and Primordial Loyalties', in *Journal of Peasant Studies*, 1, 1 (1973), pp. 23–62. Sometimes, even the work of Ranajit Guha, a fine and extremely sophisticated analysis of 'peasant insurgency' makes assertions about the 'primordial' elements of such a political consciousness. See R Guha, *Elementary Aspects of Peasant Insurgency in Colonial India*, Delhi, Oxford University Press, 1983, p. 279.

27. Kasturi, *Embattled Identities*, chapters 4, 5 and 6, pp. 137–228.

28. Mani, *Contentious Traditions*, p. 14.

29. R O'Hanlon, 'Issues of Masculinity', *IJGS*, p. 17.

30. In this context Norman Ziegler has argued that marriages provided an institutionalized means of gaining access to land, rank and *izzat*, creating 'more effective and durable bonds than vows of allegiance on the part of a client to his patron'. See Ziegler, 'Some

Notes on Rajput Loyalties', in Richards (ed.), *Kingship and Authority in South Asia*, pp. 229–30.

31. E Boserup, *Women's Role in Economic Development*, London: Allen and Unwin, 1970, p. 148.

32. Memorandum on female infanticide in Saharanpur by Mr J Kennedy, 31 March 1874, Home, Police, October 1874, no. 29, National Archives of India (henceforth NAI).

33. Kasturi, *Embattled Identities*, chapter 1, pp. 24–63.

34. *Ibid.*, chapter 1, 4, pp. 24–63, 137–71.

35. The ethnology of Ibbertson, Crooke and Blunt, among others, worked out elaborate models of hierarchical marriages, whose organizing principle was 'hypergamy', which, they argued, all Rajputs followed mechanically. While contemporary anthropologists recognize that Rajput marriage strategies are more fluid than hitherto supposed, the latter are still analysed outside the ambit of history. Recent adaptations and reinterpretations of the hypergamous model may be found in J Parry, *Caste and Kinship in Kangra*, London, Routledge and Paul, 1978, pp. 198–99; M Milner, 'Status Relations in South-Asian Marriage Alliances; Towards a General Theory', *CIS*, (NS), vol. 22, no. 2, 1988, pp. 145–69; and V D K Veen, 'Marriage and Hierarchy Amongst the Anavil Brahmins of South Gujarat', in *CIS*, (NS), vol. 11, no. 7, 1973, pp. 36–52.

36. This discussion is derived from Kasturi, *Embattled Identities*, chapter 3, pp. 102–136.

37. The confidential servant of the *raja* of Kutch admitted his master committed female infanticide. On being asked the reason why, he said 'where have they an equal to whom to be bestowed in marriage'. Memorandum by the governor of Bombay, December 1806, in J Peggs, *India's Cries to British Humanity, Relative to Suttee, Infanticide, Ghaut Murders and Slavery in India*, London, 1830, pp. 148–9.

38. N B Dirks, *The Hollow Crown, the Ethnohistory of a Little Kingdom in South India*, Cambridge, Cambridge University Press, 1987, pp. 322, 335.

39. The magistrate of Basti observed that infanticide 'is practised mainly by few of the many tribes in the district, and the practice is not universal among these tribes but confined to certain families, and, what is still more strange, to certain localities'. Joint magistrate, Basti, to magistrate, Basti, 18 June 1868, *Selections From the Records of the Government of the North-Western Provinces*, Allahabad, 1871, p. 8. The Surajbansis who exercised local power in Basti were the most addicted to the practice in the district. Specific sections of the clan, subdivided into the Babus and the Kunwars, were suspected of female infanticide. The Babus were of higher rank and consisted of sixteen families in fifty villages, while the Kunwars consisted of four families in sixty-six villages. The Surajbansis sought to marry their daughters into the families of the Kulhansis of Awadh and the Chauhan, Kaushik and Bhadauriya clans towards the west. Although they asserted that marriages did not cost them more than a hundred and sixty rupees on average, the conversations the Magistrate had with certain *zamindars* showed that many lineages spent as much as two thousand rupees on alliances. The clan did not seem to practice female infanticide beyond Amroha, but within the *pargana* virtually all the lineages (and the Babus in particular), were suspected of destroying their girl children. *Ibid.*, p. 8–10.

40. Kennedy pointed out that powerful clans alone practised female infanticide. For example, the Chauhans who were 'powerful' and 'guilty' in Mainpuri, were 'weak' and 'innocent' in Saharanpur. Memorandum by Mr J Kennedy, 31 January 1874, Home, Police, October 1874, no. 29, NAI.

41. Joint magistrate, Basti, to magistrate Basti, 18 June 1868, *Selections from Government Records*, 1871, p. 3.

42. *Ibid.*, pp. 3–4. In the village of Altheela, in the *bhaiyachara* estate of Lakhneswar, many of the 337 Sengar *zamindars* owned as little as half a *bigha*. In these estates, lineages facing a resource crunch were no longer able to afford prestigious alliances. In June 1872, there were fifty-seven unmarried men and only forty girls to eighty-four boys in this village. See letter from officiating collector, Ghazipur, to commissioner, Banaras Division, (not dated), index 18, progs. 1, North-western Provinces Judicial Infanticide Department,

(henceforth NWP JID), June 1872, vol. 55, p. 38, Uttar Pradesh State Archives, Lucknow (henceforth UPSA).

43. For details see Kasturi, *Embattled Identities*, chapter 3, pp. 102–36.

44. Commissioner for investigating the extent of female Infanticide in the Banaras Division, to commissioner, 5th Division, 28 April 1858, NWP Judicial Criminal Progs, 21 October 1858, no. 453, P/234/46, Oriental and India Office Records, British Library, London.

45. Kasturi, *Embattled Identities*, chapter 3.

46. Magistrate, Azamgarh, to commissioner, Banaras Division, 16 May 1871, index 7, progs. 21, NWP JID, 7 October 1871, vol. 54, p. 163, UPSA.

47. Civil engineer, to magistrate, Azamgarh, 22 March 1871, index 8, progs 22, NWP JID, 7 October 1871, vol. 54, p. 175, UPSA.

48. Note by Mr Turner on a bill for the prevention of female infanticide, enclosed in letter from officiating registrar, High Court of Judicature, to secretary to government, NWP, 4 March 1870, index 195, progs 42, NWP JID, 21 January 1871, vol. 53, p. 348, UPSA.

49. Magistrate, Kanpur, to secretary to government, NWP, 7 March 1870, index 199, progs 45A, NWP JID, 21 January 1871, vol. 53, p. 350, UPSA. Criminal law found it extremely difficult to prove concealment or imprisonment of the women. Consequently, the purchaser was beyond the reach of the law, for he had not abetted the kidnapper in any way. As no section of the penal code dealt with this form of kidnapping, it was suggested, with little success, that a section relating to the same be added to the Act 8 of 1870. *Ibid.*

50. W Crooke, *Tribes and Castes of the North-Western Provinces of India*, London, 1894, vol. 4, p. 220.

51. Assistant magistrate, Aligarh, to magistrate, Aligarh, 14 April 1874, index 10, progs 5, NWP JID, June 1874, vol. 59, p. 28, UPSA.

52. Officiating collector and magistrate, Farrukhabad, to officiating secretary to government, NWP, 22 March 1871, index 30, progs 83, NWP JID, 7 October 1871, vol. 54, p. 202, UPSA.

53. Officiating magistrate, Etawa, to officiating secretary to government, NWP, 3 August 1870, index 62, progs 52, NWP JID, 21 January 1871, vol. 53, p. 28, UPSA.

54. Officiating collector and magistrate, Farrukhabad, to officiating secretary to government, NWP, 22 March 1871, index 30, progs 83, NWP JID, 7 October 1871, vol. 54, p. 202, UPSA.

55. See Kasturi, *Embattled Identities*, chapter 3, pp. 102–36.

56. Similar trends have been noticed in other regions. See A Clark, 'Limitations of Female Life Chances in Rural Central Gujarat', in *Indian Economic and Social History Review (IESHR)*, vol. 20, no. 1, 1983, pp. 1–25 and J Parry, 'The Koli Dilemma', *CIS*, (NS), vol. 4, 1970, pp. 84–104.

57. Note on suppression of female infanticide by Resident, Baroda, March 1808, Peggs, *India's Cries*, p. 140.

58. Governor of Bombay, to Honourable Court of Directors, November 1827, cited in Ibid., p. 201.

59. *Ibid.*, p. 143.

60. *Ibid.*, p. 142. In Farrukhabad, in September 1806, a man was charged with committing female infanticide 'on account of the ancient customs if my tribe of not contracting our daughters in marriage with any one as well as my ignorance of the regulations of justice', Ibid.

61. Governor of Bombay, January 1821, quoted in Peggs, *India's Cries*, p. 182.

62. On the discourse of improvidence see collector, Mirzapur, to commissioner, Fifth Division, 22 November 1854, *Selections from the Records of the Government of the North-Western Provinces*, Agra, 1856, p. 229.

63. Magistrate, Mainpuri, to commissioner, Agra Division, 9 December 1851, *Selections From the Records of the Government of the North-Western Provinces*, Agra, 1852, pp. 8–9.

64. *Ibid.*

65. Rajput *zamindars* told the officiating magistrate of Farrukhabad that 'it's of no use your telling us to leave off this expenditure. We must keep up our position. If one of us gives in to please the Collector, his economy will lose him his rank among Thakoors; and he cares a great deal more about that than the Collectors praise;' Memorandum (undated) by E Buck, enclosed in letter from officiating magistrate and collector, Farrukhabad, to secretary to government, 4 August 1870, index 66, progs 49, NWP JID, 21 January 1871, vol. 53, p. 109, UPSA. Buck noted of the Rajputs that '. . . facts prove that they care a great deal more about the rank than money'. It is certain that Thakoors live very much in a Thakoor atmosphere; that they have very little sympathy with the outside non-Thakoor world; and that Thakoor public opinion is the only thing that in their hearts they respect. *Ibid.*

66. *Ibid.*, p. 108–109.

67. *Ibid.*, p. 109.

68. Settlement officer, Farrukhabad, to secretary to government, NWP (undated), index 190, progs 42, NWP JID, 21 January 1871, vol. 53, p. 344, UPSA. Also see Memorandum on female infanticide in Saharanpur by Mr J Kennedy, 31 March 1874, Home, Police, October 1874, no. 29, NAI.

69. Memorandum of 1855, *Selections From the Records of the Government of the North-Western Provinces*, Agra, 1856, p. 181.

70. See S Nigam, 'Disciplining and Policing the Criminals by Birth, Part Is–II: The Making of a Colonial Stereotype – The Criminal Castes and Tribes of North India', *IESHR*, 27, nos 2–3 (1990).

71. Kasturi, 'Crime and Law in India: British Policy and the Female Infanticide Act of 1870', in *IJGS*, vol. 1. no. 2, p. 175.

72. For details of the Female Infanticide Act, see ibid., pp. 175–9.

73. Late assistant magistrate, Allahabad, to officiating magistrate, Allahabad, 18 April 1870, *Selections from Government Records*, 1871, pp. 42–3. For details see Kasturi, 'Crime and Law', in *IJGS*, pp. 175–80.

74. Deputy Inspector General of Police (IGP), to officiating IGP, NWP, 30 October 1876, index 2, progs 2, NWP JID, February 1877, vol. 71, p. 31, UPSA.

75. *Ibid.* A closer examination of some village statistics suggests that while the male:female birthrates were often either equitable or even sometimes tipped in favour of girl children, the death rate of girls under the age of one was very high. In 454 infanticide-practising villages in Mainpuri, sixty-five males and 102 females died before they reached the age of one. See letter from district superintendent of police (through magistrate, Mainpuri), to personal assistant to inspector general of pPolice, NWP, 21 May 1872, index 36, progs 16, NWP JID, September 1872, vol. 56, p. 109, UPSA. Even if girls survived the age of one year their chances of survival were fairly slim. In Mainpuri, local investigators came upon Chauhan villages such as Ghetoule where there were forty boys and just one girl. Others reported instances of no girl births for two years. Letter from officiating magistrate, Mainpuri, to officiating commissioner, Agra Division, 10 May 1871, *Selections from Government Records*, 1871, p. 160.

76. Deputy inspector general of p, NWP and Awadh, to inspector general of police, NWP and Awadh, 16 April 1886, progs 5, serial 12, NWP JID, March 1887, vol. 87, p. 62, UPSA.

77. Officiating secretary to government, NWP, to commissioner, Allahabad Division, 15 August 1871, index 57, progs 7, NWP JID, 7 October 1871, vol. 54, p. 249, UPSA.

78. Officiating collector and magistrate, Farrukhabad to officiating secretary to government, NWP, 22 March 1875, index 30, progs 83, NWP JID, 7 October 1871, vol. 54, p. 71, UPSA.

79. Further memorandum explanatory of the appendix dividing suspected Jats into three classes by assistant magistrate, Bijnor, 7 April 1872, index 7, progs 7, NWP JID, May 1872, vol. 55, p. 25, UPSA.

80. When children died before the age of six months police officers proceeded to the village, took the evidence of *panchayats* and relatives, before the body was returned to the family for disposal. Report on female infanticide in the Agra district by assistant magistrate, Agra, 18 April 1870, *Selections from Government Records*, 1871, p. 25.

81. Memorandum on female infanticide by Pandit Moti Lal Kathju, extra assistant commissioner and Mir Munshi, Punjab Secretariat, index 219, progs 23, NWP JID, 21 January 1871, vol. 53, p. 377, UPSA.

82. Joint magistrate, Jaunpur, to officiating magistrate, Jaunpur, 13 June 1871, index 55, progs 5, NWP JID, 7 October 1871, vol. 54, p. 240, UPSA.

83. Memorandum, 11 December 1869, by magistrate, Agra, enclosed in a letter from magistrate, Agra to commissioner, Agra Division, 21 April 1870, index 49, progs 17, NWP JID, 21 January 1871, vol. 53, p. 59, UPSA.

84. Kasturi, 'Crime and Law', *IJGS*, pp. 175–9.

85. Late assistant magistrate, Allahabad, to officiating magistrate, Allahabad, 18 April 1870, *Selections from Government Records*, 1871, p. 42–3.

86. Report on the testing of the *thakur* census, by assistant collector, Hamirpur, 18 May 1871, enclosed in a letter from officiating magistrate, Hamirpur, to officiating secretary to government, NWP, 20 May 1871, index 80, progs 18, NWP JID, 7 October 1871, vol. 54, p. 325, UPSA.

87. The thakur census, by officiating magistrate, 5 February 1871, enclosed within a report on the testing of the *thakur* census, index 81, progs 19, NWP JID, 7 October 1871, vol. 54, pp. 327, UPSA.

88. Late assistant magistrate, Allahabad, to officiating magistrate, Allahabad, 18 April 1870, *Selections from Government Records*, 1871, pp. 42–3.

89. Note on female infanticide in the Agra district, by magistrate, Agra, 18 April 1870, index 50, progs 18, NWP JID, 21 January 1871, vol. 53, p. 62, UPSA.

90. *Report on the Census of the North Western Provinces of the Bengal Presidency Taken on 1 January 1853*, Calcutta, 1854, p. 216.

91. Note on female infanticide in the Agra district, by magistrate, Agra, 18 April 1870, index 50, progs 18, NWP JID, 21 January 1871, vol. 53, p. 61, UPSA.

92. Ibid., p. 64.

93. General rules proposed to be issued under Act 8 of 1870, index 65, progs 48, NWP JID, 21 January 1871, vol. 53, p. 103, UPSA.

94. Resolution of the Judicial (Infanticide) Department, 3 November 1874, index 20, progs 12, NWP JID, January 1875, vol. 61, p. 175, UPSA.

95. Kasturi, 'Crime and Law', *IJGS*, p.180.

96. Officiating magistrate, Bulandshahar, to officiating secretary to government, NWP, 14 September 1870, NWPJIDP, 21 January 1871, vol. 53, index 42, progs 53 (UPSA).

97. Many *thakur*s were upset by the system of inquests which required Rajput men to carry their daughters' corpses to the nearest police station to be examined by a British civil surgeon, before the bodies could be disposed of. See note on female infanticide in the Agra district, by magistrate, Agra, 18 April 1870, index 50, progs 18, NWP JID, 21 January 1871, vol. 53, p. 66, UPSA.

98. Officiating magistrate and collector, Farrukhabad, to secretary, Infanticide Committee, 4 August 1870, index 65, progs 48, NWP JID, 21 January 1871, vol. 53, p. 102, UPSA.

99. Judge, Moradabad, to secretary to government, NWP, 26 February 1870, index 188, progs 48, NWP JID, 21 January 1871, vol. 53, p. 341, UPSA.

100. General rules proposed to be issued under Act VIII of 1870 by officiating magistrate, Farrukhabad, 4 August 187, index 65, progs 48, NWP JID, 21 January 1871, vol. 53, p. 108, UPSA.

101. Judge, Small Cause Court, Allahabad, to officiating secretary to government, NWP, 28 February 1870, index 189, progs 41, NWP JID, 21 January 1871, vol. 53, p. 342, UPSA.

102. For a detailed discussion of the reasons for the failure of Act VIII of 1870, see Kasturi, 'Crime and Law', *IJGS*, pp. 179–84.
103. Ibid., pp. 184–86.
104. Governor of Bombay, October 1827, Peggs, *India's Cries*, p. 196.
105. Among others see P M Visaria, 'The Sex Ratio of the Population of India and Pakistan and the Regional Variations during 1901–61', in A Basu (ed.), *Patterns of Population Change in India, 1951–61*, Bombay, Allied Publishers, 1967; B D Miller, 'Female Neglect and the Cost of Marriage in Rural India', *CIS* (NS), vol. 14, No.1, 1980, pp. 95–129 and B D Miller, *The Endangered Sex*, Ithaca, London: Cornell University Press, 1981.

6. What Is Your 'Caste'?

1. This chapter is an extended version of a paper presented at the 2nd International Conference of Asia Scholars, in Berlin in August 2002. I wish to express my gratitude to Therese O'Toole, Harald Fischer-Tiné and Olaf Wall.
2. *Cf* Edward Said, *Orientalism*, London, Routledge, 1978.
3. Susan Bayly, *Caste, Society and Politics in India from the Eighteenth Century to the Modern Age*, Cambridge, Cambridge University Press, 1999, p. 4.
4. Quoted in S Bandyopadhyay, 'Caste in the Perception of the Raj', in *Bengal Past and Present*, vol. CIV, parts I/II, no. 198–9, 1985, p. 63.
5. Ronald Inden, *Imagining India*, Oxford, Blackwell, 1990, p. 58.
6. Susan Bayly, 'Caste and Race in the Colonial Ethnography of India', in Peter Robb (ed.), *The Concept of Race in South Asia*, Oxford, Oxford University Press, 1995, p. 166–7.
7. Herbert Risley, *Tribes and Castes of Bengal. Ethnographic Glossary*, Calcutta, Bengal Secretariat Press, 1891, vol. I, p. XII.
8. Montgomery Martin (ed.), *The History, Antiquities, Topography, and Statistics of Eastern India*, London: W H Allen, 1838, vol. I, p. 110.
9. *Ibid.*, vol. II, p. 415.
10. *Ibid.*, p. 414–15.
11. *Ibid.*, p. 410.
12. S Bayly, *Caste, Society and Politics*, p. 96.
13. M Martin, *Eastern India*, p. 121.
14. S. Bayly, *Caste, Society and Politics*, p. 26.
15. M Martin, *Eastern India*, vol. II, p. 120.
16. *Ibid.*, vol. I, p. 141.
17. S Bayly, *Caste, Society and Politics*, p. 95.
18. M Martin, *Eastern India*, vol. II, p. 731.
19. *Ibid.*, vol. III, p. 520.
20. *Ibid.*, vol. II, p. 733.
21. *Ibid.*
22. *Ibid.*, vol. II, p. 735.
23. *Ibid.*, vol. I, p. 158.
24. *Ibid.*, vol. II, p. 449–50.
25. H Risley, *Tribes and Castes of Bengal*, vol. I, p. 141.
26. *Ibid.*, p. 160.
27. *Ibid.*, p. 142–3.
28. *Ibid.*, p. 159.
29. *Ibid.*, p. 143.
30. *Ibid.*, p. 147.
31. *Ibid.*, p. 152.
32. *Ibid.*, p. 145.
33. M Martin, *Eastern India*, vol. I, p. 148.

34. *Ibid.*, vol. II, p. 737.
35. *Ibid.*
36. *Ibid.*, p. 466.
37. H Risley, *Tribes and Castes of Bengal*, vol. I, p. 439.
38. *Ibid.*, p. 176.
39. M Martin, *Eastern India*, vol. I, p. 187.
40. *Ibid.*, p. 190.
41. *Ibid.*, p. 170.
42. *Ibid.*, p. 171.
43. *Ibid.*, p. 168.
44. *Ibid.*, p. 166.
45. *Ibid.*, p. 160.
46. H Risley, *Tribes and Castes of Bengal*, vol. I, p. 391.
47. *Ibid.*, p. 525.
48. *Ibid.*, vol. II, p. 60.
49. *Ibid.*, p. 128.
50. *Ibid.*, p. 61.
51. *Ibid.*, vol. I, p. 181.
52. *Ibid.*, p. 232.
53. *Ibid.*, p. 246–7.
54. Lydia Icke-Schwalbe, 'Der gesellschaftliche Status der Metallhandwerker in Indien', in Cornelia Mallebrein (ed.), *Die anderen Götter. Volks- und Stammesbronzen aus Indien*, Köln, Edition Braus, 1993, p. 155.
55. H Risley, *Tribes and Castes of Bengal*, vol. I, p. 389–90.
56. *Ibid.*, p. 234.
57. Werner Danckert, *Unehrliche Leute. Die verfemten Berufe*, Bern, Francke Verlag, 1963, p. 12.
58. Mircea Eliade, *Schmiede und Alchemisten*, Stuttgart, Klett-Cotta, 1980, p. 83.
59. H Risley, *Tribes and Castes of Bengal*, vol. I, p. 359–60.
60. *Ibid.*, p. 356.
61. Narendra Nath Bhattacharya, *Ancient Indian Rituals and their Social Contents*, London, Curzon Press 1975, p. 138.
62. M Martin, *Eastern India*, vol. II, p. 746.
63. S Bayly, 'Caste and Race', p. 169.
64. H Risley, *Tribes and Castes of Bengal*, vol. I, p. VII.
65. See Kunal M Parker, 'A Corporation of Superior Prostitutes. Anglo-Indian Legal Conceptions of Temple dancing girls, 1800–1914', in *Modern Asian Studies*, 32, 3 (1998), pp. 559–663.
66. See Melitta Waligora, 'Sie änderten den ,Geist' des ganzen Systems. Zum Beginn der britischen Herrschaft in Bengalen', in *Beiträge des Südasien-Instituts*, Humboldt Universität zu Berlin, October 1998, pp. 107–34.
67. David Cannadine, *Class in Britain*, New Haven and London, Yale University Press, 1998, pp. 27–8.
68. David Cannadine, *Ornamentalism. How the British saw their Empire*, London: Allen Lane, 2001, p. 43.
69. *Ibid.*, p. 46.
70. *Ibid.*, p. XIX.
71. *Ibid.*, p. 42.
72. Uma Chakravarti, 'Whatever Happened to the Vedic Dasi? Orientalism, Nationalism, and a Script for the Past', in Kumkum Sangari/Sudesh Vaid (eds), *Recasting Women. Essays in Colonial History*, New Delhi, Kali for Women, 1989, p. 30.
73. Nicholas B. Dirks, 'The Invention of Caste: Civil Society in Colonial India', in H L Seneviratne (ed.), *Identity, Consciousness and the Past. Forging of Caste and Community in India and Sri Lanka*, Delhi, Oxford University Press, 1997, p. 125.

74. Lucy Carroll, 'Colonial Perceptions of Indian Society and the Emergence of Caste(s) Associations', in *Journal of Asian Studies*, vol. XXXVII, no. 2, 1978, p. 244.
75. S. Bayly, *Caste, Society and Politics*, p. 18.
76. See: Jan Brouwer, *The Makers of the World. Caste, Craft and Mind of South Indian Artisans*, Delhi, Oxford University Press, 1995.
77. M Martin, *Eastern India*, vol. II, p. 703.

7. Sport and the 'Civilizing Mission' in India

1. J A Mangan, 'Soccer as Moral Training: Missionary Intentions and Imperial Legacies', in P Dimeo and J Mills (eds), *Soccer in South Asia: Empire, Nation, Diaspora*, London, Frank Cass, 2001, p. 41.
2. J A Mangan. *The Games Ethic and Imperialism: Aspects of the Diffusion of an Ideal*, London, Cass, 2000, p. 5.
3. J E C Welldon, 'The Imperial Purpose of Education', in *Proceedings of the Royal Colonial Institute*, vol. XXVI, 1894–5, p. 823, cited in Mangan, ibid., p. 36.
4. Mangan, ibid., p. 35.
5. *Ibid.*, p. 5.
6. A Guttmann, *Games and Empires: Modern Sports and Cultural Imperialism*, New York, Columbia University Press, 1994, p. 6; Guttmann is explicitly drawing from A Gramsci, *Selections from the Prison Notebooks*, trans. and ed. by Quinton Hoare and Geoffrey Nowell Smith, New York, International Publishers, 1971.
7. Mangan, *ibid.*, p. 43.
8. Obituary, *British Medical Journal*, vol. 1, 1912, p. 761, cited in J A Mangan, 'Soccer as Moral Training', p. 43.
9. Obituary, *British Medical Journal*, p. 761.
10. See also J A Mangan (ed.), *The Cultural Bond: Sport, Empire, Society*, London, Cass, 1992.
11. J Rosselli, 'The self-image effeteness: physical education nationalism in nineteenth century Bengal', in *Past and Present*, 86, pp. 121–148; M Sinha, *Colonial Masculinity: the 'manly Englishman' and the 'effeminate Bengali' in the nineteenth century*, Manchester, Manchester University Press, 1995.
12. Sir G Campbell, *Memoirs of My Indian Career*, edited by Sir C E Bernard, London, Macmillan, 1893, pp. 273–4.
13. *Trust and Fear Not, Ought Natives to be Welcomed as Volunteers?*, Calcutta, Thacker, Spink, 1885, p. 18. This paper was written anonymously, however Sinha (*ibid.*, p. 82) suggests the author was Henry Harrison, chairman of the Corporation of Calcutta.
14. C E Buckland, *Bengal Under the Lieutenant-Governors: Being a Narrative of the Principal Events and Public Measures during their periods of office, from 1854 to 1898*, vol. II, 2nd edn, New Delhi, Deep Publications, 1976, pp. 117–18.
15. Cited in S Nurullah and J P Naik, *A History of Education in India (During the British Period)*, 2nd edn, Macmillan, Bombay, 1951, p. 447. The quotation comes from Curzon's Convocation Address to staff and students of the University of Calcutta, 1902.
16. A Appadurai, 'Number in the Colonial Imagination', in C A Breckenridge and P van der Veer (eds), *Orientalism and the Postcolonial Predicament: Perspectives on South Asia*, Philadelphia, University of Pennsylvania Press, 1993, p. 335.
17. Guttmann, *ibid.*, p 42.
18. A de Mello, *Portrait of Indian Sport*, London, Macmillan, 1959, p. 186.
19. *Englishman*, 5 October 1892.
20. M Nandy, 'Calcutta Soccer', in S Chaudhuri (ed.), *Calcutta: The Living City, vol. II: The Present and Future*, Calcutta, Oxford University Press, 1990, p. 316.
21. *Ibid.*, p. 317.
22. S Mookerjee, 'Early Decades of Calcutta Football', in *Economic Times: Calcutta 300*,

September 1989, p. 149.
23. *Ibid.*, p. 150.
24. It should be noted that Calcutta had a population of around 1,200,000. A crowd of the size suggested that the proportion of the total population who attended this match was of a similar ratio to a popular match in a British city around this time.
25. Mookerjee, 'Early Decades', p. 150.
26. Ibid., p. 151.
27. Nandy, 'Calcutta Soccer', p. 318.
28. 5 August 1911.
29. 14 June 1911.
30. The Bengalis did not wear boots during this period, while the British did, so boots became symbolic of British culture.
31. 30 July 1911.
32. Mookerjee, 'Early Decades', p. 151.
33. Ibid., p. 157.
34. M A Budd, *The Sculpture Machine: Physical Culture and Body Politics in the Age of Empire*, New York, New York University Press, 1997, p. 85.
35. J H Mills, *Madness, Cannabis and Colonialism, The 'Native-Only' Lunatic Asylums of British India, 1857–1900*, Basingstoke, Macmillan, 2000, p. 181.
36. *Amrita Bazar Patrika*, 1 August 1934.
37. *Hindu*, 8 December 1940.
38. *Ibid.* The irony of this vision of sport is that it echoes Nalini Ranjan Sarkar's 1934 speech when Mohammedan Sporting won the Calcutta League, but also the British public school cult of athleticism.
39. A Nandy, *The Tao of Cricket: on games of destiny and the destiny of games*, New Delhi, Oxford University Press, 2000.
40. Ibid.
41. Chandan Mitra, 'Football isn't in our blood', in *The Pioneer*, 27 June 2002 (http://www.dailypioneer. com/archives1/FORAY.ASP?fdnam=jun2702&CAT=1).
42. Indian Football Association, *Role, Achievements of the Indian Football Association (W.B.) in the Promotion and Development of the Game of Football in India* (West Bengal, IFA. 1993), p.1.

8. 'More Important to Civilize Than Subdue'?

1. The author would like to acknowledge the help of a number of individuals and organizations in the writing of this chapter. I would like to thank Dr Crispin Bates for his acute assessments of earlier versions of this work, Dr Cathy Coleborne for her methodological insights and Dr Satadru Sen for his comments. I am grateful to Dr Aditya Kumar who kindly allowed access to the three volumes of case notes that he has preserved at the Agra Mental Hospital that relate to the Lucknow Asylum for the period 1858–72. Other archival sources include those of the National Archives of India, the India Office Library and the National Library of Scotland and the staff at each deserve thanks. Finally I gratefully acknowledge the financial support of the British Academy, the Wellcome Trust and the Carnegie Trust for the Universities of Scotland that have funded my work in India.
2. Minute by President, Madras, 29 October 1865 GOI (Public) Procs, 27 February 1869, 105–107A, National Archives of India (NAI).
3. Asylums in Bengal for the year 1862, p. 66, National Library of Scotland (NLS).
4. Annual Report of the Insane Asylums in Bengal for the year 1863, p. 3, NLS.
5. For details of treatment regimes see J Mills, *Madness, Cannabis and Colonialism: the 'native-only' lunatic asylums of British India, 1857–1900*, Basingstoke, Macmillan, 2000, pp. 103–128; for a discussion of physical coercion in these regimes see J Mills, 'Body as Target, Violence as Treatment: psychiatric regimes in colonial and post-colonial India'

in J Mills and S Sen (eds), *Confronting the Body: the Politics of Physicality in Colonial and Post-colonial India*, London, Anthem Press, 2003.

6. W Ernst, *Mad Tales from the Raj: the European Insane in British India 1800–1858*, London, Routledge, 1991, p. 166.

7. S Sharma, *Mental Hospitals in India*, New Delhi, Directorate General of Health Services, 1990, pp. 52–3; for a fuller discussion of the periodization of psychiatry in India see J Mills, 'The History of Modern Psychiatry in India: 1795 to 1947', in *History of Psychiatry*, 4, 2001.

8. Case Book IA, patient no. 13, admitted 30 April 1860. These references are to the three volumes of case notes in the private collection of Dr Aditya Kumar at the Agra Mental Hospital.

9. Y Ripa, *Women and Madness: The Incarceration of Women in Nineteenth-century France*, Cambridge, Polity Press, 1990, p. 160.

10. *Ibid.*, p. 161.

11. E Showalter, *The Female Malady: Women, Madness and English Culture, 1830–1980*, London, Virago, 1987, p. 79.

12. J Monk, 'Cleansing their Souls: Laundries in Institutions for Fallen Women', in *Lilith*, 9, 1996, pp. 21–31.

13. Case Book IV, patient no. 192, admitted 11 May 1870.

14. Case Book IA, patient no. 13, admitted 30 April 1860.

15. N Rose, *The Psychological Complex: Psychology, Politics and Society in England*, 1869–1939, London, Routledge, 1985, p. 45.

16. *Ibid.*, p. 26.

17. M MacMillan, 'Anglo-Indians and the Civilizing Mission 1880–1914', in G Krishna (ed.), *Contributions to South Asian Studies* 2, Delhi, Oxford University Press, 1982, p. 73.

18. L Zastoupil, *John Stuart Mill and India*, Stanford, Stanford University Press, 1994) pp. 135–6.

19. See for example, S Alatas, *The Myth of the Lazy Native: A Study of the Image of the Malays, Filipinos and Javanese from the 16th to the 20th Century and its Function in the Ideology of Colonial Capitalism*, London, Cass, 1977.

20. R Inden, *Imagining India*, Oxford, Basil Blackwell, 1990, p. 264.

21. L Zastoupil, *John Stuart Mill and India*, p. 175.

22. J Majeed, *Ungoverned Imaginings: James Mill's 'History of British India' and Orientalism*, Oxford, Clarendon Press, 1992, p. 194.

23. E Stokes, *The English Utilitarians and India*, Oxford, Oxford University Press, 1959, p. 43.

24. *Ibid.*, p. 56.

25. Case Book IA, patient no. 114, admitted 8 June 1861.

26. For a fuller consideration of the methodological issues relating to using asylum archives from colonial India see J Mills, 'The Mad and the Past: Retrospective Diagnosis, Post-coloniality, Discourse Analysis and the Asylum Archive', *Journal of Medical Humanities* 3, 2000.

27. For more on Indian agendas on admission and within the asylum see J Mills, *Madness, Cannabis and Colonialism*, pp. 145–76; J Mills, 'Indians into Asylums: Community Use of the Colonial Medical Institution in British India, 1857–1880', in M Harrison and B Pati (eds), *Health, Medicine and Empire*, Hyderabad, Orient Longman, 2001.

28. Asylums in Bengal for the year 1862, p. 15, NLS.

29. Asylums in the Bombay Presidency for the year 1873–4, p. 16, NLS.

30. Consider the paternalistic tone of Dr Penny; 'Luxuries in the way of sweetmeats and fruit and the remains of public suppers have been constantly given in my own presence and by my own hands', in Asylums in the Punjab for the year 1870, p. 3, NLS.

31. See for example, L Zastoupil, *John Stuart Mill and India*, p. 175; A Nandy, *The Intimate Enemy: Loss and Recovery of Self under Colonialism*, (Delhi, Oxford University Press, 1983) pp. 11–16.

32. A Digby, 'Moral treatment at the Retreat 1796–1846', in W Bynum, R Porter and M Shepherd (eds), *The Anatomy of Madness: Essays in the History of Psychiatry*, vol. II, London, Tavistock, 1985, p. 68.

33. M Foucault, *Madness and Civilization*, London, Routledge, 1989, p. 252.

34. Asylums in the Bombay Presidency for the year 1874–5, p. 28, NLS.

35. Asylums in the Bombay Presidency for the year 1873–74, p. 16, NLS.

36. Asylums in the Punjab for the year 1876, pp. 18–19, NLS.

37. Asylums in Bengal for the year 1862, p. 66, NLS).

38. Asylums in the Bombay Presidency for the year 1873–74, p. 44, NLS.

39. Asylums in Bengal for the year 1863, p. 3, NLS.

40. Asylums in Bengal for the year 1862, p. 72, NLS.

41. Asylums in the Bombay Presidency for the year 1873–4, p. 29, NLS.

42. Annual Inspection Report of the Dispensaries in Oudh for the year 1872, p. 299, IOL.

43. Asylums in Bengal for the year 1862, p. 30, NLS.

44. Asylums in the Bombay Presidency for the year 1874–5, p. 28, NLS.

45. Asylums in the Bombay Presidency for the year 1873–4, p. 45, NLS.

46. Asylums in the Punjab for the year 1875, p. 3, NLS.

47. Asylums in the Bombay Presidency for the year 1873–4, p. 30, NLS.

48. Asylums in the Punjab for the year 1874, p. 2, NLS.

49. Asylums in the Bombay Presidency for the year 1873–4, p. 8, NLS.

50. See drawings in 'Reports on the Asylums for European and Native Insane Patients at Bhowanipore and Dullunda for 1856 and 1857', in Selections from the Records of the Government of Bengal no. XXVIII, IOL.

51. Asylums in Bengal for the year 1862, p. 28, NLS.

9. The Sympathizing Heart and the Healing Hand

1. Research for this article was conducted in Cambridge and London during a three-month visiting fellowship at Clare Hall College, University of Cambridge, in the spring of 2001 and a research trip to Chennai in June and July 2001. I am grateful to Clare Hall for providing access to the stimulating research environment of this institution, and to the Danish Research Council for the Humanities for financial support towards the research trip to Chennai.

2. Whitelaw Ainslie, 'Observations Respecting the Small-Pox and Inoculation in Eastern Countries; with some Account of the Introduction of Vaccination into India', in *Transactions of the Royal Asiatic Society of Great Britain and Ireland*, vol. II, 1830, pp. 52–73.

3. David Arnold, *Colonizing the Body. State Medicine and Epidemic Disease in Nineteenth-Century India*, Berkeley, University of California Press, 1993, pp. 45–7. C A Bayly, *Empire and Information – Intelligence Gathering and Social Communication in India 1780–1870*, Cambridge, Cambridge University Press, 1996, pp. 271–5.

4. Ainslie, 'Observations', p. 64.

5. *Ibid.*, p. 73.

6. Michael Adas, *Machines as the Measure of Men. Science, Technology and Ideologies of Western Dominance*, Ithaca, Cornell University Press, 1989. See also David Arnold, *Science, Technology and Medicine in Colonial India*, Cambridge, Cambridge University Press, 2000, p. 15.

7. This is the main line of argument in Thomas R Metcalf, *Ideologies of the Raj*, Cambridge, Cambridge University Press, 1995, but see in particular pp. 66, 111.

8. Adas, *Machines*, p. 57. M N Pearson, 'The Thin End of the Wedge. Medical Relativities as a Paradigm of Early Modern Indian–European Relations', in *Modern Asian Studies*, 29, 1 (1995), p. 166.

9. Pierre Sonnerat, *A Voyage to the East Indies and China*, Calcutta, English translation Francis

Magnus, 1788–9, II, p. 137.

10. Francis Buchanan Hamilton, *A Journey from Madras through the Countries of Mysore, Canara, and Malabar*, London, Bulner, 1807, vol. I, p. 336.

11. Benjamin Heyne, *Tracts, Historical and Statistical on India*, London: Baldwin, Black & Parry, 1814, p. 165.

12. Arnold, *Colonizing the Body*, p. 52. Bayly, *Empire and Information*, pp. 281–2.

13. Mark Harrison, 'Medicine and Orientalism', in Biswamoi Pati and Mark Harrison (eds), *Health, Medicine and Empire. Perspectives on Colonial India*, New Delhi, Orient Longman, 2001, pp. 50–4.

14. *Ibid.*, p. 55. See also Arnold, *Colonizing the Body*, pp. 46–7.

15. On William Jones see Harrison, 'Medicine and Orientalism', p. 58. Pierre Sonnerat was among those, who saw India as the place were 'the first sparks of reason' shone in a distant golden age. Ibid., p. 59 and Sonnerat, *A Voyage*, vol. I, p. iv.

16. Heyne, *Tracts*, pp. 166–70.

17. Whitelaw Ainslie, *Materia Medica of Hindoostan and Artisan's and Agriculturalists's Nomenclature*, Madras, Government Press, 1813, p. 64. Arnold, *Science*, p. 67.

18. I have developed this argument in greater detail in my 'Coming to Terms with the Native Practitioner – Indigenous Doctors in Colonial Service in South India 1800–1825' in S Bhattacharya (ed.), *Imperialism, Medicine and South Asia 1800–1950*, New Delhi, Orient Longman, forthcoming.

19. Arnold, *Colonizing the Body*, pp. 28–43. Mark Harrison, *Climates and Constitutions. Health, Race, Environment and British Imperialism 1600–1850*, New Delhi, Oxford University Press, 1999, pp. 11, 18.

20. Harrison, *Climates and Constitutions*, pp. 59, 92.

21. *Ibid.*, pp. 45, 81–2, 102, 142.

22. Arnold, *Colonizing the Body*, pp. 29–30, 133–4.

23. *Ibid.*, p. 134.

24. For references to resistance stemming from 'ignorance' and 'prejudice' in Germany see Eberhard Wolff, *Einschneidende Massnahmen. Pockenschutzimpfung und traditionale Gesellschaft im Württemberg des frühen 19. Jahhunderts*, Stuttgart, Franz Steiner Verlag 1998, pp. 413–46. For Sweden see Peter Sköld, *The Two Faces of Smallpox. A Disease and its Prevention in Eighteenth- and Nineteenth-century Sweden*, Umeaa, The Demographic Database, 1996, pp. 433–7.

25. Metcalf, *Ideologies of the Raj*, 27.

26. British Library, Oriental and India Office Collections (hereafter BL-OIOC) F/4/96, Board's Collections no. 1953, fols 11–12, 15. Tamil Nadu State Archive, Chennai (hereafter TNSA), Surgeon General's Records (hereafter SGR), vol. 12, fols 237–8.

27. Proceedings of the Medical Board, 6 April 1801, entered in TNSA, Madurai District records (District Records hereafter appear as DR) vol. 1181, fols 267–8. TNSA, SGR vol. 13, fol. 446. It was only thought advisable to conduct variolation in the 'cold' months between December and March.

28. Proceedings of the Medical Board, 23 July 1804, entered in TNSA, Madurai DR vol. 1190, fols 164–6. For figures for Bombay see J Banthia and T Dyson, 'Smallpox in Nineteenth-Century India', in *Population and Development Review*, 25, 4 (1999), figure 2 on p. 658. For Bengal see Arnold, *Colonizing the Body*, p. 136. The conclusions drawn from vaccination statistics must be taken to express broad tendencies only.

29. BL-OIOC F/4/268, Board's Collections, no. 5891, fols 53–5. The major change in 1805 was that indigenous vaccinators were no longer rewarded according to the number of vaccinations, but paid a fixed salary. For a detailed analysis of the debate in 1805, see Brimnes, 'Coming to Terms'.

30. Smallpox began to recede in India by 1914, although it was not totally eradicated until the 1970s. Arnold, *Science*, 75.

31. In the northernmost parts of the presidency 'Woodiah' (Oriya) *brahmin*s were reported to

have been practising variolation since – as colonial phraseology would have it – 'time immemorial'. BL-OIOC F/4/96 Board's Collections, no. 1953, fols 84–8. Whitelaw Ainslie believed the *brahmins* were *worriahs*, a brave and handsome but less-civilized tribe. Ainslie, 'Observations', p. 63.

32. BL-OIOC F/4/96, Board's Collections, no. 1953, fols 45–6.
33. *Ibid.*, fol. 107.
34. *Ibid.*, fol. 108.
35. TNSA, SGR vol. 1, fol. 194. Nicol Mein began to inoculate *sepoys* and civilians around Trichinopoly as early as the 1780s and he was probably the first Company servant to conduct extensive variolation. Baron Thomas Dimsdale emphasized the need for general inoculation in selected areas and isolation of unprotected individuals. He was famed for the inoculation of Catharina II of Russia. F. Fenner *et al.*, *Smallpox and its Eradication*, Geneva, WHO, 1988, p. 256.
36. Proceedings of the Medical Board, 3 April 1801, with enclosures entered in TNSA, Madurai DR, vol. 1181, fol. 266.
37. TNSA, Coimbatore DR, vol. 592, fol. 194.
38. BL-OIOC F/4/96, Board's Collections, no. 1953, fol. 83. Arnold, *Colonizing the Body*, p. 120.
39. BL-OIOC F/4/153, Board's Collections, no. 2613, fols 69–75. The cowpox vaccine travelled from Baghdad to Bombay through a 'human chain' of children vaccinated from arm to arm. Arnold, *Colonizing the Body*, 139–40.
40. BL-OIOC F/4/153, Board's Collections, no. 2613, fols 73–4, 82.
41. TNSA, Madurai DR, vol. 1147, fol. 218; TNSA, Trichinopoly DR, vol. 3663, fol. 199.
42. TNSA, Madurai DR, vol. 1149, fols 94–5.
43. TNSA, SGR, vol. 13A, fol. 446. Proceedings of the Medical Board, 23 July 1804, entered with enclosures in TNSA, Madurai DR, vol. 1190, fol. 166.
44. For reports about problems with the vaccine disease in the northern districts of the presidency, see TNSA, SGR, vol. 14, fols 84–9, 98–103.
45. BL-OIOC F/4/268, Board's Collection, no. 5891, fol. 67. BL-OIOC F/4/382, Board's Collection, no. 9625, fol. 30.
46. TNSA, SGR vol. 13A, fols 312–13. James Anderson, *Correspondence for the Extermination of Small-pox*, Madras, Collected and Reprinted by Francis Lawrence, 1804, p. 18.
47. TNSA, Coimbatore DR vol. 592, fols 190–4. Proceedings of the Medical Board, 21 May 1804, entered with enclosures in TNSA, Madurai DR, vol. 1190, fols 161, 163.
48. TNSA, SGR, vol. 13A, fols 456–70. Proceedings of the Medical Board, 23 July 1804, entered with enclosures in, TNSA, Madurai DR vol. 1190, fol. 166. Obviously, indigenous resistance was not the only factor determining to what extent specific groups accepted immunization. The way in which each group was targeted was significant as well. If certain groups appeared less likely to accept immunization it need not be a sign of resistance but might as well be due to lack of opportunities.
49. TNSA, SGR, vol. 14, fol. 60. TNSA, Madurai DR, vol. 1147, fols 54–5.
50. BL-OIOC F/4/96, Board's Collections, no. 1953, fol. 98. Anderson, *Correspondence*, p. 18. As the *zamindar* of Chintapilly had been variolated in 1793, subsequent vaccination would not have had any impact on his immunity.
51. TNSA, SGR vol. 14, fols 174–5.
52. Arnold, *Colonizing the Body*, pp. 120, 141–2.
53. TNSA, Trichinopoly DR, vol. 3661, fol. 159. BL-OIOC P/255/53, Madras Military Proceedings (hereafter MPP), 19 June 1805, fols 4084–5.
54. BL-OIOC P/255/53, MMP, 19 June 1805, fols 4096–7. Sawmy Naik's account of the incident is printed in *Indian Medical Gazette*, October 1902, p. 413
55. BL-OIOC P/255/53, MMP, 19 June 1805, fols 4084–5.
56. *Ibid.*
57. BL-OIOC F/4/20, Board's Collections, no. 4544, fols 39–40.

58. BL-OIOC F/4/96, Board's Collections, no. 1953, fols 2, 15–16, 97.
59. Proceedings of the Medical Board, 3 April 1801, entered with enclosures in TNSA, Madurai DR, vol. 1181, fol. 264.

10. Perceptions of Sanitation and Medicine in Bombay, 1900–14

1. The author wishes to acknowledge the assistance of the Wellcome Trust, which enabled her to consult source material in London in 2001.
2. C A Bayly, *Empire and Information: Intelligence Gathering and Social Communication in India, 1780–1870*, Cambridge, Cambridge University Press 1996, p. 282.
3. David Arnold, *New Cambridge History of India Science, Technology and Medicine*, Cambridge, Cambridge University Press, 2000, p. 212.
4. See Mridula Ramanna, *Western Medicine and Public Health in Colonial Bombay, 1845–1895*, Hyderabad, Orient Longman, 2002.
5. *Report of the Health Officer, Bombay*, 1873 (hereafter *RHO*) in General Department Volumes, Maharashtra State Archives, vol. 76, 1875, p. 165 (hereafter GD).
6. Florence Nightingale, 'How some People have lived and not died in India,' in *Report of the Sanitary Commissioner, Bombay*, 1873–74, p. 52[hereafter *RSC*].
7. *Sketch of the Medical History of the Native Army of Bombay*, Bombay, n.p., 1875, p. 8.
8. Turner was born at Portsmouth, England, and had his preliminary medical education, MB, at Aberdeen. He completed his MD from Edinburgh in Scotland, in 1882, and his degree in public health from Cambridge. He was also trained in London, Paris and Bonn. After qualifying, he turned his attention to sanitary work. His first appointment as health officer was in a district of Leicestershire and subsequently he was posted to Hertfordshire. It was from there that he came to Bombay in 1901.
9. *Some Unpublished and Later Speeches and Writings of the Honourable Sir Pherozeshah Mehta*, ed. J R B Jeejeebhoy, Bombay, The 'Commercial' Press, 1918, p. 462.
10. J A Turner, *Sanitation in India*, Bombay, Times of India Press, 1914, pp. 839–40.
11. J A Turner, 'Sanitation in India', in *Transactions of the Bombay Medical Congress 1909*, ed. W E Jennings, Bombay, The Times Press, 1910, pp. 459–62 (hereafter *TBMC*).
12. 'The Bombay Health Officer on Plague' (no author), in *The Indian Medical Gazette*, July 1906, pp. 301–2. This was the journal of the Indian Medical Service.
13. Turner, 'Sanitation', in *TBMC*, pp. 459–62.
14. *Report on Native Papers, Bombay* (hereafter *RNP*), *Bombay Samachar*, 13 January 1911. This Gujarati daily started in 1822 is still published.
15. *Pickings from the Hindi Punch*, March 1906, p. 373. *Hindi Punch* was a delightful Anglo-Gujarati weekly, which carried cartoons and caricatures of contemporary events and personalities. It was published from Bombay in the late decades of the nineteenth and the early twentieth centuries
16. *RNP*, *Native Opinion*, 10 January 1904. Viswanath Narayen Mandlik, chairman of the Bombay Municipal Corporation founded this Anglo-Marathi weekly in 1864.
17. *RNP*, *Rast Goftar*, 20 March 1904. This Anglo-Gujarati weekly from Bombay was started by Dadabhai Naoroji in 1851.
   N H Choksy (1861–1939) was also associated with the Matunga Leprosy Asylum, had edited the *Indian Medico-Chirurgical Review*, a journal for Bombay medics, from 1893–99, and contributed to the *Lancet* and the *Indian Medical Gazette*. He was a member of the Medical Society, Munich and the Medico-Physicians Academy, Florence, and was made Chevalier of the Crown of Italy.
18. *RNP*, *Indu Prakash*, 26 August 1912. Started by Vishnu Shastri Pandit in 1861 as a weekly, this Marathi paper became a daily.
19. *Speeches delivered by Lord Sydenham as Governor of Bombay, 1908–1913*, compiled by Rao

Bahadur and M G Dongre, Kolhapur, Mission Press 1913, sections I–IV, II, p. 59.

20. *Hindi Punch*, February 1905, p. 330. B K Bhatavadekar (1852–1922) was one of the fore-most doctors of Bombay, and had been chairman of the Municipal Corporation. He was also credited with popularizing western medicine in other parts of the presidency, where he had served.

21. *RNP, Jam-e-Jamshed*, 10 February 1906. This Gujarati daily from Bombay, started in 1832, was regarded as the voice of the Parsi orthodoxy.

22. *Speeches, Sydenham*, section II, p. 43.

23. The BMU was founded in 1883 as a body of Indian medical professionals and had been a forum for the expression of their grievances.

24. RHO in *Administrative Report of the Municipal Commissioner for the City of Bombay for the year 1912–13 Part II*, Bombay, The Times Press, 1913, pp. 47–9 (hereafter *ARMCB*).

    The mill-owners were B J Padshah, Tata Mills, Sir Cowasji Jehangir, Shapurji Broacha and Narottam Morarji Goculdas.

25. *ARMCB, 1917–18*, RHO, p. 9.

26. *RNP, Kesari*, 2 June 1914.

27. *RNP, Akhbar-e-Islam*, 13, 14 and 15 June 1904. This was a Gujarati daily from Bombay, catering to Gujarati-speaking Muslims.

27. *RNP, Akhbar-e-Islam*, 27 July 1915.

28. *RNP, Sanj Vartaman*, 9 March 1904. This was an Anglo-Gujarati daily. See Mridula Ramanna, 'Gauging Indian Responses to Western Medicine: Hospitals and Dispensaries, Bombay Presidency, 1900–20', in Deepak Kumar (ed.), *Disease and Medicine in India, A Historical Overview*, New Delhi, Indian History Congress, Tulika, 2001, pp. 233–48.

30. The riots in Madanpura occurred on 9 March 1898 when a Parsi medical student, a Eurasian nurse and the plague officer of the ward, Lt Warneford were refused admittance to a house to examine a suspected plague case, a twelve-year-old girl. The crowds attacked them and in the subsequent police firing five persons were killed or mortally wounded. Ian Catanach, ' "Who are your leaders?" Plague, The Raj and The 'Communities' in Bombay, 1896–1901', in Peter Robb (ed.), *Society and Ideology*, New Delhi, Oxford University Press, 1993, pp. 213–4.

31. *Hindi Punch*, May 1905, p. 445.

32. *RNP, Kaiser-I Hind*, 25 June 1905. This was an Anglo Gujarati weekly.

33. *British Medical Journal*, 7 October 1911, p. 852 (hereafter *BMJ*).

34. *RNP, Indian Spectator*, 11 June 1899. This paper was edited by the reformer, Behramji Malabari.

35. *RNP, Jam-e-Jamshed*, 30 January 1906.

36. *RNP, Maratha*, 28 January 1906. This English weekly from Puna was started in 1881 and initially edited by the great nationalist, Bal Gangadhar Tilak and often expressed his extremist views. Narsingh Chintaman Kelkar joined Tilak as editor in 1896 and remained at this post through 1918.

37. *RNP, Kaiser-I-Hind*, 23 January 1906.

38. *RNP, Maratha*, 25 June 1899.

39. *Hindi Punch*, August 1905, p. 43.

40. *RNP, Gujarati*, 28 January 1906.

41. *RNP, Jain*, 15 September 1907. This Bombay weekly was published in Gujarati and Hindi.

42. *RNP, Rast Goftar*, 24 September 1899.

43. *RNP, Kesari*, 1 August 1899. This Marathi weekly also started by Tilak, was edited by Krishna Prabhakar Khadilkar. Ghole had sent a paper to the International Congress of Hygiene and Demography, held in London in 1891, where he had credited the missionaries with having taught the people simple rules of health and the government with building roads, bridges and railways and setting up municipalities.

Nineteen persons, who had been inoculated, at Malkowal, a village in the Punjab, contracted tetanus and died on 30 October, 1902. Haffkine, who had prepared the vaccine,
was blamed for the incident when, in fact, that particular consignment had been contaminated by the forceps used to open the bottle, which had been dropped on the
ground. Ian Catanach, 'Plague and the tensions of empire: India, 1896–1918', in D.
Arnold (ed.), *Imperial Medicine and Indigenous Societies*, Manchester, Manchester University
Press, 1988, p. 160.

44. *RNP, Indian Spectator*, 4 November 1905. The BBL founded as the Plague Research
    Laboratory in 1896 by Haffkine, was the research institute where the anti-plague vaccine
    was prepared.

45. *RNP, Arunodaya*, 5 November 1905. This Marathi weekly from Thana was a conservative
    voice.

46. *RNP, Kaiser-I Hind*, 30 April 1905.

47. *RNP, Maratha*, 23 April 1904.

48. *RNP, Bombay Samachar*, 24 January 1908.

49. *RNP, Gujarati*, 2 April 1911. *Gujarati* was an Anglo Gujarati weekly from Bombay.

50. *Speeches, Sydenham*, 16 January 1908, section II, p. 15.

51. *RNP, Indian Spectator*, 29 April 1905; *Indian Social Reformer*, 30 April 1905.

52. *RNP, Indian Spectator*, 31 August 1908.

53. *RNP, Indian Social Reformer*, 22 December 1907 and 9 February 1908.

54. *RNP, Broach Samachar*, 28 September 1905; *Kaira Times*, 22 October 1905; *Shri Shahu*, 20
    September 1905; *Parikshak*, 27 July, 1905; *Indu Prakash*, 3 August 1905. The first two
    papers were published in Gujarati from Broach and Nadiad respectively, and the latter
    two were Marathi weeklies from Satara and Belgaum respectively.

55. Manjiri Kamat, 'The palkhi as Plague Carrier; The Pandharpur Fair and the Sanitary
    Fixation of the Colonial State; British India, 1908–1916', in Biswamoy Pati and Mark
    Harrison (eds), *Health Medicine and Empire Perspectives on Colonial India*, Hyderabad, Orient
    Longman, 2001, pp. 299–316.

56. *RNP, Kaiser-i-Hind*, 27 August 1915.

57. *RNP, Kesari*, 30 May 1911.

58. *RNP, Indu Prakash*, 26 July 1912.

59. *RNP Vrittasar*, 3 April 1911; *Jagad Vritt*, 10 September 1911. Both these papers were
    Marathi weeklies.

60. H N Kunzru (ed.), *Gopal Krishan Devadhar*, Puna, Servants of India Society, 1939, pp.
    134–9. Devadhar was one of Mahrashtra's greatest social reformers who founded the
    Puna Seva Sadan for women's education in 1909.

61. *RNP, Bombay Samachar*, 26 August 1908.

62. Charles A Bentley, *Report of an Investigation into the causes of Malaria in Bombay and the Measures
    necessary for its control*, Bombay, Government Central Press, 1911, p. 137.

63. *BMJ*, 4 November 1911, p. 1229.

64. *Report on Malaria Operations, April 1912–March 1913*, in *ARMCB, 1912–13*, Bombay, The
    Times Press, 1913, p. 171.

65. *Ibid.*, pp. 138–9.

66. *ARMCB, 1912–13*, p. 178.

67. *RNP, Rast Goftar*, 20 August 1911.

68. *RNP, Kaiser-I-Hind*, 8 August 1909.

69. *RNP, Indu Prakash*, 30 November 1909.

70. *RNP, Indu Prakash*, 15 July 1911.

71. *ARMCB, 1912–13*, p. 177.

72. Ibid., p. 181

73. *RNP, Rast Goftar*, 7 July 1912.

74. *RNP, Jam-e-Jamshed*, 17 July 1914.

75. *RNP, Indu Prakash*, 14 October 1914.

76. *RNP, Kaiser-I-Hind*, 6 September 1914.
77. *RNP, Indu Prakash*, 26 September 1914.
78. Bipan Chandra, *The Rise and Growth of Economic Nationalism in India*, New Delhi, People's Publishing House, 1966, p. 625.
79. *RSC, 1887*, in *GD*, 6, p. 1888.
80. Critical Remarks on Hewlett's Report, 17 July 1888, in *GD*, 6, 1888.
81. *RSC, 1888*, in *GD*, 12, 1889, pp. 59–60.
82. Mark Harrison, *Public Health in British India Anglo Indian Preventive Medicine 1859–1914*, Cambridge, Cambridge University Press, 1994, p. 186.
83. Dinsha Bomanji Master, 'Chief Defects in Present Modes of Disposal of Sewage and Town Refuse of Bombay', in *TBMC*, p. 455.
84. *RNP, Indu Prakash*, 14 August 1912. A recent paper has shown the people's resistance to the CIT's re-housing schemes, overcrowding in some CIT *chawls* and reluctance to move in others. Prashant Kidambi, 'Housing the Poor in a Colonial City: The Bombay Improvement Trust, 1898–1918' in *Studies in History*, 17, 1, n.s. (2001), pp. 57–79.
85. *RHO, 1917*, Bombay, The Times Press, 1918, pp. 62–3. During the construction of the new capital of Delhi, for colonial India, the government was guided not by what was the best system of sanitation but what the municipal funds could afford. Vijay Prashad, 'The Technology of Sanitation in Colonial Delhi' in *Modern Asian Studies*, 35, 1, (2001), p. 117.
86. *RNP, Gujarati*, 13 September 1903.
87. *RNP, Bombay Samachar*, 20 September 1904.
88. *RNP, Gujarati*, 25 January 1914.
89. *RNP, Indu Prakash*, 12 April 1912.
90. N H Choksy, ' The Serum Therapy of Plague in India', in *TBMC*, pp. 120–5.
91. Choksy, 'The Symptomatic Treatment of Plague,' in *TBMC*, pp. 125–32.
92. Jehangir Cursetji and Bomanji Master 'Unhygienic Bombay, Its Causes and its Remedies', in *TBMC*, pp. 362–82.
93. Jehangir Cursetji and Bomanji Master, 'Chief Defects in Present Modes of Disposal of Sewage and Town Refuse of Bombay', in *TBMC*, pp. 443–59.
94. Sorab C Hormusji, 'Dis-infection of Indian Houses', in *TBMC*, pp. 484–5.
95. *RNP, Indian Social Reformer*, 29 March 1908. The first Congress was held in Calcutta in 1894.
96. *RNP, Indu Prakash*, 11 January 1909.
97. *RNP, Gujarati Punch*, 17 January 1909. This Gujarati weekly was published from Ahmedabad.
98. *RNP, Maratha*, 28 February 1909.
99. *RNP, Kaiser-I-Hind*, 28 February 1909.
100. *Report of the Proceedings of a Conference on Moral, Civic and Sanitary Instruction*, Bombay, Director of Public Instruction, 1910, p. 81.
101. Ibid., p. 82.
102. *RNP, Indian Spectator*, 16 November 1912.
103. *ARMCB 1911–12*, pp. 44–6.
104. *ARMCB 1912–13*, p. 54.
105. *Some Recent Sanitary Developments in the Bombay Presidency*, Bombay, Government of Bombay, 1914, pp. 5, 17.
106. Poonam Bala, ' State Policy towards Indigenous Drugs in British Bengal', in *Journal of the European Ayurvedic Society*, 1, 1990, pp. 167–76.
107. *GD*, 76, 1882, pp. 35–8.
108. The Grant College Medical Society, founded in 1851, had been active throughout the nineteenth century as a deliberative body. Its members included both professors of the college and alumni.
109. *BMU Report*, pp. 24–26.

110. *RNP, Sanj Vartaman*, 22 November 1911, *Bombay Samachar*, 9 June 1910.

111. *RNP, Kesari*, 19 March 1912.

112. *RNP, Akhbar-e Saudagar*, 25 March 1912. This was a Gujarati daily, published from Bombay.

113. *Unpublished Speeches Mehta*, Bombay Legislative Council Meetings, 13 March 1912, pp. 289–92 (hereafter BLC).

114. *Speeches, Sydenham*, BLC, 13 March 1912, section IV, p. 205.

115. *Unpublished Speeches, Mehta*, BLC , 21 November 1911, p. 285.

116. *RNP, Kesari*, 19 March 1912. Neshat Quaiser has shown that the All India Vaidic and Unani Tibbi Conference in 1910 had mooted the idea of proper colleges for the indigenous systems. Neshat Quaiser, 'Politics, Culture and Colonialism: Unani's Debate with Doctory', in Pati and Harrison (eds) *Health, Medicine and Empire*, p. 341.

117. *RNP, Jam-e-Jamshed*, 23 January 1912.

118. *RNP, Sanj Vartaman*, 17 April 1911.

119. *RNP, Sind Patrika*, 13 August 1910. This was an Anglo-Sindhi weekly from Larkana, edited by a Hindu.

120. *RNP, Bombay Samachar*, 24 August 1910.

121. *RNP, Kesari*, 28 November 1911.

122. *Proceedings of the Legislative Council of the Governor of Bombay*, 1912, Bombay, Government Central Press, 1913, pp. 524–5. Dr Tehmulji B Nariman, founder of the Parsi Lying-in Hospital, referred to above, gave testimony in favour of the government.

123. K N Panikkar, *Culture Ideology, Hegemony. Intellectual and Social Consciousness in Colonial India*, New Delhi, Tulika, 1995, p. 150.

124. *RNP, Indian Social Reformer*, 19 November 1911.

125. *RNP, Bombay Samachar*, 17 and 18 November 1911

126. *Speeches, Sydenham*, Opening of the Central Anti-Tuberculosis dispensary and Information Bureau, 28 February 1912, section II, p. 58.

127. *BMJ*, 1 November 1912, p. 1269.

128. *Speeches, Sydenham*, BSA Meeting, 10 April 1912, section II, p. 43.

129. *Indian Sanitary Policy*, Calcutta, Superintendent Government Printing Press, 1914, p. 5.

130. *RNP, Indian Social Reformer*, 7 June 1914.

131. *RNP, Prajabandhu*, 31 May 1914.

132. *RNP, Sanj Vartaman*, 1 June 1914.

133. *Recent Developments in Bombay*, p. 22.

134. *Indian Medical Gazette, October 1904*, p. 382.

135. Ira Klein, 'Development and death: Reinterpreting malaria, economics and ecology in British India', in *Indian Economic and Social History Review*, 38, 2, (2001), p. 158.

136. Mridula Ramanna, 'Coping with the Influenza Pandemic, 1918–1919: The Bombay Experience', in Howard Phillips and David Killingray (eds), *The Spanish Flu, 1918–19*, London, Routledge, forthcoming.

137. *RNP, Kal*, 15 September 1905. *Kal* was founded by the radical journalist Shivram Mahadev Paranjpe in 1896.

138. *RNP, Rast Goftar*, 20 May 1907.

129. *Unpublished Speeches, Mehta*, p. 463.

11. National Education, Pulp Fiction and the Contradictions of Colonialism

1. This chapter is an extended and slightly altered version of a paper presented at the 2nd International Conference of Asia Scholars, in Berlin in August 2001. I wish to express my gratitude to Dr Therese O'Toole (Birmingham), Dr Margrit Pernau (New Delhi), Dr Malavika Kasturi (Toronto), Dr Michael Mann (Hagen), Thomas Bärthlein (Bonn) and

Dr Melitta Waligora (Berlin) for reading earlier drafts and making valuable suggestions for its improvement.

2. From an article in the English quarterly *The Round Table*. Cited in *VM&GS*, VII (5), 1913, p. 407.

3. *Cf* K Kumar, *A Political Agenda of Education. A study of colonialist and nationalist ideas*, New Delhi, Sage, 1991, pp. 23–34.

4. *Cf*, for example, F Hutchins, *The Illusion of Permanence. British imperialism in India*, Princeton, Princeton University Press, 1967, pp. 54–7.

5. J Kennedy, 'Indian Educational Policy', in *Imperial and Asiatic Quarterly Review and Oriental and Colonial Record*, XIX, 37, 1905, pp. 1–10.

6. T R Metcalf, *Ideologies of the Raj*, Cambridge, Cambridge University Press, 1994, NCHI, III, 4, p. x.

7. *Cf* H K Bhaba, *The Location of Culture*, London, Routledge, 1994, pp. 84–6.

8. It goes without saying that labels like 'liberal imperialists' and 'conservative imperialists' are auxiliary constructs to highlight two different strands of thought within the imperialist discourse. There are no fixed boundaries between these attitudes and – as will become obvious – even less so between two sets of colonial officials. One can detect 'liberal' as well as 'conservative' elements in the writings of the same persons. For this problematic see also Margaret Macmillan, 'Anglo Indians and the Civilizing Mission, 1880–1914', in Gopal Krishna (ed.), *Contributions to South Asian Studies 2*, Delhi, Oxford University Press, 1982, pp. 73–109, p. 83.

9. Chamupati, 'Swami Shraddhananda', in *VM&GS*, XV (8), 1922, p. 451.

10. A Nandy, *The Intimate Enemy. Loss and Recovery of Self Under Colonialism*, Delhi, Oxford University Press, 1983, pp. 2 f.

11. For details see S C Ghosh: ' 'English in Taste, in Opinions, in Words and Intellect'. Indoctrinating the Indian through textbook, curriculum and Education', in J A Mangan (ed.), *Racial Images and Education in the British Colonial Experience*, London, Routledge, 1993, pp. 175–93, especially pp. 187–92.

12. For this concept see K W Jones, *Socio-Religious Reform Movements in British India*, Cambridge, Cambridge University Press, 1989, NCHI, III, 1, p. 3 f.

13. There is a vast amount of historical research on this particular reform movement. For a short and perceptive account of the Arya Samaj, see K W Jones, 'The Arya Samaj in British India', in R D Baird (ed.), *Religion in Modern India*, New Delhi, Manohar, 1989, pp. 27–54.

14. For a brief analysis of the school's history *cf* H Fischer-Tiné, 'The Only Hope for Fallen India: The Gurukul Kangri as an Experiment in National Education'; in G Berkemer, *et al.* (eds.), *Explorations in the History of South Asia. Essays in honour of Dietmar Rothermund*, New Delhi, Manohar, 2001, pp. 277–99.

15. For biographical details see the excellent account by J T F Jordens, *Swami Shraddhananda. His Life and Causes*, New Delhi, Oxford University Press, 1981.

16. I Vidyavachaspati, 'Gurukul aur Arya Samaj', in *Shraddha*, 8 phalgun 1977 VS (18 February 1921), p. 3.

17. Gurukul literally means line or family of the teacher. It refers to the brahmanical practice that students of the Veda lived in their teachers families during the course of their studies. For details of the traditional Gurukula system see A S Altekar, *Education in Ancient India*, Benares, The Indian Book Shop, 1934, pp. 92–101; and R M Steinmann, *Guru-Shishya Sambandha. Das Meister Schüler Verhältnis im traditionellen und modernen Hinduismus*, Stuttgart, Steiner Verlag, 1986, Beiträge zur Südasienforschung, vol. 109, pp. 50–9.

18. A Basu, *The Growth of Education and Political Development in India*, Delhi, Oxford University Press, 1974, p. 77. For a similar assessment see C Jaffrelot, 'The Genesis of Hindu Nationalism in the Punjab: from the Arya Samaj to the Hindu Sabha (1875–1910)', in *Indo British Review*, XXI (1), 1996, pp. 3–39.

19. The complete course of studies extended over fourteen years The curriculum focused on

Sanskrit and Vedic literature, but English and the natural sciences were also taught right from the beginning. Later, courses in agriculture and traditional medicine were introduced in addition. All the subjects – except English – were taught through the medium of Hindi.

20. See H Fischer-Tiné, 'From *Brahmacharya* to 'Conscious Race Culture'. Victorian Discourses of Science and Hindu Traditions in Early Indian Nationalism', in C Bates (ed.), *Beyond Representation. The Construction of Identity in Colonial India*, Delhi, OUP, (forthcoming).

21. *Cf*, for example, Gurukula Kangri Vishvavidyalaya (ed.), *The Aims, Ideals and Needs of the Gurukula Vishvavidyalaya, Kangri*, Kangri, 1971 VS (1914), p. lii f. and Chamupati: 'Swami Shraddhananda'; in *VM&GS*, XV (8), 1922, p. 451.

22. On this problem see H Fischer-Tiné, 'Kindly Elders of the Hindu Biradri. The Arya Samaj's Struggle for Influence and its Impact on Hindu Muslim Relations', in A Copley, (ed.), *Gurus and their Followers. New Religious Movements in Colonial India*, Delhi, Oxford University Press, 2000, pp. 107–27.

23. The quotation is taken from an article by A G Frazer, director of the Trinity College, Kandy (Ceylon). Cited in M M Seth, *The Arya Samaj a Political Body*, Kangri s.a. (1909), p. 39. For further examples of Christian anti-Arya-agitation *cf* also J C Oman, *Cults, Customs and Superstitions of India*, London, T Fisher Unwin, 1908, p. 170; and S K Gupta, *Arya Samaj and the Raj, (1875–1920)*, New Delhi, Gitanjali Publishing House, 1991 p. 62 f.

24. NAI, Home Dept. Poll., Deposit, Proceedings April 1912, no. 4. 'Note on the Arya Samaj'.

25. *Ibid.*, p. 16.

26. S Vidyalankar, *Svami Shraddhanand* reprint, Kankhal, Hardwar, Shri Swami Shraddhanand Anusandhan Prakashan Kendra, 1995 (Dilli 1933), p. 385 f.

27. See, for instance, NAI, Home Dept. Poll. –B, Proceedings nos. 36–43, May 1908 'Weekly Report of the Dept. of Criminal Intelligence for April 1908', p. 15.

28. Vidyalankar, *Svami Shraddhanand*, p. 345.

29. S Shastri, *Bharatiya svadhinta sangram men Arya Samaj ka yogdan*, Rohtak, Haryana Sahitya Sansthan, 2046 VS (1989), p. 233.

30. I Vidyavachaspati, *Arya Samaj ka itihas*, vol. II, reprint Dilli, Sarvadeshik Arya Pratinidhi Sabha, 1995 (1957), p. 27.

31. NAI, Home Dept., Poll., Deposit, Proceedings October 1910, no. 20: 'Anti-British Agitation and some of its Causes and Means of Expression', p. 13 (italics in the original text).

32. V Chirol, *Indian Unrest*, London, Macmillan 1910, pp. 106–17.

33. The Gurukul teachers reacted against Chirol's polemic in a comprehensive apologetic article published in their English-language organ *Vedic Magazine*. *Cf* 'Mr. Valentine Chirol and the Arya Samaj'; in *VM&GS*, IV (5), 1910, pp. 65–88.

34. *Chela* (Hindi): disciple; the term was practically never used in Kangri, hence its use suggests that Sir Valentine was a rather superficial student of the Arya Samaj.

35. Chirol, *Indian Unrest*, p. 115.

36. *Aap* (Hindi): very formal and polite address.

37. NAI, Home Dept., Poll. –B, Proceedings March 1910, nos. 17–19, 'Weekly Report of the Director Criminal Intelligence', February 1911, p. 5.

38. NAI, Home Dept. Police, –B, Proceedings December 1911, nos. 19 and 20, *passim*.

39. *Cf* I Vidyavachaspati, *Amar shahid Svami Shraddhanand mere pita*, Nai Dilli, Sarasvati Vihar s. a. (1953?), pp. 99–101 and Munshiram: 'The Gulf between the Rulers and the Ruled'; in *VM&GS*, V (5), 1910, pp. 58–64. *Cf*, e.g., 'Advocate', 27 October 1910, *SNNUP*, 1910, p. 927; and *The Leader*, 20 October 1910.

40. *Cf* e. g. 'Advocate', 27 October 1910, *SNNUP*, 1910, p. 927; and *The Leader*, 20 October 1910.

41. Another example is provided by the report of district collector Ford in which Ramdev, a

teacher of history in the Gurukul, born in the Punjab, is described as the most dangerous element in the school's staff and mistaken for a Bengali. *Cf* Satyaketu Vidyalankar, *Arya Samaj ka itihas. Chautha bhag: Arya Samaj, aur rajniti*, Nai Dilli, Arya Svadhyaya Kendra, 1990, p. 208 f.

42. NMML, Meston Papers; 'Meston to Govt. of India', 21 July 1913.
43. *The Leader*, 23 February 1913, p. 4.
44. *Ibid.*, p. 6.
45. C.F. Andrews: 'Hardwar and its Gurukula'; in *Modern Review*, vol. XIII, (4), 1914, pp. 330–35.
46. The speech given in Meerut on 3 March 1913 was entitled 'More Education' and made a strong point for the introduction of physical culture, games and 'moral training' into the curricula of Indian schools. *Cf The Leader*, 6 March 1913, p. 6; and C A Watt, 'Education for National Efficiency: Constructive Nationalism in North India 1909–1916', in *MAS*, 31 (2), 1997, pp. 339–74.
47. *Indian Social Reformer*, 9 February 1913, p. 278.
48. *The Leader*, 6 March 1913, p. 5.
49. *Cf* I Vidyavachaspati, *Amar shahid Svami Shraddhanand mere pita*, Nai Dilli, s. a. (1953?).
50. A contemporary Arya journalist concludes: 'The day shall always be remembered by all Arya Samajists as a day of rejoicing, when the slur of being a dangerous set of people was removed by the merciful providence through one of the most responsible officers of the government'. L L Gupta, 'The Arya Samaj. Its Activities in the Punjab'; in *Indian Review*, April 1913, pp. 304 f.
51. M M Seth, *High Government Offcials on the Arya Samaj and its Work*, Allahabad, K C Bhalla, 1917, pp. 1 f.
52. In the welcome address Meston was even compared with the ancient *rajarishi*s who considered it an honour to patronize seats of learning and visit them time and again. The entire text of the address is reproduced in *The Leader*, 11 March 1913, p. 6.
53. *The Leader*, 6 March 1913, p. 5.
54. *VM&GS*, III (10/11), 1913, p. 882.
55. For a discussion of Victorian ideals of education and their impact on the Gurukul-experiment *cf* also H Fischer-Tiné, ' "Character Building and Manly Games" – Viktorianische Konzepte von Männlichkeit und ihre Aneignung im frühen Hindu Nationalismus', in *Historische Anthropologie*, 9 (3), 2001, pp. 432–56. A more general overview of the problematic is presented by P Van der Veer, *Imperial Encounters*, Princeton, Princeton University Press, 2001, pp. 83–105.
56. The term is borrowed from Michael Rosenthal who uses it for the Boy Scout movement. *Cf* M. Rosenthal, *The Character Factory. Baden Powell and the Origins of the Boy Scout Movement*, New York, Pantheon, 1986.
57. *Cf* Kumar, *Political Agenda of Education*, pp. 23–46. For an example from the British colonies in Africa see J Becher, K Bromber and A Eckert, 'Erziehung und Disziplinierung in Tansania, 1880–1940', in D Rothermund (ed.), *Aneignung und Selbstbehauptung. Antworten auf die Europäische Expansion*, München, Oldenbourg, 1999, pp. 299–216, especially p. 311 f.
58. For this concept and its importance in Britain see J Harris, *Private Lives, Public Spirit. A Social History of Britain, 1870–1914*, London, Penguin, 1993, pp. 233–7.
59. *VM&GS*, I (2), 1907, p. 45.
60. *Cf* NAI, Home Dept. Poll. –B, Proceedings nos.–14– 18, May 1912, 'WRDCI for April 1912', p. 14.
61. *Cf*, e.g., 'The Citizen', 19 April 1908, *SNNUP*, 1908, p. 404.
62. Lord Islington was the head of the Royal Public Services Commission, which toured India in 1913/14; he visited the Gurukul Kangri in December 1913. *Cf VM&GS*, VII (6/7), 1914, p. 572 f.
63. *Cf* Seth, *High Government Officials on the Arya Samaj*, pp. 24–43 and Munshiram (ed.), *The*

Gurukula through European Eyes, Kangri, 1917, p. 76 f.

64. Vidyavachaspati, *Amar shahid Svami Shraddhanand mere pita*, p. 113 f.

65. *Ibid.*

66. E Candler, *Siri Ram – Revolutionist. A Transcript from Life 1907–1910*, London: Constable, 1912. A brief analysis of the novel in a somewhat different context can be found in S. Chakravarty, *The Raj Syndrome. A Study in Imperial Perceptions*, reprint New Delhi, Penguin, 1991, pp. 185 f. Linguistic and literary aspects are briefly discussed in I Lewis, 'Historical Introduction'; in *idem, Sahibs, Nabobs and Boxwallahs. A Dictionary of the Words of Anglo-India*, reprint Delhi, Oxford University Press, 1999, pp. 1–43, p. 33 f.

67. In a letter written in May 1913, C F Andrews informed the Gurukul principal Munshiram about the tremendous success of the book. He mentions 'that all Shimla was reading it' and admits that the book was written so 'cleverly' that the author must be a CID officer. NAI, Chaturvedi Papers, Andrews to Munshiram, 26 May 1913. *Cf* also Lewis, 'Historical Introduction', p. 34. As early as 1914 the book went into a second edition.

68. The following is based on his autobiography: E Candler, *Youth and the East: an unconventional autobiography*, London, Edinburgh, Blackwood & Sons, 1924. Further details have been gathered from *Who was Who, Vol. 2, 1916–1928*, London, Black, 1929, p. 170; and D O'Connor, *Gospel Raj and Swaraj. The missionary years of C.F. Andrews*, Frankfurt am Main, Lang, 1990, Studien zur interkulturellen Geschichte des Christentums, vol. 62, p. 270, endnote 21.

69. *Cf* also OIOC, IOR: L/P&J/6/705, File no. 39 (1905) 'Application of Mr. E. Candler for a post in the I. E. S.'.

70. 'Letter of Recommendation by R. Carter, Rector of St Paul's School, Darjeeling', ibid.

71. Candler, *Youth and the East*, p. 219.

72. *Ibid.*, p. 215.

73. The understanding that Punjabi students showed more interest in healthy activities like football and cricket and hence were of a better 'character' was widespread among colonial educationists, See, for instance, J Kennedy, 'Unrest and Education in India', in *Imperial and Asiatic Quarterly Review and Oriental and Colonial Record*, XXXII, 63/64, 1911, pp. 81–7, especially p. 82 f.

74. Apart from *Siri Ram*, which turned out to be one of his most successful books, Candler published eleven other novels and travelogues between 1899 and 1924. The more popular include *A Vagabond in Asia* (1900) and *The Unveiling of Lhasa* (1905) In the latter book he gave an account of an expedition to Tibet, which he had accompanied as special correspondent of the *Daily Mail*.

75. For the sake of completeness a few words on Candler's further career: during the First World War he served as war correspondent in France and Mesopotamia. Afterwards he returned to India where he worked as director of publicity in the Punjab for a couple of years before returning to Britain where he died in 1926.

76. Chirol, *Indian Unrest*, p. 207.

77. Candler, *Siri Ram*, 1st edn, p. 37.

78. *Ibid.*, pp. 7–12.

79. *Ibid.*, p. 36.

80. James May, agent to the *raja* of Parlakimedi, states in his testimonial dated 8 November 1903, 'Candler is of active habits and fond of games generally, and riding and sport. He has taken much interest in Cricket, while here and coached the College eleven so successfully that they won the cup open to all Colleges in the Northern Circars'; OIOC, IOR: L/P&J/6/705, file no. 39.

81. Candler, *Siri Ram*, 1st edn, p. 191 f.

82. *Ibid.*, p. 207 f.

83. E Candler, 'The Arya Samaj', in *idem, Siri Ram Revolutionist*, London, Constable, 1914, pp. 306–308.

84. *Ibid.*, p. 307.
85. In the novel this motive reappears time and again. It is articulated most bluntly in the caustic comment by a British police officer who addresses Principal Skene as the representative of a 'westernizing' school and tells him: 'It's all you college fellows. You turn out anarchists as quick as sausages in Chicago. They ought to stop education.' Candler, *Siri Ram*, 1st edn, p. 124.
86. A similar point is made by Candler in his book *Abdication*, where he declares nationalism to be a 'perversion' of the Indian intelligentsia, who were trying to infect the masses of loyal subjects. Edmund Candler, *Abdication*, London, Constable, 1922, p. 13.
87. Chirol, *Indian Unrest*, p. 222.
88. A selection of important writings on this topic by Munshiram can be found in B Bharatiya (ed.), *Svami Shraddhanand Granthavali*, vol. X, Dilli, Govindram Hasanand, 1987, pp. 129–69. A useful overview is provided by the editor's preface to the same volume, Bhavanilal Bharatiya,: 'Sampadakiya bhumika', in *ibid.*, pp. 5–16.
89. The following is based on Munshiram, 'Mahatma Munshi Ram on 'Arya Samaj and Politics'' (The Substance of a Lecture Delivered on the Occasion of Lahore Arya Samaj Aniversary)' [*sic!*], in *VM&GS*, II (8), 1909, pp. 31–48.
90. The Lahore speech published in the *Vedic* was the first of many apologetic articles, tracts and pamphlets produced by the Gurukul authorities. The more important ones include 'The Government and the Arya Samaj'; in *VM&GS*, II (9), 1909, pp. 42–62; M M Seth, 'The Arya Samaj, a Political Body'; in *VM&GS* II (11/12), 1909, pp. 27–59; Munshiram, 'The Present Situation and our Duty' in *VM&GS* III (7/8), 1909, suppl., pp. 129; Ramdev, *The Arya Samaj and its Detractors*, Kangri, 1910; and finally M M Seth, *High Government Officials on the Arya Samaj & its Work*, Allahabad, K C Bhalla, 1917.
91. Munshiram, 'Mahatma Munshi Ram on 'Arya Samaj and Politics'', p. 31.
92. *Ibid.*, p. 32.
93. *Ibid.*, pp. 31–48.
94. *Ibid.*, pp. 41 f.
95. *Ibid.*, p. 42.
96. In his manifesto *Hind Swaraj* which was published in the same year, Gandhi presents a double concept of Swaraj whereby inner self-rule, i.e., moral-perfection, self-restraint and a complete control of the lower passions, is seen as a *conditio sine qua non* to attain political autonomy. *Cf* A J Parel (ed.), *M.K. Gandhi: Hind Swaraj and other Writings*, reprint New Delhi, Oxford University Press, 1997, pp. 73, 118.
97. Munshiram, Arya Samaj and Politics', p. 42 f.
98. Hardliners among the British bureaucrats induced the puppet *maharaja* in the princely state of Patiala to have about eighty leading Arya Samajis arrested for 'seditious activities'. It was the single most important action taken by the British against the organization. *Cf* S Shastri, *Bharatiya svadhinta sangram men Arya Samaj ka yogdan*, p. 261; and K C Yadav and K S Arya, *Arya Samaj and the Freedom Movement, vol. 1, 1875–1918*, New Delhi, Manohar, 1988, pp. 149–55.
99. Munshiram, 'The Present Situation', p. 21 f.
100. *Ibid.*, p. 16.
101. *Ibid.*, p. 9. See also Munshiram, 'Foreword'; in M M Seth, *The Arya Samaj a Political Body*, p. 1 f.
102. Munshiram, 'The Present Situation', p. 10.
103. Madanmohan Seth (1884–1956) was one of the most important Arya Samaj workers in the United Provinces. The lawyer from Bulandshahar was a member of the Royal Asiatic Society of Great Britain and Ireland and became president of the Arya Samaj, UP, in 1911. A couple of years later he entered government service as a *munsiff*, which clearly indicates that the British regarded him as loyal. *Cf* B Bharatiya, *Arya lekhak kosh. Aryasamaj tatha rishi Dayananda vishayak lekhan se jure sahastradhika lekhakom ke jivana evam karyavrtta ka vistrt vivarana*, Jodhpur, Dayananda Adhyayan Sansthan, 1991, p. 281.

104. Seth, 'The Arya Samaj a Political Body', pp. 31 f.
105. A Persecuted Arya (Pseud.), '(Swami Dayanand to John Bull) John, John, Why Persecutest Thou Me?'; in *VM&GS*, III (1), 1909, pp. 59 f.
106. See, e.g., Munshiram, 'The Present Situation', pp. 4–6; and Munshiram, 'Arya Samaj and Politics', p. 34. It is remarkable, for instance, that Munshiram had the courage to declare his sympathy for the 'notorious agitator' Lajpat Rai while the latter was banished by the British.
107. 'Swarajya', 12 February 1910, *SNNUP*, p. 209 f. Similar assessments are expressed in 'Karmayogi', 25 February 1910, *ibid.*, p. 244 f. and 'Karmayogi', 4 March 1910, *ibid.*, p. 297.

12. In Search of the Indigenous

1. For an indicative general account see H W Arndt, *Economic Development: The History of an Idea*. Arndt points to the convergence, at about the time of the end of the Second World War, of the idea of economic development under three related themes, which were often 'different labels' for the same urge: 'modernization', 'westernization' or 'industrialization'. Arndt accepts, however, that the Indian case is not quite so clearly assimilable to these categories. (He goes on to trace the idea of development in colonial theory and practice, Marxist concerns and, finally, war aims and post-war plans – which brought Third World economic development into the major interest spheres of western governments: pp. 22–9, 43–8.)

2. The importance of economics as a framework for the justification of colonial rule may be more visible in such matters as colonial development (a Colonial Office idea which never directly applied to India), where it was explicitly argued that a benevolent, improving colonialism was preferable to self-rule – especially in countries not yet 'ripe for self-government': the two strands of the argument were meant to be mutually reinforcing, and even found expression in assertions from the Labour Party that certain colonies should be given 'socialism' before they were given independence. See Partha Sarathi Gupta, *Imperialism and the British Labour Movement* (London, 1975). See also Stephen Constantine, *The Making of British Colonial Development Policy 1914–1940* (London, 1984).

3. Most importantly United States public opinion and her opposition to the British Empire and Commonwealth as a bloc which gave the US too little access to its markets – see William Roger Louis, *Imperialism at Bay: The United States and the Decolonization of the British Empire 1941–45* (Oxford, 1977)

4. This was apparently the basis of the Montagu-Chelmsford Reforms, the requirement of a Statutory Commission every ten years to review the progress of India towards fitness for self-government being built into the Act of 1919. See J A Gallagher and Anil Seal, 'Britain and India Between the Wars', in *Modern Asian Studies* 15, 3 (1981). Though the indication of the existence of such differences remained an important strategy in imperial arguments, this was expressed in a form tempered by the hope that with time things would improve. This was a useful position when it came to British reluctance to set a concrete time for its grant of self-government; but it was mainly unofficial voices among British colonial officials – speaking in their capacity as private citizens – who were permitted to express doubts as to whether the 'Westminster model' was suited to Indian society and politics at all (for instance Malcolm Darling or Penderel Moon, in their non-official capacities); it was politically incorrect to do so, although Indians were indeed expressing such doubts themselves (M N Roy, Aurobindo Ghosh or Gandhi, in varying forms).

5. This was epitomized in Nehru's view that 'communalism' would vanish with the disappearance of the economic problems which alone made it possible to delude and manipulate the masses: see Jawaharlal Nehru, *The Discovery of India* (London, 1945).

6. As Sir M Visvesvaraya, engineer, civil servant and Dewan of the Princely State of Mysore, put it: Sir M Visvesvaraya, *Planned Economy for India* (Bangalore City, 1934), preface.

7. The importance of 'economic development' in defining a role for the anticipated independent Indian state has been pointed out: see Partha Chatterjee, *The Nation and its Fragments: Colonial and Postcolonial Histories* (Princeton, 1993), Chapter 11; *Nationalist Thought and the Colonial World: A Derivative Discourse?* (London, 1986), Chapter 5. However, the complexities of what constituted the 'economic' need to be addressed. This is a notable absence in the existing literature: in much writing, the 'economic' is narrowly defined, as a result of which many ideas not assimilable to these standards are simply edited out. For an example of this, see Bhabatosh Datta, *Indian Economic Thought: Twentieth Century Perspectives* (New Delhi, 1978).

8. See Bipan Chandra, *The Rise and Growth of Economic Nationalism in India: Economic Policies of Indian National Leadership, 1880–1905* (New Delhi, 1966).

9. See for instance G D Birla, *The Path to Prosperity: A Plea for Planning* (Allahabad, 1950); P. Thakurdas *et al*, *A Plan of Economic Development for India* (2 parts, Bombay, 1944).

10. Sir M Visvesvaraya, *Nation Building: A Five-Year Plan for the Provinces* (Bangalore City, 1937), pp. 3–4.

11. M K Gandhi, *Hind Swaraj* (5th edn, Madras, 1922), Chapter VI.

12. Partha Chatterjee, *Nationalist Thought*, p. 112.

13. Ibid., pp. 93–4, 99.

14. In the work, for instance, of Ashis Nandy: see his *Tradition, Tyranny and Utopias: Essays in the Politics of Awareness* (Oxford, 1987).

15. See Bhikhu Parekh, *Colonialism, Tradition and Reform: An Analysis of Gandhi's Political Discourse* (New Delhi, 1989)

16. Partha Chatterjee, *Nationalist Thought*, pp. 50–52; for the exposition, see Chapter 4, pp. 85–130.

17. See Shahid Amin, 'Gandhi as Mahatma', in Ranajit Guha (ed.), *Subaltern Studies III* (New Delhi, 1983); G D Birla, *In the Shadow of the Mahatma: A Personal Memoir* (Bombay, 1968), and press reports of the Gandhi murder case.

18. See for instance E F Schumacher, *Small is Beautiful* (London, 1973); and various statements claiming a Gandhian lineage for movements such as the Narmada Bachao Andolan, 'intermediate technology' or environmentalism.

19. See Bhabatosh Datta, *Indian Economic Thought*, Chapter 14, especially p. 152.

20. See Ajit K. Dasgupta, *Gandhi's Economic Thought* (London, 1996).

21. *À la* Quentin Skinner: for the methodological issues involved, see James Tully (ed.), *Meaning and Context; Quentin Skinner and his Critics* (Oxford, 1988).

22. This was reflected in the organization of the Congress Socialist Party within the Congress, many of whose members were former supporters of Gandhi who broke away from Gandhian politics after the anti-climax of the Gandhi-Irwin Pact, the failure of Gandhi to secure any gains from the Round Table conference, and the failure of the second Civil Disobedience Movement. Meanwhile, Gandhi announced his retirement from active membership of the Congress, and declared it to be his intention to concentrate on 'constructive work' for the uplift of the masses.

23. Sir M Visvesvaraya, *Planned Economy for India* (Bangalore City, 1934), p. 220.

24. *Science and Culture* IV, 10 (April 1939), pp. 534–5. One of the stronger advocates of 'modern' solutions to problems of Indian development was the journal *Science and Culture* ('A Monthly Journal of Natural and Cultural Sciences'), published from Calcutta, founded and edited by Professor Meghnad Saha, well-known physicist and developmentalist, author of a scheme to dam the river Damodar, member, from 1938, of the Congress' National Planning Committee. See also Jayaprakash Narayan, *Why Socialism* (Benares, 1936), in which a great deal of space is extended to a sharp criticism of the retrogressive nature of Gandhian economic ideas and the tendency of Gandhi's idea of

'trusteeship' towards strengthening the capitalists – though Gandhi's own sincerity and good intentions are acknowledged.

25. *Science and Culture* IV, 10 (April 1939), editorial, p. 533.
26. Ibid., IV, 10 (April 1939), editorial, p. 534.
27. Ibid., IV, 1 (July 1938), editorial, 'The Next Twentyfive [*sic*] Years of Science in India', p. 2
28. Ibid., IV, 10 (April 1939), editorial, p. 535.
29. Edward Benthall, European representative at the Round Table Conference in 1931 makes several references to this dependence. See Benthall Papers, Centre for South Asian Studies, Cambridge, Box II, file on 'Ghandi' [*sic*]. Gandhi, despite his aversion to the modern industrialized world, spent his time in jail in the 1930s teaching himself economics with a little tutoring from Birla. Dietmar Rothermund, *India in the Great Depression 1929–1939* (Delhi, 1992), p. 212.
30. His method in this regard was to write a short preface explaining the author's intentions and expressing his agreement with them.
31. S N Agarwal, *The Gandhian Plan of Economic Development for India* (Bombay, 1944).
32. Biographical details are taken from K Muniandi, 'Kumarappa the Man', *Gandhi Marg* 14, 2 (July–September 1992), pp. 318–26; and Devendra Kumar, 'Kumarappa and the Contemporary Development Perspective', in *Gandhi Marg* 14, 2 (July–September 1992), pp. 294–5, except where otherwise specified.
33. Seligman also supervised B R Ambedkar's Ph.D. thesis, later published as B R Ambedkar, *The Evolution of Public Finance in British India: a Study in the Provincial Decentralisation of Public Finance* (London, 1925), and appears in the acknowledgements of Gyan Chand's *Essentials of Federal Finance: a Contribution to the Problem of Financial Readjustment in India* (London, 1930), Preface, p. viii.
34. The similarity of this tale with that of Gandhi's own description of his turning away from 'playing the English gentleman' may be noted here: see M K Gandhi, *An Autobiography, or the Story of My Experiments with Truth* (translated from the Gujarati by Mahadev Desai; edn Harmondsworth, 1982; first published Ahmedabad, 1927), pp. 60–63.
35. See K T Shah (ed.), *Report: National Planning Committee* (Bombay, 1949).
36. J C Kumarappa, *Why the Village Movement? A plea for a village-centred economic order in India*, (5th edn., Wardha, 1949; 1st edn., 1936) (hereafter Kumarappa, *Village Movement*).
37. Preface to the First Edition, reprinted in Kumarappa, *Village Movement*, p. (iii).
38. The second edition in 1937 added material on 'Barter Exchange', Education for Life', 'Democracy in the Orient' and 'Centralisation and Decentralisation'. The third, in 1939, added a chapter on 'Surveys and Plans'; the fourth, in 1945, added material on 'Schools of Economics', 'Peoples' Income', 'Moral Issues of Riches', 'Non-violent Standards of Life' and 'Planned Economy'. The book was also translated into several languages – there was a Hindustani and a Gujarati edition; and the late Professor Partha Sarathi Gupta remembered reading the Bengali edition.
39. Kumarappa, *Village Movement*, pp. 1–3.
40. *Ibid.*, p. 3.
41. *Ibid.*, pp. 4–5.
42. Indeed, Gandhi had been referring to his own ideas as 'socialistic' from the 1930s while continuing to make the distinction between Communism and *his* form of socialism.
43. Kumarappa, *Village Movement*, pp. 5–6.
44. *Ibid.*, p. 3.
45. *Ibid.*, p. 7.
46. *Ibid.*, pp. 7–8.
47. Gandhian arguments have in recent times been supported for being more culturally sensitive and less elitist than those of the 'socialists' in India. This view is not borne out by the writings of Gandhi or the Gandhians. Gandhians took upon themselves the task of convincing the 'masses' of what was good for them, and the right to guide the 'masses' to

the correct moral and material goals. The execution of this task was to be accomplished at a local level, but this was nonetheless to be done based on principles laid out by right-thinking, spiritual *brahmins*, not by precedents derived from local practices – which makes Gandhians' claims to cultural sensitivity or anti-elitism seem rather dubious. See below.

48. Kumarappa, *Village Movement*, pp. 7–8.
49. *Ibid.*, p. 8.
50. *Ibid.*, p. 9.
51. *Ibid.*, p. 10.
52. *Ibid.*, pp. 9–10.
53. *Ibid.*, pp. 10–11.
54. *Ibid.*, p. 62.
55. *Ibid.*, pp. 12, 15.
56. *Ibid.*, p. 15.
57. *Ibid.*, p. 16.
58. *Ibid.*, pp. 18–19.
59. *Ibid.*, pp. 16–17.
60. *Ibid.*, pp. 18–20.
61. *Ibid.*, p. 22.
62. *Ibid.*, pp. 22–3.
63. *Ibid.*, pp. 25–9.
64. *Ibid.*, pp. 27–8, 30.
65. *Ibid.*, p. 21
66. *Ibid.*, p. 28. Kumarappa elaborated these ideas in a later work: J C Kumarappa, *The Economy of Permanence* (Wardha, 1948). (Kumarappa recycled his writing a good deal. As he was also a prolific journalist, a great number of his articles also recycle earlier material; his main arguments remain simple, and the rest is elaboration from first princi-ples.) As the post-modernist-environmentalist connection begins to cast 'modernity' and 'development' as arch villains world-wide, there has been a tendency to reassess Gandhian economic ideas in the light of environmentalist concerns. See for instance various articles in the journal *Gandhi Marg*; or for a more well-received position Madhav Gadgil, 'On the Gandhian Economic Trail', *Gandhians in Action* April–June 1994, pp. 131–46; and as part of a larger argument, Madhav Gadgil and Ramachandra Guha, *Ecology and Equity: The Use and Abuse of Nature in Contemporary India* (London, 1995), pp. 38–9, 188.
67. See J C Kumarappa Papers: Notebooks, especially Sl. Nos. (2), (4) and (10), NML. Kumarappa seems to have read a number of extremely eclectic critiques of capitalism; and his first encounters with the ideas of Soviet Marxism seems to have come from the accounts of Fabians. His notebook for 1936 contains notes from Sidney and Beatrice Webb's *Soviet Communism* – at a time when he had presumably already written much of *Why the Village Movement?* – which he summarizes in two pages, without much interest in it. Kumarappa, Notebooks, Sl. No. (4), pp. 55–6. There is no indication that he had read much more than this, though he ought to have read a fair amount of J A Hobson, judging by the course outline provided by Professor Seligman at Columbia University. See Kumarappa, Notebooks, Sl. No. (2).
68. Quoted in Partha Chatterjee, *Nationalist Thought*, p. 93 and Note 28, p. 126.
69. See J C Kumarappa, 'The Economy of the Cross', a summary of three addresses to the Mid-India Conference of Christian Students at Nagpur, 5–7 November 1942, reprinted in J C Kumarappa, *Christianity: its Economy and Way of Life* (Ahmedabad, 1941), and other essays in that volume.
70. J J Anjaria, quoted in Bhabatosh Datta, *Indian Economic Thought*, p. 158.
71. 'Bapu' to 'Ku', 12th August 1941, J C Kumarappa Papers, Nehru Memorial Library, New Delhi, Subject File No. 5, f 75. Emphasis mine.
72. Marshall Berman has argued in this connection that the terms 'modernism' and

'modernisation' grew apart after the 1920s. The first was seen as a cultural, aesthetic and philosophical standpoint; the second was related to economics and the organisation of industry; although these two aspects of modernity were dialectically related, those interested in the one were not necessarily interested in the other. Marshall Berman, *All That Is Solid Melts Into Air: The Experience of Modernity* (London, 1983). In India, invariably the modernists were the modernizers, and the same people dominated economic and cultural life; the linking of the two positions was embodied in public phenomena such as the successful running and circulation of such journals as *Science and Culture* and the *Modern Review*.

73. Partha Chatterjee, *Nationalist Thought; The Nation and its Fragments*, Chapter 11.

74. Rather than, as in the version provided by so much Cold War era developmental rhetoric, maintain a distinction between 'tradition' and 'modernity', with the latter being identified by the former as 'western'.

75. Even though, at the level of the particular, British precedent was regularly cited as a reason to introduce a particular measure in India, this was usually by way of accusing the British of inconsistency with proclaimed values.

76. I am referring here to work following from Partha Chatterjee's *Nationalist Thought*: the phrase 'derivative but different', Chatterjee's own, has become, in the work of subsequent scholars, one which is regarded as an adequate summary of his views on the nature of nationalist thought in the colonial world – rather unfortunately, as it does no justice to the details of his arguments.

77. i.e. 'Orientalists' in the pre-Saidian sense of the term – before the publication of Edward Said's *Orientalism* (London, 1978) immensely widened the usage and the semantic range of the word.

78. The Indian case was perhaps not unique either; through the nineteenth century and into the twentieth, various nationalisms had claimed that their nation had always existed, while radical strands within them had been anxious to bury the unpleasant and undistinguished past.

79. Similarly, Gandhism's reinvention in the 1950s, in the Bhoodan movement of Vinoba Bhave, which claimed such adherents as Jayaprakash Narayan, formerly a most articulate opponent of Gandhian ideas regarding economy and society, was partly dependent upon disillusion with 'socialism' as it was experienced in the early years of independent India. For Narayan's statement of the reasons behind his conversion, see Jayaprakash Narayan, 'Letter to PSP Associates', reprinted in *Towards a New Society* (New Delhi, 1958)

80. See Sumit Sarkar, *The Swadeshi Movement in Bengal, 1903–1908* (New Delhi, 1973).

81. *Hind Swaraj* was first published in South Africa in the Gujarati section of *Indian Opinion* in two instalments, on 11 and 19 December 1909. It was first published in book form in January 1910, and in English (the translation being Gandhi's own) in March 1910, the first Indian edition not appearing before 1919. See 'A Note on the History of the Text' in Anthony J Parel (ed.), *Gandhi: Hind Swaraj and Other Writings* (Cambridge, 1997). Although written in his South African period, it also addresses Indian audiences; and from the political commentary it provides along with its attempted philosophizing, it seems apparent that Gandhi felt the need to address these general concerns. He does not, however, explicitly declare this to be his intention, but the immediate historical context seems to suggest this. This point has largely been missed by commentators – it is not mentioned, for instance, by Parel in any of his sections on the historical and intellectual contexts in his introduction – probably because Gandhi's text did not explicitly state its desire to intervene in these debates (though this would have been taken for granted by his readers at the time). In this context, Gandhi's was an extremist position on the question of the acceptability and possibility of assimilation of cultural borrowings. However, *Hind Swaraj* did not reach India till 1919 – it was banned as seditious by the Government of India in 1910 (Parel (ed.), *Gandhi: Hind Swaraj*, Note 2, p. 5) – and perhaps missed its chance to make its most profound impact.

82. See Dhruv Raina and S Irfan Habib, 'Bhadralok perceptions of science, technology and cultural nationalism', in *Indian Economic and Social History Review*, 32, 1 (1995).

13. The Civilization Obsessions of Ghulam Jilani Barq

1. Judging by his descriptions in his works, he did not engage deeply with life in the West. He believed that the Americans and British 'never deceive or cheat', and praised the institution of the supermarket and the unmanned newspaper stall. *Eik Islam*, Lahore, 1953, translated by Fazl-i-Ahmad Kuraishi as *Islam – The Religion of Humanity*, Lahore, 1956, pp. 375–6.
2. As derived from a publication list in one of Barq's most recent books, *Mu'arrakhin-e-Islam*, Lahore, 1968.
3. *Eik Islam*, p. 339.
4. Roy Mottahedeh, *The Mantle of the Prophet*, London, 1985, p.104.
5. In Kasravi's case the conversion experience was the sighting of Halley's comet over Tabriz – a spectacle that the Ptolemaic astronomy taught at his *madrasah* could neither predict nor explain. Mottahedeh, *Mantle*, p. 98 ff.
6. *Do Qur'an*, pp. 359–60.
7. The first was Rafia Badawi Rafi Tahtawi (1801–73). Similar ideas were later expressed by Muhammad Abduh and Rashid Rida. For more details on either of them see Albert Hourani, *Arabic Thought of the Liberal Age 1798–1939*, Oxford, Oxford University Press, 1962.
8. *Eik Islam*, p. vii.
9. Ibid., p. 214.
10. Ibid., p. 15.
11. 'Islami Gadagarun se Mulaqatein (1946)' reprinted in *Awaz*, October 1999, pp. 85–95.
12. Aziz Ahmad, *Islamic Modernism in India and Pakistan 1857–1964*, Oxford, Oxford University Press, 1967, pp. 233–4.
13. Interview Mian Nizam Din, Lahore 10 December 1999.
14. As expressed in his autobiographical novel *Ginster* quoted in Hans G Helms, 'Kolumbus musste nach seiner Theorie in Indien landen; er entdeckte Amerika: Siegfried Kracauers Bemühen um die Reflexion konkreter Wirklichkeit und sein polit-ökonomischer Ansatz' in M Kessler/Th Levin (eds.) *Siegfried Kracauer: Neue Interpretationen* (Tübingen 1990), S. 78.
15. *The meaning of the Glorious Qur'an*, trans. by Abdullah Yusuf Ali, Lahore, 1975.
16. See Kenneth W Jones, *Socio-religious Reform Movements in British India* Cambridge, Cambridge Univesity Press, 1989.
17. Muhammad Iqbal, *Shikwa & Jawab-i-Shikwa – Complaint and Answer: Iqbal's dialogue with Allah*, trans. Kushwant Singh, Delhi, Oxford University Press, 1981.
18. The best summary of Mashriqi's ideas is to be found in Phillips Talbot, 'The Khaksar Movement', *Indian Journal of Social Work*, 1941, vol. II, no. 2; more recently Muhammad Aslam Malik, *Allama Inayatullah Mashriqi – A Political Biography* (Pakistan, Oxford University Press, 2000.
19. Adolf Hitler, *Mein Kampf*, trans. Ralph Manheim, London, 1969, p. 88.
20. As argued by Mashriqi's mouthpiece Bakhtiar Ahmad Kabuli, Qur'an aur Musalman, *al-Islah*, 17 July 1940.
21. Ibrahim Ali Chishti, Muhammad Abdu Sattar Khan Niazi, Mian Muhammad Shafi, 'Khilafat-e-Pakistan Scheme', published in late 1930s, attached to File (Home Political) 37/2/47. National Archives of India. pp. 3, 38, 41, 42. All three authors were leading members of the Punjab Muslim Student Federation, a body associated with the Muslim League.
22. Both also mention Mashriqi by name and quote his magnum opus *Tazkirah* in the respective bibliographies.

23. *Eik Islam*, p. 295.
24. *Eik Islam*, pp. 175–204.
25. Ibid., p.p33–4.
26. Ibid., p. 324.
27. See Hamid Dabashi, *Theology of Discontent*, New York, 1993, p. 73–80.
28. The Gospel of Barnabas was first published in English by Laura and Londsdale Ragg, Oxford, 1907, and translated into Urdu in 1917. J Slomp, 'Preface' to Selim Abdul Ahad and W H T Gardener, *The Gospel of Barnbas: An Essay and Inquiry*, Hyderabad Deccan, 1975.
29. *Al-Furqan*, Lucknow, August 1975, p.48. quoted in Slomp 1975.
30. *Eik Islam*, p. 142.
31. Ibid., p. 323.
32. Ibid., p. 322.
33. Ibid., pp. 216–17.
34. Ibid., p. 311.
35. Ibid., p. 358.
36. Ibid., p. 328.
37. Phillips Talbot, 'The Khaksar Movement' in *Indian Journal of Social Work*, September 1941, vol. II, no. 2, p. 194.
38. M K Gandhi, *The Story of My Experiments with Truth*, Penguin, 1982, pp. 33–9.
39. The *locus classicus* of this argument is Ashis Nandi, *The Intimate Enemy – Loss and Recovery of Self under Colonialism*, Oxford, Oxford University Press, 1983.
40. See Lewis Wurgaft, *The Imperial Imagination*, Middletown, Wesleyan University Press, 1983.
41. *Eik Islam*, p. 37.
42. Markus Daechsel, 'Faith, Unity, Discipline – the making of a socio-political formation in urban India – Lahore 1935–1953', unpublished PhD dissertation, University of London, 2001, chapters 2 and 5.
43. Ibid., p. 99–101.
44. The Urdu popular science books published in Punjab at the time (and quoted in Barq's work) followed a standard Darwinist line, e.g., Mohan Lal Sethi, *Chaupa'e aur Insan*, Dar ul-Isha at-e-Punjab, Lahore, 1938.
45. *Eik Islam*, p. 34
46. He denounced religious piety and Sufism as useless 'monasticism'. pp. 61, 266–7.
47. Max Weber, *Wirtschaft und Gesellschaft*, Tübingen, 1972, p. 326–9.
48. *Eik Islam* p. 225.
49. Ibid., p. 231.
50. Most famous of all, Ashraf Ali Thanawi's long term best-seller *Bihishti Zewar*. Barbara Metcalf, *Perfecting Women: Maulana Ashraf 'Ali Thanawi's Bihishti Zewar: a partial translation with commentary*, Berkeley, 1990.
51. For a representative example see Khwaja Muhammad Islam, *Musalman khawatin keliye bis sabaq*, Khudian Khas, n.d., p.106–16.
52. Ibid., p. 106.
53. *Eik Islam*, pp. 69–78.
54. Ibid., p. 261.
55. Ibid., pp. 284–5.
56. The famous Islamicist scholar and Barq contemporary Abul Ala Maududi entertained very similar views. Francis Robinson, 'Islam and the Impact of Print in South Asia' in *Islam and Muslim History in South Asia*, Oxford, Oxford University Press, India, 2000,p. 92.
57. In my forthcoming book *Salvation in a Soap Bubble: The rise of consumption and the politics of radical self-expression in the Urdu middle-class milieu of early 20th century India and Pakistan*.
58. 'Between Suburb and World Politics: Middle Class Identities and the Refashioning of Space in late Imperial Lahore, c.1920–1950', in Crispin Bates (ed.), *Beyond Representation:*

Constructions of Identity in Colonial and Postcolonial India,
59. *Eik Islam*, p. ix.
60. Ibid., p. 63.
61. Ibid., p. 7.
62. Ibid., pp. 256–8.
63. Ibid., p. 282.
64. Ibid., pp. 351–2.
65. Ibid., p. 358.
66. Ibid., p. 286.

INDEX